A WRITER'S FIRST AID KIT

by

Don Rutberg

ISBN 1-58747-067-5

Copyright 2004, Pale Horse Publishing

Don Rutberg

Contact publisher at:
Pale Horse Publishing (800) 646-5590
POB 1447, Livingston, TX 77351

For B&B And My Marcia B.

Who Shine Light On Me

Foreword by A.J. Langguth

Beware.

You have in your hands a subversive book.

Not only does Donald Rutberg reveal to you the nastier secrets about writing and publishing, he tells you what most of us writers don't even want to admit. By the time you have finished the Rutberg First Aid Kit, you will have no illusions, misconceptions or impractical dreams about the life of a writer.

But you will be prepared to cope with an impenetrable and infuriating business and emerge successful.

Along the way, you will laugh a lot, usually at the author's expense. Rather than disguise his near-misses and outright failures, Rutberg treats them as badges of honor. You will seldom find such candor delivered so hilariously.

He has persevered, though, despite the mendacity and willful lack of vision around him. He will share many of the lessons he has mastered, but I can point to a fundamental one: Persistence.

Week in, week out, bubbling with fresh ideas and the talent to bring them to life, Rutberg kept working. He had faith that those projects that couldn't find a home when they left his typewriter would be adopted one day, when publishing and the television industry caught up with him.

And so it has proved.

Now it's time to turn the page and enter Don Rutberg's world--meeting former agents, loving family, ex-girlfriends and, above all, an antic imagination that will consistently amuse and inspire you.

--A. J. Langguth

January, 2004

Reader Reviews

"A Writer's First Aid Kit" is an informative compilation of the author's actual experiences in developing, writing and marketing his work. It provides many examples of how to do things, backed up by numerous illustrations of the author's actual work, trials, tribulations and, most importantly, lessons learned. It is also very entertaining in its presentation of true stories - how things happen in the real world of real writers. This is a valuable guide and a must read for novice, aspiring and experienced writers of everything from magazine articles to screenplays. -- Martin Schor, Doylestown,PA December 2003

Don Rutberg's book, "A Writer's First Aid Kit," is a multi-faceted text that serves numerous aspects of the financial world. Although it is designed as a text for the college classroom, it is delightful reading. The humorous examples and practical suggestions blended with the the technicalities of writing carry the value of the material well beyond its academic usefulness. Indeed, the book is a guide that will also serve as a valuable reference. -- Alvin Greenspan. Professor Emeritus, Temple University July 2004

Smart and irreverent ... a must read for any serious writer. One of the few books I keep returning to for advice. -- Christopher Straub, Screenwriter April 2004

There are better books on structuring your story, there are better books on layout and presentation. But, there are no better books about how things really work in the places we all want to be. "A Writer's First Aid Kit" feels like a journal, a bitch session, advice from a trusted friend, a peek into an alternative reality, and a fight I want to fight. A fight I have a better chance of winning because of "A Writer's First Aid Kit"." -- Mike Randal, Seattle, WA July 2004

"A Writer's First Aid Kit": Real examples, real answers, real world. Can't get this information any place else. -- Geneva Reynols, Honeoye, NY July 2004

I could have written this book. I have been through all the things and places he has been. I have all the rejection letters he does. I have been ignored, berated, stolen from, and survived. What I didn't do was go back for more. If "A Writer's First Aid Kit" hasn't discouraged you, you may succeed where many of us failed. At least you have a chance to protect your soft underbelly. I would have done better if I had this book when I started out. You won't see any of my work out there, but I may see yours. -- Jack Stanhope, Los Angeles, CA July 2004

Enlightening and demonstrative. -- Lee Hill Rapid City, SD July 2004

More Reader Reviews

Some things I just didn't need to know. This recent history of selling your writing in late 20th and early 21st Century America (also known as "A Writer's First Aid Kit") is brutally honest and honestly funny. In the Alice in Wonderland of Professional Writing, this is a "Read Me". -- Greg Armitage Boca Raton, FL, July 2004

They say, "Those who can write do. Those who can't teach." Don Rutberg can do both. Read "A Writer's First Aid Kit" and succeed. It will be easier for you because you will be standing on Don's shoulders and be able to reach the Brass Ring from that height. -- Betty Oliver, Nags Head, NC July 2004

Letters to Agents, Letters to Publishers, Query Letters, Rejection Letters, examples of bad formatting, good formatting, scripts, dialogue, log lines, follow up files, smart letters, stupid letters, ideas to get attention that didn't work and ones that did! I broke into song, " Who could ask for anything more?" I love it. I am so excited. I can't wait to get started. Thank you, Thank you, Thank you for "A Writer's First Aid Kit." -- Jillian Lilley, Kallispell, MT July 2004

"A Writer's First Aid Kit" would make a good movie. Adelle Dichter, Phoenix, AZ August 2004

"A Writer's First Aid Kit" allowed me to watch a mere human navigate through the treacherous caverns of publishing, movie making and television. It's amazing to hear the names of the stars and star-makers woven into a struggling writer's work day. As I came to know the author through this book I also saw a real human being make an honest effort to produce products to please the often jaded needs of others. I watched him try, try, and try yet again, succeed, venture forth again, try, fail and try again. To Don, to all writers, to those of us who wish to be writers; this book is a tribute. -- Karen Bingham, Denver CO July 2004

"A Writer's First Aid Kit" should have been required reading in my Creative Writing and Publishing Arts classes. I was taught the skills that will help me complete my projects but didn't prepare me for the world in which I would have to venture to sell them. This book is a real "Eye Opener". -- Cindy Charles, Baltimore, MD July, 2004

An excellent resource from someone who's been there. Don speaks from his experience in the trenches. The enormous amount of work that has gone into this book is clearly evident. "A Writer's First Aid Kit" in a invaluable resource. I give it 10 stars for usable information. -- James Quackenbush, Salt Lake City, UT, July 2004

This is a tour de force. -- Carol Dennis, Book Editor July, 2004

Table of Contents

Part Two - Children's Books 151

Part Three - Novels And Nonfiction Books 243

Part One - TV And Film

Introduction To Agents

I was my own funhouse mirror -- a writer-turned-literary agent.

It was like a wheeler-dealer businessman working for the IRS, undercover. Or a "Save The Whales" organizer riding the high seas with a spear gun in his hand for a percentage.

Writers and agents are fundamentally opposite. A writer distills the truth while rarely focusing on income. An agent maximizes income while rarely focusing on the truth. By that definition, agents and writers should never be in the same room at the same time. If they are invited to the same party, the host should at least keep them separated by constructing a steel cage. Through some societal oddity, like driving on a parkway and parking on a driveway, writers and agents must depend upon the other. The clearest analogy would be if a Republican New York Yankee, who played mainly for money and a Democratic Boston Red Sock, who played mainly for the love of the game, were paired in the same broadcast booth.

When business partners are fundamentally opposite, they're called complementary if business is good and incompatible if business is bad. When you get an agent, imagine that he/she is your brother/ sister-in-law and you've each inherited fifty percent of a business. Although the two of you may be incompatible and unable to relate, at least you've got complementary skills. It's like the "good cop, bad cop" scenario, with each one believing that the other is the bad, or at least the unreasonable, cop. The agent is the partner who markets the product, negotiates, handles money, cuts losses and soothes egos. A writer is the partner who creates the product, dreams, takes chances and remembers every transgression.

Without you, the writer, literary agents would have lunch every day by themselves for five hours. Aware of this, subconsciously, at least, they have been known to compensate by acting out a "Who needs you?" game. Sometimes, it is their only flash of creative talent.

Agents don't exist to flash acting talent, compose beautiful poems or churn out clever comedies. They are not in the creative department; they're in the sales and marketing departments.

To their credit, literary agents love the thrill of taking an unknown book or script and turning it into a best seller or Academy Award winner. I suspect, however, that some of them yearn to be game show hosts. (Agents will admit to the former, not to the latter.) After all, when their efforts lead to a major sale, they only get 10-15 percent of the money and almost none of the fame.(You don't see many agents' faces on magazine covers.) They rarely bask in the glory they help create. If they weren't such an insensitive bunch, you might feel badly for them.

So, the next time you want to complain about an agent ignoring you, losing your script or botching your deal, do something really nice, instead. Give them a best seller or Academy Award winner to peddle.

The next time you want to strangle an agent for ignoring you, losing your script or botching your deal, do something worse.

Let them live.

Why Did I Become An Agent?

The honest answer is: I had spent fifteen years learning the business and I thought I could identify and sell a good project.

Having been represented by many agents, I'd discovered that the most receptive ones had little clout. The unproven agents were able to submit scripts and books but producers/publishers didn't have confidence in their track records. Producers/publishers would read agency submissions because they were protected from lawsuits when an agency, rather than an unagented writer, submitted material, but they had to be blown away - shocked and awed by the story -- to seek out unproven talent.

Studios won't read an unagented writer's work, they claim, because they're afraid you'll sue them if they produce a story similar to yours. The real reason is they don't have time for new writers. When I was an agent, I actually received a letter from a new writer that began, "I'm practically illiterate but I think you'll like my book." Studios don't have time for writers like that and you can't blame them. You can blame them for thinking that all new writers are a waste of time.

The most successful, powerful agents I've worked with were not always honest and straightforward with me. They preferred to give my projects to one of their top-earning clients. The project is worth more to the agent in commissions if a star client is involved. If the big-shot writer signed on to rewrite my project, then the agent and top writer would take a meeting with my script, without me! That's a fine idea, my agents claimed, since the project would not have been seriously considered with my name attached.

That was my reward for being lucky enough to be represented by a top agent early in my writing career.

Most agents will shoo you away if you are unknown. If you get famous, they'll send a limousine to take you food shopping and forget they shooed you away when you were struggling.

Politicians and horseplayers are the only groups with worse memories than agents. If you know of any group that belongs in this paragraph -- besides lawyers -- please warn me.

Are you still sure you want an agent? Wouldn't you rather have a mean, ugly spouse or a son-in-law who's on the FBI's Most Wanted List?

I became an agent because I was signing on with the rookie agents, the ones with no clout, and realized I was training them! After years of film school (Master of Fine Arts degree in Professional Writing from USC) and living in Los Angeles, hanging around the studios and taking meetings, I was more experienced at script marketing than were my agents. If you kept training your boss, wouldn't you eventually start your own business?

In a sentence then, control over submissions was the reason I became an agent.

How I Got My First Agent

Writing good letters can open doors as well as amuse your family. When I started college, I wrote to my aunt and uncle: "Dear Uncle Myrna and Aunt Fred: College is confusing."

If a letter could get the attention of an agent, maybe he or she would read my work.

In 1981, I had written a story called "The Players' Wives" about the spouses of pro ballplayers who run the household, pay the bills, raise the kids and have to put up with the antics of their star husbands. It was a woman's story, perfect for TV.

(More than twenty years later, "Baseball Wives" will debut on HBO in 2005. Another movie, called "The Players' Wives," is also due out in 2005.)

I wrote a letter to the agents who claimed to be receptive to new writers. (The list is available from the Writer's Guild of America in New York or Los Angeles.)

"Dear Prospective Agent: Senility is difficult to cope with. I'm not saying that some of your established clients have lost their creative edge, but I am a young writer without a trace of senility... or representation."

That letter and lobster tails got me my first agent.

Maybe I should explain.

The woman agent, let's call her "Barbara," liked my letter and my "Players' Wives" story and invited me to bring it over to her office on Wilshire Boulevard in Los Angeles. Barbara had left that message with my girlfriend who, coincidentally or not, moved out of our apartment immediately after writing the message on our note pad. (Or maybe she moved out because I had taped a quote from "The Shining" on my wall: "All work and no play makes Donnie a very dull boy.")

It was as if fate had tapped my ex-girlfriend on the shoulder and ushered her out of my life so I could become closer to Barbara. It seemed akin to the theme of "It's A Wonderful Life." Later, I realized it was more like "Desperate Hours."

I met Barbara and tried to be as charming as possible. She called me at my beach apartment a few hours later, said she liked the project and asked what I was doing that night. (It was already 10 PM.) That's when I told her I was cooking lobster tails. She said she'd be over by midnight.

I knew that if she came over that night, with the moonlight on the beach, the lobster tails and wine on the table and especially the optimistic talk about getting projects sold and produced, we would be led into romance. I wondered, if I romanced this woman agent, could it ruin my chances of making it as a writer in Hollywood? Then I realized if I didn't romance this woman agent, it could ruin my chances.

It hit me: "I'm William Holden in 'Sunset Boulevard!' I'm the young, desperate writer! Where's the pool?"

Rule #1: Try not to get personally involved with your agent. It's normal, even healthy to want to grab them romantically or enthusiastically. I've done both and suggest you do neither.

What Does An Agent Do?

My first agent was habitually chased around producers' offices. Think of "9-5" with Dabney Coleman as a producer and Dolly Parton as an agent. I remember one cold day -- people's attitudes make it seem cold in L.A. -- when I drove Barbara to meet with a top producer at a major TV studio. The guy was married but still chased my agent around his desk. How did I know? I was parked on the studio lot and watched this chase scene through my windshield! Sitting in my car, I thought there was some kind of tackle football game going on in that office. He wouldn't discuss "The Players' Wives." No, all he wanted to discuss were the agent's legs.

(When Barbara and I attended a cable TV convention in Las Vegas, a network executive invited her to join a harem. A female agent who represented me in 1990 told me a producer put her in a tiny chair so he could sit up high and look down her blouse. I tried to act surprised when she told me.)

Anyway, the TV producer wasn't in the best of shape so he eventually stopped chasing my agent, Barbara. That's when she looked out toward the parking lot to see if I was still there, in case she had to jump out the window to escape molestation.

"All right, who is he?" the producer asked.

Even though he was married, he was disturbed that the female agent had a man waiting to drive her home.

I never sold "The Players' Wives" but actual wives of pro athletes (and HBO) know that it would've made a great TV movie or series. A one hour dramatic TV show with exactly the same theme was aired for a few weeks in the 1980's. Although I thought the producers had copied my idea (they had read and rejected it) the writers had changed the characters from major leaguers in Southern California to minor leaguers in Northern California, so I couldn't claim they borrowed the concept.

What else does an agent do -- besides getting chased? Barbara and I had a meeting at a major production company in L.A. with a truly miserable woman in dramatic development. She was the kind of woman who could walk away from you and still be able to watch what you were doing. Scary.

Barbara advised me to date the woman and get to know her better. Barbara knew I had a girlfriend. She was my girlfriend! Yet, she knew that by wining and dining this nasty woman executive, we could both move forward in our careers.

(The executive was nasty because she refused to watch a video presentation we had worked hard to prepare and kept bragging about her Master's Degree as if it made her some kind of scholar. The scarecrow in "The Wizard Of Oz" didn't make such a fuss about his degree but, to be honest, I thought what she needed most was a heart.)

I never dated the Hollywood executive. She wanted me to change my story -- a true story about reform-schoolers who run their own Junior Achievement company and do so well that nervous county officials shut them down -- and invent violent scenes to add drama. I guess that was why she was in charge of dramatic development.

How could I add murder and rape to the story and retain the support of Junior Achievement, whose officials we'd been taking to lunch every week? I couldn't appease both sides so I stuck to the original story (with minor changes) and no deal was offered.

What does an agent do? Usually, he or she will persuade you to add a murder or a rape scene to a script that has absolutely no reason for murder or rape.

What should an agent do? He or she should be able to judge literary talent, then recommend worthy projects, written by anyone, to appropriate producers.

Why Do You Need An Agent?

I had written a horse racing story, sort of a futuristic "Black Stallion," wherein the horse was a laboratory experiment who loved his orphaned female jockey very much. I had no agent -- this was before I met Barbara -- but if I had, I would've hoped he or she would send the script to a certain veteran actor who loved horses and horse racing.

I called the actor's agent and got him interested in the story. (This ploy seldom works.) I don't know why the agent picked up the phone to take my call. After hearing my pitch, he knew his client would have interest in the subject matter.

Six months later, still without an agent, I called back and spoke to another of the actor's agents.

"Why," this agent said, "would an important man like (our client) want to read a script by a nobody like you. Huh?"

Since I didn't have an agent, this agent believed I was probably inventing the part about someone in the agency inviting me to mail in the script. I had no credibility. If I had an agent, the actor's agent would've been more courteous and might have actually told the truth at some point, most likely after cocktails.

Still sans-agent, I met the president of Paramount Studios, Gary Nardino, at a "Laverne and Shirley" cast party. (My date danced with Squiggy.)

"Any hints for young writers?" I asked the portly president, who wore a white suit.

"Break the guild and change your name," he answered.

(Paramount was having union problems at the time.)

So I wrote him a letter, in which I told him how I had sent a letter to the guild telling them to break up or shape up because they were bothering my new pal, Mr. Nardino. When the guild asked who I was, I took his advice and barked, "John Steinbeck. If you don't comply with our demands, I won't submit my newest novel for television, ' West of Cleveland.'"

Nardino must have chuckled because he sent me to his VP, who was ordered to give my "Laverne and Shirley" script to the show's producers, but the VP's secretary would not let me in the office because I had no agent!

I literally poked her in the chest and said, "Mr. Nardino wants to help me and ... you're ... not ... helping!!!"

I had to wait until lunchtime the next day, when the assistant director of "Laverne" called me in a Paramount office and said, "Nardino's in the commissary." CLICK.

All sounds abated except for my footsteps and my heartbeat as I walked a few hundred feet to where Nardino lunched. Some of my closest friends denied knowing me as I approached the man who could kill my writing career years before it was born.

Looking back, I have only fond memories of such anxious moments, when sweat poured from my body like I was North America and my armpits were Niagara Falls. (I was also a contestant on "The Dating Game" and performed comedy acts at "The Comedy Store" -- truly sweat-stimulating experiences.)

As I walked closer to the president of Paramount Pictures Television, I tried to enjoy the excitement, the vitality, the thrill of pursuing the American dream and its possible rewards ... although it was likely that one of my best friends might shoot me in the leg for my own good.

"Remember me? (nervous chuckle)" I asked Nardino as everyone in the commissary stopped eating and talking. "I know you tried to help but ...."

Nardino promised that someone would review my script if I let him finish his lunch in peace. A few months later, I called the head of current programming at Paramount to see if anyone had read my "Laverne and Shirley" script, which I knew was better than average because, through my contacts, I had read every "Laverne" script ever produced.

I was still waking up when I called, never expecting to actually get through to the head of current programming, when the secretary said, "Mr. Barber will be right with you."

"Huh?"

I ran cold water over the back of my neck to wake up fully. My script, I was told, was being recommended to the supervising producer of the show, whom I played basketball with at (executive producer) Gary Marshall's house on weekends! Bingo!

Wrongo. That supervising producer never read the script. He trashed it. (I'm certain he checked first to make sure I wasn't Mr. Nardino's nephew.) He had his own friends who were writers -- friends with whom he could trade favors -- and knew that he wouldn't offend my powerful agent because I had no such thing.

Why Can't You Depend On Great Contacts?

My father was friendly with a man who was a childhood friend of Ed Weinberger, the executive producer of "Taxi." This friend of Dad's said he would recommend me to Ed. So, in the early 1980's, I sent Ed a letter and he promised that if I wrote a spec script (written on speculation; with the hope someone would like it) for his new show, "Best of the West," he would make sure that someone at his company read it.

So I wrote two spec scripts for "Best of the West," a silly sitcom that lasted less than a year on network television. I submitted them to Ed's company and waited for a reply. Months later, I hadn't heard from Ed or his staff. I figured that there wasn't any interest in my work, despite the personal connection.

One night, I noticed that the Emmy Awards show was on TV. Ed Weinberger was accepting an Emmy for "Taxi." I did what I always did during the award shows - I wrote. About 1:30 am, my phone rang.

"Hello, Donald?"

"Uh, yeah?"

"This is Ed Weinberger."

Ed had probably been to several parties. He sounded happy, to say the least.

"Hey, congratulations on that award," I said.

I didn't tell him that I never watched "Taxi."

"I'm not calling about that. I'm getting back to you about your work."

"Why don't you call me tomorrow?" I wondered. "I mean, it's late and you won an Emmy a couple of hours ago, for goodness -"

"No. No. I want to return all my calls tonight, tell you I read your work, or somebody in my office read your work ... and I want to ... hold on."

I heard congratulatory screaming in the background.

"Anyway, I'm sorry I can't help you. Keep trying, though."

He hung up.

So, in his greatest moment, he realized that he had to be nice to the "little guys" he met along the way, but he wasn't really interested in helping me. He was obligated to be polite because of a promise he had made to his old friend.

My uncle is very close to a woman -- she's like an aunt to me -- who shows great interest in my career and asks to read my work whenever she sees me. Coincidentally, her son is one of the main executives at a major studio.

"He had so many people help him get to where he is now," she admitted.

"Maybe he can help me," I mentioned.

"Oh, no. He won't do that."

"You said he needed help back in the day ...."

"He did. But he won't help others."

"Wait a minute," I thought. "If he did it on his own, with no help, then, maybe, he'd have a reason for not helping others. If he depended on the kindness of others to boost his career, he should want to return the favors to worthy people trying to break into the business, especially if they were close to his mother."

"I can't ask him," she told me.

This aunt-like family member recommended my work to others in the entertainment industry but she couldn't bother her busy son; a man who could almost certainly make one phone call and get me a studio job.

I'm not saying that I'd take the job, if it were offered, and move back to Los Angeles. (I now live near my hometown of Philadelphia, PA.) But I would feel better about mankind in general; place our species squarely ahead of reptiles on the evolutionary scale. I'd tone down this book's, "Almost everyone in Hollywood is a freak" sub-theme, at the very least.

Once, a friend of a friend recommended that I send my work to his agent. The agent's name happened to be Mr. List. When I started a file called "Agntlist" (to help keep track of my dealings with Mr. List) my computer told me I already had such a file. I thought it was a freaky sign from heaven. My computer somehow knew I'd be working with this agent! Soon, I realized that I had long ago started a file with a list of agents, called "Agntlist." I cupped my lips and muttered, "Hmmm, maybe it's not a freaky sign from heaven."

I was quickly rejected by the agent named List. A hundred other times, though, when I asked people I knew to recommend me to their agents, they said, "No."

If you know someone who has an agent, by all means, ask him/her if you can contact the agent and use his/her name. Don't be shocked when the "friend" invents some lame excuse as to why he/she can't help you. The odds are overwhelming that you will be told not to send your work to that agent. Why? Your friend doesn't want you to surpass him/her in the agent's stable. If you're better than your friend, you will force him/her down the ladder, on the way to a hellish obscurity. That's not high on your friend's list of things to do today. If the friend is going to fail, he/she still wants to feel more successful than you.

In other words, before you get excited about a great contact, make sure that contact is willing to help you. Sadly, it's a rare occurrence.

In the late 1980's, I had a great contact who wanted to help me. He was one of the VP's at Gulf & Western, which owned Simon & Schuster and probably half the world. He was a family friend and a wonderful guy who wanted me to publish something; anything.

I told him about my horse racing story. "Technobred" was, by then, a finished young adult novel. This friend with great contacts recommended my young adult book to a top editor at Simon and Schuster.

Six months later, I learned they had lost the book. Fine. I sent another copy of the book. Nine months after that, Simon and Schuster wrote to tell me the story was way too sophisticated for eight year-old readers!

It had been sent to the wrong department. My hair was actually a different color by the time the book came back to me. I have photos to prove it.

You could be thinking, "What if I had two great contacts; one with access to money, the other with an Oscar or Emmy in his closet?" You wouldn't need an agent to get a writing credit on a major motion picture. You'd be in great shape, right?

That's what I thought when I was the middleman between a major studio owner's business partner and an Emmy-award-winning, mini-series producer. The businessman with the strong tie to the studio (meaning he could guarantee distribution which would guarantee financing) wanted to meet with an Emmy award-winning friend of a friend of mine to make a film. I would write the script based on a paperback book ... that I didn't think was very good. A major star was attached, someone who had been in a wildly successful movie but whom ... I didn't think was very good.

As I drove around, doubting whether I should arrange the meeting, the song, "Sweet dreams are made of this, who am I to disagree?" kept playing on every station on the car stereo. I was advised to keep my mouth shut because, "Who else will give you a chance to write a script for a fully financed project?"

The truth was: anybody, as long as I supplied the guy who would supply the money and distribution deal. A basset hound could've gotten the writing assignment if he or she had sniffed out the financing. The Emmy award winner didn't care if I was a great writer or a disembodied head floating in a pot of baked beans as long as I brought him the financing.

Mr. Emmy award was planning to ask for $250,000 development money to secure, "the script, an office and a coffee maker."

I knew I wasn't going to get six figures for adapting the novel into a screenplay and I knew what offices rented for ... so how was he planning to justify the $212,000 coffee maker? Wouldn't it be obvious to the businessman that this producer was going to pocket a lot of his money and then act as if he didn't care if the film got made or was any good?

That meant the businessman was going to throw the producer out on his ear and make me look like a time-waster.

It happened just like that, but first the producer became irate because he had to wait ten minutes to make his pitch for a $212,000 coffee maker. An agent would've had more options and could've eventually sent the right producer to the businessman with the studio connection.

Years later, I asked the friend who had introduced me to the producer, "What happened to your buddy, the guy who wanted $250,000 to open an office?"

"He died."

"Really? How?" I wondered.

He answered, "You don't want to know."

If nothing else, I became acutely aware that winning an Emmy or an Oscar doesn't make a person immortal. I also learned that coffee makers cost about twenty bucks. Add filters, you're up to about twenty-two bucks, and then there's tax.

Why do you need an agent? Because these stories are only amusing if they happen to someone else. With no agent, the most frustrating job in North America turns degrading.

What About Entertainment Attorneys?

We're talking about the only humans that sharks are afraid to digest -- and sharks have the most advanced immune system on the planet. An entertainment attorney's memory, as previously suggested, can crash like an old C drive.

I was sent to a top entertainment attorney once, a man who represented major stars. He met me as a favor to an influential family friend, the aforementioned businessman with the studio connection. This guy could've put me in Caesar's Palace if I were an above-average stand-up comic.

A week after setting up a meeting with Mr. Entertainment Attorney, an L.A. production company offered to option my comedy series about children of divorce who gained custody of their home. (Based on true stories, each parent visited the children three and a half days a week.) A week later, my first agent, Barbara, and I met with this man who would "handle everything." He knew the production company's lawyer and there would be "no problem."

Barbara kept murmuring, "Pay him," and I kept telling her the Philadelphia businessman had him on retainer for doing nothing. We didn't have to pay him. He probably earned hundreds of thousands a month. What should we have done -- offered him fifty bucks? We wouldn't eat for three days.

Barbara thought the entertainment lawyer would ignore/forget our little deal (a few thousand dollars - more if the pilot was picked up by a network) since we didn't leave our wallets with him.

We didn't insult him by paying him and he never lifted a finger to sell our option to a company that wanted to buy it! The deal fell through because of entertainment lawyer apathy/ forgetfulness but he did apologize to me later.

I had to apologize to Barbara for not throwing thousand dollar bills at the entertainment attorney to ensure that he made one lousy phone call!

If you have someone helping you make a deal, ask if he or she wants money up front, even if the notion seems ridiculous.

Selling A Screenplay Without An Agent

You can do this, if you have a few years to waste.

In 1987, I submitted an original comedy series treatment (outline) and pilot script to several production companies on the East coast. Although I had no agent, I let the producers know that I knew a few agents who would handle any contract situation for me. In other words, if I did all the writing and marketing, an agent would swoop in at the last minute and pick up a ten percent cut.

A New York producer liked my proposed TV series about patriotic Soviets living in the U.S. and secretly loving it here. "Foreign Relations" (the Soviets had American cousins) was a timely story. I knew I had to sell it soon before the Soviets started World War III or communism collapsed completely. Either situation would render my script obsolete.

The producer asked me to adapt the story into a feature film. I asked for the absolute minimum in up-front money and percentage of profit that my conscience would allow (less than the Writer's Guild minimum). The producer thought I was being difficult and, after a few months of negotiating, talks broke off.

If you're an unknown writer, take the minimum number in your head and hope for more next time. But if you feel you're being out-and-out cheated on a deal and can't live with it, don't sign any contract.

This producer called me back a year later ("Donald wants everything/Donald has to get everything!") and it took a few more months to agree on -- what else? -- the minimum I would accept for writing the script. The contract appears below.

Sample Screenplay Purchase Agreement

PURCHASE AGREEMENT

THEATRICAL SCREENPLAY

This Agreement dated (day and year) between ("Producer") and ("Artist") with respect to a proposed feature length screenplay currently entitled (name of screenplay/ "Property") created by Artist and to be produced by Producer.

1. Base Compensation. Producer shall compensate Artist or cause him to be compensated for his efforts in connection with the Project as follows:

    a. $2,000.00 immediately upon execution of this agreement;

    b. $2,000.00 immediately upon delivery of first draft of script. If Producer finds script unacceptable, however, then all rights will revert to Artist, and all fees will be retained by Artist, and any and all future obligations on either party's part are forever waived and forgiven. Producer will give written notice of unacceptability within fifteen (15) days of script receipt;

    c. $2,000.00 immediately upon delivery of rewrite (or thirty (30) days after delivery of script if no rewrite requested within such period). Producer may not require more than one rewrite.

    d. $2,000.00 immediately upon delivery of polish (or $1,000 thirty (30) days after delivery of rewrite if no polish requested within such period);

    e. $10,000.00 immediately upon the earliest to occur of (i) commencement of production or (ii) sale by Producer of any interest in the Property or the Project to a third party and,

    f. $10,000.00 upon the earlier to occur of the (i) first commercial showing of the resulting motion picture, or (ii) the sale of the motion picture and/or the sale of the Producer's rights therein.

    Once Artist has received payments, Producer shall relinquish all rights and all rights shall revert back to Artist exactly twelve (12) months from receipt of the first draft, unless the Project is in production. Producer shall deliver to Artist an instrument reassigning to Artist all rights, title and interest in and to the Property. Furthermore, Paragraph 16 of this Agreement is incorporated herein by reference.

    2. Profit Participation. Artist shall be entitled to receive, and Producer shall be obligated to pay to Artist, one (1%) percent of Producer's gross income from the Project. Such gross income shall be determined in accordance with generally accepted accounting practices and procedures. Producer shall provide written periodic financial reports regarding the Project, no less often than biannually, to Artist.

    3. Screen Credit. Artist shall receive the credit of SCREENWRITER at the "head" of any motion picture produced in connection with the Project and receive prominent credit in all promotion and advertising.

    4. Subsidiary Rights. In the event that the Project results in the financing of production of a feature length motion picture prior to twelve (12) months from Producer's receipt of Artist's first draft, then Producer shall have the absolute right to produce the Project and exploit the Property in any and all media forms.

    5. Sequels. In the event that a sequel to the Property is required by Producer, Artist shall have exclusive right to write such sequel. Compensation of such Artist's performance shall be commensurate with Writers' Guild of America, West, minimums, plus one (1%) percent of Producer's gross profits, notwithstanding the above, to the extent Artist is unable or unwilling to act as scriptwriter therefore, said compensation shall be reduced by the amount which Producer is required to pay for such scriptwriting. In the event that any television series is produced pursuant to this agreement, based in whole or in part upon the Property, Artist shall be entitled to receive compensation commensurate with Writers'

Guild of America, West, minimums for series creator and/or writer. These minimums shall not be less than:

   a. $1,250.00 per each thirty minute episode;

   b. $1,750.00 per each sixty minute episode; and

   c. $2,250.00 per each ninety minute or longer episode.

Artist shall also be entitled to additional compensation for the television reuse of the above original episodes or programs to be determined on the same basis as terms set forth immediately hereabove. Artist shall in all events receive an additional one (1%) percent of the Producer's gross profits as that term is defined in paragraph 2 above.

6. Artist's Creative Role and Credit Regarding Subsidiary Rights. Artist shall be given the exclusive right to write the initial television pilot upon terms which shall be negotiated in good faith by both the parties. For a reasonable fee to be determined by both parties and negotiated in good faith, Artist agrees to sell to Producer, upon Producer's request, exclusive rights to the pilot script. Artist shall receive "Created By" credit, otherwise "Developed By" credit in connection with each television program or episode.

7. Artist's Rights Regarding Property. Artist hereby warrants and represents that he has the sole right in and to the aforementioned Property and is prepared to grant all rights, title and copyright to Producer on the basis of the terms provided herein.

8. Pending Claims Or Actions. The pendency of any claim or action shall not relieve Producer of its obligation to pay Artist any monies due hereunder and Producer shall not withhold such monies unless Producer has sustained a loss or suffered an adverse judgment or decree by reason of such claim or action.

9. Assignment. Producer shall have the unlimited right to assign this agreement in part or in its entirety.

10. Notices. All notices required by this agreement shall be given by delivery in person, or by certified or registered mail at the following locations or such other address as may hereinafter be designated in writing; to Artist (address); to Producer (address).

11. Entire Agreement. This agreement is entire in nature and all negotiations and understandings with respect to the subject matter hereof have been merged herein. This agreement may be amended or modified only by an instrument in writing executed by Artist and Producer.

12. Treatment. Subject to the above-referenced agreement, a treatment for the screenplay which has been submitted by Artist to Producer, and of which is material part of this agreement, has been attached hereto and made a part hereof, and marked as Exhibit "A".

13. Governing Law/Binding Arbitration. This agreement shall be governed under the laws of the state of New York. Should any dispute arise concerning the validity of this agreement and/or the breach of any term(s) thereunder, the parties shall agree to binding arbitration.

14. Waiver. No waiver, whether it be expressed or implied, of any breach of any term, condition or provision of this agreement shall be construed to be a continuing waiver or consent to any subsequent breach on the part of either party to this agreement.

15. Section Headings. The captions of the sections of this agreement are inserted solely for convenience and are not a part of the agreement and/or the construction of any provision hereof.

16. Separation of Rights. The parties hereto understand and agree that upon the payment of $2,500.00 (or $3,000.00) pursuant to Paragraph 1, the Artist will have transferred to Producer the exclusive right to market said screenplay, and Producer shall have the exclusive right to make, publish and copyright, any material referred to herein including photoplay, feature length motion picture or television movie and

may exploit the screenplay for such use or any other appropriate use. Therefore, upon payment by Producer to Artist of all monies as specified in Paragraphs 1(e) and 1(f), Artist will have transferred all rights to screenplay, including dramatic rights and any other rights which exists for all time, subject to Artist's rights under this agreement. Artist and Producer agree and understand that the screenplay will have no separable material which has not been assigned, and transferred wholly to the Producer.

IN WITNESS WHEREOF, the parties hereto have executed this agreement as of the day and year first written above.

(Artist) _____

(Producer) _____

The film was never made. When communism collapsed, so did all chances of my seeing "Foreign Relations" on the big screen. World peace, I learned, does have a price.

It is possible to sell a script without an agent by Attending Pitch Sessions in Los Angeles and telling producers about your project. If the right people get excited over your five-minute pitch, your two page synopsis and your screenplay, you're on your way to a sale. You can also find yourself an agent at one of these functions.

Pitch sessions are reviewed later in this segment.

There are writers who sell projects without agents but, in many cases, after negotiations are finished, the writers can't stand the people who hired them. (It's similar to the arbitration process in baseball; the main difference being writers won't tell reporters, "They insulted me with an offer of $16.5 million!")

An agent acts as a buffer between writer and producer so writers can plot stories, not revenge.

Keep Your Expectations Realistic

Your expectations must be in line with your track record. Try not to be overly demanding, as in calling the agent or producer twenty-four hours after he/she received your work and saying, "Are you interested or not? Huh?"

Metaphorically speaking, when you poke a finger in someone's chest, you'll get your eyes poked out by that person. Don't wait meekly by the phone for eight months either, canceling all social plans and holiday dinners, hoping today will be the day an agent calls you back. To paraphrase Stephen King, sort of, celibacy and leftovers from holiday dinners will make you all very dull boys and girls.

As you make more submissions, you'll acquire a better sense of what is right or wrong, normal or abnormal.

Of the people whom you contact, expect a very low percentage of respectful, cheerful, constructive, hopeful replies. When you do receive an encouraging letter, respond to it at once and submit something new.

Don't get too depressed over the plethora of rejections. My reaction to generic rejections was usually, "What's the use?" The voice in my head, sounding much like Livia Soprano, said, "Oh, poor you!" I sucked it up and kept trying. It was my only option if I wanted to be a writer.

Also, don't under-react to an encouraging letter. It's easy to say, "Close but no banana. They liked it but rejected it anyway. Who cares?"

Once, I wrote,

> "Hope ... comes and goes consistent with the sacrifice;
>
> Hope itself well may suffice."

About a year later, I said, "(Stuff) that! Hope isn't enough. I want results!"

About a year after that, I started thinking that hope was pretty good, after all. Hope was enough to keep me going, whether the results were encouraging or not. I still feel that way. If I was starving to death because I hadn't achieved any positive results, well, I might have to reevaluate my approach.

So, for the most part, when you are submitting without an agent, expect to be ignored. Remain hopeful that, eventually, someone will like your work and offer a contract.

When Is A Script Ready To Submit?

If you are afraid to show your script to anybody, including your mother, then the script is not ready to submit. You must let other people see your work and you must learn to accept constructive criticism.

Many of my writing students say the same thing: "I wrote it and threw it in my closet for a few years."

The last time I checked, closets can't read. They don't produce motion pictures, either. Show your work to a writing instructor, writing group members, your spouse; somebody. It's up to you to decide who will read your first draft. Somebody has got to go first. Tossing the script in the closet is your last option, unless, of course, you're suicidal.

Rule #2: Never let the bastards wear you so far down that you consider committing suicide. If you are totally depressed because no one wants to buy your work, write a nasty letter to someone who has crossed you. That will get you back into a creative mode and, while you're sitting at the computer, you can start on your next project.

Make sure your script has page numbers, is typed in Courier #12 (or #11) bold font, is written in three distinct acts, spell-checked and bound in some manner. The title page should have your name, address, email and Copyright (©) symbol. You can create the symbol by typing a left parentheses followed by a c followed by a right parentheses ... so it's (then c then). The © symbol will appear like magic. Typing the © symbol always brings a smile to my face because, for years, I couldn't make one appear on the page.

You don't have to go crazy and print the © symbol everywhere on your script. The artist who drew my comic book (details to follow) placed a © on every page of the book! He would've drawn the © symbol on every panel if I hadn't stopped him. Years from now, scientists may discover that typing the © symbol is addictive. It appears four times in this paragraph, a warning sign.

If you know your copyright registration number, include that on your title page, too.

Make sure you have no more than 120 pages in your dramatic screenplay and no more than 110 in your comedy.

Further information on copyrighting and formatting appears later in this book.

What About Agents Outside LA And NY?

I'm based in Philadelphia so don't expect me to trash this group en masse, although most of them deserve it. The nicest things I can say about them is they're better than no agent at all and they don't have access to the strong intoxicants served up in the big cities. They don't have access to the really good mental health facilities, either.

A small town agent will probably have a shorter-rap sheet and fewer ex-spouses than their big city counterparts.

When I moved back to Philadelphia from L.A., I found that these small-town agents were a bit more interested in my work than New Yorkers. (That means one in ten answered my query.) I almost had luck with a woman agent in Minnesota; let's call her "Carol."

When Carol first called me about possible representation, I didn't thank her for her interest or beg her for her time. I asked a simple question that may have endeared her to me: "Is this agency some kinda toy from your husband so you can appear to have a career? I don't have a year to waste, if ya know what I mean."

Poetry does not have to be pretty to be effective.

She got angry but realized that I had self-esteem; I couldn't afford a lazy agent. Maybe I was offensive, but I had to be sure that she was totally committed to this endeavor like I was. As it turned out, her commitment was laudable.

We spoke often via telephone and the producers liked her immensely because she had mid-western charm and honesty. Los Angeles producers were used to sleazy, slimy, gimmicky come-ons -- probably because that's what they knew best -- and this woman was as honest and unassuming as a corn field. She hadn't been through the battles in fancy Rodeo Drive restaurants and she conveyed a freshness that hadn't been seen in Hollywood since Samuel Goldwyn was a herring salesman. (He was, no kidding, until "The Squaw Man" became a hit.)

We set up meetings in the city that never weeps (L.A.) and actually met in person for the first time in June, 1990. I believe it was still snowing in Minnesota. How did we hook up after we landed separately at LAX? We only recognized each other's voice. Simple. We were the only ones in the L.A. airport without magnificent suntans.

We got our bags, then sat outside in the sun for an hour. Carol asked me, "What's that big, round, yellow thing in the sky?"

We took meetings with "important" producers. She didn't fully comprehend that I was her protection from aggressive male producers. I spent half my time pitching projects; the other half giving off vibrations that conveyed, "Keep your slimy mitts off this lady."

Carol never suggested that I date a female producer to get an edge because that concept never occurred to her. The producers tried to help her whenever they could.

She needed help. The average "TV Guide" reader knew more about entertainment industry people than she did. She had to be an actress to be a credible agent.

One producer told us a dramatic tale of how Michael Ovitz (Hollywood's most powerful agent at the time and now a man who publicly wonders why no one will take his calls) had called about a project. This young producer paced around his office for a minute muttering nervously, "What do I say? Suppose I say something wrong?"

Carol had absolutely no idea who he was talking about. I made wild facial expressions, trying to convey to her it was someone presidential -- as presidential as an agent can be. Clasping her hands together in awed delight, she said, "It was really him?" Then she looked out of the corner of her eye for my approval. I expressed the idea that she should tone it down and save the act for a screen test later that day.

Gene Wilder's company was interested in my story about the only lawyer in heaven. John Candy, who sadly passed away soon after, had a production company which was curious about my "Superfan" project. Producers who didn't know us and couldn't use my scripts recommended us to other companies. All we needed was one producer who wanted to buy something I'd written. We were in the right place with the right stuff ... was it the right time?

It was exciting, but I reminded myself that Charlie Sheen was excited after meeting Gordon Gekko, the guy who said, "Greed is good," in "Wall Street."

I remember vividly that I bought new, summer shoes before the trip -- I was still wearing snow boots in Philly -- and wore them for the first time in L.A. My feet were killing me the first two days of meetings. I had more blisters than Minnesota had lakes.

I also remember shouting out at studio buildings, "I'm BAAAA-AAACK!". The city of Los Angeles was like an old foe whom I had vowed to defeat in time. If it wasn't then, it would be later that decade.

I had spent many sleepless nights dreading the notion that a big earthquake would turn the town to dust before I could return victoriously. The strangest thing was ... I knew I wasn't alone in that kind of deranged thinking. Not at all.

I lived in a town that gave bad Karma a good name.

As we entered the new millennium, I realized I had forgiven the old gal, California. She hadn't singled me out for punishment; she abused everyone equally. She broke everyone's heart without malice. She was like a cat kidnapping a baby rabbit -- it was what she did. What could we do about it -- sue her? We'd have better luck suing the rabbit-napping cat.

When I visit L.A. nowadays, I smile nostalgically at many happy memories from my youth ... and mumble, "I'll have the last laugh on you, yet ... but have a nice day." To be truthful, that coveted last laugh may wind up being only a minor chuckle, as satisfying as a mustard burp ("Momentarily tangy," like the dying man said in "Things To Do In Denver When You're Dead," "but quickly forgotten in the wind.")

Anyway, Carol and I got a break. I had written a domestic comedy TV movie script that I had expanded from a film treatment and a female director liked it. This woman had directed a similar kind of TV movie, had a deal with the networks to develop projects and had recently completed the AA program, just as Carol had done! They were talking about "Bill this" and "Bill that." I didn't know what was going on, but the successful director and my agent were hugging twenty minutes after they had met.

The director had a male assistant, twenty years her junior, with her at lunch and I knew this guy was selling his body and soul to get a break in show business. I was doubly happy because I was getting a break without stooping to his level.

We gave this duo a copy of my script and they promised to send us a contract the following week for, what else, the minimum I would accept.

I returned to Philadelphia, triumphant. We were a hit. I had paid off as a longshot winner for my wonderful agent, who had signed me to a contract although I was a nobody. Now both of us were somebodies.

I wrote a poem:

I'm just another player in the exhibition game,

Out there on the field between rejection and acclaim.

And this, like any movie, has a message in each frame:

The bottom line is money ... and under it is fame.

Unhappily, the contract sent by the director and her assistant/sex slave was completely ludicrous. It called for no up-front money, as promised, and only a fraction of the money we verbally agreed on in-between the ladies' hugs! Meanwhile, this director was pitching my project, which she didn't own even a little bit, to the networks! The director kept stalling, then pitching the project, over and over again until the project was dead. If a network had said "yes," then she would've been forced to pay something to us or steal it outright.

My small-town agent could not stop the Hollywood types from doing what they do best; steal, lie and sleaze around with underage wannabes. (I'm sure adultery was part of the package, too.)

How often can you afford to fly to California, take meetings for two weeks, get legitimate interest and good feedback, then be disappointed? It gets old and gets you old quickly. When you live in L.A., you can repeat this process every month and you might be lucky and have a deal go through.

Small town agents can take you to a certain point and then either you or the agent better have the experience to get a deal finalized.

It's like being turned down for fire insurance, then you smell something burning. You don't know the origin of the fire, but you're sure it's about to go "boom." You douse your home with water, call the fire department and before the fire trucks can get there, you're standing on a pile of ashes and everyone's crying and blaming each other. Then the crying stops and everyone is still blaming each other.

Your only solace is the fact that you've learned something ... and you've gotten a good poem out of the experience.

Agents I Have Known

When my first agent, Barbara, started a literary wing of an established theatrical agency, it meant I was accepted into the Hollywood community and I would get to meet Adam West, star of the 1960's "Batman" TV series.

I wasn't, and I wouldn't, but I did get out of the starting gate quickly with a race track script. "The Jockettes" was the true story of a female jockey who overcame sexual discrimination and harassment to succeed in a man's world. I had written a treatment (more information on writing treatments appears later in this book) after wandering in to the jockeys' quarters at a Pennsylvania race track and chatting amicably with the riders. I had no credentials or press pass but I looked like I might be important. When the conversation was over, I had a condensed life story on my notebook and a handshake agreement with the girl jockey.

My agent, who had been with the established agency less than a month, sold the project to a producer who had secured the interest of a female TV star, Cheryl Ladd, one TV's original "Charlie's Angels."

My biggest concern that week was buying new clothes so I would look good when I went to a party at Ms. Ladd's home. (Hey, I had already met Bo Derek at the supermarket in Marina del Rey; maybe I was on a roll!)

In moments like these, breaking into the entertainment business seems easy. Too easy.

It's never that easy. The jockey never responded to the contract offer because ... wait, let my lawyer approve this first ... OK? ... because ... she had been busted on pot charges five years earlier and someone told her I would exploit her. I could never sell a story about a drug-crazed jockey. I had no problem selling a woman-succeeds-in-a-man's-world story.

The only reason I discovered the jockey's reason for stonewalling me was because I was involved in owning a race horse. I found out about the jockey's concern over publicizing her past problems through a race track employee. I saw the woman jockey in the paddock years later and she looked at me as if to say, "I know I did something bad to this guy but I can't remember what it was."

She wouldn't even tell me she had changed her mind when ABC offered a deal. She just agreed to work with me during our first meeting, asked me to send her a good faith check, which I did, then ignored me, making me look like a compulsive liar to ABC.

The jockey's agent also ignored me, probably following his client's orders. At that point, I vowed never to work with agents who lived and worked out of cheap motel rooms. What really annoys me is that I drive past the motel all the time; constantly reminded of the lying jockey's agent, named Dick. Often, I shield my eyes while driving so I don't have to see the motel sign.

The worst part about that failed movie deal was returning all those nice clothes to the stores on Rodeo Drive in Beverly Hills.

My most vivid memory of those meetings with the producer was that the owner of the agency was more nervous than me. Another detail I haven't blocked out was the reaction of the producer who had gotten ABC's interest after I let him read, "A Decent Man," my compassionate poem about alcohol abuse. He patted me on the back and looked at me as if to say, "This guy will survive in Hollywood about a week." If I read him any more poems, he probably would've bought me a one-way bus ticket to Utah.

It was looking like I wasn't cut out for the Hollywood lifestyle. The double-dealing, an industry staple, seemed to bother me more than most. But I couldn't leave when I was so close to getting a script produced. As a matter of fact, I kept getting closer.

Barbara and I moved, as a writing/producing team, to a major agency in Los Angeles. Our agent, who referred to Barbara and myself as, "The Dynamic Duo," represented Ron Howard, who had just directed "Splash" and "Cocoon."

Our agent hung up on Ron Howard, saying, "Ron, I gotta go now, Don and Barbara are here."

That was the highlight of my career, thus far.

I suspect this agent took us on because of my friendship with the influential Philadelphian, who worked closely with a studio owner on oil deals. So, the best agent I ever had probably didn't really want me; he wanted my friend's friend as a business ally. Or he wanted Barbara and I to acquire the rights to life stories, then turn over those rights to his major clients. People would demand more money for their life stories if they knew the rights were going to a successful director instead of unknowns like us.

I wanted to get a personalized license plate that read "Writer/Sucker" but there were too many letters to fit on the plate.

The life story angle almost worked for us when we closed in on signing two athletes for a movie deal. We would've acquired the rights, then given them to a director in exchange for associate producer credits on a feature film. I was to put up the relatively small sum ($10,000) to get the rights, then Barbara, who had developed a good relationship with the athletes, and I would both be associate producers; that's how it worked.

Not that our imagined success went to our heads, but Barbara and I argued for days about the design of our corporate logo.

Before I invested any money, I happened to ask Barbara, "What if this director turns the project into a TV show or animated series, then what?"

She said that she would have a job on the show, but I was promised absolutely nothing.

I said, "How would that make you feel if I put up the money and made nothing and you worked on the show for ten years?"

She said, "That would be great for me!"

I packed, sold my car and left L.A. I didn't want to adapt to that way of thinking.

I had ignored nine-hundred-and-ninety-nine-thousand, nine-hundred-and-ninety-nine (my editor tells me I must spell out numbers and it's getting on my nerves) omens telling me to get out of L.A. before I turned into a reptile. This omen, number one million for those of you keeping score, motivated me to fly out of town before I needed a special airline seat to accommodate my tail.

It's possible that, when they made the film, "Godzilla," the main character was not the only one on the Hollywood set with a tail. No wonder the film laid an egg and sunk to the bottom of the pond.

I signed with my next agent after I had moved from Los Angeles to my home town of Philadelphia. This man in Arizona liked my Superfan screenplay, a parody of a futuristic sports society, but admitted, "I don't understand it, but I like it."

He acted like a scorned lover when I told him I was giving a New York City agent/producer a one-time shot to sell the Superfan project. If either person sold the project, I'd pay two commissions, which seemed fair to me. Call me a relic, but when everyone wins, I consider it fair. The Arizona agent called me a two-timer so I was left with the New Yorker.

Mr. New York told me he didn't want to be my agent, per se. He was going to be my personal manager, my producer, my lawyer, my pimp; my reading service, financier, accountant and architect.

"Anything else you want to tell me?" I asked.

"Yeah. I just stopped drinking again and got married for the sixth time."

I needed representation so we shook hands on a Manhattan street so cold that I briefly missed the city of Los Angeles.

This New York fellow liked my project, "Hidden Star," which was a true story based on the book about the discovery of the planet, Pluto. In 1930, a young man went to work in the Lowell observatory, searching for planets. While all the European experts couldn't locate the ninth planet, this twenty-one year old discovered Pluto, a needle in a planetary haystack.

Mr. N.Y. told me to redraw my contract with the publisher, who signed a new agreement granting me full rights to market a movie based on the book written by the twenty-one year old (now eighty-something) who discovered Pluto. The publisher had full rights, now I had 'em; that's how it worked.

We signed contracts. Mr. N.Y. sent my screen treatment (more on that later, honest) to studios who liked the project, but were only interested if the main character was a teenager. Twenty-one years òld was too old for young audiences.

I wrote a full screenplay, subtracted two years from the main character's age (now he was 19) and a major studio wanted to buy it! One problem -- the publisher told me matter-of-factly that the contract between author/publisher had unexpectedly expired and we (including me) don't have any rights anymore. I called the author in Arizona and explained that I had done everything above-board in securing rights only to find I now needed his approval. I also mentioned how, after all my research, done in good faith, I felt as if I knew him. I really did respect his dedication. The author didn't want to lift a finger to read my script because, "We're busy people."

He and his wife were pushing ninety! How busy could they have been?

The N.Y. producer/personal manager/private eye called me an "amateur" for botching the contract. The only preventative measure available to me was going to the publisher's office, opening the files and demanding to see their contract with the "busy" author. Basically, I would've had to call them liars and demand they prove otherwise which isn't a great way to conduct business, even in the entertainment industry.

You can do everything right and end up with spit ...

But you only really lose if you quit.

I looked for another agent by knocking on doors in New York City. One agent invited me into his tiny apartment/office in a high-rise security building. He wore a neck brace so I asked him how he got hurt and how he felt. As it turned out, he was separating from his wife who, the week before, had worn a perfume that "she knew" made him sneeze. He sneezed so violently that he threw out his spine and was now suing her for damages.

"Maybe you should avoid her altogether," I suggested.

"Can't," he answered. "She's still living here with me. Part of the settlement."

Then he showed me the article in that day's New York Post about his problems with his wife. It was like living a scene out of "The Fortune Cookie" which is a lot better than feeling like William Holden at the end of "Sunset Boulevard."

(I recently corresponded with the neck-braced agent. He remembered me and wrote back, "I've had massive, unsuccessful surgery." I didn't ask if his ex-wife still lived with him in his tiny apartment.)

Writers can be quirky, demanding, unreasonable and, in a rare congruency, so can agents. A top agent will not want to work with a new writer because he/she will consume too much time. A new writer must settle for a new or unproven agent -- which can be good enough if that agent submits a great project to the right person at the right time.

An Agent's Typical Day

My first agent, Barbara, had a typical day in the mid-1980's. She accompanied me to a major TV studio for a meeting with the studio's VP.

I trusted her with directions and we got lost. While unintentionally cruising the barrio, I told her, "You know, they asked to see us and we're guessing it's because of the 'Superfan' script we sent them but ... I did mention that we were very close to the studio president's uncle -- "

"Personal contacts don't mean squat!" she screamed. "They want to meet with you because they love the script!"

So we walked into the office, late, and the VP threw my script into my chest like a frisbee.

"We didn't like the script but the president wanted me to talk to you out of respect for his uncle."

Barbara looked at me like she knew he was going to say that. I was prepared, however, and I pitched other projects. While I pitched, this VP took a large bullwhip and began whipping his own hand, then bragged about the immense sum he had won betting Monday night football. (I'm not sure of the year but it was definitely a Tuesday afternoon in a strike season.) Each time he cracked the whip, Barbara's shoulders twitched up to her ears. She didn't say a word the entire meeting.

This executive was testing my recuperative powers and my toughness. He started to like me when I answered impudently. He didn't pursue anything I'd written. That could have meant he was a bad judge of talent, the ideas were bad, the writing spotty, the subject too similar to what they already had; they were broke, indifferent or ... great contacts are not always great.

My guess is he was indifferent.

Months later, I was at a party and mentioned the VP to a stranger, who said, "Oh yeah, the guy with the whip."

So it was a typical day, after all.

I once had a typical day as an agent. A scorned boyfriend walked into my office building in downtown Philadelphia and shot his girlfriend to death near the water cooler in her office. I was reviewing a book on illegal arms sales.

The point is: don't expect agents to read your script or book in a day. They have distractions, like everyone else.

In a typical day, I might get a call from a writer with whom I haven't spoken for a year.

"So, any nibbles?" the writer asks.

"On what?" I reply.

"On my book."

"We haven't spoken for a year. In our last conversation, you said you'd try to finish the book."

"All finished. I thought you sent out query letters."

"Why didn't you mention we were working together?"

If I had sent out letters of inquiry on his behalf, it would guarantee that the writer's response would've been: "I haven't called you for a year. That means I'm working with someone else, dummy!"

He probably got booted by the agent whom he'd worked with for the past year.

Sometimes, an agent sends out a book to a dozen logical publishers and all twelve hate the book a lot. Then the writer yells at the agent for being a bad agent. They want to break the contract, they want all copies of the contract returned along with all their work, even rough copies, via overnight mail, at once.

Those writers eroded my enthusiasm for new talent.

On a typical day, I received a query letter regarding a book about wimpy guys and how to avoid being one. I liked the premise and agreed to read the book.

The author was clearly a misogynist. I'm no feminist, but I thought that the writer's touch was a little heavy. He thought I was close-minded. Typical.

Don't be a writer who expects the agent to do everything immediately. An agent is not going to make one hundred copies of your book, one hundred phone calls, one hundred follow up calls, then drive in a thousand mile loop to make personal presentations on your behalf on the first day you sign a contract. If you're a new writer, expect your agent to test your material somewhere and expect a reply from a publisher within a few months.

If you call your agent every day and ask, "What have you done for me today?" the answer will be, "I mailed your book back to you. We're no longer working together!"

What Is Going On In That Fuzzy Agent Head?

Most agents look for this type of opportunity: a world famous individual turns down millions from the tabloids to write a book that everybody wants to read. A dozen publishers start the bidding with the agent at one million dollars.

Agents are like bankers. They want dead-sure-shots with no possible risk. In this manner, they are again the exact antithesis of writers who must take chances to get at the truth.

I represented a woman who had written a children's book about the sibling rivalry between her cocker spaniels. I love animals so I sent the book to children's publishers, who hated it a lot. That's what agents fear most: a publisher writing back, "I have no need for sibling rivalries between cocker spaniels." It's like buying a new car and everyone says, "What a horrible color."

So what's worse: hearing that the book you've chosen to represent is a dog or hearing that the movie deal you successfully arranged is dead because a publisher botched the rights' agreement?

The first scenario is worse because you made a bad decision. If you keep doing that, you'll never make a sale. If you keep Acquiring Rights To Interesting Books that will adapt well to film, you'll eventually get a movie made. You just have to find that special someone who doesn't assign expired book rights or try to steal from you outright. This task is harder than it seems.

It's important to note that signed contracts guarantee nothing except that lawyers will be paid. A handshake agreement with someone you know and trust usually works out better.

It's important, also, to remember why I took on the cocker spaniel story. It appealed to my taste. The best way to get an agent's representation is to write about something that appeals to the agent.

For example, if you had written to me describing your story about race tracks, animals, the environment, planets, sports, the future, scam artists and other topics which interest me, I'd have probably invited you to send the entire book/script. So it would be helpful if you knew agents well enough to send them a story they would be preconditioned to enjoy. I don't know how you would elicit this information without living in their homes for a week or dressing up as a Gallup Poll representative, but you're a writer so be creative.

Getting back to taste, I once sent my project list (synopses of about two dozen of my projects) to a Los Angeles agent who called me back immediately and declared, "We have the same taste!" At her request, I Fedex'd about a dozen scripts to her office, at a cost of about one hundred dollars.

I never heard from her again.

Let's analyze the situation. She called me the moment she read my project list, which is extremely encouraging. She insisted I send my best twelve scripts at once, overnight mail, which is flattering. She said we had the same taste which is lucky as hell. I knew she was inclined to like at least one of my projects and sign me on as a client.

I bet she never read a word. I suspect she works for an overnight delivery company and is personally responsible for a few hundred thousand dollars in business each year. She may have simply thrown my twelve scripts and my return postage in the trash can.

Before I was an agent, I thought agents kept and used the stamps that writers provided for return postage. Now I believe stamps are lost or misplaced by agents who fail to return material. So, to balance my antagonistic statements regarding agents, let me admit they are more likely to be slobs than thieves.

Remember, even if you're good and lucky enough to motivate an agent to ask for your work, don't be so sure the agent will read your work. Agents have been known to not only distort the truth but also to toss the truths you've written into a trash can, unread. Ironically, you need these truth-challenged salespeople to sell your truths.

I once wrote,

"A writer tries to mine the truth

And distill it until it turns pure;

But are truths that go unnoticed

Still worthwhile? I'm not sure."

Now I am sure. They are worthwhile, just hard to sell when you're unknown.

Should You Send An Agent Money?

The natural tendency, if you have self-esteem, is to dismiss the idea, then lose self-esteem for having briefly entertained it. No one wants to be a struggling writer/sucker. An insulted/injured lover would be preferable.

If you're any good, you'll get noticed without paying a fee, right?

Of the writers who pay for critiques, seminars, etc., ninety percent of them will never finish their second book because they have no clue and too much disposable cash -- is that what you're thinking?

If you expect to live two hundred years, you'd be right. The cream would rise to the top and you'd never need to spend money on anything but postage. If you know that you're a natural talent, don't pay professionals to analyze your work. Just keep writing and you will be successful in your two hundred-year lifetime.

For the rest of us, there's always that fear of bad timing. Example: The studio chiefs, all born in the 21st century, suddenly love your work and visit you at the old age home. They're adapting every book you ever wrote into major motion pictures and you can't remember one word you wrote.

"How did you manage to stay unknown?" the studio chiefs ask, as if you wanted to be a well-kept secret so your art didn't suffer, although you suffered plenty.

Don't spend ten thousand dollars a year on reading fees but don't be close-minded to spending a few bucks for consultation.

For example: I wrote a parody of sports society, "Superfan 2020," which was later adapted into a nationally distributed Comic Book, and I didn't know where my story was centered until the third draft. That's when a paid consultant told me, "you've got a buddy-movie about the immature adult fan and the mature child fan. That's what works."

I had been focusing on the relationship between the team and the fans when the real story concerned the lonely man and neglected boy. I had spent a few hundred dollars wisely.

If you think everyone is out to rip you off, you'd be right much of the time, but that attitude would sink you like a torpedo to the ocean floor, where it's hard to breathe without help. You'd be stuck in a reef, waving to the blue fish in "Finding Nemo." Remember the blue fish? She was better off having a horrible memory. She was full of trust and devoid of paranoia because she couldn't remember all the occasions when she had her fins picked by unscrupulous bottom feeders.

So, when you're not sure whether to send an agent or a script consultant money, listen to your own common sense. Take a few intelligent chances.

One beginning writer sent a $50 check to my agency and asked me to critique his work. He wrote that he knew I would probably cash the check and ignore his work (because that's what other agents had done) but, hey, it was only 50 bucks.

A final note for those of you who will live to be two-hundred years-old. Write a nonfiction book entitled, "How To Live To Be Two-Hundred, Guaranteed" and an agent will happily represent you without charging a fee ... if you're one hundred-and-fifty years-old, walk vigorously and look good.

Earning An Agent's Attention And Respect

If you're planning on living two-hundred years, you shouldn't send agents money for any reason. Why not? Because, by your one-hundredth birthday, you'll figure out for yourself how to get an agent's attention.

First, you have to become a method actor and imagine yourself in the role of an agent. If you're a serious writer, this will cause you to sweat and become confused. You may not be able to drive. It's always helpful for a writer to experience and appreciate acting, directing, agenting and other facets of the business. You'll know more about the other person's job and receive fewer overall surprises in the industry. For unknown writers, surprises are usually bad.

For example, in 1992, I was unpleasantly surprised by a publishing contract. The company that offered to publish my book was not listed in the "Vanity Press" section of the Writer's Market; it was listed with other legitimate publishers. But when the contract arrived, I learned that I had to pay all production costs! Surprise! I reacted by riding up and down an elevator for an hour in my future mother in law's apartment building, muttering. She had to send a search-and-rescue team to drag me back to the holiday dinner, where I muttered at the table while stabbing my fork into the mashed sweet potatoes.

Imagine yourself in my old office in downtown Philadelphia. Paramount in your mind is, of course, the big question: Is anyone being murdered in my building at this moment? Has any jealous, heavily armed boyfriend barged through security to shoot an unarmed woman at the water cooler because she had the nerve to date other men?

Ask yourself: have I dated any women with a jealous, heavily armed boyfriend in this building?

OK, your conscience is clear. Now you can read mail from writers you've never met.

Have these strangers read the Writer's Guild list, specifying that you only read letters of inquiry? If someone sends you an unsolicited three-thousand page script on the Roman Empire, then demands that you read it immediately and spend seventy-five dollars on postage to mail it back, you will throw the entire package in the trash can.

You'll want writers to include a SASE to make it easier to respond. If one hundred writers fail to include a SASE that day, you will spend that day typing labels and waiting in line at the post office. Unknown writers must make everything easy for an agent. Try including a stamped post card with blocks to check off if the agent is interested.

Try to propose a project that appeals to the agent's own taste or to his/her business sense. Even if the agent doesn't like your idea, he/she may believe there is a strong market for your book. When it comes to new writers, one of two elements must be present in their work:

1. agents love the subject matter and would write their own book on this subject if they woke up one day possessing talent of their own.

2. agents know they can sell this story no matter whose name appears on the title page because it's a hot subject.

So your job is to convince agents that either of these conditions exist: they love the project personally or they know it's an easy sale.

You also must convince them that you're easy to work with; not an agitator, instigator or litigator. Present yourself as humble, professional and appreciative. Act as if you know exactly how to present your material to the marketplace. Don't insist that the agent send your script to Mr. X at studio Y but suggest that your project would be well received at a certain studio because of specific, irrefutable reasons. If you've written a great script and have a good hunch who will be interested, you'll be making the agent's job easier.

Assume that all agents are lazy and will be receptive to brilliant marketing suggestions. Without calling anyone lazy, convince them you've got a great project and great plan and you'll get noticed. That's all it takes to get an agent.

If you don't follow their suggestions (like including a SASE) they will assume you're hard to work with and ignore you. It's like driving down the boulevard. You see fifty green lights ahead of you and if any one of them turns red, you'll have to stop. Don't change the color on any of those green lights. You need all fifty to stay green or your project is stopped cold.

When the agent signs you on, there are more lights ahead of you, all of which must stay green for your project to succeed.

So, to recap, write a great story, be humble, show appreciation, make it easy for an agent to reply, explain why the project is viable and likely to sell, be patient and get lucky.

It also helps if you exhibit a sense of humor. If you've never had one and want to survive your writing career, you'd better find one quickly. Rent one or something.

You may be thinking: how can I be nice to people if they act like haughty, lazy, front-running slobs? The answer is: make believe you're dealing with a loan officer at a bank. If you didn't need the services of an agent or banker, you'd probably roll your eyes and cross the street to avoid them. You'd be doing the right thing. As writers, we need agents to peddle our work. If there were other options, I'd have explored them and told you about them. Hey, having an agent is better than having a parole officer, or so I'm told.

A good way to get an agent or producer's attention is to produce a videotaped presentation of your story. It could be a ten-minute recap of the Junior Achievement program, a few minutes of athletes competing or a scene from your proposed sitcom or children's show. I know a young producer who spent a few hundred thousand dollars (of other people's money) making a six minute trailer for his proposed film. Investors are taking him seriously now because of this trailer. If he didn't have an agent, he could probably have his choice of agents simply by mailing them his trailer.

If you're a comedy writer and you send an agent your ten minute act on videotape, it will have more of an impact than if you'd sent only the written material.

It's a cheap way of attracting attention, but it works.

If you want to break in as a television writer, write a spec script, which is a script written with the hope that someone will recognize your talent. Maybe it should be called a "hope" script.

You can write an episode of your favorite sitcom or drama and get yourself noticed as someone who can write within the framework of an existing show. This can get you a job on another show or an upcoming one. It isn't written solely to impress the producers of that particular show. It's something you write to impress every TV producer.

After you've written a spec sitcom/dramatic script, I suggest writing an original pilot script, to prove you can create your own characters and comedic/dramatic situations, not just imitate others.

Most agents will tell you to write an episode of an existing TV series, like "Smallville" or "The Simpsons." I've always felt that it's more difficult to create an entire universe, i.e. an original TV series. Even though the odds are against getting it produced, you can get noticed quicker.

Here is what the producer of the "North Shore" TV show said (in Creative Screenwriting Magazine's daily newsletter) about writing spec scripts for existing series versus writing a pilot script for your own series:

"You should write a sample of an existing show, to show you have the chops to write professionally. So if somebody picked up that script and read it, they would say, 'Wow, this really feels like a Six Feet Under to me, that's terrific.' You want that, but you also want a piece of work that shows evidence of how clever, original, and what a great writer you are."

Recently, I wrote a spec script for my favorite show, "Curb Your Enthusiasm." I am trying to motivate my agent (details about how I found one appear later) to submit that script along with my original pilot script, "When Angels Speak," to TV producers, so I can get paid someday for my TV writing.

I have written many spec sitcom scripts over the years. Besides "Best of the West," I wrote an episode of "Barney Miller," "Laverne and Shirley" and "Married With Children."

The "Barney Miller" episode was about cops who arrested a major bookie. Meanwhile, the same cops were playing the bookie's football pools at the police station.

My "Laverne and Shirley" script was called "Animal Crackers - Is Your Pet Nuts?" It was about Squiggy's crush on a pretty veterinarian.

In my "Married with Children" episode, "Earth To Bundy," Al thinks he's discovered a planet. As it turns out, all he discovered was a spider egg on the telescope lens.

One day, in the early 1980's, my first agent, Barbara, received a call from a producer at a major television production company. She had previously sent them my spec sitcom scripts.

"Would Don be interested in a staff position?" they asked.

I heard this on the phone extension and started jumping up and down, nodding with vigor.

"Does a clam want to go to the beach?" I thought. "Yes!"

I was twenty-six years old and would be making a thousand or two per week.

My agent said she would run the idea past me and give them an answer soon. She didn't want to sound over-eager, but she wanted to put me to work and take a ten percent cut of my weekly earnings.

A few weeks later, a producer called back and said, "Sorry. One of the partner's nephews just graduated from college and he wants to give the staff job to the kid."

The encouraging part of this story is that a completely unknown writer can impress an agent with a spec script and, with a little luck, get hired as a staff writer on a TV show. If your agent has a stable of twenty writers working at staff jobs, he or she will earn thousands a week without doing much. So agents are always looking for writers who can display a flair for writing TV spec scripts.

Other Ways To Get Your Scripts Read

Eva Peel lives in Los Angeles, charges writers to promote their work and is a really nice person. You didn't expect that last part, did you? Well, neither did I. She admits that she would be better off in some ways if she mastered the art of the "hard sell."

Eva once owned THEWRITEWAYIN.COM and charged about thirty-five dollars to writers who wanted their one page synopses pitched to publishers and producers. She charged about twenty-five dollars for a chance to get noticed by agents and managers. Managers are more interested in finding new talent, she claims.

Screenwriters pay about one-hundred dollars to personally pitch scripts to producers in meetings, organized by Eva several times per year. I constantly send money to Eva, hoping that a producer likes my one-page synopsis and asks to read my script.

Now, Eva charges $150 to help writers target producers who produce the same type of material. Since I have two true stories, "The Jockettes" and "The Money Machine," Eva will soon be sending me a list of companies that produce real-life dramas. I will send them each a letter and a synopsis of my story. By November, 2004, Eva will be selling a list of entertainment industry contacts. If you buy her list at evapeel@earthlink.net, you will be able to contact the agents of certain actors or directors and attempt to pitch your story to those folks. Eva specializes in helping unknown writers get their scripts noticed.

Natalie Rothenberg owns THE INSIDER'S SYSTEM. For a few hundred dollars, she critiqued my screenplay, called "The Money Machine" and gave it a box-score (a 1-10 scale for premise, dialogue, character development and other story elements.) Then she published a magazine with dozens of synopses, critiques and box-scores and sent it to three-hundred producers and publishers. The theory was, if a producer liked my synopsis, he or she would call Natalie and request the script. Then Natalie would call and tell me where to send it.

I chose to promote "The Money Machine" because a similar caper film is in the works at HBO. (Details appear later in this section.) I thought that, maybe, producers would notice that my story was similar to the HBO film and would want to read my script. If my screenplay had suddenly become marketable, I thought I should find out about it. (If one caper film does well, producers will hunt for more of the same.) I paid for a critique and an opportunity to reach elusive producers.

(Both Eva Peel and Natalie Rothenberg have turned over control of their critiquing services to others but their companies continue to serve writers. You can call Eva Peel at 310-396-1662 and ask how she can help you contact producers.)

"The Money Machine" screenplay is described below, along with my other screenplays, teleplays, TV series and books on my project list.

Do not copy the format for this list. I correct the mistakes later in this chapter.

The Project List -- Screenplays/ Novels

Donald Paul Rutberg

Email: DPRinnet@aol.com

CURRENT LIST OF PROJECTS

SCREENPLAYS/ NOVELS:

"THE JOCKETTES": In the late 1960's, no female jockey had ever ridden in a thoroughbred horse race. The men who controlled the "Sport of Kings" considered women too weak to control an 1,100 pound animal running at 35 miles an hour. That didn't stop women from seeking out jockeys' licenses. Men barred them from applying. They went to court and got their licenses. Men boycotted the racetracks. They began to ride horses in actual races. Men threw stones at their trailers. Finally, in 1969, female jockeys started winning races at North American race tracks. This is the inspirational true story of Diane Crump, the first female jockey to ride in the U.S., and the other pioneering women who overcame incredible obstacles to win equal rights on the racetrack. (The exclusive rights to Diane Crump's life story are attached to this project.)

THE MONEY MACHINE: In 2002, computer hackers altered "Pick 6" tickets worth $3 million. But in 1970, there were no computers to hack. Crooks had to use a more hands-on approach ... so they stole a tote machine, hand-cranked it and printed winning tickets after the races were over! For several months, the race track was giving money away to its patrons and it didn't know why! When the crooks were finally caught due to their own error, they exchanged the money machine -- for freedom. In essence, the advancing computer age was delayed just long enough to ensure this "Sting"-like perfect crime. (Based on a true story)

WHEN ANGELS SPEAK ... (THEY ARGUE): An outgoing, arbitration lawyer dies and is disappointed to learn that he's been assigned a similar job in a dull, sterile world known as heaven. With no chance to enjoy the Earthly pleasures his spirit craves, the only lawyer in heaven enters the game of angelic politics, hoping to add some life to his death. (Also a TV series)

SUPERFAN 2020: It is 2020 and sports society has gone beyond escapism to insanity ... on its way to the unnatural. A sports nut named Murray joyfully jeopardizes his marriage, his job and his life in order to win the Superfan trophy. He and his 11 year-old protégé prove that the heroes are in the cheap seats after the pampered players are forced to play in a "Real" World Series. (Also a comic book -- nationally distributed)

SUMMER AT SARATOGA: A young man quits his "perfect" job in the family dress business and takes his chances, acquiring two race horses and falling in love with the horses' trainer. In one frantic summer, he's stalked by the trainer's telepathic, telekinetic, terribly jealous ex-boyfriend and discovers the horses are superstar clones, who may be worth millions.

HANGIN' WITH HOMELESS OTIS: Tall, lean, black, 50'ish, bug-eyed, drug-free, high-strung Otis is homeless by choice. He applies his intelligence and communicative skills in the city streets, "developing relationships" (not "panhandling") and dodging death. Otis is considered a nuisance by everyone in the street, except for the young man who knows him best. (Based on a true story; also a stage play)

Donald Paul Rutberg

Email: DPRinnet@aol.com

CURRENT LIST OF PROJECTS

NONFICTION BOOKS:

<u>A WRITER'S FIRST AID KIT</u>: A writer-turned-literary agent discovers unsettling truths about each profession and, from a dual perspective, offers advice for unagented writers. (Includes chapters on how to write and market TV/film treatments, children's books, magazine articles, etc.) (Published by Pale Horse Publishing, 2004)

<u>WHEN BABY BOOMERS WERE YOUNG</u>: A collection of stories and poems from Baby Boomers' childhoods; while we can still remember them.

NONFICTION -- TELEPLAYS/ BOOKS

<u>OUT OF THE WILDERNESS</u>: During WWII, an orphaned, Polish, Jewish teenager miraculously eludes the Nazis, joins the Russian army, gets arrested for "Counter Revolutionary Propaganda," nearly starves to death in prison; survives in a wilderness commune, escapes to and from the Polish army posing as a Greek concentration camp survivor and finds his family in America.

<u>HOT PEPPERS FOR POP</u>: During the Great Depression, a 15 year-old boy earns enough money in hot-pepper eating contests to attend a major league baseball game, where he sits on the field with Dizzy Dean and drinks from the dugout water fountain.

<u>TWENTY MILLION NICKELS</u>: The true story of Sigmund Lubin, an immigrant optician who transforms a flash-in-the-pan sideshow act called "Life Motion Pictures" from a lower-class amusement into a world-wide industry. Competitors with Thomas Edison, partners with Samuel Goldwyn -- then vice-versa! -- Lubin is the first to make millions in the movie business ... and the first to lose millions.

<u>LIFE AFTER DEATH</u>: Imagine a place where there is total peace, love, knowledge and wonder; where there is no violence, hatred or greed and where no one judges you. Millions of near death survivors claim there is such a place -- and the only way to get there is to die. Do we live many lifetimes, do Beings of Light exist in heaven, do ghosts walk among us ... or are they all just products of our wildest dreams?

<u>EXTERNAL REVENUE SERVICE</u>: Like any organization which loses billions to delinquent accounts, yet survives, the IRS has its share of heroes and victims. In this, the biggest corruption case in IRS history, an honest-yet-flashy agent is pressured to work undercover for the IRS' internal investigation of corruption. With no undercover training, he must deal with an alarming abundance of bribery-minded accountants, businessmen and respected civic leaders as well as elite IRS supervisors with hidden agendas.

<u>WHY HOMING PIGEONS COME HOME</u>: Descendants of the dove, Homing Pigeons are known as war heroes and bad housekeepers ... who have a special gift that allows them to flow with the Earth's magnetic fields.

Donald Paul Rutberg

Email: DPRinnet@aol.com

CURRENT LIST OF PROJECTS

YOUNG ADULT FICTION/ TELEPLAYS

TECHNOBRED: Cloning can eradicate disease and famine or introduce problems even more deadly. It can also bring together an orphaned girl and a loving pet. "TECHNOBRED" is a contemporary "boy and his horse" story about the abandoned and unwanted triumphing through love and courage. The "boy" is an orphaned girl and the "horse" is a secret genetics experiment. When these two team up with a down-on-his-luck trainer, they win the most prestigious race in the world. But there is some concern when they realize the entrants in the race are all the same horse; all cloned from the same illegal embryo. The heroes decide to stop the conspiracy, even if it means losing their own champion runner.

COMMUNITY PROPERTY: Children of divorce sue for, and win, custody of the home. In this story about children's rights, the ex-spouses are forced to share the home equally and independently, confronting responsibilities they ignored while married.

OVER-ACHIEVEMENT: Reform-schoolers run their own "Young Achievers" business and do so well that nervous city officials halt the program.

TECHNOPHOBIA!: Children of divorce move in with their grandparents; into a test home with a Home Nerve Center -- a computer brain that does all household tasks. The children soon notice that their grandparents have gotten carried away with the new technologies -- and the Home Nerve Center has a mind of its own!

HIDDEN STAR: A dedicated yet under-qualified teenaged astronomer, using his late uncle's telescope, accomplishes what few have done since Galileo's time: he discovers a planet. But will his newfound celebrity impress the girl of his dreams and procure a scholarship?

TV COMEDY SERIES

ELIJAH'S BACK!: After 2,800 years as an alien abductee, Elijah, the Biblical prophet, is returned to Earth for the new millennium, no worse for wear. When he moves in with his black descendants in New York City, he finds it difficult to adjust or remain even remotely low-key.

BREAKIN' NEW GROUND: An innovative real estate developer pioneers a self-contained community built underneath New York City, where social deviants form their own society -- with a very different set of ground rules.

About The Project List

The project list has one job to perform -- obtain the interest of a producer or publisher who is seeking a certain type of story. If they are looking for a comedy, a true story, a social drama, whatever; all they have to do is scan my project list to find it quickly.

Some professionals claim they can't gauge a project's merits by one paragraph but most prefer to read or hear one snippet about the story. If your synopsis hits them just right, they will ask to read the entire script or book.

Often, an agent will simply read a synopsis to a producer when pitching a project. The agent will suggest casting decisions (casting is vital to a film's success) or mention other marketing angles, but the synopsis is what wins or loses the producer's favor.

Make sure the project list is crisply written and well-organized. At times, I've written a synopsis and added it to my project list months before actually writing the project. If enough producers or agents ask about the story, I know it's time to write it.

I've opened letters and shouted, "Great! They want to read my work! Yippee! ... uh-oh ... they want the script I've just started to write!"

I calm myself down and go to work, knowing that the idea must have some merit; also knowing that no one would have requested the project had it not been added to my project list.

Some of you may are asking, "What if I'm a slow writer?" That's not a problem. I'm betting that a script request from a studio or agency will speed up your writing.

Think back to the Coen brothers' film, "Barton Fink." An important man, a studio chief, who happened to be insane (not exactly a stretch for the imagination) gave Barton an assignment to write a wrestling picture. There was no way he could meet the deadline. He had never even seen a wrestling picture. He did the best he could, despite getting drunk, jailed and accused of murder.

If you think there is no way in the world that you'll be able to finish what a studio or agency has requested ... lie! Assure them you'll deliver what they need and then find some way to do it!

Write Stories *About* Your Stories

I wrote an article, "How Crimes Have Changed," to help sell my related script, called "The Money Machine." The idea was to get it some exposure through the print media, along with exposure through The Insider's System.

Years ago, I did the same with my Pluto story. I have come close to selling both the Pluto screenplay and article. Selling the article will probably be a much easier task.

Hold the presses! I sold the Pluto article to Horizon Air Magazine. It was published in December, 2003.

My chances of selling the screenplay were hurt when Pluto was downgraded by some scientists to a non-planet; an icy, rocky, "thing" that was sucked into our solar system. What were the odds that I'd spend years writing about one of only nine planets in our solar system and then have that one planet downgraded to an "icy thing"?

Oddly, the setback, Pluto's downgrade to non-planet status, helped me sell the Pluto article. I rewrote it, added the part about how a new scientific theory had turned my screenplay into one hundred pages of irrelevant trash, and turned it into a more poignant article. Setbacks, I've found, can be our friends. The theory is developed later in this book.

The late, great songwriter Harry Chapin once said that he had trouble selling songs about a heroic narrator; about a guy who got all the girls. When he started writing about loveable losers ("Taxi," "W-O-L-D," and others) he became quite successful. I agree that the public wants to read and watch movies about flawed people in precarious situations. It's easy to root for the loveable losers because everyone is flawed. My advice to you is: no matter if you're writing a screenplay, book or article, employ a main character who has lost something valuable. He or she should have a demeanor that shouts, "Give it back to me!"

I wrote a poem about it:

"And I Knew, Then ...."

I was talking to a child

And the look on his face said, "Amuse me."

And I knew, then, that he'd be all right.

I didn't worry; that kid was all right.

I was talking to a woman

And the look on her face said, "Abuse me."

And I knew, then, I'd wait for a wife.

Shouldn't hurry when choosing a wife.

I was talking to a maniac

And the look on his face said, "Attack me."

And I knew, then, that wasn't my fight.

Got to have a good reason to fight.

I was talking to a senior citizen

And the look on his face said, "Give it back to me!"

And I knew, then, the meaning of life.

I knew, then, the meaning of life.

With regard to writing stories about your stories, my hope is that the following article about "The Money Machine" screenplay will facilitate an option deal or, at the very least, lead to a magazine publishing credit.

"How Crimes Have Changed"

It's discouraging when the three guys who scammed the public out of three million dollars spent seven years in college, each, without graduating. For those of us who did graduate or learned to count somewhere else, that's a total of twenty-one years in college with zero college degrees. Yet they were able to steal from us.

Who were those guys who took three million dollars from fans betting at Arlington Park in October, 2002, during the Breeder's Cup, the World Thoroughbred Championships and racing's richest day? Was it John Belushi and his frat brothers from "Animal House"? Going by the twenty-one combined years of zero-degree college, they couldn't have been the hottest lights in the buffet bay. Yet Moe, Larry and Curly scammed the racing industry and the betting public, yes, you and me, several times prior to their three million dollar computer-con job at Arlington Park.

All three of the twenty-nine year-olds were once members of Tau Kappa Epsilon fraternity at Drexel University. They are facing ten-twenty years in jail each; the equivalent, for them, of a semester and a half of college.

Figuring out the young men's plan was easy. Their bets were made at Catskill Off-Track-Betting in New York State. Their accounts were opened one week before the big day, October 26th, 2002.

Dropout #1 got a job working with a national computer firm, Autotote, that was updating its system. Dropouts #2 and #3 placed bets on their accounts; not win, place and show bets but Pick 6's, in which the bettor has to pick the winner of six consecutive races.

Since the information from Pick 6 bets isn't transferred electronically until the fourth race is over, the Drexel University frat boys didn't have to worry about the first four races. They waited until they knew who won those races, then inserted the winning numbers into their Pick 6 ticket. The inside computer man had the password to change the numbers electronically.

Why is information from tracks throughout the U.S. (eighty-five percent of all bets originate from out of town) transmitted after the fourth race of the Pick 6? It's delayed to reduce traffic on the information highway. Only tickets that are still "alive" after four races are transmitted.

The computer worker showed up on Breeder's Cup Day, although it was his day off. Phone records indicate he was talking to his two buddies on a cell phone all afternoon.

Guaranteed to be 4-4 after four races, the frat rats took all the remaining horses in the final two races and ensured a winning Pick 6 ticket, which was certain to pay six, if not seven figures. (The pool was overflowing with $4.6 million on Breeder's Cup Day.)

So, after cheating for the first four races and wheeling the last two, the guys knew they would win. Why have only one ticket to split three ways? Why not have three winning tickets? Why not six? Six it was; a twelve dollar straight ticket (six times two dollars worth) that cost over a thousand dollars.

Later, one of the cheaters said he intended to bet only one hundred dollars but didn't have time to correct his error. Yet, telephone records prove that he made his original bet a half-hour before the first race was run! If you intended to bet a hundred dollars and were told by a teller or phone operator that the ticket cost over one thousand dollars, wouldn't you straighten things out immediately?

Put another way, has anyone ever purchased one-hundred-thousand dollars worth of stock when they intended to purchase ten grand's worth?

The clowns had no qualms about investing a grand since they were cheating (a supposedly uncheatable system, by the way). It was like betting on a fixed boxing match, where you knew the champ was going down in the third round. Why bet a gold nugget on the challenger when you have a suitcase full of gold in your hand?

The scam worked at least twice earlier in 2002. In test races at other tracks (Hawthorne Race Track in Illinois and Belmont Park in New York) the dropouts won at least one-hundred thousand dollars on Pick 6's. Then came Breeder's Cup Day and, as Lee Marvin said in, "The Dirty Dozen," the only thing they did wrong was get caught. They must never have taken the senior level course, "Don't let anyone catch ya."

To the surprise of few, evidence is missing in this case. There are no security logs for technicians that day; no audio tapes of the actual telephone bet. It wasn't erased, like Nixon's oval office tapes. (Coincidentally, the dropouts were born around the time of Watergate.) It turned out that Catskill OTB had not installed the security device to record conversations made through their touch tone system.

"The system is relatively new," an insider admitted.

Recording bets on audio was an extra cost no one wanted to incur.

"They went in through a weak link," an Autotote official said.

Ya think?

Autotote stock dropped seven percent in the first week after the scam. There is no truth to reports that, the day before the scam took place, Martha Stewart sold all of her Autotote stock.

What experts are telling us is that outsiders can't hack into the computer system and change their bets after the races are official. The only people who can steal millions from us, the betting public, are the thousands of Autotote employees. Is that supposed to make anyone feel better?

Two days after the Breeder's Cup, the Autotote corporation fired their employee for altering the suspicious winning ticket. All three guys were arrested and released on $200,000 bond. They had much of the cash lying around from their previous scams; those winning Pick 6's from Illinois, New York and who-knows-where. To their credit, only two of the three scammers had cocaine in their systems in post-race, post-arrest drug tests.

If they weren't greedy, betting a twelve dollar ticket on Breeder's Cup Day, trying to have every winning Pick 6 ticket sold in the world, they may have succeeded the third time. But their charm ran out. Somebody figured out that one guy owning all six tickets couldn't be real. The FBI froze the three million dollar payout.

Many bettors, their confidence shaken, have threatened to boycott the racing industry. The integrity of the sport depends on someone's proving these dropouts hacked into the computer system and made bets after the first four races were over.

Their lawyers claimed the guys were innocent. One of their lawyers said, "Can the government show the bets they placed are different from the bets they won? I don't think so."

Think again. Chris Harn, the autotote employee, pleaded guilty in late November, 2002, to federal charges of wire and computer fraud and money laundering. He implicated his two frat brothers in more than one scheme. They will all be going from the frat house to the Big House.

Also, the racing industry has hired former New York Mayor Rudolph W. Giuliani to look for more fraud and suggest ways to improve security. Giuliani, a horse racing fan, said, "You need to be able to say to people making wagers on horse races that they are getting fair treatment."

Of the frat boys scam, he said, "It's an example of exceeding 'the pig factor.' Somebody goes too far and it becomes obvious."

The Pick 6 bets, "Stuck out like a sore thumb," said Tim Smith, commissioner of the racing association.

One of the other frat boys' lawyers said that Harn implicating the other two was, "Like getting John Gotti to testify against a busboy who was skimming tips."

Oh, now I get it. I must have forced you to eat that box of donuts so it's my fault you're fat.

Giuliani must accomplish two tasks. Ascertain exactly how many times the public was conned and pay the people who deserved to win the consolation Pick 5 their forty-four thousand dollar prize. (They only collected four thousand dollars each.)

When I heard about this scam, I burst out laughing. (I wouldn't have won the Pick 6 anyway.) When Baby Boomers were young, we didn't have to hack into any damn computer system to change a losing ticket into a winning one. We stole the whole ticket machine and printed our own winners after the race!

In 1970 (true story) the computer industry was in its infancy, looming large on the horizon. Computer manufacturers said their systems were unbeatable (insert laugh track here). Race tracks agreed their old tote machines were vulnerable but worried they'd have to lay off a ton of employees. The unions weren't happy. There was chaos. There were hard feelings. Decisions regarding the installation of computers were being made slowly.

So, a bunch of crooks from the Baby Boomer and Pre- WW II generation went about proving that tote machines were, indeed, vulnerable. They broke into a betting area of Santa Anita racetrack and lifted a machine out through a tunnel and over a fence near the parking lot. They left behind the electrical system, which bypassed the alarm. The first machine dropped and shattered but they went back and got another one. One crook was crushed when the tote machine fell on him by the fence, but he was fine. All they had to do was get the thing hand-cranked and replace some aluminum letters. In a week or two, they had the machine working, ready to print winning tickets after the races were over. (Notice a common theme here?)

The race track officials thought the crooks would never get the machine working so they didn't worry. Well, they worried, but they never thought it would actually cost them money.

The crooks printed winning tickets, then dropped them on the floor. Eager spectators, looking on the ground and in trash cans, picked up the tickets and cashed them. No teller could detect the counterfeits. Many tickets had mustard stains on them. Almost everybody with decent eyesight was winning and no one was going to get singled out as the real crook.

The crooks cashed tickets for months! The race track was giving away money to its patrons and it didn't know why. All it knew was that, if $20,000 was bet on a race, it was paying out $21,000 -- after the takeout!

Sounds like a perfect crime, right? Well, it was.

It was so perfect that, when the crooks printed the wrong code on the tickets and when the ringleader was caught with a stack of phony tickets, no one was sent to jail. The racing industry couldn't afford to have a renegade machine traveling from state to state, damaging its integrity. The crooks returned the machine in exchange for amnesty.

They say nostalgia isn't what it used to be, but I find the 1970 scam much more appealing. I'd pay eight dollars to see that movie. (I admit I've already written the screenplay and am trying to sell it.) It has the charm of "The Sting", the 1970's film that had us rooting for the bad guys to get away with the crime. Like "The Sting," this scam did not hurt the average person, only the rich, haughty, possibly corrupt figures of authority. In the 1970 Santa Anita scam, the two dollar bettors were actually making money along with the crooks by picking up winning tickets off the ground.

In the 2002 Breeder's Cup scam, the crooks/dropouts were stealing money, not from Autotote or Arlington Park, but from other two dollar bettors. If you picked five winners on your Pick 6 ticket, you collected four thousand dollars instead of forty-four thousand. That's a once-in-a-lifetime thrill, negated by ninety percent! That's like bowling a 299 game and losing to a creep who used magnets to bowl 300.

U.S. Attorney James B. Comey was asked if the 2002 scam sounded a little bit like "The Sting."

Comey answered, "Paul Newman and Robert Redford were much better looking people."

So the Drexel dropouts were stupid, greedy, drugged-up and ugly. They stole from the little guys. Who would want to see that movie?

Apparently, HBO thinks you would like to see that movie. The cable giant has signed a deal with actor Robert Wuhl to produce a film about the 2002 Breeder's Cup scam. I doubt it will be called, "Despicable Drexel Dropouts Defraud da Public by Deliberately Diverting Digits During Distaff Dash." Maybe they'll call it, "Dopey Dormitory Dreams."

Whatever the title, the cable movie won't elicit audience sympathy for the main characters, who, in real life, will be viewing from the prison TV room, right after a rerun of "Oz". These caper films have always depended on audiences rooting for the bad guys to get away with the crime. I don't know about you, but when I watch this film, I'll be rooting for the FBI.

A Story *About* The Story About The Story!

The story at the end of the above heading is "The Money Machine" screenplay. The story about it is the article above, called "How Crimes Have Changed." Moving right to left here, which should be natural to any of you who have studied Hebrew, here is a story about how I pitched both the screenplay and article to an agent.

I sat down with a young man, maybe he was twenty-five years old, who worked with an established Hollywood talent agency (Writers & Artists Agency). I showed him the synopsis for "The Money Machine" and the article, "How Crimes Have Changed." I told him how my screenplay was better than the movie in production at HBO, produced by and starring Robert Wuhl. In my movie, the audience roots for criminals; in Wuhl's movie, the audience will despise the criminals.

"That's a bad thing," I explained, since the criminals are the main characters.

The agent got all excited ... but for the wrong reasons.

"Our agency represents Robert Wuhl!" he screamed. ""We're doing that movie!"

Oops.

I knew I had to pitch another project to him before he got really pissed. I had basically told him that I thought his movie had little chance for success.

"What do I know?" I said, like a guy who had just raved about a Michael Moore film to a Republican boss. "Maybe the time is right for audiences to root for the FBI."

Not surprisingly, he didn't ask to read any of my scripts. It is never a good idea to denigrate someone's project in development. It's better to suggest their child is stupid than hint that their film will be a bomb.

I focused on my next pitch session. What are pitch sessions? I will describe them later in this section.

Is Extra Exposure Worth The Extra Cost?

To an unknown extent, my synopsis in The Insider's System has proven worthwhile. So far, months after the magazine was distributed, two producers have asked to read "The Money Machine."

One producer is also an actor who was featured in "Pulp Fiction." The other company is in Beverly Hills and has produced several horse-related films. It would have been difficult to find these producers by myself.

Months later, I called the producer from the Beverly Hills company and told her I'd be coming to Los Angeles and would like to pitch "The Jockettes" project to her. She said she'd be glad to meet. We spoke in person for an hour and a half in July, 2003.

This young, female producer liked the story about the first female jockeys ("The Jockettes" was a demeaning term used by the male-dominated media in 1969) and told me, "Would you be upset if I try to sell it as a TV movie to HBO or TNT, rather than as a feature film? I think both those companies will like the story." (A feature film could take years to finance and, by then, the momentum created by "Seabiscuit" could be gone.)

I told her, "If 'The Jockettes' is on HBO next summer, I promise I won't be mad at you!"

So, if you spend wisely, it is a good idea to pay someone like Eva Peel, who can help expose your projects to producers.

Technical Aspects Of Writing A Screenplay

The format for screenwriting is very easy to learn. If you have problems picking it up, it can still be easy. Load a software package like Final Draft into your computer and follow the prompts.

Does the part about following the prompts scare you? Well, here's the technical theory.

You've got to use certain elements. The first element is your scene heading. You want to "Fade In" and tell the reader where the story begins; inside or outside, where and when.

It looks like this:

FADE IN:

EXT. BALCONY -- DAY

EXT means it's an outside or exterior scene; INT means it's an interior scene.

Your screenplay is in progress. That's all there is to it.

You've got another element, action, going in your script, right? That's the part where your hero jumps off the balcony to, let's say, save the children from the flying dinosaur. It reads from far left to far right, all across your page, single-spaced, like this:

HARRY, a short 40 year-old wearing a cowboy hat, leaps off the balcony, scoops up the children, and ducks into a sewer, just before the flying dinosaur can attack them.

When you type Harry's name for the first time, capitalize his name on the action line. After you introduce a character, you shouldn't capitalize his or her name. When you write dialogue (another element) capitalize all names (do not capitalize the actual dialogue) and write down the middle of the page, like this:

> HARRY
> Watch out, kids! Those dinosaurs haven't
> eaten since the Ice Age!

> LITTLE JOEY
> (whispers)
> We should take them to the school cafeteria.
> They won't ever want to eat again!

Notice the parenthetical expression above. It is indented (approximately 2.5 inches from the left margin) beneath the character's name (which is indented about three inches).

Those elements are the basic ones and, for the most part, the only ones I use.

To review: Fade in to where your action takes place (EXT. or INT.) and start writing dialogue.

I was recently told that screenplay format had changed since I was a film student at USC in the 1980's. Here are a few of the changes from older reference books you may already own.

- Producers nowadays expect to see a script printed in
`Courier 12 Point (bold) font.`
- They don't want to read more than three lines of description (action) at one time. (So don't write a half-page describing the scene.)
- Don't use "CUT TO" when you jump from an exterior scene to an interior scene. When the dialogue ends and the producer reads "INT," they'll know that the action has moved to another location.
- Only use continued ("CONT'D") to indicate the character is still talking when you jump between pages. Example: Harry says something, then, in the action line, a dinosaur flies by, then Harry says

something else. Don't use ("CONT'D) after Harry's name in the dialogue line. The reader will know that Harry is continuing his dialogue.

- Don't use a parenthetical expression ("angrily") unless the word is counter to the character's emotion. Use ("Fuming") if the character is talking sweetly but fuming inside.
- Remember that producers will usually read only the first ten pages of your script and the last ten pages.

Here Are Some More Hints About Screenplay Format:

- The left side of the script should have a 1 ½ inch margin.
- The right side of the script should have a one-half to one inch margin.
- Top and bottom margins should be one inch.
- Scene headings are spaced 1 ½ inch from left side of the page.
- Dialogue should start two inches from the left margin. Do not center the dialogue; align it about two inches from the left margin and 1 ½ inches from the right margin.
- Characters' names should be three inches from the left margin.
- If you use Final Draft or a similar software package that formats scripts, these rules will be followed automatically and you won't have to waste time on measurements.
- Try not to have your character's speech spill over to the next page. If you can't help it, you can put "CONT'D after the character's name on the top of the next page. (Final Draft will do this automatically.)
- Never turn in a script that is longer than one hundred-twenty pages; calculate it as one page per minute. Producers will be turned off, thinking your script is ponderous and expensive to shoot.
- If you are writing a low-budget screenplay, avoid scenes in which high-tech helicopters chase the bad guys through an underground city. You could unintentionally produce the world's most expensive movie. No one is going to spend two hundred million dollars to shoot a screenplay written by a previously unknown writer.
- If your script is longer than one hundred-twenty pages, try clicking on the "very tight" mode of the Final Draft software. This will squeeze the script down in length several pages and sort of cram the words closer together.
- Use (V.O.) after the character's name if it is a voice-over; that is, if the character is talking from a distant location on the phone. Use (O.C.) if the character is slightly out of the camera's view (in the kitchen).
- Always use page numbers.
- I put the screenplay title on every page, in the upper right corner next to the page numbers. When I use Final Draft, the software doesn't do that for me, probably because I don't know how to communicate my instructions to the computer.
- Don't overuse camera directions, such as "CRANE SHOT FROM ROOF" followed by "CLOSE UP FROM ZEPPELIN OVERHEAD" followed by "EXTREME LONG SHOT FROM SURFACE OF THE MOON." Directors call those shots and shoot films their way. They don't want you to do their job while you're doing your job. If you want a second job, buy a fleet of catering trucks.
- You can use "ANGLE ON …" when, for example, you want to show an intimate conversation in a corner booth of a restaurant. So, if the scene takes place in a crowded restaurant, you can tell the reader that, way off in the corner, these two lovers are really getting cozy.

Example: ANGLE ON Bill and Monica, making out in the corner booth, as federal agents saunter onto the dance floor.

- Whether you print your screenplay from your own computer or copy it at a printing shop, always bind the script. Most people use three-hole punch paper and brass fasteners. I don't like those fasteners; they rip holes in envelopes when I mail the scripts. Instead, I have the scripts spiral-bound at the copying store, with a hard back cover and a clear plastic front cover (so the producer can read the title page).
- Use twenty-four pound paper. It feels more substantial than thinner paper. I use twenty-four pound laser paper, with a ninety-two or higher brightness factor. I also use a heavy duty copier that is designed to make large amounts of copies at one time without melting.

I am including the first pages of my "SUPERFAN 2020" screenplay so you can visualize the format. For clarification of the TV format, I have included (in the appendices of this book) a sample of "WHEN ANGELS SPEAK ...."

For now, here are the opening pages of "SUPERFAN 2020." Following this scene, we'll deal with the creative aspects of writing and researching a screenplay.

Getting Started -- Sample First Scene

"SUPERFAN 2020"

Original Screenplay

by

Donald Paul Rutberg

(address, phone number)

DPRinnet@aol.com

© 1999

Registered WGAW

FADE IN:

EXT. STREET -- AN EARLY SPRING DAY

We're flying above a quiet street. The snow is melting on the modest lawns.

GRAPHIC: "THE STORY YOU'RE ABOUT TO SEE IS TRUE. IT

JUST HASN'T HAPPENED YET."

We land near a satellite dish on the lawn of one modesthome. we can hear a televised baseball game; the unmistakable sound of a baseball bat connecting with a pitched baseball, the fans screaming and the announcer describing the action -- in spanish.

> ANNOUNCER (V.O.)
> La bola esta saltando contra el pared. Dos jugadores llevaran ventaja. (The ball is bouncing against the wall. Two runs will score.)

GRAPHIC: "PHILADELPHIA, PA EARLY SPRING, 2020"ROLL TITLES

INT. MURRAY KRANEFIELD'S LIVING ROOM -- CONTINUOUS ACTION

It feels like we're in a stadium at night. the living room is illuminated only by three giant TV screens which dominate the wall   s, glowing blue. MURRAY KRANEFIELD, yawning on the only chair in the room, watches a diving competition. The TV displays the word "AUTOGRAZE."

> ANNOUNCER (V.O.)
> And it comes down to the last dive of the afternoon. She'll need a perfect score to catch the Canadian for the gold. Here it is.

Murray tilts his head, watches the three giant screens as a large pig dives into the Olympic pool. The crowd cheers wildly.

> ANNOUNCER (V.O.)
> What a beauty! Silver medal, at least!

We PAN Murray's living room, furnished with a dozen DVD's, blank discs, beer cans; objects which promote dedicated sports viewing. and nothing else except for the one cozy chair.

In the near darkness, we see that Murray is chubby, in his late thirties and half-asleep. "Autograze" CLICKS the TV back to the Latin baseball game. The videophone rings.

Murray ignores the call but sees the caller, LENNY, in the upper corner of giant screen. The videophone prints out "ANSWER RECORD" on the TV screen as murray continues to watch the Latin baseball game.

> LENNY
> (on TV screen)
> Pick up the phone, Murray. I know you're
> up; I see your dish rotating!

Murray continues to watch the baseball game.

> LENNY
> (on TV screen)
> All right. You're missin' it.
> There's somethin' on that you'll want to see.
> And it's not the pig diving!

Lenny hangs up; DISAPPEARS FROM SCREEN. Murray CLICKS to another channel. We can see a sign on the talk show's set: "SPORTOHOLIC."

> GUEST (V.O.)
> Yes, Japan is suing the United States. So is
> the Dominican Republic.

> HOST (V.O.)
> Then be honest. Is it really a *World*
> Series?

CLICK. Murray changes the channel. he watches a man on a podium.

> MAN ON PODIUM (V.O.)
> I want to talk to you about money!

CLICK. Murray turns on a sports highlights show. He grimaces as he watches violent collisions on ball fields.

> SPORTSCASTER (V.O.)
> "This Week In Crashes" is next.

The videophone rings again. Lenny is seen in the upper corner of the giant screen TV.

> LENNY (V.O.)
> Murray, you're really gonna be mad if ya
> miss this.

Murray opens the drapes and bright sunshine replaces the dark stadium effect. He pushes a button on his Home Nerve Center.

> MURRAY
> Yeah, Lenny, what is it?

LENNY (V.O.)
Turn to channel 197.

Murray quickly enters "197" on his remote control cube. He goes face to giant-sized face with EDDIE "BEAK" BEACON, the man we recently saw on the podium talking about money.

MURRAY
Some kind of get-rich-quick program?

LENNY (V.O.)
Don't you know who that is? You really
were sleeping.

MURRAY
He looks familiar ....

LENNY (V.O.)
That's Beak. He's the guy who bought all
those sports franchises and kept movin' 'em.

MURRAY
Oh, yeah. The guy who kept gettin' sued and
then counter-sued.

LENNY (V.O.)
He won every case; made a fortune. He
moved to Las Vegas, Honolulu --

MURRAY
So what's the big deal?

LENNY (V.O.)
(melodramatically)
Didn't ya hear? He's bringin' baseball back
to Philadelphia!

We hear angelic music.

MURRAY
(collapsing from emotion in
the only chair; near tears)
Baseball's comin' back to Philly?

> LENNY (V.O.)
> They're callin' it America's Team. It's a national team that everybody can root for; especially guys like us who's favorite team moved away.
> (ironic laugh)
> Dee was so happy when the Phillies left town, because all you used to do was watch baseball. But now baseball's back; it must be fate.

END TITLES

> MURRAY
> It's history!

> LENNY (V.O.)
> They're putting every game on TV; every inning, every rally ....
> (voice rises an octave)
> Every pitch!

> MURRAY
> Shut up! Let me listen.

Murray hits the MUTING BUTTON on his videophone answering machine. Lenny is silenced in the Kranefield living room but his lips keep moving in the upper corner of Murray's giant screens. Lenny apparently doesn't know he's muted.

INT. AMERICADOME MEDIA CENTER -- CONTINUOUS ACTION

The room is packed with reporters and cameramen. the walls are covered with life-sized murals of baseball players in action. A ten-foot sign instructs us: "AMERICA'S TEAM IS YOUR TEAM!"

The TV cameras zoom in on the podium, where twelve unshaven athletes sit with America's Team Owner, EDDIE "BEAK" BEACON and his overdressed, once-glamorous wife, ZSA ZSA BEACON.

> BEAK
> I'm doing this for the fans. Hell, I am a fan. Can I say that? Why not, it's my network.
> (chuckles loudly)
> So I took my hard-earned money and got us some players. On this platform are some of the greats you'll see this year -- on this network. First, to my right, is Marty Mason, formerly of the Indians, where he was the league's Most Valuable Player five years in a row.

ANGLE on MARTY MASON and his teammate, fellow superstar free agent VANCE CONLIN.

Marty and Vance play with a child's toy, a hologram box that's shaped like a baseball diamond. They ignore Beak's introduction and whisper to each other.

> VANCE
> How much you makin'?

> MARTY
> Twenty five-point-five.

> VANCE
> Million?

> MARTY
> Yeah. But it's spread out over
> the whole year.

> VANCE
> Me too. And he threw in a bunch of thor-
> oughbreds.
> (scratches his head) What are they?

> MARTY
> I dunno. Some kinda sandwich? Hey, what's
> it mean, "Spread out over the whole year"?

ANGLE on Beak as he speaks into dozens of microphones.

> BEAK
> Next is Vance Conlin. He hit .321 for New
> Orleans last year.

INT. MURRAY'S LIVING ROOM -- CONTINUOUS ACTION

Murray shakes his head at the giant screens.

> MURRAY
> (mumbles to himself) He hit
> .322 last year, led the league in
> triples.

Lenny, still muted in the upper corner of Murray's giant screens, desperately tries to get Murray's attention -- no easy matter under the circumstances. Lenny, who seems to be looking out his window, jumps up and down, points, screams silently; obviously afraid. Murray keeps his eyes and ears riveted on Beak.

> BEAK (V.O.)
> We've also signed as free agents slugger
> Moondance Taylor along with pitcher
> Roscoe McCormack.

> MURRAY
> (eyes bulging; sotto)
> Roscoe McCormack: averages 34 wins a
> season! And Moondance Taylor - the man
> who hit six home runs in one game and it
> was shortened by rain!

Murray semi-notices that Lenny is holding up a sign which reads: "TURN OFF MUTING!" Murray hits the REVERSE MUTING button. The press conference, not Lenny, is muted.

> MURRAY
> Lenny, this is the greatest. We'll never lose a
> game.

Before lenny can reveal the danger, the danger reveals herself. DEE KRANEFIELD SMITHERS, Murray's spouse of five years, enters the house. Dee is cute, energetic, well-directed ... and mad as hell.

> DEE
> You're still watching that TV? One day,
> you're gonna blend right into it!

DEE bashes in the power switch. The TV goes off, momentarily, then turns itself back on with impulse power via the Home Nerve Center (as per Murray's instructions).

Dee doesn't realize that the press conference is still on the screen, muted, or that Lenny, back from the MUTING ZONE, is still listening.

> DEE
> (to Murray)
> Why don't you get a J-O-B instead of sitting
> around here all day? Have you been bred for
> fandom or something?

Murray starts to say yes, pushes REVERSE MUTING button instead and stares at screen intently.

>   DEE
> You drink your beer, you make your bets;
> you call and order the fan kit and the steak
> knives with the team logo.

Murray stares at a shelf; spots the steak knives, grunts.

>   DEE
> It's gotta stop, Murray.

>   MURRAY
> But --

>   DEE
> You're regressing! You must act like an adult
> if you want our marriage to work.

Murray turns up the volume on giant screens TV.

>   BEAK (V.O.)
> If I lose twenty million a year, so what? Ha!
> I can afford it. I've got 51 cameras covering
> all the games. Cameras in locker rooms, the
> umpires' room, the visitors' dugout; I've got
> cameras under home plate and in space!

Murray whistles in appreciation. Dee glares at lenny on the videophone screen.

>   DEE
> What are you laughin' at?

Dee savagely rips the plug from the wall; the TV goes off.

Murray grabs his jacket, walks quickly to the door.

>   MURRAY
> I'm goin'. I'm goin'.

>   DEE
> Get a job!

Dee kicks the door closed as Murray exits.

EXT. MURRAY'S DRIVEWAY -- CONTINUOUS ACTION

Murray races by his lawnmower and sporting goods, which are thawing out on his lawn. he gets into his van, starts the ignition, then turns on one of his van's TV sets. We hear the van's dish click.

INT. VAN -- CONTINUOUS ACTION

Murray looks closely into his rear view mirror. he watches beak on a giant screen; the image projected from the back of the van. The image is backwards but, since he's looking at it through a mirror, it's right-side up. Murray turns up the volume, drives away.

> BEAK (V.O.)
> I bought the most popular team mascot, The
> Animal, from the California club that folded
> last year.

THE ANIMAL, dressed in a bright yellow chicken suit with a large snout, four eyes, a couple of tongues, etc., dances across Murray's giant screen van TV.

> MURRAY
> (screams)
> He has The Animal, too!

> BEAK (V.O.)
> Plus, I'm doing something for the fans that
> has never been done in professional sports.

> MURRAY
> What's he gonna do? Let us in for free?

> BEAK (V.O.)
> I'm letting the fans in for free!

Creative Aspects Of Writing A Screenplay

My strong advice to you is: write about yourselves. Why are so many of you detached from your stories? You should be writing what you know, not avoiding what you know.

You must train yourselves to think visually. For example, before I wrote the first scene of "Superfan 2020," and bear with me here because I wrote it twenty years ago, I visualized what the scene would look like on the screen. I must have "taken" the helicopter ride over Murray Kranefield's neighborhood about five hundred times. I could actually see the snow melting on the lawns of the modest homes. I visualized exactly where Murray's satellite dishes were located on his lawn, his roof, around his home and on his van's roof. I put myself into his van and "saw" where the giant screen TV would be located. It was in the rear of the van, projected backward. When he looked at it through his rear-view mirror, it was right-side up.

I know exactly how Murray will react in all situations because, like Murray, I'm a sports' nut. It was as if Murray were a real person, and it was my job to study his tendencies. He is obsessed with sports and that thread has to be woven throughout his personality; it has to take precedence over all other activities, even his marital duties. Later in the script, the needs of his little buddy, TJ, become more important than his fan activities. In effect, his desire to take care of TJ changes him. He realizes that he loves TJ more than the team he follows so passionately.

Characters should be taken out of their normal routines, either willingly or unwillingly, in the first 30 pages of your script. Murray is taken out of his normal routine three times; when the team offers him a chance to become famous, when he stops being the obsessive-compulsive Superfan and when he saves the day in the last scene. This is called character escalation. Think about Jim Carrey in "The Majestic." He loses his memory and lives a completely different life, complete with a new father.

Perhaps the greatest example of character escalation is Michael Corleone in "The Godfather." Once he pulls that trigger in the restaurant and kills the police captain (who deserves it!) his life is changed forever. In my story about the only lawyer in heaven, "When Angels Speak....," my hero, Charley Merriweather, goes though an abrupt change in the first few pages. He is pulled far out of his normal routine -- because I kill him! For him, a fun-loving, win-at-all-costs attorney, following the strict rules imposed in heaven is certainly abnormal.

Researching Your Original Screenplay

Let's assume you've got the talent and determination to become a successful screenwriter. You've even got a great idea, a true story that is commercially viable and perfect for the screen. Where do you start?

The first thing to do is stop shaking. I will try to explain the process in a clear, calm manner. You see, I stopped shaking years ago.

Like you, I am a Hollywood outsider. I do not go to L.A. parties, overhear conversations about which studio is seeking a certain type of project, then show up at the studio a week later to pitch to corporate big-wigs, all of whom call me their friend. I live far away from Hollywood and recommend you do the same.

Hey, I have nothing against the folks in Tinsel town, other than not trusting them. I lived there for seven years and loved every day of it, except for the last twenty-four months or so. My reasons are listed throughout this book. For now, let me take you step by step through my latest screenplay project. I haven't sold it to a studio yet, but I am hoping that I will be able to update readers on this subject. I'll even leave space later in this segment to tell you what happened to "The Jockettes" script. (See "Updates". In the meantime, try not to elevate your hopes.)

In early 2003, I decided to write a screenplay that had been on my mind for decades, a story about female jockeys. I had written this story as a contemporary piece in the 1980's and actually had an offer from ABC to produce it. Cheryl Ladd was interested in playing the lead role. The deal fell through when the 1980's jockey reneged on her agreement with me. She wanted to give me the rights to tell her life story, then she didn't. Oh, well. At the time, I was devastated. The setback may actually help me now or later in my career. (More on "Setbacks Are Your Friends" later in this book.)

I decided, after months of negative thought, years of second guessing and decades of assessing blame, that the best story to tell would concern the original female jockeys, circa 1969.

Barbara Jo Rubin was the first female jockey to win a thoroughbred race. She had spoken to me twice in the early 1990's and read my sample stories. She invited me down to Florida to chat with her about her life. So I called her in early 2003. Unfortunately, or so I thought, her number had changed.

I wrote to her. I looked up her new, married name, Warman, but still couldn't locate her. I met a lot of nice people named Warman but not Barbara Jo. One lady with the last name of Warman said she was overweight and would crush a horse. Another Warman, named Earl, had recently retired and spent a lot of time trying to help me track down the ex-jockey.

By the way, when you write sentences like "track down the ex-jockey" without realizing the word-play dynamics until later, that is a good thing. "Racing to track down the ex-jockey" would be even better, but I wasn't really rushing to find her so I didn't force it into that last paragraph.

It soon became clear that Barbara Jo was avoiding me. She had changed her mind about working with me, as the other jockey had done in 1983. I still wanted to write the story. "Seabiscuit" was being made and it was going to be a big hit. The timing was right to tell the tale of how sexist men had prevented female jockeys from riding in real races and making a living. This was similar to Jackie Robinson's story; with sexism replacing racism as the main theme.

Diane Crump was the first woman to actually ride in a race, in February of 1969. A year later, she became the first woman to ride in the Kentucky Derby. I got her number from the Jockey's Guild or the New York Racing Association and called her, told her what I was trying to do.

"Why don't you call Julie Krone?" Diane asked.

Krone is a female rider who came along after the 1970's. She didn't have to struggle to get her chance on the track like the original girls. She got her license with no problem. She showed up and went to work. She was no Jackie Robinson. Besides, I had spoken to her two nights in a row in the early 1990's and, on the second night, she had no idea who I was.

"Julie, I spoke to you last night for twenty minutes," I told her.

"You did? Who are you again?"

I told Diane that I didn't particularly like Julie or want to write about a female jockey from the 1980's. I didn't know that, on one occasion, Julie had refused to take a picture with Diane at a charity event, thinking she was too good for her. Julie won many more races; even became the first female jockey to win a Triple Crown event, the Belmont Stakes. She won a Breeder's Cup race in 2003, becoming the first female jockey to win a World Championship race.

So Diane disliked her - a lot. When I said I didn't want to work with Julie, Diane immediately trusted me. How bad could I be, right? She invited me to Virginia for a chat.

I drove from Philadelphia to Diane's home in Virginia one weekend in April, 2003. My wife wanted to see the caverns there, anyway. (They were neat.) I brought my mini-tape recorder and recorded two days worth of conversations about Diane's childhood, career and life, concentrating on her rise from exercise rider to Kentucky Derby jockey.

Diane gave me her entire life in boxes; all the articles, photos and memories of her career. I was taken aback by her trust in me. I wasn't sure she should've entrusted those personal, irreplaceable items with anyone, not even her brother. When I left, I told her I would write her story within a year. I completed the task in less than three months.

Here's how I did it. I listened to all the tapes and took notes and arranged them in chronological order. Then I went through the boxes with the articles and added to my notes. Next, I reviewed the videotapes I had taken. They were mostly filled with scenes of her two dogs, Buggy and Josie. So I couldn't use the videotape.

I added to the mix all my preliminary notes regarding the overall story. These were notes I had taken as I unsuccessfully tried to track down Barbara Jo Rubin, proving that setbacks were my friends! If I had been successful in tracking down Barbara Jo, I never would have accumulated information from dozens of people who "were there" in 1969, and I never would've spoken to Diane Crump, who had the best story to tell of all the female jockeys.

When I interviewed an assistant trainer on the telephone, the man told me, "The trainers were high, the jockeys were high and the horses were high" on certain occasions. I was shocked but, if the man were telling the truth, it would explain why some of the jockeys ignored my phone calls.

I didn't start writing the screenplay. Instead, I wrote a treatment. Later in this book, I will explain how to write one of these outlines. Basically, a treatment is a short outline explaining how the movie would unfold in terms of concept, main characters and story outline.

The treatment was completed by late July, 2003, and was fifty pages in length. That's a long treatment, but I had an intricate story to tell - about all the jockeys, male and female and all the horse people, male and female, who were involved in this story over thirty years ago.

I wrote a letter agreement between Diane Crump and myself. In this agreement, Diane promised to give me the exclusive rights for two years to try to sell her story as a movie or book. I promised to bring any deal back to her and, at that point, we would both have to agree on the terms before any deal was signed. In other words, we were cemented together in this project. She couldn't cut me out or make a deal behind my back nor could I pull any tricks on her. A sample "life rights" letter agreement appears later in this book. You don't need an expensive lawyer to work on this for you. Remember to copyright or register your material with the Library of Congress or the Writer's Guild of America. That helps protect your project. Pay the thirty dollar fee and send in your forms as soon as you complete your treatment, screenplay or book. The copyrighting process is explained in detail later in this segment. Don't skip that chapter!

Rules For Writing Screenplays

Certain rules for writing screenplay structure have been around since dinosaurs roamed the earth. You remember that first script - boy meets pterodactyl, boy loses pterodactyl, girl clubs boy over the head when she finds out about the pterodactyl. When boy invents the wheel and gains fame and fortune, girl forgives boy and they live happily ever after in trendy neighborhood, near Hef's cave. The rules were probably rewritten a few eons later by mogul Irving Thalberg.

The film, "The Last Tycoon," starring Robert DeNiro, was an adaptation of F. Scott's Fitzgerald's last book and was based loosely on Irving Thalberg's life. Thalberg was one of the first movie moguls. On an old Dick Cavett show, I heard Groucho Marx speak about Thalberg. Groucho said the mogul lived in Malibu, right off the ocean. When Groucho went to visit, he kept opening the sliding door to get a whiff of the refreshing ocean breeze and Thalberg kept closing it.

"Why do you keep closing the door?" Groucho asked him.

Thalberg replied, "I can't stand the sound of that damn ocean!"

That allegedly true scene never made it into Fitzgerald's book or the DeNiro film. I'm not completely sure if these rules were around before Thalberg's time, despite the fact that I wrote about the very first mogul, Sigmund Lubin, who produced movies before Thalberg was born, in the late 1890's. (Details about the Lubin project appear later in this book.) I do know these rules will be helpful to anyone considering writing a screenplay. You don't have to adhere to every one of them. Simply use them as a guide.

1. Develop the screenplay in three acts.

2. Grab the reader's attention on page one.

3. The hero is pulled out of his normal routine, either willingly or unwillingly, in the first thirty pages.

4. Introduce a major plot point by page thirty.

5. Act One ends by page thirty.

6. At the end of Act One, the hero cannot "walk away" with a clear conscience.

7. Hero rethinks his options.

8. In Act Two, the hero has to learn new skills.

9. A subplot depicts another version of the hero's story.

10. Establish the antagonist between pages forty to fifty.

11. The bad guy always thinks he is doing the right thing.

12. The hero moves to a different location and, between pages fifty to sixty, completes his first task.

13. Problems escalate on pages seventy to eighty.

14. Give the antagonist more screen time.

15. Reveal the hero's secret.

16. An ally challenges the hero's values.

17. Pages eighty to ninety: Hero starts to fail, the love story collapses, a lie is exposed.

18. In Act Three, put the hero in a limited arena of action (courtroom, boxing ring)

19. Re-examine hero's values and priorities.

20. Direct confrontation between hero and protagonist.

21. Hero must be the underdog.

22. Maximum chaos - things are out of control. Darkest moment.

23. The hero is about to fail totally but devises a desperate plan.

24. Hero makes a hard choice.

25. Hero defeats the villain.

26. Hero has changed.

27. Add a twist to the end.

28. Closure.

29. Make sure you finish your first draft, no matter what.

After you've finished, go back and make sure that you have kept the story in motion at all times. Then cut out the scenes you don't need.

A comedy should be no longer than one hundred and ten pages; a drama no more than one hundred and twenty pages. Never submit a screenplay that is less than ninety pages or less than your best work!

How To Sell A Screenplay

Now I had to convince movie producers to read my "Jockettes" treatment, no easy task since I had, as usual, no agent. So I called the people who had asked to read my other screenplays.

How did I get them to read my work initially? I spent one hundred dollars or so and had my work reviewed by people who publish newsletters or magazines with screenplay synopses (Eva Peel, Natalie Rothenberg and others). You pay them for a review and they recommend your work, if they think it's good. Producers read their publications and request scripts that fit their needs.

I had a script under consideration by Irwin Winkler Productions (the company produced "Rocky" and "Goodfellas") and Rope the Moon Productions. The lady from Winkler Productions, June, ignored me. The lady from Rope The Moon, Amanda, said she would "love to" meet with me to discuss the jockey story when I was in Los Angeles, in July, 2003.

I called my ex-agent, Barbara, in Los Angeles. She told me I'd be better off pitching a full script, not just a treatment. I finished the screenplay in four weeks and took it with me to California.

Amanda met with me for an hour and a half, discussing my story, which clearly captured her interest. She said she'd call me in a few weeks. Months later, I was still waiting for her call. (A year later, I was still waiting.)

No biggie. I made plans to return to L.A. to attend pitch sessions with producers. If you have no agent, these pitch sessions - five minutes to pitch your story verbally to producers - are about the only way you can create interest in your work and make a sale.

Before I went, however, I rewrote my project list.

Rewriting Your Project List

I sent my original screenplay project list, the one that appeared earlier in this book, to Eva Peel at evapeel@earthlink.net. She suggested I shorten it to give myself a better chance of making a sale. She thought that if I brought twenty unsold scripts to the table, I would look like someone who couldn't sell anything; like I could just fill up pages without writing anything worthwhile.

So I cut out a few of my lesser-regarded projects. The rewritten project list, streamlined and designed to maximize my strengths, follows. I include descriptions of my completed screenplays and some book projects that could be adapted into screenplays. If enough people ask to read, "Out of the Wilderness," for example, I will adapt the book into a script.

I put the more polished projects on page one and the less polished projects on page two.

Notice that I cut out, "Current List of Projects" and the category called, "Teleplays."

"How do you know if a producer wants to make your story into a feature film or a telefilm?" Eva asked me. "What does 'current list' mean? Do you have a non-current list?"

What was I thinking - "Current List"? I had used that heading on my project list for over twenty years, despite the fact that it made no sense!

Donald Paul Rutberg

DPRinnet@aol.com

USC screenwriting graduate (MFA)

Published book author, comic book author, children's book author.

Published Journalist and Playwright.

Writer/Producer of children's TV shows and commercials.

"A Writer's First Aid Kit" due out in 2004; Pale Horse Publishing.

SCREENPLAYS

THE JOCKETTES: (True drama with rights) The inspirational true story of Diane Crump, _the first female jockey to ride in the U.S._, and the other pioneering women who overcome incredible obstacles to win equal rights on the racetrack. In 1969, female jockeys start winning races at North American race tracks and by May, 1970, Diane Crump becomes _the first woman to ride in the Kentucky Derby_.

SUPERFAN 2020: (Comic book comedy) It is 2020 and s_ports society has gone beyond escapism to insanity ... on its way to the unnatural_. A sports nut named Murray joyfully jeopardizes his marriage, his job and his life in order to win the Superfan trophy. He and his eleven year-old protégé prove that the heroes are in the cheap seats after the pampered players are forced to play in a "Real" World Series. (_Also a nationally distributed comic book and comedy series_)

THE MONEY MACHINE: (True crime caper) In 2002, computer hackers alter "Pick 6" tickets worth three million dollars. But in 1970, there are no computers to hack. Crooks have to use a more hands-on approach ... so they steal a tote machine, hand-crank it and print winning tickets after the races are over! For several months, the race track gives away money to its patrons and it doesn't know why! When the crooks are finally caught due to their own error, they exchange "The Money Machine" -- for freedom. In essence, _the advancing computer age is delayed just long enough to ensure this "Sting"-like perfect crime._

WHEN ANGELS SPEAK ... (THEY ARGUE): (Comedy-Fantasy) An outgoing, arbitration lawyer dies and is disappointed to learn that he's been assigned a similar job in a dull, sterile world known as heaven. With no chance to enjoy the Earthly pleasures his spirit craves, _the only lawyer in heaven_ enters the game of angelic politics, hoping to add some life to his death. (Also a comedy series)

SUMMER AT SARATOGA: (Romantic Comedy-Drama) A young man quits his "perfect" job in the family dress business and takes his chances, acquiring two race horses and falling in love with the horses' trainer. In one frantic summer, he's stalked by the trainer's telepathic, telekinetic, terribly jealous ex-boyfriend and discovers _the horses are superstar clones, who may be worth millions_.

A Writer's First Aid Kit

Donald Paul Rutberg

DPRinnet@aol.com

SCREENPLAYS

HOT PEPPERS FOR POP: (True coming-of-age story with rights) During the Great Depression, a *15 year-old boy earns enough money in hot-pepper eating contests* to attend a major league baseball game, where he sits on the field with Dizzy Dean and drinks from the dugout water fountain.

OUT OF THE WILDERNESS: (True drama with rights) During WWII, an orphaned, Polish, Jewish teenager miraculously eludes the Nazis, joins the Russian army, gets arrested for "Counter Revolutionary Propaganda," nearly starves to death in prison; survives in a wilderness commune, *escapes to and from the Polish army* posing as a Greek concentration camp survivor and finds his family in America.

EXTERNAL REVENUE SERVICE: (True drama/comedy with rights) Like any organization which loses billions to delinquent accounts, yet survives, the IRS has its share of heroes and victims. In this, the biggest corruption case in IRS history, an honest-yet-flashy agent is pressured to work undercover for the IRS' internal investigation of corruption. With no undercover training, he must deal with an alarming abundance of bribery-minded accountants, businessmen and respected civic leaders as well as elite IRS supervisors with hidden agendas.

TECHNOBRED: Cloning can eradicate disease and famine or introduce problems even more deadly. It can also bring together an orphaned girl and a loving pet. In this "boy and his horse" story, the "boy" is an orphaned girl and the "horse" is a secret genetics experiment. When these two team up with a down-on-his-luck trainer, they win the most prestigious race in the world. But there is some concern when they realize the entrants in the race are *all the same horse; all cloned from the same illegal embryo*. The heroes decide to stop the conspiracy, even if it means losing their own champion runner.

COMEDY SERIES

BREAKIN' NEW GROUND: An innovative real estate developer pioneers a *self-contained community built underneath New York City*, where social deviants form their own society -- with a very different set of ground rules.

ELIJAH'S BACK!: After 2,800 years as an alien abductee, Elijah, the Biblical prophet, is *returned to Earth for the new millennium, no worse for wear*. When he moves in with his black descendants in New York City, he finds it difficult to adjust or remain even remotely low-key.

Writing Loglines and Expanded Synopses

Before I pitched the above project list to producers, I had to be ready for anything, even success. In the event of a successful pitch, I would have to be prepared with an in-between element; something longer than a one paragraph logline and shorter than a full screenplay. That is something called an expanded synopsis.

Let's be perfectly clear about Screenplay Development:

- A logline is a two sentence description of your story, like on a digital TV info guide.
- An expanded synopsis is a two-to-three page version of your story, which describes the genre, locale, period and outline.
- A treatment is a ten-twenty page outline, consisting of concept, characters descriptions and story outline.
- A screenplay is a ninety to one-hundred-twenty page script, complete with action and dialogue.

In the expanded synopsis, you must describe, in two to three pages, what happens in your story. Don't do what I did initially - try to sell the story to the reader. (In my first two page synopsis for "The Jockettes," I tried to inform the reader how well "Seabiscuit" did at the box-office and why that would carry over to my story.) Keep it simple and write the story outline and describe your main characters. In effect, it is really a mini-treatment. If the producer likes you, your pitch, your short logline and your expanded synopsis, he or she will ask to read your screenplay. That's all there is to it.

In other words, if you're driving and you make the light at the end of your street and make the light at the first intersection, and then you make the light at the boulevard and make the light at the turnpike, you'll be allowed to enter the interstate. You'll still have to travel cross-country but are ahead of most of the traffic and out of gridlock.

Here are four examples of my screenplay loglines and expanded synopses of projects described on the project lists. Don't be confused when you read two versions of "The Jockettes," "The Money Machine" and "Superfan 2020." I correct my mistakes in the latter versions.

Also, after my synopsis of "Out of the Wilderness," I attach the table of contents from the book. Producers don't know it, but, at this point, I haven't written the screenplay, only the book. Let's keep that our little secret, OK?

SCREENPLAY LOGLINE:

(First version - not to be imitated)

"THE JOCKETTES": The inspirational true story of Diane Crump, the first female jockey to ride in the U.S., and the other pioneering women who overcome incredible obstacles to win equal rights on the racetrack.

Format: Screenplay

Length: 116 pages

Genre: True Story (rights acquired)

Locale: Kentucky, Florida; some foreign scenes

Period: Mainly 1969-1970

(First version - not to be imitated)

It is the late 1960's. No female jockey has ever ridden in a thoroughbred horse race in the U.S. The men who rule the "Sport of Kings" consider women too weak to control an eleven-hundred pound animal running at thirty-five miles an hour.

This doesn't stop women from seeking out jockeys' licenses. Men bar them from applying.

Women go to court to get their licenses. Men boycott the race tracks. They prepare to ride in actual races. Men throw rocks at their trailers.

Finally, in February, 1969, female jockeys ride -- and win -- at U.S. tracks.This is the inspirational, true story of Diane Crump, the first female jockey to ride in the U.S., and other pioneering women who overcome incredible obstacles to win equal rights on the racetrack. Unlikely heroes and villains litter the trail these female jockeys blaze. The casualties they inflict are profound and, for the most part, directed at themselves.

The story begins in the 1950's, depicting a little girl's (Diane's) obsession with horses. Her parents think it will be a passing phase but the obsession grows. Diane hurries to finish high school in Oldsmar, Florida, so she can work with a stable of horses in Ocala. Eventually, she becomes an exercise rider for a powerful stable in Kentucky.

The trainer, Don Divine, is an ex-jockey who takes a special interest in Diane's career. Don is not well-liked among his peers, however. He is considered a great trainer but a hot-head. The two eventually marry. This helps and hurts Diane's career.

Meanwhile, other female jockeys decide to sue for the right to ride in thoroughbred races. A female attorney, Audrey Melbourne, aided by the Marjorie Cook Foundation, which was founded to assist bullied women, wins the case.

In early 1969, when it looks as if a particular woman will be the first to ride, circumstances keep preventing it. Diane is in the right place at the right time to break the sport's sex barrier when she's hired to ride by a trainer she's never met. (The trainer's wife orders him to hire Diane.)

Diane is befriended by a fourth generation, highly respected veterinarian in Kentucky who is banned in other states. She is also admired by horse owners Warner Jones and Lyons Brown. Jones, however, owns historic Churchill Downs and does not want Diane riding at his track. He doesn't want any riots.

Most of the other female jockeys are hard-living cowgirls from broken homes. One is a daredevil who will do anything to ride the best horses. Another invents a happy childhood, college degree and movie studio contract, then marries a movie star. When these two travel to Venezuela with other female riders for a week of racing, an insanely intense rivalry develops. Diane rises above their antics. Years later, when the daredevil becomes too ill to ride, she commits suicide.

Male jockeys, meanwhile, boycott the races in which women are entered. When they do compete against women, they whip them in the face. Female trainers, like Mary Keim, lend their support, having faced sexism years earlier. The media swarms to the racetracks, demeaning the female jockeys by referring to them as "Jockettes." Sportswriter Red Smith asks, "Would you want your brother to marry a jockey?"

In 1970, with Lyons Brown ailing, Diane agrees to ride his horse, Fathom, in the Kentucky Derby. She becomes the first woman to ride in the world's most famous race and as she enters the racetrack, one hundred thousand fans erupt in spontaneous applause.

Here is a rewritten version of my logline and synopsis for "The Jockettes."

<u>SCREENPLAY LOGLINE:</u>

<u>"THE JOCKETTES"</u>: The inspirational true story of Diane Crump, the first female jockey to ride in the U.S., and the other pioneering women who overcome incredible obstacles to win equal rights on the racetrack. Diane goes on to become the first woman to ride in the Kentucky Derby.

Format: Screenplay

Length: 116 pages

Genre: True Story (rights acquired)

Locale: Kentucky, Florida; some foreign scenes

Period: Mainly 1969-1970

"THE JOCKETTES" -- <u>SYNOPSIS</u>

In the early 1960's, young Diane Crump is obsessed with horses and wants desperately to become a jockey. At age eighteen, she becomes an exercise rider for Don Divine, a trainer in Kentucky. But that appears to be as far as she can go in her career. The Jockey Club will not allow females to ride in actual races. The men who manage the Sport of Kings consider women too weak to control an eleven-hundred pound animal running at thirty-five MPH.

When one female jockey wins a court case, Diane and the other women are granted licenses to ride in bona fide races. But male jockeys boycott those races and fans riot. Diane and other female jockeys are continually harassed, forced to dodge the rocks and bottles of irate men.

In February, 1969, Diane becomes the first female jockey to ride at a U.S. track. But life is still difficult for her and the other female jockeys, most of whom are hard-living cowgirls from broken homes who will do anything to get the best mounts. Male jockeys, forced to compete against women, whip them in the face during races. Female trainers lend their support, having faced sexism years earlier. A few male trainers are ordered by their wives to hire female jockeys.

In 1970, Diane is offered the opportunity to ride in the Kentucky Derby. She becomes the first woman to ride in the world's most famous race and as she enters the racetrack, one hundred thousand fans erupt in spontaneous applause, forever changing the face of the sport.

SCREENPLAY LOGLINE:

(First version - not to be imitated)

"THE MONEY MACHINE": In 2002, computer hackers alter "Pick 6" tickets worth $3 million. But in 1970, there are no computers to hack. Crooks have to use a more hands-on approach … so they steal a tote machine, hand-crank it and print winning tickets after the races are over! For months, the race track gives away money to its patrons and it doesn't know why. When the crooks are finally caught due to their own error, they exchange "The Money Machine" - for freedom. In essence, the advancing computer age is delayed just long enough to ensure this "Sting"-like perfect crime.

Format: Screenplay

Length: 119 pages

Genre: True Crime

Locale: Southern California

Period: 1970

"THE MONEY MACHINE" -- <u>SYNOPSIS</u>

(First version - not to be imitated)

In 2002, computer hackers altered "Pick 6" tickets worth three million dollars but in 1970, there were no computers to hack. Crooks had to use a more hands-on approach to change losing tickets into winners ... so they stole a tote machine, hand-cranked it and printed winning tickets after the races were over!

In 1970, the computer industry was in its infancy, looming large on the horizon. Computer manufacturers claimed their systems were unbeatable. (Insert laugh track here.) Race tracks agreed their old tote machines were vulnerable but worried they'd have to lay off too many employees. The unions were unhappy and delayed the installation of computers.

So, a bunch of loveable crooks, track "regulars" with a grudge against management, proved that tote machines were, indeed, vulnerable. They broke into a betting area of Santa Anita racetrack and lifted out a machine through a tunnel and over a fence near the parking lot. They left behind the electrical system, which bypassed the alarm. The first machine dropped and shattered, but they went back and got another one. One crook was crushed when the tote machine fell on him by the fence, but he recovered. All they had to do was get the thing hand-cranked and replace some aluminum letters. Soon, they had the machine working, ready to print winning tickets, after the races were over.

The race track officials thought the crooks would never get the machine working so they didn't worry. Well, they worried, but they never thought it would actually cost them money.

The crooks printed winning tickets, then dropped them on the ground. Eager spectators, looking for tickets on the ground and in trash cans, picked up the tickets and cashed them. No teller could detect the counterfeits. Many tickets had mustard stains on them. Almost everybody with decent eyesight was winning and no one was going to get singled out as the real crook.

The crooks cashed tickets for months! The race track was giving away money to its patrons and it didn't know why. All it knew was that, if twenty thousand dollars was bet on a race, it was paying out twenty-one thousand -- after the takeout!

Sounds like a perfect crime, right? Well, it was.

It was so perfect that it withstood an insider's double-cross and another insider's error. He printed the wrong code on the tickets, a red flag. Even when the ringleader was caught with a stack of phony tickets, no one was sent to jail. The racing industry couldn't afford to have a renegade machine traveling from state to state, damaging its integrity. The crooks simply returned the "Money Machine" -- in exchange for freedom.

They say nostalgia isn't what it used to be, but this story has the charm of "The Sting", the 1970's film that had us rooting for the bad guys. Like "The Sting," this scam did not hurt the average person, only the rich, heartless, possibly corrupt figures of authority who were trying to evict the "regulars" from "Mom and Pop's" backstretch kitchen. In the 1970 Santa Anita scam, the $2 bettors were actually making money along with the crooks.

In the 2002 "Pick 6" scam, the hackers were stealing money, not from the computer company or the race track, but from other two dollar bettors. Caper films have always depended on audiences rooting for the loveable "bad" guys to get away with the crime.

In this true/perfect crime story, they will.

Here is a rewritten version of my logline and synopsis for "THE MONEY MACHINE."

SCREENPLAY LOGLINE

THE MONEY MACHINE: (Comedic crime caper, based on a true story) In 1970, some down-on-their-luck gamblers steal a race track ticket machine and use it to blackmail a ruthless track owner in order to reclaim their cherished way of life. When the well-intentioned crooks are finally caught due to their own error, they exchange "The Money Machine" -- for freedom. In essence, the advancing computer age is delayed just long enough to ensure this "Sting"-like perfect crime.

Format: Screenplay

Length: 119 pages

Genre: True Crime

Locale: Southern California

Period: 1970

"THE MONEY MACHINE" -- SYNOPSIS

The story opens at Santa Anita race track in 1970. Mike, the owner of a small, backstretch diner patronized by race track regulars and employees, learns he is losing his lease.

The track owner, an old friend of Mike's, has passed on; replaced by his ruthless, gold-digging widow, Ellen, who decides to close the diner.

Mike and his friends from the diner decide to teach Ellen a lesson. They steal a ticket printing (tote) machine and start printing winning tickets after the races are over. Initially, the scam works because track cashiers do not realize the tickets are coming from a renegade machine. But soon, a sharp accountant alerts Ellen to the fraud. Meanwhile Mike's partner, Hawk, decides that the machine has tremendous value on the open market and arranges to secretly betray Mike and the gang and sell the machine to the highest bidder.

Mike gets caught with a stack of phony tickets and is held by race track security. He eventually convinces Ellen that a renegade machine could cripple the entire racing industry. The public would perceive the problem as a lack of integrity on the part of the race track. Hawk and Mike's friends execute one last scam in an attempt to free Mike and save the diner.

SCREENPLAY LOGLINE

(First version - not to be imitated)

"SUPERFAN 2020": (Baseball Comedy) It is 2020 and sports society has gone beyond escapism to insanity ... on its way to the unnatural. A sports nut named Murray joyfully jeopardizes his marriage, his job and his life in order to win the Superfan trophy. He and his 11 year-old protégé prove that the heroes are in the cheap seats after the pampered players are forced to play in a "Real" World Series. (Also a nationally distributed comic book & comedy series)

Format: Screenplay

Length: 120 pages

Genre: Comic Book Comedy (based on a nationally distributed comic book)

Locale: Washington, D.C.; Caribbean island; small town in the Midwest

Period: The year 2020

"SUPERFAN 2020" -- SYNOPSIS

(First version - not to be imitated)

The screenplay you're about to read is true. It just hasn't happened yet.

It's 2020 and sports society has gone beyond escapism to insanity ... on its way to the unnatural. Baseball has returned to Washington, D.C., where America's Team beams its games via satellite to fifty million homes every night. Fan involvement has progressed to the point where adoring local fans receive free admission to The Americadome and TV viewers worldwide are encouraged to advise the Team, via home computer, when to bunt or pinch-hit. The maverick Team owner, who asks fans only to subscribe to his cable network, promises that the fan who makes the best managerial choices and displays the most team spirit will be proclaimed Superfan and become richer and more celebrated than the players.

A Superfan named Murray joyfully jeopardizes his marriage, his job and his life in order to win the coveted Superfan trophy. The only one who appreciates Murray's dedication is an attention-starved, upper-class black youth, TJ, who runs away from home to join Murray at the World Series. The child-like adult and mature kid meet privacy-minded players who prove that the fan/player love affair is one-sided. Distraught, yet bonded, they drive home, no longer fans of the most popular Team ever.

When Murray, feeling snubbed, wins the Superfan award, he doesn't want it. When an island dictator/baseball fanatic forces the Team ("You call it a World Series and don't let anyone else play!") to play in a "Real" World Series, the players need Superfan support. It is Murray and TJ who prove more valuable than the pampered players, suggesting that the heroes are not on the field -- they're in the cheap seats.

This screenplay is designed to appeal to sports fans worldwide, as well as to people who think that sports are a waste of time. It is a parody of a futuristic sports society that pokes fun at everyone and everything in that futuristic world. At its core, however, is a touching story about faith, dedication and the bond between a lonely man and neglected boy.

As a TV series, "Superfan 2020" follows Murray and TJ into a futuristic society which puts a little too much emphasis on sports. As the winner of the prestigious "Superfan" trophy and the new Fan Commissioner, Murray becomes a consumer advocate, a watchdog for all sports fans. He and TJ infuse perspective into a futuristic sports society that has lost all sense of sanity. They are the "Superfans" deep inside the psyches of all fans as well as heroes in the sports community.

There will never be a shortage of story ideas because we can take today's headlines and project them into the future. This method has already been proven effective. Many of the wild scenarios written into the screenplay in the early 1990's have actually happened in recent years.

A "Superfan 2020" TV series, like the movie, depicts a world in which fans are rewarded for their obsession with their teams. If we even hint at the possibility of rewarding fan loyalty, we'll be rewarded with obsessively loyal viewers.

Here is a rewritten version of my logline for "SUPERFAN 2020."

<u>SCREENPLAY LOGLINE</u>

<u>"SUPERFAN 2020"</u>: (Baseball Fairy Tale) It is 2020 and *sports society has gone beyond escapism to insanity ... on its way to the unnatural*. A sports nut named Murray joyfully jeopardizes his marriage, his job and his life in order to win the Superfan trophy and the title of greatest baseball fan. He and his eleven year-old protégé prove that the heroes are in the cheap seats after the pampered players are forced to play in a "Real" World Series, which closely resembles a life-or-death grudge match. *(Also a nationally distributed comic book & comedy series)*

Format: Screenplay

Length: 120 pages

Genre: Comic Book Comedy (based on a nationally distributed comic book)

Locale: Philadelphia, PA; Caribbean island

Period: The year 2020

<u>"SUPERFAN 2020"</u> -- <u>SYNOPSIS</u>

The story opens in the year 2020, when a sports nut named Murray learns that baseball is returning to his hometown of Philadelphia and that fans of "America's Team" will be admitted for free and be asked to dictate game strategy via computer. The maverick team owner/cable TV magnate promises that the fan who makes the best managerial decisions and shows the most team spirit will be proclaimed Super-fan and become richer and more celebrated than the players.

Meanwhile, an island dictator and failed major league ballplayer makes plans to kidnap the team after the World Series and force them to play in the "World Game" - a game that he will rig in his favor.

Murray joyfully jeopardizes his marriage, his job and his life in order to win the Superfan trophy. The only one who appreciates his dedication is an attention-starved, upper-class black youth, TJ, who runs away from home to attend the World Series. The childlike adult and mature kid quickly have their hearts broken when they meet the selfish, dim-witted, privacy-minded players.

When Murray wins the Superfan trophy, he doesn't want it. When the island dictator/baseball fanatic forces the team to play in the "World Game," it falls upon these two fans to save the lives and dignity of the pampered players.

This screenplay/TV series, based on a nationally distributed comic book, will appeal to sports fans, as well as to people who think sports are a waste of time. It is a parody of a futuristic sports society and a story about faith, dedication and the bond between a lonely man and neglected boy.

SCREENPLAY LOGLINE:

"OUT OF THE WILDERNESS": During WWII, an orphaned, Polish, Jewish teenager miraculously eludes the Nazis, joins the Russian army, gets arrested for "Counter Revolutionary Propaganda," nearly starves to death in prison; survives in a wilderness commune, escapes to and from the Polish army posing as a Greek concentration camp survivor and finds his family in America.

Format: Screenplay

Length: 115 pages

Genre: True Story (rights acquired)

Locale: Eastern Europe, Russia, Central Asia

Period: 1930's & 1940's

"OUT OF THE WILDERNESS" -- SYNOPSIS

Chaim Pacowsky (pronounced Pah-sov-sky) was born in Vilnius, Poland (now Lithuania) in 1920. His poor, Jewish family was all alone (relatives had moved to the U.S.) in an anti-Semitic environment. In 1925, Poles nearly beat his father to death. A few months later, they finished the job, locking his father in a freezing lumberyard. Months after that, his mother died during childbirth.

Chaim attended a Jewish orphanage and took a menial job at age thirteen. Starvation, isolation and fear of the future were the major aspects of his youth. He didn't know that the worst war in human history was only a few years away from blasting through his part of the world; a war in which six million of his people would perish.

In 1937, Chaim got lucky. Someone who worked at a flour mill in Tabrushuk drowned and Chaim was offered the job. He was paid twenty-five zloty (dimes) a month and worked six days a week, from six am to ten pm.

"Those two years, from 1937-1939, were the best years of my youth," Chaim would say later.

The "fun" was about to end. The Russians were coming.

On September 1st, 1939, the Nazis attacked Poland from the West. Sixteen days later, Russia invaded Eastern Poland. Fortunately for Chaim, he had advanced notice and fled to Belarus, where his sisters lived. His zloty were worthless and he had no rubles. He stayed in Belarus, in a one and a half room shack with five relatives, until 1940. There was no future for him there, either.

Since he would've been drafted into the Russian army within a year anyway, Chaim enlisted. The Russians were happy to have him; they wanted Polish soldiers to "liberate" Warsaw after the war was over and transfer the capitalist regime to communist. A year after he left Belarus, the Nazis attacked the area. Leaving there in timely fashion saved his life.

A soldier deep in Russia, surviving on soup, Chaim complained about the Russian economy. "At least in Poland, if you had money, you could buy things. Here, money is a joke."

He was sentenced to ten years in prison for making that comment. Just before he starved to death in a labor camp, during the wintertime, he was released - so he could be redrafted at a later date. In April, 1942, he walked slowly into the wilderness. Farmers invited him into their houses to eat - they were more afraid of the Russian soldiers and police than of ex-convicts.

Chaim worked on a commune, harvesting vegetables with old men and women. His surviving family members (many were already dead, hunted down by "dogcatchers") were sent to Auschwitz. The Nazis picked out the young, single Jews and put them to work. All others were killed. Chaim's single, twenty-four year-old sister, Minka, did not want to live without her sister and nephews. She took one of her nephews as her own child and was killed, too.

Meanwhile, Chaim, a soldier, was arrested again, this time for walking around without official papers. He had been working on a barge on the Volga River, loading wood. He was soon free ... to freeze in the Russian winter of 1943.

He and a friend headed south, hitching a free ride on a train to Tashkent, the capital of Uzbekistan. They survived by stealing apples from people in train stations. In March, 1943, Chaim's friend was dead but Chaim joined a Polish unit of the Russian army.

Marching back toward Poland as the war was winding down in 1944, Chaim was to cross the Visla River in a boat, to help retake Warsaw from the Nazis. Boat after boat was blown up. Just before his suicide mission, the boats were called back. The Russians would wait for the river to freeze and roll in their tanks. Chaim took another of his ill-advised walks and was hit by shrapnel. He wasn't a war hero, however, he was just "Someone who got shot." A few months later, he was hit again by shrapnel, in the jaw, and barely survived.

In 1945, Chaim was offered officer's training in Lodz, Poland's second largest city and a place barely affected by war. At age twenty-four4, he simply went AWOL from the Polish army and was put on a train back to Germany, to the DP camps. He had to pose as a Greek concentration camp survivor. The border guards stopped the train and checked everyone's identification. These were the same guards whom Chaim had trained! If they recognized him, they would have shot him instantly. Luckily, they did not, and Chaim's life was miraculously spared, again.

Chaim thought of emigrating to Israel. He still had family in America, however, and remembered getting treats like shoelaces and candy from aunts in Philadelphia. He didn't know anyone's last name. The family in America was no longer called Pacowsky.

Chaim put an ad in a Jewish newspaper and his aunts eventually found him.

"My brother's son - he's alive!" the American aunts screamed.

When Chaim finally arrived in Philadelphia in 1948, his wealthy, American cousin greeted him with ... a five dollar bill. Chaim changed his name to Herman Ruthberg, to match, or nearly match, his cousins' name. At age twenty-nine, he had his first date -- with a woman named Beatrice. They married and had four children.

Chaim/Herman admits that miracles kept following him. Although his family was killed by anti-Semites, he was seldom bothered because he was a Jew. He was tormented for being Polish.

The man who should've been killed countless times before, during and after World War II is still alive at age eighty-three.

"I didn't choose anything. It all just happened," he said recently.

He never returned to Vilnius.

Don Rutberg

"OUT OF THE WILDERNESS"

TABLE OF CONTENTS FROM THE BOOK

PART ONE

PART TWO

Pitching To Producers At Pitch Sessions

I was finally ready to promote my work to producers. There were two pitch sessions offered in Los Angeles in October, 2003. I signed up for both. One was sponsored by Eva Peel (when she owned a company called Thewritewayin.com) and the other by Creative Screenwriting Magazine. One was situated on the West side of town; the other was held downtown at the Expo center.

On the West side, writers paid $109 to get four guaranteed appointments with producers for five minutes each. If, however, a writer left the table early, another writer could jump in and take the remaining two minutes or so. It was a chaotic scene. Here is what happened and here is what to expect if and when you go.

The session was scheduled to start at seven pm but I arrived two hours early with a writer, Demetric, I had met at my hotel. Demetric was an ex-marine who had been stationed in Guantanamo Bay, Cuba. One day, he was on a bus heading to a dance when he felt a strange sensation. A voice in his head told him to get off the bus. He couldn't -- there was no time -- so he moved forward about ten rows. Then the bus was hit by a car and exploded, killing everyone in the rows behind him.

After he told me his story, which was the subject of his screenplay, I told him, "You have no third act." He had the beginning (he's blown up), middle (he struggles to overcome his health problems) and no ending. When you outline your screenplay, make sure it has all three elements: beginning, middle and end. Despite what Meat Loaf sang, two out of three is bad.

To simplify, in act one, your main character's cat gets stuck in a tree. In act two, all efforts to rescue the cat fail and it looks hopeless. In act three, the cat is saved by your main characters.

I selected four meetings with producers who were seeking my type of scripts; comedies and true stories. A bell rang and we ran to individual tables to sign up for the meetings. I was able to get all four that I had selected, but three of them were crammed into the second hour; only one was to be held in the first hour. The producer I was scheduled to meet in the first hour didn't show up so I was minus one pitch session and had nothing to do, formally, at least, for an hour.

When a writer left a meeting early, I zoomed into his seat, like a wolf after a fresh veal chop. The producer, Brad Pollack from Skylark Films, remembered my name from a letter I had sent him years earlier. I was amazed, knowing that he received hundreds if not thousands of queries from unagented writers around the world. He took my project list and said he'd call me if he wanted to read anything.

A few minutes later, I catapulted into a seat at Sub-Rosa Productions' table for a bonus mini-appointment. The producer, who seemed to be the boss, Sherilyn Moore, didn't like "The Jockettes" story. So I pitched "Superfan 2020." She clearly liked the idea and the related Comic Book I handed her. She asked if it would adapt into a TV series. I said I had already written it as such. She wondered if it would do well as an ESPN cable movie. I said, "Of course." She gave me her email address.

When I returned home, I sent a two page synopsis of "Superfan 2020" to her company. A day later, they asked to read the script. An hour after that, I had mailed it to them.

If I had simply mailed or emailed a query letter to this company, or just about any production company, I never would have gotten a reply. Sherilyn told me up front, "Write 'Requested Material' in the subject line of the email and say I told you to submit the synopsis or it will never get read!" My note would've been one of a thousand in a slush pile or electronic phantom zone. That is why I consider these pitch sessions valuable.

My aggressiveness landed me the bonus appointment with Sub-Rosa. My flexibility allowed me to move on to the next project, after they said "No" to "The Jockettes." I was ready to pitch five to six projects to them. I knew that producers often hated what I loved the best, just as they often loved what I considered weakest. If you go in expecting to sell your murder mystery, the odds are that the producer will love your romantic comedy - and vice-versa. A writer never knows what to expect in these meetings so prepare yourself for some kind of surprise.

I started to feel guilty for jumping in front of my peers, wolf-style, to get these bonus appointments. (As a hockey goaltender, I am a lot quicker than most folks.) So, when I noticed two ladies pitching to Marty Katz Productions, with one lady crouching uncomfortably because she had no seat, I brought over a chair for her. A few minutes later, the producer sent someone to get me, so he could listen to a pitch from that "chivalrous guy with the gray hair."

After that bonus meeting, I gulped down another triple espresso and circled the tables, smiling at my fellow writers, all of whom, I knew, would spray chloroform in my face in order to beat me to a bonus appointment. There was an uneasy camaraderie in the room; the kind that is only palpable when chloroform and Hollywood ambitions get together. I struck up a conversation with an aspiring agent, David Freedman.

David was already a successful businessman, having been involved with MovieFone, a service that informs moviegoers about where and when their favorite films are playing. David told me he was looking around for potential clients. I gave him my project list. A week later, he asked to read two of my screenplays.

David did not like the title, "The Jockettes." I told him the title captured the sexist environment which prevailed in 1969, when female jockeys couldn't get their licenses. He liked "Running Against The Wind." (We later compromised on "The Jockey Club.")

A month later, David read two of screenplays and offered criticism. He had applied for his agents' license by that time. After I re-wrote my scripts, I planned on signing a contract with him. He was the first agent in twenty years whom I actually liked! I should have known that he would do something I didn't like in a matter of months. (See "Updates" later in this section.)

I met with a producer, Stephen Graham, who was producing a film about the first female umpires. So I pitched "The Jockettes" to him and he asked to read it. Writers were asked to mail the scripts to producers after the pitch sessions were over so they didn't have to carry two hundred pounds of screenplays out to their cars.

Some producers treated me like a pest; others seemed very interested in my work. I gave my "Superfan" comic book to just about everybody I met. "Superfan" is a baseball comedy and the World Series was being played that evening. Even better, a few nights earlier, a Chicago Cubs' fan had interfered with the home team's left fielder and indirectly caused the Cubs to lose the game and the playoff series! So baseball and its fans were very much in the public eye that evening.

Later, I followed a producer named June, from Winkler Productions, out the door.

Do you remember June from the last section? She requested my script, "The Money Machine," then ignored my calls for six months.

"Hi, June," I said with a smile. "Remember me, the Philly guy?"

(June was born in Philadelphia, too.)

June looked nervous. She knew I knew something that she didn't.

She smiled patiently.

I reminded her, "You asked to read my screenplay and never responded. Then you asked to read my jockey treatment and never responded. I know you're busy ...."

"Oh, yeah," she stammered. "Didn't I send that back to you?"

"Noooooooooo."

"Did you ever write the full script for the jockey story?"

"Yeaaaaaaaaah."

"I'd love to read that. Send it to me."

That was when I should have said, "Sure, thanks."

I should have said that to the agent from Minnesota in 1990 when I asked her instead, "Is this agency some kind of toy from your husband to make it seem like you have a career?"

Like the undercover IRS agent I interviewed in the 1980's, I guess I'm brash.

So, I didn't thank her for the opportunity and smile like a dummy. I asked, "What can I do to motivate you to actually read it this time?"

Her cell phone rang and all I got was a nod and a smile. I sent her the script. I will be very surprised if I hear from her again or if I get invited to a pool party at Mr. Winkler's home. (I'm guessing that the producer of "Rocky" and "Goodfellas" has a pool at his home.)

Note: I never heard back from June. But I do scan the trade papers so I'll know if she ever gets fired, or better yet, blackballed from the industry. To be serious for a moment, she could have sent me an email advising that she was passing on the project. Most of her peers who had requested my scripts took a few seconds to reply via email. If I saw her again, she would probably ask me to send the jockey script for a third time - and, if I were foolish enough to submit it, she'd ignore it for a third time. When you are an outsider, you will be treated disrespectfully. Deal with it.

With the first session over and a dozen or so script requests to show for it, I prepped for the second session at the L.A. Expo Center downtown. This was a major event. William Goldman (author of "Butch Cassidy and The Sundance Kid," "The Princess Bride" and "Adventures in the Screen Trade," the book which inspired me to write this) would be speaking. Thousands would attend seminars. Hundreds would attend pitch sessions, paying twenty-five dollars each to pitch to two or three producers. I paid for fifteen pitch tickets. For every five sessions, the discounted price was only a hundred dollars. What the heck.

After meeting with the first three producers, I had three script requests. Then I made the mistake of telling my peers that I had a success ratio of 1,000% and was three-for-three. The next few producers didn't ask to read anything. I vowed never to brag about anything again.

Many interested parties gave me their email addresses and told me to remind them of their interest in my specific project. One lady suggested I see a company called, "Circle of Confusion" because they adapted comic books into films. How was I going to get an appointment with them at the last minute?

I met with two German ladies from Romano-Shane Productions, the company that brought you, "Catch Me If You Can." That film was based on a true story and I had true stories to pitch. The ladies, who were very, very thin and spoke with heavy German accents, kept asking each other when they could sneak out for a smoke. I was trying to pitch; they were trying to puff. Still, they asked to read my true stories.

Then I got a break. At 11:40 am, when I went to pitch my low-budget story, "Ghetto Princess," to a low-budget producer, Leo Grillo, I learned that he made movies about endangered animals.

"I'm Mr. Endangered Animal," I told him, my new-found kindred spirit. "I've written a dozen children's books about kids saving whales, butterflies, goats, bears; you name it. I could adapt them to film."

My five minutes were up at that time. No one had an appointment for 11:45 am so we kept talking. At 11:50, there was a scheduled break. (The German girls flew out the door, cigarettes in hand.) We spoke some more; twenty minutes in all. Leo, a stocky man who made movies with European financing, told me, "You're a real writer - the second one I've met today." (He had been meeting a dozen people per hour, for several hours.)

I had no idea that Leo produced animal films. That's why I didn't even bring my children's book project list. Signing up to pitch to him was a lucky coincidence.

After I met with one producer, I noticed him doing one-handed push-ups. I made a note to mention the push-ups to him in the email he asked me to send. "Maybe you could join the circus," I later wrote to him, "if this producer gig doesn't work out."

A seventeen year-old boy, named Ari, was attending the pitch sessions. I put him under my wing and offered encouragement. He was a brave soul, risking rejection and seeking knowledge in an adult environment.

"You'll be successful," I told him. "I can feel it in my bones."

He was probably the other "real writer" that Leo Grillo had referred to earlier.

At the Twilight Pictures table, I met Andrea Spiegel, a young producer from Calgary, Alberta, Canada. Her company worked with the Canadian government to produce high-quality TV shows and movies.

I told Andrea about my cousin's Holocaust survival story, "Out of the Wilderness." She was interested and said she had a family Holocaust survival story, too.

"You're paying to talk to me so I'll tell you later," she said. "At the party."

I was glad I had paid the extra fifteen dollars to attend the post-expo party at the Figueroa Hotel.

As I pitched to agent Marc Hernandez, my energy was starting to wane. It was like appearing as a guest on fifteen talk shows in one day. So I let my project list do my talking for me. Marc said he liked my lawyer in heaven story, "When Angels Speak..." and "The Money Machine." But he only wanted to read one of my scripts.

"Which is more polished?" he asked.

I had rewritten "The Money Machine" several times. The plot was much more intricate so I told him I was more comfortable sending that script.

"OK, send it," he replied and we were done.

"Thirty seconds left in this session," a voice called out.

I had finished the pitch in under five minutes - a first for me!

Marc looked like he had somewhere else to go.

"So how long have you been an agent?" I asked.

"Six years on my own."

"I hate to waste fifteen seconds but I think we're finished," I said with a smile.

Marc has since rejected, via email, my script called, "The Money Machine." He left the door open for me to pitch to him again, via email. I tried again with the man. I remembered he liked the concept for "When Angels Speak..." so I sent him the logline and a few more loglines. The respectful rejection led me to more opportunities with this particular company. Sometimes, it takes three-four rejections for a writer to figure out what the agent/producer is seeking and finally send an appropriate story.

I still hadn't seen Circle of Confusion, the company that handled comic books. I had one more pitch ticket, but the producer had not shown up. I needed to trade with someone who was going in to pitch to Circle of Confusion.

When a worker asked if anyone would trade with me, little Ari raised his hand! He gladly traded Pitch Tickets (he would get to see El Rey Pictures, whom I had already seen) with me and was even happier to accept a comic book for his good will.

Circle of Confusion took my comic book and promised to get back to me. I left hoping that Ari had sold a script to El Rey Pictures.

I drove back in fifteen minutes from the downtown Expo to my hotel at Sunset Blvd. and the 405 freeway. I showered, ate, watched a little of the World Series, then drove back downtown to the party at the Figueroa Hotel, near the Staples Center. The return drive, at 7:30 pm -- the same trip that took fifteen minutes at 4:30 pm -- took seventy-five minutes on the L.A. freeways! While driving in my rented Volvo with the giant sunroof, I could not pick up the World Series game. Yet I was able to pick up two soccer games loud and clear, proving, to me at least, that L.A. was some kind of a parallel universe.

Out of curiosity, I would like to drive around L.A. on Super Bowl Sunday to find out if I could pick up the Super Bowl on radio … or if I'd only be able to pick up the broadcast of a rugby match out of Sydney and a bullfight from Tijuana.

I exited the freeway and drove into the first parking lot I could find.

I asked the parking attendant, "Is the Figueroa Hotel anywhere near here?"

"It's right there," he replied. "Across the street."

"Oh."

I saw Andrea, from Twilight Pictures in Canada, at the party. She was talking with Eric Reid, a young agent from the Writers and Artists Agency.

"Don't tell your client, Robert Wuhl, what I said about his new caper flick," I told Eric.

Eric laughed at the irony of me pitching a project that was similar to a film they were committed to making. (The story about how I unintentionally demeaned their project appears earlier in this section.) He soon walked off to chat with partygoers, all of whom were desperate to meet a real-life agent.

I then turned my attention to sweet, pretty, young Andrea. Twenty years ago, I would have been more interested in her social life then her professional life. But I'm married now and twice Andrea's age, so I asked about her family's Holocaust story.

Andrea relayed a story about how her great-aunt had escaped from a camp by bribing a guard with smuggled diamonds. We talked for twenty minutes. I reminded myself I was old enough to be her father and tried not to flirt. As you know from the early chapters of this book, I was too eager to flirt with producers and agents when I was in my twenties. I should have had less romance back then; maybe I would've sold more scripts.

So there I was, a rarity; a healthy man in Los Angeles who was not there to cheat on his wife. I felt as though I had lost my knack to charm young, female producers … and had subconsciously acquired "hands-off, I'm married" mannerisms. (I think John Lennon felt the same way after he met Yoko.) There was nothing wrong with these internal changes. How can we grow if we don't make them? In all likelihood, I had succumbed at an appropriate time. I would have to get by on my talent from that point forward, a noble if isolated practice.

"Less romance; more script sales" became my mantra, along with, "More tequila, less thinking."

Here is another thought about setbacks and how they can become our friends. I teach screenwriting, children's book writing and magazine writing at Bucks County Community College near Philadelphia. (Now, I also teach in the MFA in Creative Writing program at Rosemont College.) I asked the staff at Bucks if I could miss a week of class to attend the pitch sessions in L.A. and they said, "Sure, just teach an extra twenty minutes to make up for the time missed." Fair 'nuff.

In July, a few months earlier, I was asked to interview for a university teaching job. I was in California and said I couldn't come in for two weeks. There were four open freshman English teaching jobs but they were going quickly. In two weeks, they could be gone.

When I called two weeks later, they were all gone. I didn't get the university teaching job that was sitting there, waiting for me. A setback, right?

No it wasn't. If I had not been in California in July, I would've probably been offered and accepted that job. There would have been no way I would have been able to go to Los Angeles to meet with producers in October. I could not have missed my fourth week of teaching, during my first semester at a university. I probably wouldn't have even bothered to ask. (The university president wrote to me in July, 2004, and demonstrated an interest in hiring me for the Fall, 2004 or Spring, 2005.)

If I manage to sell a screenplay or acquire an agent based on what I did at those October, 2003, pitch sessions, it will be a happy result of a major setback.

More examples of how setbacks can be helpful are described later, in the children's book writing section.

Pitch Sessions In Smaller Venues

Not all conferences will elicit desirable results. In fact, some will be a waste of time. I left a recent conference gnashing my teeth, regretting that I hadn't lashed back verbally at an arrogant clown on the panel.

I had spent fifty dollars or so to attend a writer's conference in New Hope, PA; an artsy town twenty-five miles north of my village on the Delaware River. The promise of a pitch session motivated me to attend.

There were only about 100 people in the old firehouse. Almost none of them signed up for the pitch session. They were afraid to pitch their script ideas to a panel of experts in a cozy room. That's a silly approach. Any feedback from a producer is worthwhile.

Let me amend that to almost any industry feedback is worthwhile.

With my friend, script consultant Jim Breckinridge sitting nearby, cheering me on, I walked to a microphone and addressed the "distinguished" panel. The panelists had gleefully shot down the first five writers but I knew I had more interesting projects to promote ("The Jockettes," "Superfan 2020," etc.). I was different. I wasn't afraid of these panelists, who were like hyenas and actually fed off the fear of the writers in the room. I knew they weren't going to have me for lunch. I could actually sense that other writers were fearful for me; like they felt sorry for what could happen if I pitched bad stories. Many came up after my pitch session and praised me for my courage. Huh? Soldiers have courage. Writers just have to do a little PR work.

The first panelist, who had briefly worked with a New York production company, advised that I change the sports setting in "Superfan 2020" from baseball to slamball. What the hell is slamball? That trash sport we see on TV once a year at 3 am? The whole point of "Superfan 2020" is that the main character has been weaned on baseball; he's followed the game for decades and loves it more than anything. How could anyone love slamball? My movie would make no sense if the Superfan idolized a slamball team.

I quickly turned the conversation to "The Jockettes," explaining how I had written the first draft of my female jockey story way back in 1984. One panelist, a fat guy with hair plugs and an ugly, orange scarf, who had written a few really bad monkey movies (apes, gorillas; whatever) had an insult waiting for me. But that insult had to wait for his first insult. After I mentioned to the panel that I had written the book you are now reading, Mr. Orangutan said with a chuckle, "Yeah. I wanted to write a book called, 'How to write a book about how to write a book about how to write a screenplay.'" Then he laughed out loud at his own wit and wisdom.

I turned to Jim Breckinridge, mouthing to him, "What's wrong with this guy?" Jim didn't want to get involved. He later admitted that the monkey man's insult was completely mindless.

I guess I threatened this ape man because he then retorted, "I don't know why some people have to imitate other successful movies and can't think of a good story on their own."

"Excuse me?" I muttered.

"You're just trying to piggyback on 'Seabiscuit's' success."

I yelled back, "I told you that I wrote the first draft of this story 20 years ago! How could I be imitating something that was produced this year?"

He just waved me away.

The rest of the panel sat there with stupid expressions on their faces. For this, I gave up four hours of sleep? I left, went home and took a nap. I dreamt about monkey poachers.

If you decide to go to a writer's conference or a pitch session, do yourself a favor and attend one in Los Angeles or New York City. The panelists at the small-town conferences, from my experience, are not there to help you develop your script or consider it for representation or production. They are certainly not there to encourage you. They go so they can gloat about their own successes and dismiss you as an outsider with no clue.

This is not a case of sour grapes. I highly recommend the L.A. and New York City conferences/pitch sessions. Many of the panelists there were open-minded and helpful. If you are ever asked to appear at these conferences as a panelist, try to be a positive influence. And don't get hair plugs in your head; your hair looks just fine the way it is.

Keeping Track Of Your Submissions

An unagented writer must be his/her own sales force. To a creative, talented person like yourself, wearing this extra hat will seem trivial and repulsive.

Well, you're more right than you'll ever know, but look at the problem this way. Somebody's got to do it; why shouldn't the responsibility fall to the person who created every character and every scene in a script? Why not take the initiative to promote your script's virtues to as many potential buyers as you can find?

If you've completed a script, you've achieved some level of success. If you sell it, you could earn a few hundred thousand dollars. Seems to me, getting to that next level is worthwhile.

As mundane and non-creative as it may be, it is imperative for you, the salesperson, to keep track of submissions. When you receive a positive reply ("Please send us a logline or the script") you will be able to quickly locate your original letter to the company, see what they produce, where you met them or found the listing.

A Close Look At The "Expect Reply" File

I keep an "Expect Reply" file in my computer. When "XYZ" Productions asks to read my logline or script, I ask the computer to search for "XYZ." Then I read my own notes, such as, "Superfan logline and cb (comic book) handed to XYZ Prods at L.A. expo, 10/19/03, to Jane Doe. They produce comedies -- feature and TV films."

After I've sent the script to "XYZ Prods," I add to the paragraph, "On 11/11/03, they asked to read Superfan 2020 screenplay. Sent 11/12/03 with release form."

If a production company returns my script, I scan my "Expect Reply" file before opening the package. By the time I read their letter, I have refreshed my memory with regard to the company's needs. If their rejection letter states, "We enjoyed reading your script and hope you will keep us in mind with other comedies," I send the information to my "Try Again" file. A few weeks later, I mail them another comedic screenplay, along with a short letter thanking them for their interest in my work.

If they send me a form rejection letter after six months, which is common, I send the information to my "PRODX.doc" file, which could be called "TRASHEDBYPRODS.doc". If I see the name of a producer that I don't even remember, I scan the profoundly dead-end file, called "UR.doc" for "unlikely replies". (My "UR" file has information on producers who have died, been fired for their involvement in embarrassing incidents, been incarcerated in federal prison, had nervous breakdowns or who have steamed the stamps off my SASE. Often, it is a combination of three or more of these factors.)

Here is my current "Expect Reply" File. It is hard to believe that I've wasted so much time trying to promote my work to a group of mostly, let's be kind here, apathetic recipients. It's clear that they don't have time for new writers yet they solicit scripts from them. (Rarely should you contact a company that seeks only agented submissions.)

Think of the following as an experiment: what would happen if you had ample amounts of time and money to reach out to producers and publishers? Would it be worthwhile? Even if the answer is no, you have to do something to promote your work. You can knock on doors, call friends of friends, attend conferences, produce your own work or take other steps. I chose to throw out a wide net and see what I could catch.

I will explain these notes, the actual (though abridged) shorthand, unedited notes from my computer file, as they are presented.

EXPECT REPLIES FROM EVERYBODY!: (FROM OCT 2002? THRU OCT, 2003) :)

(160? ARE READING AS OF 11/22/03)

expect reply, lev sp & satch sp samples emailed to alliance theatre group 11/11.

(This is fairly straightforward. I emailed two of my children's stage play samples, "A Leprechaun Named Levity" and "Satchel Paige … Did What?!" to a theater group.)

expect checks from Jewish journal & horizon air -- by 12/1. if not, call these people!

(This is something to which everyone can relate. When will I get paid for articles that have already been published?)

EXPECT REPLY, GOATS REWRITE SENT TO ANN RIVERS GUNTON 10/28 AS PER HER SUGGESTIONS! VIKING CHILDREN'S BOOKS. prev: letr telling her she'll have goats rr by mid nov sent 10/13. See PUBS SEP OCT 03: prev: xlev, xihs, xsb x'd 10/9. prev: CHAIM BK was sent 9/2. xx'd 10/15. I accidentally sent her goats, lev, ihs, sb on 9/2 and she liked goats!!! LATER? Hope it's not necc: otisnf, pignpam. prev: xxHP BK x'd 8/30, sent 5/6 at her request. Prev: X'D LIFE INTRO, 1 PG NF PROJ X'D 5/5/03, ORIG SENT 3/11/02! IT TOOK 14 MONTHS TO REPLY! "HP VERY INTERESTING."

("Prev" means what had happened previously. Goats "rr" means a rewrite. Chaim bk is "Out of the Wilderness" and was sent 9/2; rejected 10/15. This is a good sign. She reviewed and returned my book in only six weeks. "Later" means what I plan to send her if and when she rejects what she's currently reading. She took 14 months to reply to my "Life After Death" book. But, to be fair, I had sent the book to her predecessor at Viking.)

EXPECT REPLY, TRICYCLE PRESS, ABAGAIL SAMOUN. IN A LETTER 11/03, I ASKED IF SHE READ OTISJUVSH? SENT IN JUNE, '02. AT HER REQUEST!

(Here is another publisher who has still not reviewed my work - the work she requested and asked me to rewrite! - after 16 months!)

?expect reply, to my email sent 11/2. go to induction ceremony in feb? $150? Does he want to implement my superfan contest for the philly hall of fame? EXPECT REPLY, SUPCON/CB SENT 6/18 TO KEN AVALLON, PHILLY SPORTS HALL OF FAME. 6/17, I PITCHED SUPCON IN EMAIL. HE ASKED ME TO SEND ANYTHING THAT CAN HELP OUT HALL OF FAME. I CALLED 8/19. ur.

(This is an example of trying to sell a project to an unorthodox buyer. I am trying to get The Philadelphia Sports Hall of Fame to pick up my "Superfan" project as a reality show or a contest. In response, he asked me for $150 to attend his banquet. UR means this is an unlikely reply and I shouldn't expect much interest from him -- other than soliciting my $150 check.).

expect reply, Jockettes sent 11/5 to Ksana Golod, intercom ent., inc, at her request. no release form. Re Eva's NL. Ksana was w/warner bros. now has deal w/other studios. Is it a feature or TV film? We spoke for 15 minutes 11/4.

(This is a good opportunity. Ksana is an experienced producer who was inspired to ask for my script and actually talked to me on the phone for 15 minutes. Phone calls from producers or publishers to unagented writers are extremely rare and should be celebrated. "Re Eva's NL" means Ksana found me in Eva Peel's newsletter.)

(EXPECT REPLIES FROM L.A. PITCH SESSIONS; 6 EMAILS SENT 10/22

expect reply, Jockettesff, supff & supcb, 2 signed release forms & letr to Signe Olynyk. At her request. 11/4. (re andrea Spiegel), Twilight Pictures, Inc.

also, on 11/6!!!, andrea asked me to send her logline for chaim ff. I did 11/7. But she said supff not right? but signe likes it! Andrea said she was just a "worker ant" for signe so superfan is still alive. Supff & jockff arrived there 11/12. ok. they do cable, feature, ½ hr tv series, I reminded her that sup also ½ hr tv series. (EXPO) Recap: 10/22: I sent email, 2 pg synopsis, Jockettes & sup. (reminded her re chaim on handout). 11/3, signe at twilight sent email requesting sup & jock ff's. 11/6: andrea at twilight asked 4 chaimff logline. On 11/12, andrea asked me in email if signe liked chaim. I said she doesn't know about it. Maybe andrea will tell signe about chaim. Andrea "loved" chaim logline.

(Here, I explain the whole scenario to myself. Expo means I met her at the L.A. Expo pitch sessions.)

By 12/15: "sit tight" and expect call from nina davis platinum sky pics/Major league prods, re how we could possibly proceed." (we spoke 11/17; she called orig 11/13). she does sports marketing! 323-960-

2887. Nina loves sup & likes angel! I told her Sup & angel tv series, too! Sup is contest, reality show, vid game... nina said 11/17 that she likes idea of tv series, etc. ask if she wants to read supcon.

 after I speak to nina in mid dec, if she wants to do something with sup & angel, call david freedman & get # of his entertainment attorney. Maybe a dollar/day option contract??

prev:10/24 jockff, supff, angelff, mmff to andra-nina davis (eva's pitch session)

(This producer called me! and expressed interest in two of the screenplays I sent to her. So this is a triple green light. She liked my pitch in person, she liked my synopses and she liked my screenplays. She wants to "proceed!" I have a plan re proceeding: to call agent David Freedman's entertainment lawyer if and when Nina actually does proceed. "Eva's pitch session" means I met her through Eva Peel.)

expect reply, SUPFF & CB & SIGNED RELEASE FORM to Sub-rosa's Virginia Romfh on 10/29. on outside of ENV, I PUT "REQUESTED MATERIAL", "SUPERFAN 2020" & "ATTN VIRGINIA ROMFH". prev, IN 10/22 EMAIL, I SENT 2 PG synopsis for supff. Describe what would happen if sup were a series and if sup were a mow on espn. Sherilyn moore asked me to send this. (eva) ON 10/29, I SENT VIRGINIA EMAIL SAYING SUPFF IS EN ROUTE, AS SHE REQUESTED.

call if I don't hear from leo grillo by 12/1. expect reply, lubintrt & summer help bk synopses (pg 2 of juv proj) emailed 10/26 to leo grillo. Great meeting!!! He does animals are people too. Family action adventure. He wants animal related thrillers. Save animals in danger. Expose type theme. Baby boomer dad w/ his little girl save butterflies or whales etc. maybe he'll ask to read juv bks from summer help series, adapt em into treatments/scripts. Send his card w/my materials. leo grillo prods. now that I've sent lubintrt & juv proj w/ summer help synopses. Which juv bk story does he like best? I pushed Pigns!!!! Whales? (EXPO). Eva says Imdb.com. google him.

(IMBD.com is a website where you can check up on producers; see what they've done and if they are legitimate. Google is the search engine needed to do the task..)

expect reply, 10/24, angelff, jockff, chaim bk, "re eva peel" to Mr. Stephen Graham. (he's doing 1st female umpire.) honored by women in film. (eva)

(Since this producer is making a movie about the first female umpire, he should be interested in "The Jockettes.")

expect reply, 10/24, jockff, jock 2 pg synopsis to Barbara Hiser, Backlot Prods. Looking for strong female roles. (eva)

expect reply, 10/24 JOCKETTES FF TO JUNE CZERWINSKI. She is slowly reading mmff & has jock trt. This is a long shot. (eva) WINKLER FILMS. SHE'S VP OF DEVELOPMENT. fax sent 7/9 to June re jockettes ff. She has my email & phone. I CALLED 8/19. & 9/16.

(In this paragraph, I tell myself not to expect much from this producer. I could really write, "This is a long shot" about every producer in this file.)

expect reply, 10/24 angelff to Karen loop, el rey pictures. (expo)

It should be clear by now what I am trying to do in this file. When someone contacts me, I can quickly refresh my memory and talk about the work I submitted.

expect reply, 10/24 mmff to marc Hernandez, crescendo ent. Managers. He also liked angel but only wanted 1 script. Mmff more polished, right? (expo) I dreamt I was working with him!!!

(That's a new angle - I dreamt that I was his client. Maybe it's a good omen.)

EXPECT REPLY, OK 10/23. JOCKETTES FF & SIGNED RELEASE FORM TO lacy boughn at escape artists. She asked for release form so I can send jockff at her request.

EXPECT REPLY, OK 10/23. 2 pg synopses for mmff & jockff to Nadine at romano/shane prods. Maybe she'll ask to read scripts later. Euro girl. I gave her crimesart. (expo)

expect reply, ok 10/22, I sent email to Clinton Huling, regent pics. Reminded him he liked mmff, supff, jockff on my proj. he did 1 handed pushups. Tell him he has a future in the circus if this producer thing doesn't work out! He has cb, proj. (expo)

("MAYBES FROM CAL TRIP") (if they're interested, they'll ask to read by thanksgiving)

Maybe chris kachel at licht meuller will ask to read supff. He has proj, supcb. He's a big baseball fan! From seattle. Harvard grad. Nice kid. (eva)

Maybe Mike Schwartz at industry ent will ask to read from proj. xsup. He called Jockettes "interesting". Agents. Tough sell. (expo)

Maybe Dwayne Smith at circle of confusion will ask to read supff. He has cb. They make films from comic books. Maybe he'll call or email and ask to read supff. Karen loop at el rey pics recommended me to circle of confusion. comic books -- films. (expo)

EXPECT REPLY, JOCKETTES SCREENPLAY 8/4 TO MR. STEVE LEON, AT HIS REQUEST. COLLABORATIVE ARTISTS. GREG LIKED JOCKETTES MINI-TRT (5 PGS) & FIRST 15 PAGES OF SCREENPLAY 7/15; (XCHAIM MINI-TRT(TABLE CONTS & 1ST 4 PGS AT HIS REQUEST 7/ 14; X8/3). ORIG PROJFF SENT 10/21/02 TO Barry Perelman). THEY'RE AGENTS WHO PACK-AGE SCREENPLAYS.(NEW WM)

(The assistant, Greg, who originally liked my synopsis and sample pages, has left the company. That's a very bad thing. I sent my query in October, 2002. They asked to read my work nine months later! It is now five months after I submitted the requested material. I will probably never hear from them. "New WM" means I found the company in the Writer's Market.)

EXPECT REPLY, (I CALLED 9/16) MMFF, LETR (RE EVA) & SIGNED RELEASE FORM 8/4 TO MS. BETH DAGITSES, MOCEAN PICTURES. "REQUESTED MATERIAL" ON ENVELOPE. SENT PRIORITY. THEY LIKED MM SYNOPSES FROM EVA. EVA" "DON'T UNDER-SELL MM!"

EXPECT REPLY, SUPFF/CB 8/4 (FOR ESPN?!) TO AMANDA MICALLEF, ROPE THE MOON PRODUCTIONS. I HANDED HER Jockettes FF/TRT MON 7/28. does she like it?

ALSO EXPECT REPLY, MMFF & CRIMES ART & LETR 3/10 TO AMANDA MICALLEF AT HER REQUEST TO READ MMFF THRU INSIDER'S SYSTEM MAG. I TOLD HER BOUT ROBERT WUHL MAKING MOVIE RE 2002 BC SCAM. I PUT "REQUESTED MATERIAL" 7/15, I pitched Jockettes ff to Amanda on answer machine. WE MET IN LA 7/28!

(Amanda met with me for 90 minutes in L.A. on July 28th , 2003. She asked to read a few of my screenplays, then completely forgot about me. This stuff happens.)

Ur? EXPECT REPLY, JOCKETTES TRT, LETR, SASE SENT 6/17 TO AGENT ADAM MEYER. (ASST. KIMBERLY GOODEN) LITERARY & CREATIVE ARTISTS HE ASKED TO READ 1/30. PREV:X 3/31. 93 PGS XANGNOV. ORIG Q (BK PROJ,1PG PASGS 1/17/03. FROM AAR AGENT LIST:

(This agency waited 10 months to request a script. Eight months later, I still have not heard from them. That's why the UR, unlikely reply, is typed before the passage.)

Ur? EXPECT CALL, LINDA MURRAY SR Editor TROLL COMMUNICATIONS. RE HP SENT 5/6 AND RETURNED 6/11. SHE LOVED HP! "STORY HAS SO MANY GOOD ASPECTS, GLIMPSE AT IMMIGRANT LIFE, THE GREAT DEPRESSION, YOUNG BOY'S DISCOVERY OF AMERI-CAN PASTIME, ALL THESE THINGS WORK TO MAKE A FINE STORY BUT WE'RE IN CHAP 11 BANKRUPTCY!" juv fic & nf. XCHAIMBK 3/10.(1/30 AT HER REQUEST) ORIG: juvproj 12/24 (JAN RM). SHE WROTE THAT CHAIM IS "INSPIRING" "FASCINATING." "AMAZING; HIS LIFE A BEACON OF HOPE FOR OTHERS. HIS STORY SHOULD BE TOLD"

(Can you believe that a book can be praised so highly and not be published by the infatuated editor? The lady really liked my children's book but her company was in bankruptcy. What could I have done - lend them $100,000? I recently heard that Scholastic Books took over Troll's assets. That doesn't help me at all.)

Here are some magazine notes:

(EXPECT REPLIES, MAGS CONTACTED 6/6/03):

EXPECT REPLY, 6/6, HYBRID, CUFFS, NEWLAW peyote silver TO GORDON MOTT, EXEC ED, CIGAR AFICIONADO. PREV SENT TO xMarvin Shanken Xcrimes, Xnielsen, Xgolf.Xpuck,Xpro-jarts. X'D 3/25 (11/22. WM MENS.

(These people take five months to read and reject. I'm not getting my hopes up. Besides, I've already had the "golf" article, which they rejected, published elsewhere.)

EXPECT REPLY, 4/15 LETR TO MR. STEPHEN C. GEORGE. BETTER HOMES & GARDENS. PITCH STORIES FOR THEIR LAST PAGE, "THEN & NOW." (NO FIRST PERSON!). STEPHEN SENT SAMPLES OF THEN & NOW. NICE LETR. 4/4: "NOT RIGHT BUT WE LIKE YOUR STYLE" "SEND IDEAS OUR WAY." KEPT MY ARTS ON FILE. ORIG TO XRichard Sowienski. Xnielsen, Xandrea, Xsilver, Xproj SENT 12/24. (JAN WD)

EXPECT REPLY, LARRY GERBER, EMMYMAG. HE LIKES NIELSEN ART, SENT 11/27? & RESUBMITTED 3/7; EXPANDED TO 1,250 WORDS FOR HIM. BUT HE NEEDS TO RUN A

COMPANION, STRAIGHT PIECE ON NIELSEN. IT WORKS AS HUMOROUS PIECE 4 EMMY. 1K-1500 WORDS .

(Larry Gerber has published me in the past so I will try to sell him another article.)

EXPECT CALL DAVID KNOX & SANDIE SHARKEY-KNOX, OBLIO PRODUCTNS, RE SUPCB/ COMIX/TRT/JUV & VID 2/20 & ABOUT ME SELLING THEIR 1ST CD 4 EM IN THIS AREA IN SCHLS, BK FAIRS, DAYCARE CNTRS,LIBS,ETC. THEY LIKED THAT!

PREV: SF, BEAR, BF, RN, WHALE SENT 8/6 AT HER REQUEST! FOR THEIR "ARE WE THERE YET" PROGRAM. 1ST LETR 8/5: "BKS SOUND INTERESTING & POTENTIALLY USE-FUL" FOR SEGMENTS OF THEIR PROGRAM. SHE READ THOSE 5 TO SEE IF THEY WORKED AS AUDIO PROGRAMMING. ON 8/19: "WE CAN USE THEM IN FUTURE! VERY INTERESTING & THOUGHT PROVOKING." DELAY -- DOING YOUNGER STORIES 1ST. SHE'LL LET ME KNOW SCHEDULE FOR MY BKS. THEN SHE'LL SEND CONTRACT! ORIG PRJQ 7/17 TO DAVID KNOX. I PUSHED DIDWHAT. LOOKING 4 SERIES! GRADES K-6. FROM CHILD'S POV. (from CBI)

(These people never called me back. "CBI: is Children's Book Insider newsletter.)

(EXPECT REPLIES, PROJ, ASSORTED ARTS TO 18 SYNDIES IN WM): (SENT 1/30)

(Every one of the newspaper syndicates ignored my query letter.)

EXPECT REPLY, 1/22, YOOCLAH, CUZ PHYLLIS, NIELSEN 100 WRDS TO "LIFE IN THESE UNITED STATES" EDITOR, READER'S DIGEST. PAYS $300.

ALSO EXPECT REPLY, 1/22, '62 CADDY & BEN STORY ("NO REST FOR THE FRUGAL") TO ALL IN A DAY'S WORK EDITR, READER'S DIGST. 100 WRDS. $300

(Reader's Digest editors must have a pile of my SASEs on their desks from the 1980's and 1990's. Why can't they just write, "No" and return my SASEs? Are they working with a short staff? To read about my dealings with this company, see "More About Great Contacts" in the magazine section of this book.)

(EXPECT REPLIES, 24 AAR AGNTS GOT 1PG BKPROJ, 1PG PASSAGES 1/17):

Donna Bagdasarian DAVID VIGLIANO AGENCY.AAR AGENT LIST: PROJ, 1/17

Ms. Paula Balzer SARAH LAZIN BOOKS. AAR AGENT LIST: PROJ 1/17

Ms. Faye Bender DORIS S. MICHAELS LIT. AGENCYAAR AGENT LIST: PROJ 1/17

Ms. Linda Chester AAR AGENT LIST: PROJ 1/17

Mr. Thomas Grady AAR AGENT LIST: 1PG BK PROJ, 1PG PASSAGES 1/17

Ms. Maxine Groffsky AAR AGENT LIST: 1PG BK PROJ, 1PG PASSAGES 1/17

Bert Holtje ORION ASOC, AAR AGNTLIST: 1PG BKPRJ, 1PG PASSAGES 1/17

Mr. Chris Lotts RALPH M. VICINANZA, LTD. AAR AGENT LIST: PROJ, 1PG PASSAGES 1/17

Mr. Jed Mattes AAR AGENT LIST: 1PG BK PROJ, 1PG PASSAGES 1/17

Ms. Shawna McCarthy AAR AGENT LIST: 1PG BK PROJ, 1PG PASSAGES 1/17

Ms. Anita McClellan AAR AGENT LIST: 1PG BK PROJ, 1PG PASSAGES 1/17

Mr. John Michel HOWARD MORHAIM LIT. AGENCY AAR AGENT LIST: PROJ 1/17

Mr. Craig Nelson AAR AGENT LIST: 1PG BK PROJ, 1PG PASSAGES 1/17

Ms. Helen Pratt AAR AGENT LIST: 1PG BK PROJ, 1PG PASSAGES 1/17

Mr. Mark Ryan NEW BRAND AGENCY GROUP AAR AGENT LIST: PROJ, 1PG PASSAGES 1/17

Mr. Raphael Sagalyn AAR AGENT LIST: 1PG BK PROJ, 1PG PASSAGES 1/17

Harriet Wasserman AAR AGENT LIST: 1PG BK PROJ, 1PG PASSAGES 1/17

Ms. Audrey A. Wolf AAR AGENT LIST: 1PG BK PROJ, 1PG PASSAGES 1/17

Ms. Denise Marcil AAR AGENT LIST: 1PG BK PROJ, 1PG PASSAGES 1/17

(Most of the book agents from the Association of Authors' Representatives (AAR) completely ignored my query letters.)

(EXPECT REPLIES, 9 AAR SCRIPT AGNTS; MMLETR,PROJFF,CRIMES 1/15):

EXPECT REPLY, Mr. John Buzzetti THE GERSH AGENCY. AAR AGENTS WHO HANDLE SCRIPTS. MM/FF LETR, PROJFF & CRIMES ART 1/15.

EXPECT REPLY, Mr. Ben Camardi HAROLD MATSON COMPANY. AAR AGENTS WHO HANDLE SCRIPTS. MM/FF LETR, PROJFF & CRIMES ART 1/15.

EXPECT REPLY, Susan Schulman SUSAN SCHULMAN LIT AGENCY. AAR AGENTS HANDLE SCRIPTS. MM/FF LETR, PROJFF & CRIMES ART 1/15.

EXPECT REPLY, Mr. Michael Valentino CAMBRIDGE LITERARY. AAR AGNTS WHO HANDLE SCRIPTS. MM/FF LETR, PROJFF & CRIMES ART 1/15.

EXPECT REPLY, Mr. Bruce Ostler BRET ADAMS LIMITED AGENCY. AAR AGENTS HANDLE SCRIPTS. MM/FF LETR, PROJFF & CRIMES ART 1/15.

(Most of the script agents from the Association of Authors' Representatives (AAR) completely ignored my query letters.)

(EXPECT REPLIES, 33 PRODS FROM NEW WM, SCREENWRITING SECTION CONTACTED 12/4; I PUSHED MM!):

EXPECT REPLY, 2 PG PROJFF, CRIMES ART (PUSH MM!) 12/4 TO Ms. Sarah Schuster ALEXANDER/ENRIGHT & ASSOC.

EXPECT REPLY, 2 PG PROJFF, CRIMES ART (PUSH MM!) Mr. John Nichols ALLIED ARTISTS, INC.12/4

EXPECT REPLY, 2 PG PROJFF, CRIMES ART (PUSH MM!) Ms. Isabel Casper AMERICAN MOVING PICTURE CO., INC.12/4

EXPECT REPLY, 2 PG PROJFF, CRIMES ART (PUSH MM!) Mr. Richard Hull AVALANCHE ENTERTAINMENT12/4

EXPECT REPLY, 2 PG PROJFF, CRIMES ART (PUSH MM!) Mr. Michael Cargile BIG EVENT PICTURES12/4

EXPECT REPLY, 2 PG PROJFF, CRIMES ART (PUSH MM!) Ms. Peggy Chane CPC ENTERTAINMENT12/4

EXPECT REPLY, 2 PG PROJFF, CRIMES ART(PUSH MM!) Lou DiGiaimo 12/4

EXPECT REPLY, 2 PG PROJFF, CRIMES ART (PUSH MM!) Mr. Steve Rubin FAST CARRIER PICS; C/O SHOWTIME12/4

EXPECT REPLY, 2 PG PROJFF, CRIMES ART (PUSH MM!) Ms. Layla Bennett GINTY FILMS12/4

EXPECT REPLY, 2 PG PROJFF, CRIMES ART (PUSH MM!) Mr. Andy Cohen GRADE A ENTERTAINMENT12/4

EXPECT REPLY, 2 PG PROJFF, CRIMES ART (PUSH MM!) Mr. Christopher Tipton A HAPPY PLACE12/4

EXPECT REPLY, 2 PG PROJFF, CRIMES ART (PUSH MM!) Mr. David Sheldon JOADA PRODUC-TIONS, INC.12/4

EXPECT REPLY, 2 PG PROJFF, CRIMES ART (PUSH MM!) Ms. Katherine Kramer KN'K PRO-DUCTIONS INC.12/4

EXPECT REPLY, 2 PG PROJFF, CRIMES ART (PUSH MM!) Mr. Brian K. Schlichter LANCASTER GATE ENT.12/4

EXPECT REPLY, 2 PG PROJFF, CRIMES ART (PUSH MM!) Mr. Kevin Biegel DAVID LANASTER PRODS.12/4

EXPECT REPLY, 2 PG PROJFF, CRIMES ART (PUSH MM!) Mr. Harvey Bloomstein LAST MINUTE PRODUCTIONS12/4

EXPECT REPLY, 2 PG PROJFF, CRIMES ART (PUSH MM!) Mr. Steve Lustgarten LEO FILMS12/4

EXPECT REPLY, 2 PG PROJFF, CRIMES ART (PUSH MM!) LICHT/MUELLER FILM CORP. ATTN: QUERIES12/4

EXPECT REPLY, 2 PG PROJFF, CRIMES ART (PUSH MM!) Ms. Nancy Johnson LOCKWOOD FILMS. KIDS FILMS. juv proj & projff.12/4

EXPECT REPLY, 2 PG PROJFF, CRIMES ART (PUSH MM!) Mr. Max Goldenson MWG PRODUCTIONS12/4

EXPECT REPLY, 2 PG PROJFF, CRIMES ART (PUSH MM!) Mr. Mark Costa NHO ENT. 12/4

EXPECT REPLY, 2 PG PROJFF, CRIMES ART (PUSH SUPCB & MM!) Arnold Leibovit THE PUP-PETOON STUDIOS. supcb q. they do animation 12/4

EXPECT REPLY, 2 PG PROJFF, CRIMES ART (PUSH MM!) Mr. Tom Kageff RANDWELL PRODS., INC. 12/4

EXPECT REPLY, 2 PG PROJFF, CRIMES ART (PUSH MM!) Ms. Holly Anderson SHORELINE ENT., INC.12/4

EXPECT REPLY, 2 PG PROJFF, CRIMES ART (PUSH MM!) Mr. David Kohner Zuckerman SILVER LION FILMS 12/4

EXPECT REPLY, 2 PG PROJFF, CRIMES ART (PUSH MM!) Mr. Brian McNeal STARLIGHT PIC-TURES 12/4

EXPECT REPLY, 2 PG PROJFF, CRIMES ART (PUSH MM!) Mr. Terrence M O'Keefe VANGUARD PRODS.12/4

(Almost all of the producers listed in the screenwriting section of the Writers' Market completely ignored my query letters. That is as bad as it gets)

EXPECT REPLY, 10/30/02!!!, TRY AGAIN. LEV, BEAR, SQUIRL, ELIJAH BKS TO MS. MEGAN KEEFE, HARPERCOLLINS. I SENT SOMETHING THAT'S NOT TOO ADULT. THAT'S BEEN HER REASON FOR X'ING. LATER: SEND OTISJVSH! MOSES? WHALE? GOATS? PREV: XOTISJUV X'D 10/26 (5/22). (SHE "ADMIRED THE INTENT BEHIND OTIS." BUT TOO ADULT FOR SHORT CHAP BOOK. PREV: XLIFE ("INTELLIGENTLY ARRANGED & QUITE INTERESTING BUT TOO ADULT"); XCHAIM ("FASCINATING"). XHP ("TONE TOO DRY") X'D 5/20. (3/6) PREV: xSF, xBF, xPIGNFIC, xSATCH & PROJ x'd 2/28. (1/22) RECOMMENDED BY CAROLINE BELTZ AT DUTTON. PREV: Ms. Alix Reid HARPERCOLLINS xx'd 3/23/02 (10/26/01) xSEPT xchaim & xsf; PREV: X'D XELIJAH, XLEV, XIHS

(HarperCollins is one of my least favorite companies. They used to respond to my books in two months; then it became five months. Now it's up to infinity. I was recommended to Megan Keefe by her friend at Dutton Books, Caroline Beltz. This is very unusual, to have one editor recommend that you send your work to a peer at another company. Was Caroline pawning me off because she was tired of hearing from me? Was she too nice to tell me to just go away? Megan Keefe, in effect, told me to go away, simply by tossing my books and my SASE into the trash can. One of those books has been published by another company. By the way, if you find the $3.95 in stamps on an envelope in a New York City trash can, use them. They're still good.)

(EXPECT REPLY, 22 SCREENPLAY AGENTS CONTACTED 10/21; ALL NEW WM):

EXPECT REPLY, PROJFF 10/21 TO Kelvin Bulger. comedy. family saga.

EXPECT REPLY, PROJFF 10/21: Robin Swenson CLIENT 1ST/HAFFEY AGNCY

EXPECT REPLY, PROJFF SENT 10/21 TO Ms. Susan Gurman

EXPECT REPLY, PROJFF SENT 10/21 TO Ms. Dorothy Palmer

EXPECT REPLY, PROJFF SENT 10/21 TO Mr. Jack Scagnetti

EXPECT REPLY, PROJFF SENT 10/21 TO Ms. Camille Sorice

Note: I have been waiting over a year to hear from the above screenplay agents.

Try Again

Don't waste your time on companies that treat you poorly. Be persistent (pester) with companies which seem willing to read more of your work and respond to your submissions with personal, respectful letters.

In addition to the "Expect Reply" section, I have a "Try Again" section of my Agenda. Here are a few samples:

Try Again. Barbara Hiser, Backlot Prods. Looking for strong female roles. Xx'd jockff, jock 2 pg loglin 11/23, sent 10/24. (eva). "Enjoyed reading Jockettes. Please keep in touch. I'm most available by email. Even though we're currently passing, things change, you know."

(The first thing to notice is the date of rejection. This producer read my work in just four weeks! That is a terrific response time, especially from a film producer. She told me she was "glad I had a chance to learn about your work … would always like to hear about your new work" and asked me to "please keep in touch." She gave me her email address in her email rejection. Producers don't give out their email addresses unless they like you! So, this is a great rejection letter. This is someone who will read any emails I send and consider any scripts that fit her needs -- no small accomplishment when you are an unagented writer.)

Try Again, email loglines for angel, sup sent 11/20 to marc Hernandez, crescendo ent. Managers. Mmff mailed to him 10/24, xx'd 11/19.

(Crescendo passed on "The Money Machine" screenplay but invited me to submit other loglines, which I did right away.)

Try Again. Send goats to Ms Randi Rivers CHARLESBRIDGE PUBS. also send RN, BF, moses but they need to be shorter! Prev: ON 10/13, (xx'd 11/17) I SENT xIHS, xSB, & SHORTER 7 PG VER-SION OF xLEV. Short bks 4 younger kids. xx 9/6, (6/6), PIC BKS ONLY! xsquirl, xlev, xsneeze, xonion, xxotisjvshfic PREV: xx HP BK 6/4 (5/6). THEY DON'T DO CHAP BKS. XCHAIM BK X'D 4/29/03. (2/19). CHAIM "POWERFUL & INTENSE; NOT A PIC BK, THO; MID GRADE." HUH? I KNOW THAT! PREV: XXbann. Xjuvproj. X'D 2/1. (1/9). bios of people who made difference. not well known. fun bios. dec jr . FIC; ADVENTURE, CONTMPORARY MCULT, HISTORY. NF: ANIMAL, BIO, HEALTH, HISTORY, MCULT, SCIENCE.

(This is a children's book publisher who always sends me positive rejection letters. She is open to my unsolicited submissions in a big way. Look, I mailed her my books on 10/13/03 and received her reply on 11/17/03. That is so quick and respectful, I should really send her a bouquet of flowers. An "x" before the title of a book , for example, "xSB," means she rejected "Sloth Bears.")

Only good leads should be listed in your "Try Again" section. These are high percentage compa-nies, meaning your odds of selling them a book or script are better than one in a hundred. Can you imag-ine what your odds would be if they didn't already like you?

Good Things Happen Without An Agent

First of all, if you have no agent, it is always good to have your work considered by producers. It means that you have risen from the vast wasteland of nobodies to be a somebody with a worthwhile script. You are way ahead of the pack. You've moved up a million places in line, like "Beetlejuice" tried to do in the final scene of his movie. (I've always suspected that "Beetlejuice" was based on the true life story of an agent or producer.)

If you send a query letter to a producer and it gets read, that's a good thing. If you receive a response of any kind, that's also good. If the company asks you to submit your logline or script, that is very good. Any type of phone call you receive from the producer's office is fabulous.

Check around your home town and see if there any aspiring filmmakers looking for writers. Maybe they hang out in coffee shops or in TV commercial production companies or with local casting direc-tors. Introduce yourself and hand them your best script.

One time, I walked away from a paying job, a screenplay assignment, because the local producer wanted a slasher film. (My wife offered me more money not to write it; to continue writing children's books instead.) The film was eventually written by another writer and completed. When I saw the pre-view of the movie, I was grateful my name did not appear anywhere on the credits.

(Note: I recently re-wrote/expanded a novel for an ex-student because I thought the story was worthwhile. I was paid by the hour and my wife did not offer me more money per hour to stop writing.)

It's good to get feedback on your script from someone in the entertainment industry. Paul Newman's secretary is currently reading one of my scripts. (The script is about the secretary's niece, jockey Diane Crump. Diane sent it to her.) My aunt sent one of my scripts to a friend of hers, who is an actress. If an insider likes your work, they could recommend it to someone influential.

When you solicit the aid of Hollywood insiders, be mature about it. Make them understand that you know they're doing you a big favor. Don't be pushy. Tell them how much you appreciate their interest. Expect nothing but a courteous rejection. Then, no matter what happens, send them a thank you note.

The openings in this industry are miniscule. When a sliver of light is seen, hundreds of thousands of people rush to the light. Some of them are wonderful writers and even they can't find their way into the Hollywood inner circle.

If I wrote, in this sentence, that I would recommend the work of anyone who sent me a great script to an agent, I would be inundated with scripts. I wouldn't even have to give my address or my last name. People would find me. They'd search the name "Don" until they did. They'd find my publisher or track down my wife at work. (It's a good idea for writers who are "outsiders" to have working spouses, if you haven't already figured that out.)

If I asked you to send me a great script, it would be like, "Night of the Living Dead" in my neighborhood. Zombies would walk through the streets at night, scripts in hand. It would be like Halloween 365 days a year.

I wouldn't blame you for doing that. You must be persistent and aggressive. (Although pestering is good, I'd prefer you not pester me.)

What good things can happen when you don't have an agent? The obvious answer is - you can find an agent! Submit your query letters to agents and impress them with your professionalism. Maybe you can convince one or two to read your work.

Bad Things Happen Without An Agent

You've read about the female jockey story and Diane Crump earlier in this book. It seems that Diane's career intersected with a woman jockey named … oh, her name isn't important. It is relevant to note that when this woman experienced hard times, she stayed at Diane's house. Diane treated her well over the years. The woman owed Diane many favors. Besides, they had been dear friends for decades. Recently, this woman married a man with multiple Academy Awards in his living room.

Why not ask the friend and her Oscar-winning husband to take a look at the jockey script, right? The subject matter was certainly relevant to her life - she had been a female jockey, like the main character in the script. There was nothing about the other jockey in the screenplay - she had started her career after my version of the story ended in 1970. No conflict occurs about what to leave in the script and what to take out.

If you're hoping for a cheerful story, skip over this page. The heading above should reveal the unhappy outcome.

I spoke to the ex-jockey's husband, and he was very friendly.

"Send me the script and we'll meet when you get out here next month," he told me.

If he liked the script, he could recommend it to very important producers. Who would ignore a multiple Oscar winner?

I sent him my script immediately. He never called me back. Finally, a day before I flew to California on vacation, in July, 2003, I called him and he said he had just received my script. I guessed he was stalling. He asked me to call him before I drove into L.A. (from points north and east) and set up a lunch appointment for the four of us.

It doesn't sound so bad, does it? My wife and I, having lunch with Diane's dear friend (by this time, Diane was our dear friend, too) and her big-shot husband, talking about a movie deal.

I called the man from Lancaster, California, where my wife's aunt lives. The lunch was scheduled for Friday. All I had to do was call him on Friday morning.

I couldn't reach him on Friday morning. My wife and I checked into a hotel in Redondo Beach. We swam in the pool and relaxed in the Jacuzzi all day. There were no messages waiting for us. My wife was upset.

"Forget about it, Jake," I told her. "It's Chinatown." (We were only a few miles away from that section of Los Angeles but my wife's name is not really Jake.)

The next day, the man called. He apologized for the delay but would meet us on Sunday.

"Where?" I asked.

"We live 45 minutes away," he told me. "Without traffic."

That meant he lived 90 minutes away.

"I'll be glad to drive -"I began.

"No, no," he said, a real gentleman. "You stay there. We haven't been to the beach for a while, anyway. See you at four PM for a late lunch, so we don't interfere with your dinner plans."

I knew the guy was full of crap. He didn't want to interfere with our dinner plans? He meant that he didn't want us to interfere with his plans. By this time, my wife wanted to make other plans. We both knew this couple was less than sincere.

We rescheduled all other plans with family and friends and prepared to meet with the influential couple. In retrospect, that made no sense. We had 100 clues that these two were going to cancel on us.

The message light was blinking when we walked into our hotel room at three pm.

The man left a message saying that his wife had "food poisoning" and they couldn't have lunch with us. At that point, I was happy to be rid of them.

I called Diane and asked if she wanted to try to contact these people again.

"No!" she said, coldly.

I couldn't have agreed more.

Typically, a non-agented submission receives a non-response. In other words, you send out unsolicited query letters or submit scripts to producers at their request ... and that's the end of it. Years pass, your family grows, interest rates rise and fall, animals become extinct, genders become interchangeable, the stars realign, the universe bends, expands, then bends back again ... and you still don't hear from the producer who "loved" your idea. When you call to get an explanation, the name of the company has changed. The producer has been fired. No one will pick up the phone and release you from hold.

When this happens, forget about it and move on. Create more marketing opportunities. It's never appropriate to sulk or scream.

Well, there are times when it's appropriate to sulk and scream. Indeed, I have been inclined to act that way.

The worst thing that can happen when you submit a script without an agent is that some sleazy producer tries to take your project and leave you in the dust. If he/she makes the movie, all you can do is sue him/her. The cost of suing could be in the hundreds of thousands of dollars.

What do you do about it? You copyright or register the script (see details later in this section) so you can prove that you wrote it before the thieves stole it. Most companies will ask you to sign a release form, wherein you promise not to hold the company responsible for anything they do in the future. You have no choice but to sign this form. It is the only way your script will get read.

Next are two sample release forms from producers and one from an agent:

Sample Producer/Agent Release Forms

SUBMISSION RELEASE FORM

Gentlebeings:

I am submitting to you, XYZ Productions, Inc., its producers, employees and owners (hereinafter referred to as XYZ Productions, Inc.) the following material (hereinafter referred to as "material"):

TITLE: _____

AUTHOR: _____

FORM OF MATERIAL (e.g., screenplay, teleplay, treatment, novel, short story): _____

_____

PRINCIPAL CHARACTERS _____

: _____

_____

BRIEF SUMMARY OF THEME OR PLOT _____

_____

_____

_____

WGA REGISTRATION NO. (if registered): _____

COPYRIGHT NO. (if copyrighted): _____

This material is submitted on the following terms and conditions:

1.   I agree that I am voluntarily submitting the above material. I request that you read and evaluate said material with a view to deciding whether you will undertake to option it, and you hereby agree to examine it. I understand that XYZ Productions, Inc. shall have no obligation to me in any respect what-soever with regard to such material until each of us has executed a written agreement which, by its terms and provisions, will be the only contract between us. I agree that any discussion between XYZ Productions, Inc. and myself with respect to such material shall not constitute any agreement expressed or implied as to the purchase or option of such material.

2.   I represent and warrant that I am the author of said material; and/or that I am the present and sole owner of all right, title and interest in and to said material; that I have the exclusive, unconditional right and authority to submit and/or convey said material to you upon the terms and conditions set forth herein; and that all important features of said material are summarized herein. I will indemnify you from and against any and all claims, expenses, losses, or liabilities (including, without limitation, reasonable attorneys' fees and punitive damages) that may be asserted against you or incurred by you at any time in connection with said material, or any use thereof, including without limitation those arising from any breach or alleged breach of the warranties and promises given by me herein.

3.   I realize that many ideas, treatments, teleplays, screenplays and stories in other formats are submitted to you and that many such submissions heretofore or hereafter received by you are similar to material previously used, previously submitted by others, already owned or under development by you, or identical to those developed by you or your employees, or otherwise available to you. If such material submitted by me is not new or novel, or was not originated by me, or has not been reduced to concrete form, or is not protected as literary property under the laws of plagiarism, or which is in the public domain; or if because other persons including your employees have heretofore submitted or hereafter submit similar or identical material which you have the right to use or if XYZ Productions, Inc. otherwise has the independent right to use the material without acquiring the rights from me, under the law or otherwise, then I agree that XYZ Productions, Inc. shall not be liable to me for its use of such material and shall not be obligated in any respect whatsoever to compensate me for such use.

4.   I further agree that if XYZ Productions, Inc. hereafter produces a film(s), television program(s), or other form(s) of artistic expression based upon the same general idea, theme or situation and/or having the same setting or background history as the material, then unless XYZ Productions, Inc. has substantially copied the expression of such idea, theme or situation, including the characters and story line thereof, as submitted by me, and unless XYZ Productions, Inc. does not otherwise have the right to use such expression under law or otherwise, XYZ Productions, Inc. shall have no obligation or liability to be obligated to compensate me in connection therewith.

5.   I understand and agree that you are not responsible for the return of any material submitted. I acknowledge that I have retained at least one copy of said material, and I release you from any and all liability for loss or other damage to the copy (or copies) of said material submitted to you hereunder. I agree that if I want the material returned I must include with the submission a self-addressed script-sized envelope with $3.20 per script postage on it.

6.   Should any provision or part of any provision be void or unenforceable, such provision or part thereof shall be deemed omitted, and this agreement with such provision or part thereof omitted shall remain in full force and effect. This agreement shall at all times be construed so as to carry out the purposes stated herein.

7.   This agreement shall be governed by the laws of the State of California.

8.   I hereby state that I have read and understood this agreement and that no oral representations of any kind have been made to me and that this agreement states our entire understanding with reference to the subject matter stated herein. Any modification or waiver of any of the provisions of this agreement must be in writing and signed by both of us.

9.   I further acknowledge that but for my agreement to the above terms and conditions, XYZ Productions, Inc. would not consider the material hereby submitted.

Very truly yours,

_____ Date: _____

Signature _____

Print Name _____

Street Address _____

City/State/Zip _____

Telephone E-Mail Address _____

ACCEPTED AND AGREED TO:

Signature _____ Date: _____

Print Name _____
on behalf of XYZ Productions, Inc.

SUBMISSION AGREEMENT

Date: _____

BLANK Pictures Inc.

Attention: President

Dear President:

I am submitting to you herewith certain materials described as follows:

PROPERTY TITLE _____

In consideration of your examining said material, I hereby represent, warrant, acknowledge and agree as follows:

1. I am either the author or owner of all rights to said material, or the duly authorized agent of the lawful owner of said material: and that I have full power and authority to submit said material to you on the terms and conditions hereof, each and all of which shall be binding not only on me but on any and all persons for whom I am acting. This Agreement shall inure to your benefit and to the benefit of your parent, subsidiary, and affiliated corporations and their, and each of their, officers, directors, employees, and agents.

2. Said material has been, and is hereby, submitted with the understanding that you will not use the same or any part thereof unless either: (a) you shall hereafter enter into a written agreement with the lawful owner of the materials or rights involved for the acquisition of rights therein, it being understood that in no event shall any agreement be implied in act or in law; and that you shall not become obligated to pay anything to me or any other person, firm, or corporation in the absence of such written agreement executed by you; or (b) you shall determine in good faith that you have the right to use all or any part of the materials without obtaining clearance, either because the material so used is not new or novel, or is in public domain, or otherwise not legally protected or protectible, or was not reduced to concrete form, or was obtained by you from other sources, including your own employees, or for any other reason, it not being made in confidence.

3. Should you proceed under 2(b) above, and should I dispute your right so to do, I undertake the entire burden of proof of originality, access, copying and all other elements necessary to establish your liability, and agree that my submission of said materials shall not give rise to a presumption or inference of copying or taking, or a presumption or inference that anyone, other than the particular individual to whom such material is delivered to me, had access to the material or examined the same.

4. Should I bring any action against you for wrongful appropriation of said material or any part thereof, such action should be limited to an action at law for damages, which shall in no event, under any theory, exceed the fair market value of the material on the date hereof, and I specifically waive statutory damages and attorneys' fees under Sections 504 and 505 of Title 17 of the U.S. Code, 1976, and agree that I shall in no event seek or be entitled to an injunction or any other relief. Should I be unsuccessful in any such action, I assume and agree to pay, upon demand, all costs and expenses entailed in defending or contesting such action, including all court costs, costs of discovery and depositions, attorneys' fees, and

all the fees or charges of any experts engaged by you to ascertain originality, public domain status, or any other facts or factors deemed necessary or advisable by you in the defense of such action. As a condition of precedent to any such action, I will give you written notice of my contention that you have no right to proceed under 2(b) above, stating the particulars in complete detail; and any such action shall be, and is hereby, waived and barred unless filed within six months after your first public release or use of the material, or thirty days after you notify me in writing that you deny liability to me, whichever is earlier.

5. Any dispute, claim cause of action, demand, grievance or controversy of any nature regarding this Agreement, including without limitation the construction, application, or performance of any term or provision hereof, or arising out of or relating to the material, shall be submitted to binding arbitration. The arbitration shall be held in Los Angeles, California, as set forth below:

The arbitral panel shall consist of three arbitrators, one of whom shall be appointed by myself and one of whom shall be appointed by Blank Pictures, and one who shall be appointed by the first two arbitrators or, in case such two arbitrators cannot agree, by the American Arbitration Association which shall administer the arbitration proceeding under its Procedure for Cases under the American Arbitration Association Rules. The Arbitrators shall hear and dispose of any dispute in such manner as they, in their discretion, shall determine, but in so doing they shall be required to receive my submissions and the submissions of Blank Pictures Inc., with respect to the dispute. The arbitrators may, for their convenience, my convenience, or the convenience of Blank Pictures Inc. take evidence at places other than the situs of the proceedings without changing the situs of the proceedings. The arbitrators shall base their award with respect to the matter before them on the contents of This Agreement and on the law of the state of California as applicable to disputes between California domiciliaries based on acts or omission occurring or not wholly in California, except as preempted by federal law. The arbitrators may issue interim awards. The final award shall assign costs of the arbitration to Blank Pictures Inc., and me. The decision of the arbitrators shall be rendered in writing with all reasonable expeditiousness, shall set out the reasons therefore and, except as set forth below, Blank Pictures Inc., and I agree to exclude any right of application or appeal to any court in connection with any award made.

Judgment upon the arbitration award may be entered in any court having jurisdiction. The losing party shall also bear the fees and costs of the prevailing party including without limitation, those incurred in any legal action to enforce this Agreement, including without limitation, a petition to compel arbitration or to enter judgment on the arbitrators award.

6. You may, but shall not be obligated to, return my material to me, and shall not be liable in any way if it is lost, misplaced, stolen, or destroyed.

7. I acknowledge that you must disclose the materials to your various employees, and possibly even to those outside of your employ, to determine the material's value to you. Accordingly, I acknowledge that no confidential relationship is entered into by reason of my submission to you or by reason of any oral discussion that you and I at any time may have with respect to the idea.

8. I understand that you shall give my submission such consideration as it merits in your sole judgment. I agree that you assume no obligation to evaluate the submission. Moreover I agree that you are under no obligation to reveal to me either your actions in connection with the submitted idea or any information regarding your activities in either the general or specific field to which the submitted idea pertains.

9. I agree that any consideration of the submitted idea or negotiations to purchase the same shall in no way prejudice you. I further agree that you do not waive your right to contest the validity of any copyright, trademark, patent or other intellectual property rights I may claim have in the submitted idea. Consideration of the submitted idea is not an admission by you of the novelty, propriety or originality of the idea.

10. No modification or waiver of the foregoing conditions is valid unless such modification or waiver is in writing and is signed by an officer of Blank Pictures Inc.

Very truly yours,

Signature _____

Name (Print): _____

Telephone: _____

Email: _____

Agreed to: _____

VIA EMAIL by President - Blank Pictures Inc.

Below is a shorter release form, this from a literary agent.

LITERARY RELEASE

Dated: _____

To Whom It May Concern:

In submitting my accompanying screenplay, treatment or manuscript, I appreciate the fact that at all times you have many stories and projects in being read, and that it is quite possible that ideas, themes or story plot included in my material are at this time being used by you or are under consideration by your company. I appreciate also your concern that an examination of my material without a full release of liability to me might expose you to a plagiarism claim or litigation.

Therefore, as an inducement to you to examine, and in consideration of your promise to examine, the project entitled: _____

_____

Which I submit herewith on my own initiative, and not under a confidential relationship, I hereby unconditionally and fully release you from any claim that I might have or might otherwise assert against you by reason of your claimed use of any ideas, plots, situations, stories, treatments, themes or schemes which might be identical or similar to those contained in my said material.

I hereby warrant that I have full power and authority to submit said material and hereby bind myself and all parties claiming under me to adhere fully to the terms and conditions specified herein.

Although I have retained a copy of said material, it is agreed that the submitted copy is non-returnable to me, and I assume full responsibility for any loss, theft or destruction of it while it is in your possession or in transit.

Signature _____

Name (please print) _____

Address _____

City, Stat, Zip Code _____

A Reunion With "Barbara"

On Friday, the day between Eva Peel's pitch sessions and the L.A. Expo sessions, I had time to catch up with an old war buddy, my first agent, Barbara. She was now producing TV films for the Lifetime Network and others.

I refer to her as an old war buddy because it seemed like we were in a foxhole together, dodging the grenades launched at us by the entertainment industry cretins when we were young and idealistic. A few months after I left L.A., she married a lawyer and found security. She had a few more kids and continued trying to get films produced. She has had some success and I'm happy for her.

"How is the kid?" I wondered.

The kid is her thirty-year-old son who was a pre-teen when I knew him. I would take great joy in pitching baseballs to him in a batting cage or coaching his soccer and little league teams. The kid appreciated it and always ran to hug me whenever I'd see him in the 1990's.

"He has his own company that raises capital for feature films," Barbara revealed.

It became clear that, if my screenplays appealed to him, the kid could help get my screenplays produced!

I was noticing a pattern. Bring a chair for a woman who is forced to stand during a pitch session and you will be rewarded with a meeting. Be a big brother to a child of divorce and you might get repaid with a movie deal twenty years later.

I sent my scripts to the kid with a letter stating I didn't care whether he helped me or not; I was very proud of the man he had become. My theory is, if you are kind to a child, the child will forever appreciate it. This was proven to me in the 1990's when I would speak to youngsters in schools and book stores about my children's books. After story time, they would often come up to me and hug my kneecaps.

Barbara and I had lunch overlooking the L.A. basin. We were both relaxed, in stark contrast to how we acted in the early 1980's.

"Keep your eye on the prize," she repeated.

"I'm going to keep doing what I love to do, regardless of any prize," I replied.

She looked at me like I was crazy.

I told her that, when she arrived in heaven, no one was going to ask her how many Emmy's she had won. Her spiritual advisors would ask what had she done for her fellow human beings; how much love was in her heart.

She answered that her only spiritual advisor was her agent. (As a producer, she now had an agent.)

I told her it was the first time in history that "spiritual" and "agent" had ever been used in the same sentence.

"What will you do next?" I wondered. "Compare sharks with bananas?"

She said he didn't like "The Jockettes" because Diane Crump's life was "boring."

"Diane was the good girl, working hard to fulfill her dreams," I explained. "Her life is balanced by the other girl jockeys who were mostly wild products of broken homes who would do anything to get the best horses to ride."

"Kill Diane," she suggested.

"What?!"

"Have her get thrown from her horse and killed at age twelve. The audience will say, 'What a shame. She never lived to see her dream.' Then tell the story about the wild girls. Lots of action and sex and violence and drugs and cheating and ...."

"Hold on," I begged. "How am I going to get the rights to that kind of story?"

"Make everything up. Call it fiction."

"Then it's not an inspirational, true story!"

"So what?"

"The sexism really affected those women and I want to tell that story."

"Forget about sexism. That's not important."

I stabbed a fork into my eggs and told her, "If it weren't for sexism, the girls would've simply gotten their licenses and started their riding careers. I'm yawning just thinking about it. The whole point is that they overcame sexism!"

"Lifetime will never want it," she said blandly. "No one will want it, but it's a nice story, from a nice guy."

If you knew Barbara like I did, you'd know that this was the cruelest insult she could ever deliver. It was akin to saying, "You are not cut out for this business. Try to borrow money to open up a Taco Bell or something."

Barbara and I had once argued about the design of our proposed corporate logo, before we had a deal finalized. If I was brash, she was just plain belligerent. So it wasn't surprising to find myself arguing with her. If she stopped making controversial statements with complete confidence that she was right and I was wrong, I would have assumed something had struck her on the head and she needed to be rushed to the hospital.

"Remember that time when you were almost broke and your wealthy girlfriend spent three hundred dollars on a champagne lunch for you?" I asked. "I couldn't believe she wouldn't lend you a hundred dollars to buy food for you and your son."

"Oh, I remember that lunch. She gave me $10,000 to option rights for the cowboy movie."

"She did what?"

"I never told you?" she asked innocently.

Barbara was admitting that she had intended to play a little game with me in 1984 if she ever got a producer to sign a deal memo. I would have handed her a check for $10,000, to secure the rights, and she would've said, "Sorry. I have the money. I don't need you."

I never knew this until nineteen years had past. While she was holding the $10,000, I was helping her pay for food and utilities. Now, this wasn't L.A.'s fault. The city wasn't plotting against me to see just how many walls I could punch in a single year. It's clear to me that so many people there would do the same thing; say, "You take care of me and I'll help you later, if I can, maybe."

I forgave her. Then I paid for breakfast.

"Forget about it, Jake. It's Chinatown," I thought.

We hugged goodbye, not remembering our minor squabbles, but instead acknowledging that, between 1981 and 1984, we were fighting the world together. No one in L.A. cared about us ... but us. It's possible that neither of us would have survived without the other. She was my first aid kit and I was hers.

"I may write a movie about our lives, back in the '80's," she told me with a wicked smile.

So now she was an agent-slash-producer-slash-writer. I had the feeling she would omit the part about how she plotted to cut me, her partner and best friend, out of a movie deal.

"Don't worry," she continued, "it will be fiction."

"Oh, yeah," I said with a sly wink. "I'm, uh, writing something about us, too, and it's non- fiction!"

Updates On Producers

Here's an update on Leo Grillo Productions. If you recall, Leo produced movies about endangered animals. I met with him for 20 minutes at the L.A. Expo pitch sessions. I wrote how it was a lucky coincidence that I had signed up to pitch to him. "Great meeting!" I wrote in my notes.

When I returned home, the first thing I did was email Leo my project list with descriptions of endangered animal stories. Then I sent him a treatment he asked to see, a story about the first movie mogul. That was in October, 2003.

A few months later, as per my notes in my "Expect Reply" section, I called Leo to see if he had read my materials. His telephone was disconnected.

So, what seemed like the most meaningful session I had at the Expo Pitch-A-Thon was really the least meaningful session. Looking at it from a positive viewpoint, that could mean that a one minute meeting with somebody who seemed apathetic could lead to a future sale. A writer has to keep trying to reach producers because he or she never knows when the "interested party" will have his phone disconnected and when the "disinterested party" will ring in with good news.

One of the producers from the pitch sessions who expressed interest in my work was Stephen Graham. He said he was making a movie about the first female umpires in baseball so I pitched my female jockey story and he asked to read it. Here are my notes regarding my efforts with Stephen as of 5/2/04:

call producer Stephen Graham by 4/6 (4/30 latest); (I called him 3/16 and he told me to call back in 3 weeks). expect reply, 10/24, angelff, jockff, chaim bk, "re Eva Peel". (he's doing 1st female umpire; was honored by women in film.)

So, on May 4th, 2004, I called Stephen to see if he liked any of the three scripts he requested six months earlier. (This was my third follow-up phone call.) I left a message.

On May 6th, I called again.

To recap: Stephen met with me, showed interest in my work, asked me to send him three screenplays, then, six months later, told me to call back. I called back and he ignored me. That's the way it often works.

"Check, please."

Producer Nina Davis, who asked to read "Superfan 2020" and other screenplays, called me to say she liked the baseball comedy and that I should call her back in a month. I called back and she told me to sit tight. I called back and she advised me to call in three weeks. After a while, I stopped calling.

Did I just repeat a story? The answer is yes and no. It was the same story, with different characters.

Twilight Pictures called my jockey story "fragmented." That piece of constructive criticism will help me rewrite the script. I thanked them for their review. Everyone else from the L.A. pitch sessions ignored my scripts. But the trip was worthwhile because … I found myself an agent!

Update on Agent David Freedman

After many months of review, David suggested changes to three of my screenplays. I made the changes and signed with his new agency. He began pitching my scripts to Hollywood producers - the same people who ignored me for decades.

Also, David sent two of my nonfiction children's books to publishers who only read books submitted by agents. For the first time, companies like Random House and Simon & Schuster began reading my books, stories I had come very close to selling without an agent. I felt as though I have taken a step up a ladder. Who cared if the step was tiny and the ladder enormous? I didn't.

Update to previous paragraph: Two of my nonfiction books were rejected recently by Ms. Mallory Loehr, the editor-in-chief at Random House. I was elated! I had never been considered by someone at the very top of a publishing house. Without an agent, I could try for a hundred years and never get to the boss.

Here Is Another Example Of How An Agent Can Promote An Unknown Writer.

Last week, David said he had met the head writer of Saturday Night Live and, if I wrote comedy sketches, he would send them to SNL. Again, I was more than pleased. For years, I had been writing funny articles, knowing that I could not get my sketches read by TV producers. I adapted the articles into sketches for David to submit.

One sketch that was submitted to SNL, a mock interview with Pete Rose's little league manager (the manager has the kids betting on how many soft drinks are in the water cooler) was rejected as "passé."

"Does SNL know that ESPN is producing a movie, directed by Peter Bogdonovich, about Pete's post-career gambling problems?" I asked David. "Do they know he may finally be admitted into the baseball Hall of Fame later this year? If he is, or even if he isn't, it will be front page news."

David knew little about baseball and even less about Pete what's-his-name. He knew a lot about classic cars because he owned at least three. That was a bad omen, a sign that he was a show-off. Of course, I ignored the omen. David gave me all kinds of advice on "Superfan 2020" despite not knowing nor caring about baseball. That, too, was a bad omen. I agreed to make the changes he suggested anyway. What was I thinking? I guess I was trying to show my agent that I was open-minded. In retrospect, I should have told him to submit the screenplay if he liked it and not interfere with the writing process because he wasn't a writer and even if he were, he didn't have a feel for the subject matter.

Anyway, the reader at SNL wasn't in touch with popular culture, a scary thought, but at least he was reading my sketches. The only reason he was doing so was because they were submitted through an agent.

Now that I had an agent, I had a legitimate chance to sell a screenplay. I could concentrate on one thing -- my writing.

Agent/ Writer Contract

Agent/ Writer Contract

CONTRACT BETWEEN ARTIST AND TALENT AGENCY

1. I hereby employ you as my nonexclusive talent agency for a period of _____ years (not to exceed 7 years) from date hereof to negotiate contracts for the rendition of my professional services as an artist, or otherwise, in the fields of motion pictures, legitimate stage, radio broadcasting, television, and other fields of entertainment.

2. I hereby agree that you may advise, counsel or direct me in the development and/or advancement of my professional career.

3. As compensation for your said services agreed to be rendered hereunder, I hereby agree to pay you a sum equal to TEN percent (10%); not to exceed maximum rate shown on fee schedule of all monies or things of value as and when received by me directly or indirectly, as compensation for my professional services rendered or agreed to be rendered during the term hereof under contracts, or any extensions, renewals, modifications, or substitutions thereof, entered into or negotiated during the term hereof and to pay the same to you thereafter for so long a time as I receive compensation on any such contracts, extensions, options, or renewals of said contracts; and for so long as you remain licensed. It is expressly understood that to be entitled to continue to receive the payment compensation on the aforementioned contracts, after the termination of this agreement, you shall remain obligated to serve me and perform obligations with respect to said employment contracts or to extensions or renewals of said contracts or to any employment requiring my services on which such compensation is based.

4. I hereby agree that you may render your services to others during the term hereof.

5. In the event that I do not obtain a bona-fide offer of employment from a responsible employer during a period of time in excess of four (4) consecutive months, during of which said time I shall be ready, able, willing, and available to accept employment, either party hereto shall have the right to terminate this contract by notice in writing to that effect sent to the other by registered or certified mail.

6. Controversies arising between us under the provisions of the California Labor Code relating to talent agencies and under the rules and regulations for the enforcement thereof shall be referred to the Labor Commissioner for the State of California, as provided in Section 1700.44 of the California Labor Code.

7. In the event that you shall collect from me a fee or expenses for obtaining employment for me, and shall fail to procure such employment, or shall fail to be paid for such employment, you shall, upon demand therefore, repay to me the fee and expenses so collected. Unless repayment thereof is made within forty-eight (48) hours after demand therefore, you shall pay to me an additional sum equal to the amount of the fee as provided in Section 1700.40 of the California Labor Code.

8. Subject to my availability, you hereby agree to use all reasonable efforts to procure employment for me in the field or fields of endeavor specified in the contract in which you represent me.

9. This instrument constitutes the entire agreement between us and no statement, promises, or inducement made by any party hereto that is contained herein shall be binding or valid, and this contract this contract may not be enlarged, modified, or altered, except in writing by both the parties hereto; and provided further, any substantial changes in this contract must be approved by the Labor Commissioner.

10. You hereby agree to deliver to me an executed copy of this contract.

Page 1

DATED: _____

AGREED AND ACCEPTED:

Principal Agent _____

Name of Artist_____

Street Address _____

City, State, Zip _____

THIS TALENT AGENCY IS LICENSED BY THE LABOR COMMISIONER OF THE STATE OF CALIFORNIA.

This form of contract has been approved by the state Labor Commissioner

on the _____ day of _____, _____.

By: _____

Page 2

Update On "The Jockey Club" Screenplay

Since Twilight Pictures called my script fragmented and David thought it read too much like an MTV video, I knew what I had to do - remove some of the quick scenes. I believe, while writing the first draft, I tried to stay true to the actual story and crammed too many anecdotes into one-hundred-nineteen pages. Less could prove to be more.

I am in the process of fictionalizing some of the characters (so I won't get sued by people who broke the law - even though multiple sources saw them do it) adding some scenes that involve scandalous behavior (I had originally dropped them at Diane Crump's request) and deleting scenes that do not have a direct impact on the climax -- when Diane becomes the first female jockey to ride in the Kentucky Derby. I will no longer be a slave to the truth. I am going to change time lines, invent names and embellish the darker side of the sport. I am writing this for producers and moviegoers, not for Diane or myself. You can't say that success has changed me because I haven't yet had a film produced.

I Changed The Title From "The Jockettes" To "The Jockey Club" because my agent hated the first title and I wanted to prove to him that I was willing to compromise. The new title was suggested by Jim Breckinridge, whom I had paid to review the first draft. Jim's critique was inexpensive and very helpful. He knows his craft. If you need your screenplay or stage play reviewed, call Jim at 888-399-2506. His address is P.O. Box 1403, Doylestown, PA 18901.

My first agent, Barbara, who is now a producer, keeps emailing me to check on the progress of "The Jockey Club." This tells me that she smells a successful project. She is not emailing me to reminisce about the early 1980's, when she had no phone or car. When I finish the rewrite, Barbara will probably be the first to read it. Then we can argue about the deal-making process, like we did in the good old days.

(Note: only a writer can get sentimental about old arguments.)

Agent David Freedman Says "Goodbye"

It was late June, 2004 and I was excited because David had promised to submit "The Jockey Club" to producers who had requested it after they had read the expanded synopsis. David had also promised to submit my "Curb Your Enthusiasm" spec script to TV producers, which I knew could lead to a script sale, assignment or staff position.

I had a direct line to Hollywood although the line was more like a slender thread.

David said he would call me after he returned from a writer's conference in Calgary, Alberta, Canada. He would either tell me that "The Jockey Club" was ready for submission or ask for more rewrites. I was absolutely sick of his rewriting requests and didn't think it was normal for an agent to act like a fastidious editor. I wanted to tell him, "Either you like it or you don't. If you think you can sell it, submit it. Otherwise, submit the other scripts."

The "other scripts" were "Superfan 2020" and "The Money Machine." David had asked for abundant changes in those scripts but was finally happy with the most recent drafts. In fact, he said I had hit "home runs" with these rewritten screenplays.

David emailed me and said he had a bad cold. Then his cold worsened, according to him. Then he sent me the following letter, approximately four months into our one year contract:

Dear Don,

It is with great regret that I inform you of my decision to discontinue representation of your literary works. In the certified letter that I sent to you, I expressed my feelings that you would be better served by an agent that has time to work with you on your features and TV scripts.

Specifically, while I believe that you are a good writer that is very committed to the craft, I feel that you are stuck on The Jockey Club and not making any progress.

Even though I have been actively shopping your scripts since we signed, I feel like I have served in a much larger capacity as a free script consultant, which I no longer have any time to do.

It is very difficult for me to do this, but I have no choice.

Best of luck to you.

Sincerely,

David Freedman, Principal Agent

Hollywood View

Let's review. When he writes that I am "stuck," he means that I didn't change the script enough to suit him. He ordered hundreds of changes! I wasn't going to make the script worse to make him happy.

Here is an example. There is a scene in "The Jockey Club" where a veterinarian takes a horse out of the starting gate, leads him behind a bush and gives him a needle full of dope to slow him down. The vet had bet on another horse in the race. David said that the scene wasn't realistic and I should move the action to the barn area an hour earlier. Well, three people who were present told me it happened that way. Despite the fact that it was true event, David said it couldn't have been true. He wanted me to make the scene false and less interesting. If an agent asks you to do something like that, argue with him and stand firm.

While he writes that he has been "actively shopping" my scripts, the truth is that he sent out two of my screenplays in four months.

He has the nerve to write that he has been acting as a "free script consultant" when I never wanted his advice on writing! It's like your barber telling you that he can't cut your hair anymore because he's spending too much time giving you free fashion advice, when you never wanted his semi-professional fashion advice.

Meanwhile, David told me last month that Paramount and Warner Brothers, among other studios, had read my expanded synopsis of "The Jockey Club" and asked to read the script. What happens to those leads?

I called the Writer's Guild in Los Angeles and a young man named Ryan said it was odd that an agent would drop me when studios had expressed interest in reading my work. Either David was lying about the studio interest or he thought the screenplay was so terrible that he didn't want his name associated with its submission. He signed me because he liked the first draft of that same screenplay!

Ryan advised me to send David a nice email and ask for the names of the interested producers, so my next agent can contact them. I am very skeptical about the chances of David complying with that request. I doubt he'll mail back the "Superfan" comic books I sent to him at his request, either. If he throws out those rare, first edition comic books, that will help illustrate one of the main points of this book; that is, agents, in general, are an extremely disrespectful lot. I mean, even my ex-girlfriends returned my record collection when they were immensely miffed at me.

Most of us are extremely careful when choosing a mate. We want someone who will show loyalty and class, even in bad times. When we sign with an agent, unless we're famous writers, we partner with anyone who sends us a contract. I'll bet some of you will sign with the Attila the Hun Literary Agency and travel to a high security Roman prison to do so. (Read more about Attila in the magazine section of this book.)

Eva Peel said this about my experience with David: "He expected to have immediate success with your work, and when he didn't, he dropped you. He'll probably have a new stable of writers every year."

Agents should change their group name to "Frontrunners." Their motto should be, "We will bet on you after you've already won" or "Loyalty is for our clients, not us."

This setback can help me in the long run. My next agent will not bully me into rewriting scenes I know are good. My next agent will not act like his or her time is more important than mine. Well, one out of two isn't bad.

Now I am going to Writersmarket.com and checking the Writers Guild list, looking for a new agent. I'm sending email queries and a short project list to dozens of these less-than-loveable characters. I'm pushing the jockey story, now known by its original name, "The Jockettes," to "honor" David Freedman, who hated the title.

Bandage Your Wounds & Get A New Agent

It was relatively simple to locate the names and addresses of literary agents. As a subscriber to www.writersmarket.com (which costs about thirty dollars per year), I was able to search for agents and found about seventy from which to choose. Next, I went to www.wga.org and printed out a list of agents from the Writers Guild of America.

Some of these agents accepted email queries; others only accepted snail-mail queries. I sent the following letter and one-page project list to forty-one agents:

Subject line: Blue Sky Query.

Dear (Name of agent):

My screenplays and TV scripts have been represented by the Hollywood-View Agency in Los Angeles for the past several months. In what Wall Street would call "light trading," the agency submitted two scripts and released me from the contract. The agency never got around to submitting my screenplay, "The Jockettes," a true story with rights attached, set in 1969, about the first female jockeys to ride in the U.S. I believe this script will generate a great deal of interest from producers. As a matter of fact, I was told by my ex-agent that Warner Brothers, Paramount and other entities requested the script after reading a two page synopsis.

I am soliciting your interest in "The Jockettes" screenplay or any of my other completed projects, which are described below.

I will also be happy to send you my latest work, a spec script for HBO's, "Curb Your Enthusiasm."

I know that, from your perspective, the odds are slim that a well-executed screenplay can come from out of the blue like this. Maybe Neil Young was referring to us when he sang, "Out of the blue and into the black."

I will be happy to sign any release forms you send. I look forward to hearing from you.

With Appreciation,   Don Rutberg

A Writer's First Aid Kit

Donald Paul Rutberg

DPRinnet@aol.com

USC screenwriting graduate (MFA)

Published book author, comic book author, children's book author

Published Journalist and Playwright

Writer/Producer of children's TV shows and commercials

"A Writer's First Aid Kit" published September, 2004; Pale Horse Publishing Publishing

Professor at Rosemont College's graduate school; MFA in Creative Writing program

SCREENPLAYS

"THE JOCKETTES": (True drama with rights) The inspirational true story of Diane Crump, *the first female jockey to ride in the U.S.*, and the other pioneering women who overcome incredible obstacles to win equal rights on the racetrack. In 1969, female jockeys start winning races at North American race tracks and by May, 1970, Diane Crump becomes *the first woman to ride in the Kentucky Derby*.

SUPERFAN 2020: (Comic book comedy) It is 2020 and *sports society has gone beyond escapism to insanity ... on its way to the unnatural*. A sports nut named Murray joyfully jeopardizes his marriage, his job and his life in order to win the Superfan trophy and the title of greatest baseball fan. He and his 11 year-old protégé prove that the heroes are in the cheap seats after the pampered players are forced to play in a "Real" World Series, which closely resembles a life-or-death grudge match. (Also a nationally distributed comic book & comedy series)

THE MONEY MACHINE: (Comedic crime caper, based on a true story) In 1970, some down-on-their-luck gamblers steal a race track ticket machine and use it to blackmail a ruthless track owner in order to reclaim their cherished way of life. When the well-intentioned crooks are finally caught due to their own error, they exchange "The Money Machine" -- for freedom. In essence, *the advancing computer age is delayed just long enough to ensure this "Sting"-like perfect crime.*

TELEVISION SCRIPTS

CURB YOUR ENTHUSIASM: "Man of the Year" (Spec Script): Larry is honored by his synagogue, discovers a stock that earns a fortune and helps Cheryl save endangered whales ... *all of which guide him to disaster*.

WHEN ANGELS SPEAK ... (THEY ARGUE): (Original Comedy-Fantasy Pilot) An outgoing, arbitration lawyer dies and is disappointed to learn that he's been assigned a similar job in a dull, sterile world known as heaven. With no chance to enjoy the Earthly pleasures his spirit craves, *the only lawyer in heaven* enters the game of angelic politics, hoping to add some life to his death. (Also a screenplay)

Agent Replies To "Blue Sky" Queries

As of July 7th, 2004, a few days after sending queries to agents, I received ten replies. Most told me nicely to go away. I expected that kind of response. I also expected at least one pleasant surprise and I got that.

The Hudson Agency in Montrose, New York, indicated on their website that they were not looking for new writers. They described their agency in such a wonderful way, however, that I had to try to reach them. I added a line in my email telling them how impressed I was with their self-description. I wasn't begging. I was saying, "Just in case anything jumps out at you, maybe you'll take a look at a new writer." This was a flare sent to people with their eyes firmly closed shut. Maybe they would hear the sizzle of the flare. Any way you approach it, this was a long shot but since it took less than a minute to send, it was worth the effort.

A few hours later, a woman at the Hudson Agency wrote this email to me:

"You can send 'The Jockettes' for review. But only because I love horses."

This is a perfect example of a theory I offered earlier in this book; that, in order to hook an agent, he or she must think that your script is an easy sale or the story appeals to his or her own sensibilities.

I sent the requested script to this agency a day later. I had eight bound copies of "The Jockettes" lying around because, a week earlier, Diane Crump had asked me to send her a few copies, to distribute to people she knew in the entertainment industry. It could be Diane's connections, wealthy horse breeders with ties to movie makers, who eventually produce the film about her life. If she shows the script to the right people, we could achieve our goal without the help of an agent.

While the Hudson Agency asked to read my script, other agents deleted my entire query. One agent, Peregrine Whittlesey, sent this nice letter to me via email:

Dear Mr. Rutberg,

Thank you for your email asking about representation. Normally, my response is to say that I am not the best person for screenwriters and you'd do better with a Hollywood agent. It is true. I'm a signatory to the Guild but what I really represent is playwrights -- one of my clients won last year's Pulitzer Prize and my focus is entirely on theatre. I work with a very good agent in Hollywood for my clients. Frankly, what I think you will need to do is to get another agent in Hollywood. If what you have is a mainstream screenplay that should be produced by mainstream producers, that is what you will need in representation. Sorry not to be more helpful. What you might want to do is to buy a book by K Callen called, "I've written this script now what do I do with it?" She details the credentials and interests and successes of a bunch of agents and you might want to see if your work seems to be the kind of thing any agent has succeeded with.

All the best,

Peregrine Whittlesey

The above is an example of how a negative letter can be good, just as a positive letter can be bad. This agent represents a Pulitzer Prize winner yet he took the time to reply to my letter. This was something to savor. I was compelled to reply with a heartfelt, follow-up, thank-you note, which follows:

Dear Peregrine Whittlesey:

Your kind letter is forcing me rethink all the agent bashing I do in my soon-to-be-published book, "A Writer's First Aid Kit." As a writer-turned-agent-turned writer, and as a graduate school professor (one class is called, "Working with agents and editors") I am supposed to be an expert on matters covered in K Callen's book. Twenty-five years after graduation from film school, I may have to admit that I dislike the business side of the writing life. Perhaps it's because of all the emotional groin-kicks that I, and every other writer, has taken, usually when I'm not looking.

My mentor, Jack Langguth ("Our Vietnam") has worked with an agent in NYC for thirty years. Her name escapes me (Trudy?) but you may know her. I am not a jealous person but I think about their trusting relationship and wonder if I will ever find a representative that I respect. I've had agents who told me, "I just got married for the eighth time and stopped drinking for the ninth time." On the other side of the coin, when I was briefly an agent, I received a letter that started, "I'm practically illiterate but I think you'll like my book."

Ah, I'm sure you are right. I need an agent in Hollywood. I left that town in 1984, after seven years (felt like seventy) hoping that I would never again have to live amongst the fear and loathing. In LA, I didn't get a straight answer -- like the letter you just emailed to me -- in all those years.

So when I find a savvy, respected, kind person like yourself, my first instinct is to try again; tell you that I am, by nature, a playwright. For example, my story about the only lawyer in heaven, which I've been pitching as a TV series, is and always has been a stage play. There are scenes on Earth, in heaven and hell. I know it would work best on stage. I've come very close to selling "When Angels Speak" as a one-act play. However, I've had to concentrate on other forms of writing (such as children's books, a field in which an agent isn't required to get published) so I wouldn't spread my marketing efforts too thin.

Yeah, I know I'm not emotionally cut out for this business. But I love to write and will never stop. If you'd like to take a look at "When Angels Speak," I would, of course, be happy to send it to you. If you have any suggestions about Hollywood agents, or know of any that would read my work with a referral from you or Jack Langguth, please let me know. Meanwhile, congratulations on representing a Pulitzer Prize winner. That is wonderful news. It is also wonderful to come across a person like you with such obvious integrity.

Good Luck! Warmest Regards, Don Rutberg

That letter could be called, "Pouring my heart out to Peregrine." I could plug the lyrics right into a country music song. I admit I groveled a bit in the letter. I knew Peregrine would respond and I was hoping to get a recommendation so I could contact that partner agent in Hollywood -- the "very good" one who handled screenplays. Here is Peregrine's reply:

Dear Mr. Rutberg,

Gosh what a lovely letter. And, of course, I know how very hard it is to survive -- emotionally, if not artistically. And I also know that I am hugely lucky to be able to do this in a way that has to do with conviction. I wish I had a ready answer as to who I should recommend as an agent. It is hard to trust people and I am very grateful to have found a "partner" in Los Angeles that I can trust. Having worked with others before her, I know how hard it is to find another person to work with who has integrity and will be honest with me. I unfortunately can't recommend you to her because I have to reserve this relationships for my existing playwright clients. Anyway, truly the best to you. I hope you find the right person to represent your work.
                                                        Peregrine Whittlesey

I almost had a recommendation from the New York agent to the Hollywood partner agent. I sensed that Peregrine wanted to help me. I didn't care that I had to pester and grovel for sympathy. My words were honest. At least I learned that the Hollywood agent was female, which narrowed down the search to a few thousand. (It would not be appropriate to try to find the partner in Hollywood and tell her how Peregrine and I were hanging out recently and we both thought it would be a good idea for me to contact her. If I were that sneaky and crass, I'd still be an agent.)

Here is the odd part of this story. While I know that Peregrine is a terrific, compassionate person, I don't know if Peregrine is a man or a woman!

Update: One of the forty-one agencies who received my blue sky query was a company called Circle of Confusion. I had remembered them from my trip to the L.A. Expo pitch sessions. Their representative took my "Superfan" comic book and said that, if he liked it, he would request the "Superfan 2020" screenplay. I never heard from him.

In my July, 2004, email to Circle of Confusion, I pitched "The Jockettes" screenplay. That was silly because I knew they were best at adapting comic books into movie projects. That was why I rearranged my schedule to pitch to them at the L.A. Expo pitch sessions in October, 2003. This time, they quickly rejected my jockey story but left the door open for me to pitch something else.

In my follow-up email, which was sent a few moments after I received their rejection, I told them, "What I meant to do in that last email was pitch my screenplay/comic book project to you."

Trust me, I was shocked when David Mattis at Circle of Confusion asked me to send him the "Superfan 2020" screenplay and comic book. From my first fifteen blue sky queries, I had received two script requests. The odds of that happening were about as good as getting hit by lightening twice in fifteen minutes, in Alaska.

Before I start strutting around in triumph, however, I will remind myself that I might not hear from any of the remaining agents I recently contacted. It is worth noting that, in dealing with both The Hudson Agency and Circle of Confusion, I behaved like a pest. Hudson warned me on their info page not to contact them -- they were not looking for new writers. Circle of Confusion rejected my first pitch, which included the description of "Superfan 2020." In order for me to eek out two small victories, I had to employ one of my, or any writer's, most desirable qualities -- a bad memory. I diligently forgot that Hudson didn't want to hear from me and Circle of Confusion didn't like my projects. Being a pest with a bad memory served me well.

How To Write A Screen Or TV Treatment

There are various reasons why it's important to write treatments -- that is, ten-twenty page outlines of a full-length script. The most important reason is the likelihood that many producers have Adult Attention Deficit Disorder. They can't read one-hundred-twenty pages in one month. They can skim a ten page treatment and get an idea whether they like or dislike a certain project.

Another reason is time management. If you have three great projects in mind and don't know which is most marketable, write three great treatments and you'll have three viable projects instead of one script. If someone wants you to expand a treatment into a script, fine; let them pay you to do so.

That doesn't always work.

I once wrote a true story about the largest corruption case in IRS history. I worked with the undercover IRS agent who risked his life for the government and was treated like the enemy by his bosses.

One producer liked the story treatment but wanted me to change the focus from the honest IRS agent to the famous guy who bribed the IRS agent and went to jail.

"Will you pay me to rewrite it?" I asked humbly.

"No," they replied, "but there are only three of us here and we all like it, so it's very likely we'll pay you to write the script."

I rewrote the story, although I knew the better story involved the unknown IRS agent who went through hell with his good intentions. The famous guy offered a bribe, went to jail ... so what?

I sent the story to these L.A. producers who suddenly had a major box office hit in the theaters, had moved offices and returned my treatment "to sender." They requested I rewrite the treatment and send it to them, which took me a month, then they wouldn't accept the treatment in the mail!

If ten producers want you to expand a certain treatment but no one will pay you to do so, at least you'll know which project is your best.

I've written treatments that attracted interest from a few producers. I knew then it was time to write the full script. Plus, I knew that producers had the capability to read ten whole pages in a single sitting. I've sold some of those treatments.

Also, writing treatments for original feature films or TV films is more practical than writing treatments for original TV series. It's more likely that someone will buy your proposal for a film than your proposal for a TV series.

The sample treatments, which appear later in the appendices, are blueprints to help you adapt your story or your notes into a cohesive outline. They should make producers think, "These could be expanded into good scripts."

Please note, however, that it is better to have a great script to show to producers, rather than a great treatment.

The first appendix, Appendix "A", in the back section of this book is for a TV comedy series treatment. It is followed by the script for the series' pilot episode, Appendix "B". You don't need a completed script if you just want to submit a treatment but this appendix illustrates how a treatment can be expanded. The next treatment, Appendix "C", is for a feature film.

In the TV comedy series treatment, I present the concept, format, main characters, pilot episode story outline and future story ideas followed by the pilot script.

In the feature film treatment, I present the concept, main characters and detailed story outline.

Skip ahead to the appendices if you like. Many readers, including my mother, prefer to read the final pages of a book first.

In the pages ahead, I'll explain the thought processes involved in the creation of such projects.

Copyrighting Your Work

As soon as you finish your treatment or script, you should copyright your material with the Copyright Office at the Library of Congress in Washington, DC. This is the best place to protect your material because you will be protected longer. (The laws may be changing so you may own the copyright for thirty years or seventy years or as little as seven years from the creation of the project.) Use the TX form for treatments, PA form for scripts. The cost is thirty dollars per script or treatment. (The cost may be changing soon, too.)

The Copyright Office website is www.loc.gov/copyright or call 202-707-3000. The Library of Congress receives 10,000 books per day! It has accumulated 127 million items. The library is building thirteen more warehouses in Maryland to handle the written material and even more in Virginia for audiovisual material. Ten years after it opened (in the Capitol building) in 1802, British forces set fire to the Capitol during the War of 1812. Soon after, Thomas Jefferson gave the building a new foundation by selling it most of his personal library. The Jefferson Building, which is still in use today, was completely full within a decade. Between 1960 and 1970, the collection of manuscripts and other artifacts grew by 50%. The library said it was, "heartening to the nation's scholars but also a cause of dismay to the staff, staggering under the responsibility of finding a place to put them."

If you call, be prepared to wait a while on hold. Ask for several forms in each category (TX and PA) and the copyright basics form, which explains how to fill out the short form.

By copyrighting or registering your material, you are proving that you created the work at a certain point in time. If someone steals it, you have a fighting chance to win in court. The bad news is that you could spend a fortune on legal fees leading up to that courtroom triumph.

By the way, if your projects are worth stealing, that's a positive sign. The same company that tries to rip you off may eventually decide to pay you for your next project. They'll say, "Oh, sure, we remember you. We love your work" and then take credit for discovering your talent. Consider yourself lucky if the projects stolen from you are not your favorites.

Title Page For A TV Series Treatment

Titles can't be copyrighted so call your story anything you want. Pseudonyms are OK so call yourself anything you want. Put your title, your name and copyright notice on the title page and your treatment is off to a good start. Type "Copyright 2004" (or "© 2004") if you copyright your material with the Library of Congress in Washington, DC . Type "Registered WGA" if you register your treatments or scripts with the Writer's Guild of America (East or West). The cost is also thirty dollars.

Your title delivers a message about your work that can help or hinder you. That means the reader can love or hate your treatment/script before turning to page one! Sometimes, you can lose out to an admittedly inferior project because the other was, "All title." The boring story on the same subject as yours can win out because of the title.

When a writer has experienced that circumstance, and I have ("Kidco" was selected over my "Over-Achievement," about reform schoolers who go into business) he or she becomes very careful when it comes to choosing titles. Often, a title comes to me as I'm finishing the first draft so don't panic if it seems fuzzy to you while you're writing.

This book was first titled, "Confessions Of A Literary Agent (And How To Get One)." Later, it was known as "A Writer's Survival Guide" because the publisher wanted the word "guide" in the title. Just before this book was to be printed, I noticed that a writing instructor at a college very close to Rosemont College, where I teach, was signing her book at a conference. (I saw her photo in the newspaper.) Her book was called "The Writer's Survival Guide."

I knew that I could legally keep my title but doing so would cause confusion. Even worse, I feared that someone would accuse me of being lazy and stealing the title. After a few minutes of deliberation with my publisher, Charlotte Hardwick, we agreed on "A Writer's First Aid Kit."

With regard to my comedy series, which I refer to quite a bit in the next few pages, I call the project "When Angels Speak" (see Appendices "A" and "B") because that's part of my concept; when they speak, they argue, mostly. The tone is consistent with the subject matter.

Refer to the title pages of my treatments (in the appendices) for examples. Try to use a clear plastic cover so producers can read your title without turning the cover page (to lessen their load). Then pray that he or she is in the mood to read.

Writing The Concept

The concept is a synopsis of your story, with emphasis on the story's essence rather than the plot. This first page of the treatment is your most important page. Whatever you do, don't offend anyone on page one. Starting out with "Everyone knows that all people who eat meat should be electrocuted" is the kind of opening Zero Mostel's character, Max Bialystock, wanted in "The Producers." Unlike Max, you won't make any money if you offend a significant portion of your audience. Your first page should be so good that the producer reading your treatment could get development money based solely on that page.

There is only one sure way to get a movie/TV deal based on the first sentence. It should read like this (and don't be skeptical because this will work):

CONCEPT:

To whoever reads this, I will give you $100,000 in cash if you secure $50,000 from a studio for me to develop this project.

Powerful first sentences like that will get you a studio deal and much more. The "much more" was explained to me in detail by my friend, the IRS agent whom I wrote about.

So, although that line will work, it will cost you $50,000 in the long run and get you in trouble. We'll take the old-fashioned approach -- creating a terrific, original concept.

As an outsider, you must develop something original because all the stupid ideas that get developed are created and approved by insiders. Hollywood doesn't need outsiders to create boring stories (beach bum inherits fortune, lonely old maid becomes beautiful); they have plenty of their own people doing that. The only chance people like us have to sell to Hollywood is to create an original project that Hollywood can't buy from their sister-in-laws and mistresses (who are sometimes the same person).

Let's use my comedy series, "When Angels Speak ... (They Argue)" as an example.

Start with one good sentence that would fit into a typical newspaper TV supplement: "The only lawyer in heaven."

If that is a good idea, and I know for a fact it's better than some ideas I've seen produced on television (in no way is this a knock on "My Mother The Car") the work is halfway completed. A writer finds out if the idea is solid through the development of this one sentence into a few pages.

Let's start at the very beginning of this project. My first thought was, "What would happen to a fun-loving fellow if he were forced to exist in a dull, sterile world known as heaven?"

Inasmuch as it was a random thought in the shower, it was worth pursuing.

He'd be happy to have made it into heaven, of course. He'd be rewarded for his humanitarian efforts and good intentions. He'd also be bored out of his mind. The alternative would be getting sent to hell, where there's always a party in progress, but where everyone is decadent and out of control. This raises inherent conflict and irony which means the concept could work!

OK, this guy is a ... lawyer. Perfect. He's trained himself to be sneaky, and here he is with all those dirty tricks at his fingertips -- and he's in heaven. What if the angels finally tired of being abused by demons and decided to send for a good-hearted, crafty lawyer to fight the fair fight for them?

My only lawyer in heaven would spend every week in sitcom-land trying to locate some excitement, either in heaven (where debate is the only allowable vice) in hell (where excitement is way too easy to find or be any fun) or on Earth.

The answer to the question, "What happens when angels speak?" is, "They argue," since that's their excitement, their entertainment and their frolic rolled into one.

Hollywood defines "High Concept" as an inherently funny situation, like a crook hiding in a police station. Producers feel safe when a project can be described as "High Concept."

In 1982, I co-wrote and co-produced a twelve minute, "High Concept" sitcom (shot on videotape, as a sample) about a divorce attorney and a marriage counselor who shared the same office. No one bought, "For Better Or Worse," which starred Linda Goodfriend, from "Happy Days." Today, I read about "Miss/Match," an upcoming NBC sitcom pilot about a divorce attorney who is also a matchmaker. I was hip to "High Concept," just twenty-one years too early, as usual.

I was only nineteen years ahead of my time with a sit-com about a game show. That's right, "Finder's Keepers" was created to appeal to viewers who enjoyed both genres (Similarly, "The Larry Sanders Show" appealed to folks who liked sit-coms and talk-shows). In the scenes that were written about the game show, I employed a format called, "Face Your Phobia!" Contestants with claustrophobia were locked in tiny closets and so forth. This was exactly like "Fear Factor," produced nineteen years later. I was parodying a society that actually enjoyed low-brow shows that tortured contestants for fun and profit. Now, nineteen years later, I find myself living in that society!

Try to create an original story with inherent conflict that Hollywood can't buy from anyone but you. Don't be surprised if you are only given a story credit, instead of credit for the final draft. After you're successful, you'll be asked to write final drafts. Until then, think "High Concept" and make your material hard to steal (by copyrighting!) without being paranoid.

This just in (January, 2004) from the Hollywood Reporter: F. Murray Abraham and Sean Patrick Flanery will star in "Dead Lawyers" for the Sci-Fi Channel. It's about an arrogant lawyer sent back to Earth, after he dies, to work on pro bono cases.

It's OK. "When Angeles Speak" is a comedy, not a Sci-Fi flick. It is a movie as well as a comedy series. It takes place in heaven, hell and Earth, not just Earth.

This happens to me quite a bit. I create a story, can't get it to the right people and then, 15-20 years later, a similar story gets produced. This is no reason to feel sorry for myself. Well, maybe it is a reason to feel sorry for myself. I just don't. I'm either a pragmatist, the numbest guy in America or a happy fool who loves to write.

Damn. I think I'm the third one.

Writing The Format

This step is not always necessary. If your comedy series takes place in a living room, your format is a given.

In "When Angels Speak ..." there is a need to explain where all the conflict takes place. After all, most of the characters do not exist on Earth.

My lawyer, the main character, will be bored in heaven so he must invent excuses to visit Earth (to do some saintly deed) or conduct business in hell. So he'll be jumping from heaven, to hell, to Earth and back; a format that needs to be explained more than the "all action takes place in the living room" format.

Temptation is the common theme, no matter where the action takes place.

Now, I've got enough to write the concept and format, but I must bring it all together with interesting characters and good story ideas for the first season.

The green light/red light analogy applies once more. Everything in your treatment must be acceptable or else someone will give you a red light and your project will get trashed.

Writing Character Descriptions

I was thinking about a religious figure in this story. I needed one that absolutely no one had ever heard of. A man named Muck.

Muck was bigger than Jesus, Buddha, Moses; bigger than Elvis. His problem was one of timing. He couldn't stand the heat in the Middle East so he set up his church in Alaska, where practically no one lived. Only one rendition of him was ever drawn and, as of the early 21st century, never discovered. He's revered in heaven but unknown on Earth ... and it drives him crazy!

When asked if serenity is important to angels in heaven, Muck starts crying.

The serious angels and the decadent devils are necessary characters in this story. I also needed an angelic wannabe who insists he should be an angel but, because of a clerical error, was sent directly to hell. He's the lawyer's tour guide during frequent business trips to hell.

The lawyer's loyal secretary, still alive on Earth, adds more conflict. How can she get any closure when her late boss/boyfriend keeps appearing from another world?

The point is, if appropriate characters keep popping into your head, you've got a fertile story. In this case, I've got a lawyer in heaven who's trying to have an interesting afterlife without getting banished to hell. I need characters who will help him and others who will prevent him from attaining his goals.

Writing A Pilot Episode Story Outline

I had to start the first episode off by killing the lawyer. No problem -- he had to die trying to get rich. So I had him fall off a ledge trying to save a suitcase filled with money.

Since the lawyer dies through a mistake made by a clumsy janitor, we add a constant theme to the show: should the lawyer get revenge on the janitor if he gets the chance?

The angels say, "Forgive and forget" while the devils say, "Turnabout is fair play and encouraged here!"

So, in the pilot episode, the angels decide to recruit this lawyer and the devils assume that, since he's a lawyer, he's destined for hell. It's like a small university signing a star football player that a Florida State or Michigan assumed would be theirs on the half-shell.

By the first commercial, halfway through the first half-hour episode, the lawyer decides to add a little life to his death by accepting a job as heavenly counsel. Remember, something dramatic must always happen right before that first act break.

In Act two, the second half of the script, the lawyer gets acclimated to heaven and then learns how the other side "lives." He visits the dark world and sees many lawyers he used to know. He opens negotiations with the devilish "boss" and finds him to be a scary, yet entertaining leader with a well-stocked bar.

As the first episode ends, I have to establish the conflicts which will permeate the entire season and beyond.

Please note that I omit the pilot episode story outline in the treatment (Appendix "A") because it's repeated in the pilot script (Appendix "B") and you read about it in this chapter.

Writing Future Story Ideas

These few pages are incredibly important because producers want you to prove that your show will not run out of ideas after two seasons. You must present a trunk full of story ideas that would be appropriate and hilarious for many years or else it's red light time!

I once lost out to another proposed TV series because the producer thought my story wouldn't last ten years. The show he produced ("AKA Pablo") lasted a few weeks before it was cancelled!

The studio executive had to choose between an idea he liked (proposed by me) or an idea he didn't like (proposed by Norman Lear). He choose the idea he didn't like, from a star producer, because if the series stunk, no one would blame him for believing in Norman Lear more than me. Choosing my story could've gotten the studio executive fired; choosing Norman Lear's story could not.

If your concept is good, story ideas will pop into your head. Like ... heaven and hell play a Thanksgiving day football game every year and our lawyer is heaven's quarterback. (He's one of the few angels who's shown much toughness.) Or else the lawyer has a chance to get revenge on the clumsy janitor who ended his life. Does he kill the janitor?

I can explore reincarnation, examine the lives of people on Earth the lawyer left behind; focus on the changing politics in heaven (where debate, after all, is the only vice and the dress code is extremely important.)

After I wrote a nonfiction book about life after death, I added many of the theories I'd read about to this sitcom, to make it more realistic. In that regard, this became a well-researched sitcom!

If you struggle to find more than a handful of future story ideas, you don't have a TV series to write. You have an article or short story.

Suppose You Can't Find A Good Premise?

Ok, I'll get you started. The following premise is my newest idea for a comedy series and it's registered so please don't submit it to me or anyone else, especially anyone else. It should serve as an excellent classroom device. Develop it in your own way to see if you have the knack for writing a screenplay or TV series treatment.

"Mobil Mike and Homeless Otis" is about two diverse characters who are forced to coexist. Mobil Mike works the graveyard shift at an urban gas station. Homeless Otis lives outside the gas station, earning more in handouts than Mike earns on the job.

Mike is a redneck, wears the confederate flag on his hat, drives a truck, is missing an eye from his tour in Vietnam nearly forty years ago and, as he tells the court when he goes for jury duty, "I want to do my civic duty, but I should tell you, I am a Klansman." Mike is a terrific father and isn't really a Klansman because he gives everyone a chance to prove themselves good or bad. Mike is an ex-outlaw biker who drove for seventeen years without a driver's license -- without getting caught -- and always has at least three guns with him. He plans to get a permit any day now. (That would be one story idea for an episode.)

Homeless Otis describes himself not as a panhandler but as someone who "develops relationships." He has a better vocabulary than most college graduates. He's black and is the most street-smart person we'll ever meet. He does not take drugs.

Mike would love to shoot Otis for being on the street and living off donations from Mike's customers. Otis would love to get rid of Mike so he can make business deals with another employee who would let Otis fix flat tires for a fee in the wee hours of the morning. When Otis gets a department store wool hat from a stranger, he checks out the label: "Only 75% wool?" he wonders derisively.

Through these characters, we can explore the comical side of almost every important societal issue, especially homelessness. Why does Otis refuse to get a job and live indoors? Why did Mike give up his outlaw biker lifestyle? How can these two misfits be so darn loveable?

If this is the start of an interesting TV series or movie, story ideas should pop into your head. Maybe the local, friendly cop drops by for coffee and reports that he has found Mike's motorcycle, stolen ten years earlier. Maybe Otis hits the lottery.

Try to develop this idea and then you'll be better prepared to develop your own original treatments. If you ever see this story on TV, don't accuse me of stealing your idea, please.

Note: I used Mobil Mike and Homeless Otis as supporting characters in one of my novels, Summer at Saratoga, a sample of which appears later in this book, in Appendix "G".

Sad note: The real Mobil Mike passed away in June, 2004. At the time of his death, he finally had a gun permit and a driver's license. If you always find yourself rooting for the outlaws in Westerns, Mike was your kind of guy.

Common Mistakes To Avoid

The ex-marine, Demetric, sent me his script for a proposed thirty minute show. I read it and found many problems.

First of all, he centered the dialogue, instead of aligning it 2 ½ inches or so from the left margin. He single-spaced the dialogue when he should have double-spaced it. He had way too much filler in his dialogue. Characters were saying "Hi" and "What's new?" and "How are things?" for pages at a time. Worse, they were saying things simultaneously. Two characters were placed on the same line, saying different things. If you want you characters to both say "Hi" at the same time, do it like this:

JOE/ CINDY

Hi.

Demetric's script was not paced properly. He had scenes that were very long or very short. That made it choppy to read. He included a phone conversation that cut between the two parties every time they spoke. Jerome's room, Stacy's room, Jerome's room, Stacey's room ... I was getting dizzy reading it.

Demetric's act break, about halfway through the show, was dramatic. You must have an interesting break there to bring viewers back after the commercial. In Act Two, his characters started giving sermons. The dialogue was too preachy. You should try to avoid this.

Common mistakes in TV writing include poor pacing/choppy scenes, scripts that run longer than twenty-eight pages (for half-hour shows), filler for dialogue, lack of comedy or drama, lack of natural commercial breaks halfway through the script and predictable story lines. Make your scripts sharp, clever, stimulating and full of inherent conflict or comedy so the scenes practically write themselves.

It is important to remember that each page of your TV script must represent about one minute of TV air-time. Read each page out loud and make sure the action/dialogue unfolds in about one minute.

Final Thoughts On Writing A TV Treatment

I've tried to explain my thought processes while writing "When Angels Speak." It's really a combination of getting a good idea and using common sense when evaluating your potential customers. The producers who will read your treatment have short attention spans or undiagnosed adult attention deficit disorder. Avoid writing a treatment about a producer with this affliction.

Once, in the early 1980's, my writing partner and I pitched story ideas for a popular sitcom to the head writer of that sitcom. The only reason he met with us was because my partner was an assistant director on that same show ("Laverne and Shirley").

This head writer, who made a few thousand dollars a week, listened indifferently and then told us what he thought of our story ideas. The only thing I'm changing is the guy's name.

"Greg doesn't like your story ideas ... but Greg REALLY likes them!"

Look up psychosis is the medical textbooks and I dare you to tell me that "Greg" is healthy. I didn't want to sell a story to the man; I wanted to leave his office before his delusions focused on me. It's mind-boggling when a writer creates his best work, then manages to get into high level meetings only to find that the head writer of a successful TV show should be in a mental hospital.

In the early 1980's, I had a meeting with a woman who was a writer on a popular sitcom. She got the job because her husband was a good friend of the executive producer. She didn't know how to write a treatment or a script. She asked me to leave behind samples of my treatments and scripts so she could learn how to write them herself someday.

Getting an agent and writing a good script won't help you make any money if you take meetings with Greg" or the producer's friend's wife. If you have never been to these types of meetings, expect one soon after you land an agent. Don't think of them as unique cases, either.

If you take a meeting with someone who is genuinely talented, you will need a good treatment or script to get noticed. A good rule of thumb is to take 100 meetings and hope you meet one important producer who isn't unqualified or psychotic.

You think I'm exaggerating? I once had a meeting at a major film studio scheduled for 10 am. I arrived at 9:30 am and waited until four pm. He was too busy to see me.

I told the secretary, "I'm leaving." As I headed outside into rush hour traffic I was told to come inside, he would see me.

In the inside offices, petite female secretaries typed in a row. The producer with whom I was meeting had a seven foot tall male secretary, who crammed his legs under a tiny desk. Was the producer having problems with loan sharks? I wouldn't even venture a guess.

I do know for certain the producer could not find an electrical outlet in his own office. He did not know his own zip code. He pointed to me (about eight hours after I arrived at his office) and said, "Go."

"Do you have any interest in nighttime soaps?" I asked.

"Absolutely not. I can't stand the whole genre," he answered firmly.

"That's a shame," I said, "because I have one set in Atlantic City's embryonic gaming ndustry."

He shouted, "I wanna see that right away!"

He wandered out of his office fifteen minutes later, muttering to himself, and I knew the meeting was over.

While he chatted amicably with the row of female secretaries, I screamed to him, "Great to see you again" and he waved back as if I were his favorite nephew.

He was in better shape than "Greg."

Also, if you have a gut feeling about your project -- I don't care how ridiculous it seems -- you must get at least a few pages written.

I experimented with automatic writing once, in L.A. -- where else? -- and scribbled some unintelligible notes on a yellow pad. Years later, I picked up the pad and could only make out one sentence from all the scribble: "When Angels Speak, They Argue."

The punctuation was not perfect, but I had accidentally/unconsciously scribbled the title of a project I would not start writing until years later.

Title Page For Your Feature Film Treatment

Titles should be consistent with your subject matter so don't use a funny title for your serious film.

In the film treatment that follows, in Appendix "C", "Techno" was not my first choice as a title. I was told by an agent that "Technobred" was too intimidating to teen-aged viewers/readers. Technobred is an appropriate name for a technologically created thoroughbred so it seemed like a good title to me. It was a scientific title which was consistent with the subject matter.

A real life racehorse named "Technology" won several prestigious races, and I thought, "Someone read my work and went out and copied the idea! That horse is probably a clone!"

The horse didn't perform very well after that so now I think the horse was ... a horse.

I still don't know which title to use.

Writing The Concept

Sometimes you get an idea which could make you a lot of money and, if you're a writer, you don't have to go through the machinations of bringing the idea to fruition -- you just write about it. If the idea is an illegal one, writing about it is a much safer option.

I was driving to the race track one day after watching a PBS special on new technologies in horse breeding and I thought, "What if I stole the reproductive materials from two champions and created the embryo in a laboratory?" Heck, I could clone this embryo and have ten future champions for the same cost as ten milk cows. Sure it would be illegal, but a desperate man, say, a dairy magnate who isn't rich enough to buy the best young horses, would take that chance and probably get away with it if he implanted the embryos in obscure surrogate mothers on obscure farms.

This story would have the same theme as The Black Stallion and other "boy and his horse" movies but this would be an updated, 21st Century kind of story. Potentially, it had the best of both worlds; a tried and true theme of a child-horse bond and an original twist that would've been science fiction thirty years ago.

Because I was involved in owning race horses, I knew the industry from the ground up. I knew that when a horse worked out in 1:10 seconds in morning drills, the official clocker would call out, "1:13" so he could hide the fast horse from the public. Then he'd bet on that animal.

Being a naive sort, I actually went to the official clocker and tried to explain to him that his $100,000 timing device must've been broken because all of our stopwatches indicated the horse was actually moving at a much quicker rate of speed. I wasn't supposed to do that because clockers have been lying about workouts since Damon Runyon and Charles Bukowski were watching horse races in short pants. I was able to write about that and my main character does exactly the same thing.

My main concept in this project is the ethical question: what would you do if you stumbled onto a ten million dollar asset, you were desperate for a champion, yet you knew something was crooked? Would you zip your mouth and retain your chance at fame and fortune or would you do the right thing and risk losing everything?

I enjoy writing about how new technologies impact on the average person. When I write this type of story, no one tells me it's a tired, old plot they've seen before.

Writing Character Descriptions

My main characters are the "boy," who is a girl and the "horse," who is a clone. They act like siblings because they were raised together. The horse is extremely intelligent but that's based on research; one of our horses was smarter than most of the people who handled him. This colt knew whether I had brought him apples or carrots before I got out of the car!

After killing off the dairy magnate who created the clones illegally and killing the girl's abusive stepfather, I introduce the down-on-his-luck trainer who's desperate for a champion. Through him, I examine the moral dilemma. His wife is a equine bone specialist and has the equipment to test DNA. She learns that at least two horses have the same DNA, which is impossible unless someone's cheating.

I also employ a veterinarian who delivers the foal and suspects that something is wrong from the start. (The supposed sire was sterile, for beginners.) There's also the dairy magnate's vet who steals the reproductive materials, then vanishes. This guy hides for most of the story.

The villain is the wife of the dairy magnate. Once she learns these clones are worth millions and are avoiding detection, she becomes quite interested in owning race horses; so interested that she kills her husband.

If your story is solid, good characters will pop into your head as you're writing.

Writing The Story Outline

I knew from the start that the girl and her horse would meet on her stepfather's farm, move to an orphanage after someone tries to kill the horse by setting fire to the farm, then move together to the trainer's house. Clues would pop up as to the horse's origin as the girl jockey and fast horse were prepping for the world's richest-race.

As I finished writing the race scene, I realized the story was only half over! That had never happened to me before. I still had to explain what happened after the trainer exposed the scam, what happened to the villain and what happened to the horse and jockey after they're banned from the sport. Characters had to come out of hiding, old crimes had to be solved and the horse had to be hidden and overcome physical problems. (Fast horses almost always have leg problems because, at eleven hundred pounds, they run thirty-five miles an hour on legs no wider than our wrists.)

So I hid the horse, exposed the crimes and brought 'em all back for an unprecedented second victory in the world's richest race.

Final Thoughts On Writing A Film Treatment

It helps when you know enough about your subject to logically and effortlessly lead your characters through the story, all the while bringing in other characters who help or hinder their plans. Although comedy is hard to write, when you're writing drama, you can't throw in a hilarious joke that covers the fact you're out of story ideas.

Try to break down your story into three acts (unless you're writing a thirty minute TV show, which consists of two acts) and have the excitement build at the end of every act. (Act three coincides with the final fade out). Remember the most basic story: in act one a cat gets stuck in a tree, in act two all efforts to rescue the cat fail and in act three, through some miracle or surprise, the cat is saved.

In "Techno," my girl and her horse survive a fire and run off from the orphanage, finally on their own as act one ends. They win the four million dollar race but have to hide in Canada to ensure they aren't split up as act two ends. They experience more highs and lows before winning the big race again as the story winds down. The story ends as Techno's friend, a mare, delivers Techno's foal. I've seen foals being born on film. They are so helpless and cute that audiences will want to adopt one on their way home from the theater.

They may write to the studio and insist a sequel be made.

The feature film treatment is published later in this book, in Appendix "C".

Performing Stand-Up Comedy Acts

Are you the opposite of the guy or girl who tosses the script in the closet to prevent anyone from reading it? Are you fearless when it comes to accepting criticism?

Have I got a gig for you.

In 1978, I was a theater arts student at Cal State Northridge. (The following year I enrolled in USC's film school and earned an MFA in screenwriting.) During my year at Cal State, I performed comedy acts for fellow students and teachers. Everybody laughed at my routines, despite the fact that I performed while wearing an old rugby shirt (I had traded my official Philadelphia Flyers' shirt for it years earlier at summer camp) and looked like a giant bumblebee. Maybe they laughed because I was wearing the rugby shirt. Either way, I believed that most of the adoring audience was hoping I would return the favor -- laugh and applaud for them when they performed, minutes later.

I didn't see how this system (friends critiquing friends) could provide an objective review of my writing. I wanted to be critiqued by total strangers, to discover whether or not I was really good.

Besides, I was a writer who happened to be performing comedy skits. The material was important, not my performance.

I went to Hollywood. To the town's credit, there were no crack vials on the streets. (This was about a year before the invention of crack vials.) I parked my car near the female hookers, walked past the male hookers and signed up to perform at The Comedy Store.

I waited for my time slot while listening to Rod Stewart's "Maggie May" on my cassette deck: "I laughed at part of your jokes." I had that lyric on an endless loop on my tape deck. (It wasn't a Walkman or micro-recorder; it was one of those large, clunky 1970's tape recorders.) Other aspiring comedians thought I was wacky. I felt more tense than wacky.

The emcee introduced me at about 8:30 pm.

"Here's a new performer. He took a pill at eight o'clock and he's ready to go on now. Please welcome Dan Rutborg!"

I told the emcee that he had mispronounced my first and last names. He shrugged and handed me the microphone.

I remember one joke from that evening.

"I'll name one guy who has premarital sex all the time and no one thinks he's crude or immoral -- Secretariat, but he's been a failure at stud. Why? He's a little naïve. He thinks that 'Coming from behind' means running real fast at the end of the race."

One drunken lady kept laughing. She was the only one doing so.

"I'm gonna marry this girl," I ad-libbed.

I learned that I wanted to be a writer, not a stand-up comedian. Through this harrowing experience, I understood more about the writing-performing relationship. A bad actor can mess up a great script, just as a bad script can foil the work of a great actor.

Looking at the situation more positively, a weak script can be improved by a talented performer and a good script can make a weak actor look good.

In other words, all the elements are tied together; script, acting, directing, casting, lighting. If the finished product turns out great, everyone involved has done great work, much like a baseball team. In fact, the theory is that casting is similar to pitching in baseball; it's seventy-five percent of the game. (Connie Mack declared that pitching was 75 percent of baseball.)

Some people don't want a harsh spotlight shining on their work. (The comedy clubs would do that - shine a spotlight in your face when your time was up.) I recommend doing something drastic, like performing what you write, to elicit instant feedback.

You want drastic? I'll give you drastic. In 1978, I went on, "The Dating Game"!

How did I get talked into that? I didn't. I was watching the show on TV, admiring the three bachelorettes, all Los Angeles Rams cheerleaders. (Remember the L.A. Rams?)

"How do you get a date with them?" I asked a friend.

"Look at today's paper. They advertise for contestants every day," she said.

So I called and took a practice test.

During the test, I was asked, "What do you think about disco?" (Remember disco?)

"I think it sucks," I said, tastefully. "The guys go to get laid and the girls go to dance and drink."

When the practice game ended, I was called over to the side.

"We're going to use you next Thursday," the producer told me.

"Next Thursday!" I yelped. "I'm gonna be on national TV in six days?"

"It will be aired a few months later."

"Oh."

"But don't say things like 'suck' and 'laid.' It will get bleeped out," the producer advised.

"I can understand that."

So, a few days later, in an attempt to gain some experience in the television industry, in what had to have been the worst imaginable way, or at least the most humiliating, I was on stage, next to Jim Lange.

"Never walk in front of Jim!" the producers reminded us twice a minute. "Ever!"

I didn't want to have anything to do with Jim. I suspected he was some sort of hologram anyway; not real. I wanted this to be over.

Cathy, a pretty, blonde bachelorette, asked me, Bachelor #3, "How would you use your clone in social situations?"

I didn't hesitate.

"Well, if I didn't like the girl, I'd split," I told Cathy, Jim Lange, the studio audience and millions of people who would eventually be watching on TV, for unknown reasons.

The audience laughed about ten seconds later. The girl didn't know what I was talking about. I didn't know what she looked like. The director didn't know which camera to use. I was hoping I wouldn't be asked any more questions in our abridged segment. One of the actors from "The Waltons," I think it was "John Boy" (remember "John Boy"?) was featured in the longer, second segment.

Is this getting weird enough for you?

I answered another question competently, then lost to Bachelor #1, Pinky. The winner was no taller than 4', 11". He arrived in a Cadillac and got out of the car with eight or nine family members, all of whom were old ladies with blue hair. He won because he had told Cathy he liked ballet and horses. He was lying and, later, didn't even remember saying those words to her.

Cathy gave me a little peck on the cheek and stared at my backside as I walked, happily, off-stage. When Pinky came to greet her, she groaned at the midget and wouldn't stand next to him.

"I would've picked you," some women from the audience told me.

If I had won, I would've been whisked off to a vacation in San Diego. I was living one hundred miles away on the beach in L.A. It wasn't like I had missed out on a unique opportunity.

Upon reflection, I knew that I wanted to be a guy who sat in the audience and heard a professional comedian deliver my material. A comedian would've gotten a lot more laughs and applause delivering the same lines I had delivered on stage at The Dating Game and The Comedy Store.

Why am I so certain? Because during a college performance I had a firsthand look at a talented performer and saw the difference he provided.

In a playwriting class, students such as myself would write a two-person scene and then choose a classmate to be one of the performers. The teacher would choose the other performer from the class talent pool.

On one occasion, I wrote a skit for two characters - Richard Nixon and Bob Haldeman. The setting was Haldeman's jail cell. The big joke at the end was about Haldeman complaining that he had nothing and Nixon, the bigger crook, still had almost everything. Nixon denied it.

"That's not true, Bob. You have three squares a day, your own room -"

"Name one thing I have that you don't have, Dick," Haldeman shouted to the former president. "Go ahead, name one!"

"That's easy, Bob - a prison record."

The students roared with laughter while I tried to figure out what had happened. The student who played the role of Nixon was so good, so deep-voiced and deep-jowled, that he made my skit one hundred times better than it looked on paper. I was overjoyed.

A few weeks later, I directed my own play in a stage directing course. The main character would deliver his lines and no one would laugh - not even me, and I had written the jokes! He mumbled so terribly that no one understood the punch lines. I was horrified. A massive amount of a writer's success or failure depended on the performers. The fine line between being hailed as a genius or an idiot was manipulated less by the critics and more by the actors. That's why my advice to you is: learn all you can about acting and directing and producing.

You may even want to try to learn about a craft that is a first cousin to Screenwriting - comic book writing.

Adapting A Screenplay Into A Comic Book

I parked myself in the corner booth at the Country Club Diner in Northeast Philadelphia. It was dinner time -- three am. The 1980's were over and I was depressed, not because the bloom was off the rose of my youth, well, that was part of it, but mostly because I still hadn't sold my "Superfan" screenplay.

Like I had a real shot of selling it from Northeast Philly.

Another night-owl, Big Lee, sat across from me. He knew I was upset because I hadn't ordered any food.

"How's the writing going?" Big Lee asked.

"The writing is fine. I can't sell anything. I can't give the stuff away."

"You know what the Zen Buddhists would say?"

"I really don't give a shit what the Zen Buddhists would say, OK?"

"Of course. Relax," Big Lee said.

He always said that.

I wrote a poem that night. It began with:

> Years from now when we're fallin' apart
> We'll look back on these days with only fondness of heart.
> Of course. Relax.

Every verse ended with, "Of Course. Relax." Think of Joe Pesci's character in the "Lethal Weapon" movies complaining that they "(screw) you at the drive-in window." Of course it's true, but what can you do about it? You might as well relax.

I couldn't relax. I couldn't eat. I was eating myself up because "Superfan" was unsold, seven long years after I had written it.

Now, of course, I realize that seven years is a short period of time to wait to sell a screenplay. It is now fourteen years after the original seven years and I still haven't sold the thing.

"Why don't you adapt it into a comic book?" Big Lee asked casually.

As Jack Nicholson did in "The Shining," I tilted my head and said, "I'm intrigued."

Big Lee, I should mention, owned a comic book store. I would make fun of comic book geeks who wore "Punisher" t-shirts and he would take off his jacket and show me that he was wearing one! He knew everything about comic books.

"Talk to my buddy, Al Weisner. He puts out a book called, "Shaloman."

"'Shaloman?'" I quizzed.

"He's a good artist. And he's got national distribution."

So I approached the 64 year-old artist, Al Weisner, who wrote, sketched, printed and distributed his labor of love, "Shaloman."

"What is 'Shaloman?'" I asked, to be polite.

"He's a Jewish superhero," Al explained.

"Not an overworked concept," I told him. "I don't see a lot of them on billboards or in pop culture."

Al nodded. I quickly sold him on the concept of "Superfan." He agreed to replace the August edition of "Shaloman" with the first edition of "Superfan." His national distributor, Diamond, would have no problem with the switch. Al always sold a decent number of his comic books.

Al sketched the story as comic strips and a comic book. I broke down the final third of my "Superfan" screenplay and he arranged it in thirty-two page comic book format. The cover and inside cover, back cover and back inside cover were in color; the rest of the comic book was in black and white.

We only had one major disagreement - when he drew home plate as a square and insisted it was drawn accurately.

"Home plate is a plate!" I insisted. "It's not a bag."

After checking out the sports page, he reluctantly agreed to redraw home plate with five sides.

So, in August of 1991, "Superfan 1999" was distributed in all fifty states. Thousands were sold, and I'm sure many of them were scooped up by collectors who would buy any first edition comic book.

We didn't make a fortune, but I had what I wanted - a visual aid to help sell my screenplay. I know one of those comic books is like a magic bullet and will, one day, impress a producer, who will, in turn, produce the screenplay. Don't ask me when this will happen. I just feel it will.

I went to comic book conventions and sold many more copies of the comic book. Major comic book publishers wanted nothing to do with acquiring the project. Believe me, I tried to get them to look at it. Without an agent, without sales in the millions of copies, without t-shirt sales, no one wanted to take a chance on publishing a second edition.

I met the man who licensed the "Teenaged Mutant Ninja Turtles" and "Barney the Dinosaur" and convinced him to read the comic book. He handed it over to his "people" who wondered if I was the man's nephew.

"No, I met him in the horse parlor at the casino," I explained.

"Well, without sales in the millions, we can't get behind this project," the readers told me.

"If I had sales in the millions, I wouldn't need you," I replied.

Like so many times before, people were polite to me, in case I was related to the man in charge. When they found out I wasn't, they had no reason to help me because I wasn't pitching a guaranteed winner.

The only time we ever heard from a major company was when the attorneys from DC Comics sent us a threatening letter. DC thought Al's "Superfan 1999" logo was similar to their "Superman" logo. Come on! How much of a threat could we have been? Were millions of people going to confuse the names each month and buy our book instead of DC's book? It was an example of a giant corporation flexing its muscles with the little guys. We ignored them. The last DC comic that I bought was purchased in the 1970's - and it will stay that way! (I still have an early edition copy of DC's "Swamp Thing," printed in December, 1974. If that's worth anything, please email me and let me know.)

At the comic book conventions, I would bring a "lovely assistant" and the young lady would invite all the men to my table. The female assistant ended up with a serious boyfriend through one of these table gatherings - Big Lee! Maybe it was his "Punisher" t-shirt that attracted her.

I paid a few hundred dollars to place the comic strips in artistmarket.com but no one asked to carry the strip in their newspapers. The minimal exposure gained through the Internet Marketing Service Was Definitely Not Worth The extra cost. I seriously doubt whether artistmarket.com is still in business.

The contract I signed with Al Weisner is printed later in this book. I made it clear to him that he was simply the artist on the first comic book; he had no other interests in my "Superfan" screenplay, novel, video game or children's book. If the screenplay gets produced, I expect him to come calling anyway.

He might say, "That's my story!"

Well, I had it copyrighted nine years before I met him so I should be covered.

You probably have noticed that the story is called "Superfan 1999" in some places and "Superfan 2020" in others. That's because it's a futuristic story that I haven't been able to sell! The script is set in the future so, the more time that passes, the more I have to push back the date after the title. I hope that I don't have to change the title to "Superfan 2047" because it remains unsold for thirty + more years. In the early 2040's, the script will be sixty years old! That's retirement age. By then, I'll have spent almost a thousand dollars keeping the copyright up to date and thousands more printing, copying, binding and mailing out the script! When you consider the time I've put into the project, I'd need to be paid about $100,000 to break even!

At the very least, my comic book is something I can hand to producers to demonstrate my commitment to my own project. Like a videotaped TV show or a self-published book, it is a worthwhile promotional gimmick.

If you do produce your own comic book, however, make sure to get it nationally distributed, somehow. You could make a few bucks by selling the comic books at book fairs. If you do show up at these fairs, expect folks to ask for your autograph. That's always fun.

Q & A

Q: How many screenplays are written in the United States every year?

A: One hundred thousand.

Q: How many screenplays are actually purchased every year?

A: A few thousand.

Q: Of scripts purchased and developed, how many of them actually get made?

A: One out of ten.

Q: Why write screenplays in three acts?

A: Developing your stories in three acts allows you to clearly define the beginning, middle and end.

Q: How long do I have to deliver a script to the producer who purchased it?

A: Ten weeks or less.

Q: What is a spec script?

A: It is a script that is written speculatively. No one has commissioned it, but you write it anyway, hoping that someone in the industry will buy it or recognize your writing talent.

Q: How long will it take producers to read my spec screenplay after they have requested it?

A: Ten weeks or more; sometimes, much more.

Q: How will I know if my script actually got read?

A: You won't.

Q: Who is the most likely person to read my spec script?

A: A young, inexperienced reader.

Q: How much do these young readers make a year?

A: Slightly more than a young, inexperienced gas station attendant.

Q: Should I send a query letter or full screenplay?

A: If you do not have an agent, send a query letter. If the producer or agent indicates, "No unsolicited scripts" - and almost all do - send only a letter with a brief description of your screenplay ideas. At most, send a two-page synopsis. Only submit a screenplay when a producer or agent has asked to read it.

Q: Will the producer or agent mind if I call them?

A: They will more than mind - they will want to hurt you. Do not call them unless there is a special reason for doing so. If they accepted unsolicited phone calls, they would never have time to represent their clients ... or go to the bathroom ... or sleep.

Q: Can I send emails to producers?

A: Yes, but many of them guard their email addresses closely. If you truly believethat you can make an agent or producer laugh or say, "Wow!" and want to read your work, gamble by sending emails.

Q: Should I submit my requested scripts via overnight mail?

A: It won't help much. Sometimes, it seems as if the more I spend on fast service, special handling and return receipts, the slower it takes for my material to arrive at its destination. If you are sending a package to Canada, I wish you luck, no matter how much you pay for "Guaranteed mail" or "Express mail" or other Canadian expressions that mean "It will take two weeks to deliver if the lead mush dog is feeling OK."

Q: When should I use self-addressed stamped envelopes?

A: Use them whenever you send unsolicited material. However, if someone asks to read your work, and then they reject it, let them spend money to mail it back to you. They rarely do, but that's not the point.

Q: What happens if I never get my script returned?

A: Deal with it, kid. Roll with the punches. Get a dog. Try again with another producer. There are plenty of producers (and dogs) out there.

Q: Do I pay for services such as Reading, Editing And Promoting?

A: Some services are worthwhile, others are rip-offs. Make a common sense decision. When you gain more experience, you will better recognize when to spend on writing services and when to laugh at a scam.

Q: Are writing contests worthwhile?

A: Some are OK. The only one I've entered is the "Set In Philadelphia" screenwriting competition, sponsored by the PA Council of the Arts.

Q: Did you win?

A: Not only didn't I win, I failed to get an invitation to the party that "everyone is invited to."

Q: How could you be left off the guest list if "everyone" was invited?

A: Possibly because I wasn't a PA Council of the Arts "insider." When you are an outsider, whether you live in Hollywood or your home town, you don't get many breaks or party invitations.

Q: What was their explanation for leaving you off the party list, although you paid the entry fee and were on the official list?

A: Human error. I made the error of not kissing up to the right people.

Q: How do I contact the right people?

A: Get a reference book, like Writer's Market or various guides to producers and agents, or search the internet. The Writers Guild Of America has a list of agents at www.wga.org. Eva Peel can help you reach the right producers at evapeel@earthlink.net. See what these people produce or develop. If you have a script that is consistent with their needs, let them know about it.

Q: What's the best way to do that?

A: For me, it's been through pitch sessions or writers' conferences. Producers and publishers seem to treat me better when they know I've spent time and Money On These Conferences. It's as if they're saying, "You're here. You must be serious about your work and really believe in yourself." Plus, they are geared to consider new ideas from new writers at these conferences/pitch sessions. That is not the case on a normal Tuesday morning, when they receive your unsolicited query letter and put it in a pile with hundreds of other unsolicited letters.

Q: So, meeting with producers is a major step in the right direction, right?

A: It's a rare window of opportunity that you must dive through.

Q: Suppose the window of opportunity is only open an inch or two?

A: Put on a helmet and use your head to break the glass.

Q: Don't you break the glass "in the case of emergency" only?

A: That's for fire alarms. Besides, it is an emergency because you need to aggressively pursue every marketing opportunity if you want to sell a screenplay in your lifetime.

Q: How do I assess an agent?

A: Check their list of prior sales on the Internet. If you are starting out and one agent sends you a contract, no assessment is needed. If you have a choice of agents, select the one who seems most willing to spend time promoting your work. A big agency is not likely to spend a lot of time on you or me. Most of them send me rejection letters that begin with, "Dear Paul." (My middle name is Paul.) It is better than "Dear ____" (blank). I've gotten some of those, too.

Q: How does a writer get into the Writers' Guild?

A: You must earn a screen credit, such as "Screenplay by" or "Story by" to be accepted into the guild. It is a quintessential "Catch -22" because you can't get into the guild if you haven't sold a screenplay and it's nearly impossible to sell a screenplay unless you're already in the guild. It's my belief that, by the time I am accepted into the guild, I won't need the guild.

It was always my goal, to be a Writer's Guild member.

If they want me, it's just for the dues that I'll tender.

Of course; relax!

Q: What's the difference between a "Screenplay by" credit and a "Story by" credit?

A: The story is simply the basis of the screenplay. "Story by" means someone else wrote the script but it was based on your initial outline.

Q: If you can't get a "Screenplay by" or "Story by" credit on a film, what should you try to get?

A: Like a dog who can't reach the turkey on the table or the scrap of beef under the fridge, aim for the bread and butter -- an "Associate Producer" credit. Often, you won't have to do anything for the credit, other than bringing the project to the producer's attention.

Q: What is an option and how much does that pay?

A: When a producer or film studio options your script, it means they are acquiring your property (controlling its rights) for a given period of time (one year is typical) and will decide later whether they want to produce it or not. Thousands of writers make good livings through option deals, even though their scripts never get produced. When the option period expires, the rights to the project are either extended or returned to the writer. The Writers' Guild sets minimums with regard to the price of option deals. If you're not in the guild, ask for the Writers' Guild minimum. Usually, the standard option agreement is ten percent of the purchase price. If the script is produced, the option money is deducted from the purchase price of the script.

Q: Suppose I have an offer for my script but don't have an agent?

A: Contact an entertainment attorney or use the opportunity to call agents (if you have a deal pending, they will be happy to take your call) and ask one of them to represent you on all of your projects. They'll figure if you can get a deal without an agent, you've beaten the odds and must be talented ... or lucky.

Q: What does a producer do?

A: Producers seek out great properties and take them to meetings. In that regard, they are salespeople. They also coordinate the project; attach talent, help decide whom to hire from top to bottom, etc. Rent the movie, "The Kid Stays in the Picture," which is about the career of producer Robert Evans. (Evans produced "The Godfather," "Chinatown," "Love Story" and many, many other films. Don't envy him, though, until you see the movie about his life.) A "Line Producer" works on more technical aspects of filmmaking.

I see the studio door, but when I get there, they shut it.

I've got deadlines; do they just wanna see how close I can cut it?

Of course; relax!

Here are a few questions from my students: The ex-marine from Atlanta, Demetric, emailed me this question:

Q: "How many acts and pages is a thirty minute script for television? I know they figure on one page per minute but should it be exactly thirty pages? I have to send some work out and I'm building a TV show from the feature script, "The Journey." I have already written three episodes and before I go any further, I wanted to know how many acts I should include in each script. Thanks, Demetric."

A: There are two acts and twenty-four to twenty-six pages in a TV script. These scripts have to leave room for commercials. Some have a two minute (two page) teaser scene, commercial break, then about eleven pages in act one. After the halftime commercial break, there should be eleven more pages in act two. Some shows have twelve minutes, commercial break, then twelve minutes -- and that's all. It's up to you how you want to present the script. If you write thirty pages it will be too long for a half-hour show. (Double-space the dialogue in TV scripts; it should still translate to one page per minute.)

Act one takes you to a commercial at, say, 8:15. Act two takes you to the end at 8:30. The drama must peak just before your act breaks. Leave the audience hungry to return for the second half of the show. Don't have major breaks at 8:09 or 8:23. It must be paced properly for television.

Paul Simon wrote that the people bowed and prayed, to a neon god they made. For some reason, his words just popped into my head. I'm sure it's nothing to worry about.

The odds are stacked against you seeing your original series on TV but, if you write one, you can impress people with your ability to create a whole universe. Everyone has advised me to write spec scripts for existing shows, but I keep writing original series anyway, in addition to spec script for existing shows.

Q: Why do TV scripts have lettered scenes?

A: Some TV shows have lettered scenes - (A), (B), etc. so the director can easily follow the script. No one puts a scene F after scene E because the letters look too much alike. Remember, a half-hour TV show has two acts, not three. Bring the drama or comedy to a high point exactly in the middle of your script, at the end of act one, to segue into a commercial break. Do not write more than twenty-six pages because there will be no time to fit it all into the show. Someone will cut out five minutes or so and the script won't make any sense. Also, if you are adapting a screenplay into an original TV series, be prepared to have a dozen great future story ideas ready to go. If you only have a few good ideas for future shows, you'll get rejected faster than you can say, "A.K.A. Pablo." Producers want to hear how your series can be sustained for five years. They can't make a fortune on five good episodes. They exist to make fortunes. Give them what they want.

Jay, a student in my screenwriting class, asked this question:

Q: "How do I describe a fight scene in a screenplay?"

A: Imagine how the scene would look, frame by frame, in your head. Does one guy smash his opponent's head against a wall? Does the other combatant pick up a broken bottle? Are there children watching the fight from a third story window? Think of all the details in your scene. Is one fellow heavy-set? He'd be sweating, right? Is anyone bleeding? Who gets the upper hand? Tell the director in your script exactly what you see in your head. Don't be long-winded in your description. If the fight takes forty-five seconds of screen time, don't write five pages worth of fighting action.

Jay also wondered:

Q: "How do you make a character, who is sort of a blind fool when it comes to a certain matter, not look foolish?"

A: Make the audience feel sympathy for him. Whatever you do, don't influence the viewer to sneer at the main character and think of him or her as a sucker. Give the main character a valid reason for not seeing the truth, or don't reveal the truth too early, simply hint at it. Nobody will root for your hero if he's criminally stubborn or stupid. In the TV series, "24," starring Kiefer Sutherland as Jack Bauer, Jack's daughter may be the dumbest character ever created. I watch her on screen and, instead of cheering for her to survive a kidnapping or car crash or bomb scare, I think, "What is this moron doing now? Can't they just kill her off and put the character out of her misery?" I expect the character to light a match near a gas pump in every scene. Or tell a government secret to the bad guy who is torturing her father and preparing to unleash a virus in Los Angeles. Don't write a scene that will influence the viewer to root for the wrong side. Your characters should be flawed (Jack Bauer, for example, has a serious drug problem) yet capable of sustaining an emotional bond with the viewer.

Final Thoughts On Everything -- Part One

I know what you want -- a literary agent. You know that most agents don't want to hear from you because you can't guarantee that they'll make millions from your writing in the first year.

You can give up or keep writing and get better. Don't give up. Writers don't need to audition to get work, they can just work. Think of each project as something that will produce income at a later date; before your death, after your death ... sometime. What's your priority: making big money today or producing stories that people will enjoy forever?

Remember:

You're Just Another Player In The Exhibition Game,

Out There On The Field Between Rejection And Acclaim.

And This, Like Any Movie, Has A Message In Each Frame:

The Bottom Line Is Money ... And Under It Is Fame.

Do you need more reminders about the importance of The Three "P's"? (They are, of course, Persistence, Perseverance and Pestering.) Go to www.picturediscovery.com. At that website, you will find mini-movies that remind you to follow your dreams, never look back, hold your head high, smell the roses … don't actually use those clichés in your writing but apply those positive messages to your writing.

At this time, I have one hundred and sixty UR's. UR is my abbreviation for "Unlikely Replies" from publishers, editors, producers, agents and similar entities. What does that mean exactly? It means that I typed four hundred individual letters (some were duplicated to save time) during the course of 2003, stuffed them into envelopes with project lists and/or books/scripts, waited in line at the post office and mailed them out. (I was compelled to put stamps on the outside and the inside of the large envelopes -- no one would ever return my work without an enclosed self-addressed, stamped envelope, called an SASE). I couldn't guess how much time, effort and expense I put forth in trying to promote my work this year. (I do have receipts, but I never look at them.) Still, nearly half of the hand-picked people whom I chose to contact, who claimed in legitimate publications that they were willing to read unsolicited work, never bothered to respond!

Of the half who did respond, many sent letters that included the words, "Dear (Blank): or "We only publish nonfiction" (when I had sent nonfiction) or "I am longer be accepting (sic) unsolicited manuscripts." Many rejections were received fourteen months after I had submitted my work.

One publisher, whom you'll read about later in this book, had no mailbox!

I also sent out scores of emails. Those queries were answered a lot quicker, on the whole, than mailed queries. That's not really an endorsement for emailed queries, though. Plenty of companies won't read them. Others guard their email addresses like state secrets. They'll tell you code words to use if they want to read your query. They don't guard their phone numbers as closely because if you call them, you'll never get through to pitch.

How do you pitch? You promote yourself like a salesman with a good product. Put yourself in their shoes and get right to the point. Don't be nervous. If you are nervous, pitch to people continuously, until you get bored with being nervous.

Let's say that if I came to your college to speak, I'd be nervous. After speaking to an auditorium full of students one hundred days in a row, I wouldn't be nervous by the last day. A roller coaster might scare you at first and so might an advanced ski run. The fear subsides in time.

I appeared on "The Dating Game" and at The Comedy Store in Hollywood. I was a bit sweaty. The more I performed, the less sweaty I became. Like lawyers, a good writer must learn to relax under pressure.

I once heard that the feat of accomplishment lies in composure and you are most composed when you know your subject. Who knows your story better than you do? Not the producer or publisher, that's for sure.

When you go to pitch, dress like a professional. Don't do what I did as a young man - dress like a playboy surfer in heat. I actually went to meet my first agent wearing shorts and a mesh t-shirt! What was I thinking? I wanted to come across as bright, eager, talented and alluring to the opposite sex. Well, if you are all of those things, no one is going to believe you anyway! Don't go in to pitch humming the words to "Hot, Hot, Hot."

Even if you go to pitch meetings dressed like a monk, there are predators who will try to take advantage of you. One macho fellow, a tough-looking Italian actor, was propositioned by a male casting agent. The actor punched the agent in the nose! Don't fool yourself into thinking that you can advance your career by giving in to predators. There are a million ways to get embittered by Hollywood and that is probably the worst of the lot. If you must give something away, make sure it's something that you can replace. Remember, predators are everywhere in Hollywood. If you know any predators in your home town, the odds are good that the person will someday move to Hollywood. It's a natural progression. If the devil really did go down to Georgia, it was a side trip on his way back home to Hollywood. I'd bet if you tried to get a personalized license plate in California that read, "PREDATR," it would already be taken.

To recap, when you pitch, Look and Act Like a Professional. Don't try to make the producer love you. Get him or her to love your script. If your script is criticized, consider yourself lucky that you received some feedback. Often, several producers will offer the same bit of criticism. That's a good thing. You'll have a consensus about how to change the script to make it saleable.

Don't argue with people who denigrate your script. Tell them why you made the choices you did and why you think they work. Go home and think about what was said. Be confident that your script is OK the way it is, yet open-minded to making a few changes. If you think that personality traits like confidence and humility don't exactly mesh, you're right. I've read books by successful writers and those are exactly the traits they say we must possess.

Do you think that successful screenwriters just showed up in Hollywood one afternoon and started working by sunset? Here is what Oliver Stone wrote recently, to Erik Bauer in Creative Screenwriting Daily (thanks Eric) about his troubles getting "Platoon" produced:

"It was another heartbreaker --- either you give up or you become very cynical. I don't know what kept me going through all that. I've had so much rejection in my life and so much failure. It's ironic that most people think of me as a tremendous, powerful person and as a success. If you looked at my life in detail you'd find most everything has been failure. And I think probably that's true about a lot of people.

"I think the rejections in those years steeled me, my character, in a way that I've been able to survive criticism of the worst kind. I've probably had as rough a criticism as any director's ever had. Even my screenplays. They singled me out. Pauline Kael [movie critic for the New York Times] would write diatribes about how awful I was. Mean stuff that would destroy a lot of people who didn't believe in themselves. It's hard. I think there is some truth to that Nietzsche line: 'That which doesn't kill you, does make you stronger.' But, I came very close to giving up. Very close."

Any one of you could be the next Oliver Stone so don't give up a month or a year before you sell a script. Keep trying to market your work no matter what everyone tells you about the severity of the odds against success.

Before you get to the submission phase, however, and I know you're just hankering for the chance, you must finish your projects. I once had a screenwriting partner, an assistant director of "Happy Days" and Laverne and Shirley," who said to me, "I wish the script wasn't finished so we could keep working on it."

I shouted, "What? Are you crazy? We have to finish one, start the next, and so on until we sell one of them."

He shook his head. He felt safer re-working the first screenplay until the polar caps melted. Maybe he had a fear of rejection. After all, no one can criticize your work if you never show it to anyone but that is self-defeating. Train yourself to finish, move on; rewrite the first one a few months later if necessary, but move on again. If someone wants you to rewrite a script for the fifth time, great. Just make sure they pay you to do it.

How can I help you get an agent? Well, I teach screenwriting, children's book writing and magazine article writing courses at Bucks County Community College near Philadelphia so if you live in the area, call the college at 215-968-8409, say you've read my handbook and want to take my class. I can't sign you as a client because I'm no longer a licensed agent but at least you'll have a chance to impress someone who can suggest where to submit your material. That's better than the deal I had at USC where they basically told me, "Good luck. You're on your own. If you happen to get famous, give us all the credit!"

A Writer's First Aid Kit

One day, I would love to re-establish the agency I incorporated in the 1990's. I'd hire a really big staff to read inquiries and scripts from every undiscovered writer who contacted me. To me, unknown writers are brave, determined jewels; consummate underdogs. It would bring me great joy to discover writers who couldn't get the time of day in Los Angeles or New York. (No one in New York has a moment to give you the time and no one in L.A. will tell you the real time because, "Like, you could be after my job, man, but have a nice day.")

For now, I am writing screenplays, children's books, magazine articles, novels, stage plays and nonfiction books. The writing is easy; the marketing is not.

Rudyard Kipling wrote about success and failure and cautioned us to treat both impostors just the same.

Print that on a poster and hang it up by your computer because it's the best advice anyone can give you.

Part Two - Children's Books

Writing Children's Books -- Getting Started

One day it occurred to me that I could get my children's books read by most children's book publishers without the aggravation of a middleman, which meant no agent would be involved.

On that day, I became a children's book author.

I had moved from a smoggy, sleazy, soulless city to a wholesome, woodsy, river town. Now, when I look out my window, I see a running river instead of a dancing devil. When I go outside, it's to feed the wild geese on the nature reserve, not to stop transients from swiping the newspaper at my door.

From that day on, I wouldn't have to depend on agents to peddle my projects (which, for a decade, were mostly screenplays). I could write children's books and market them myself to publishers. I'd control who read a certain book, how many were reading it and what kind of query letter they'd receive. The necessary evil I'd been forced to regularly approach and coddle, whose ranks I even chose to (briefly) join -- agents -- were magically excised from my professional life. They were apathetic-at-best, evil-at-worst entities in my rearview mirror. Or so I thought.

My first job, naturally, was to write some children's books. Luckily, I had already written three. I didn't wake up one day and say, "Hey, how 'bout if I write a couple o' books for kids?" While I was trying to make it as a screenwriter and/or TV writer, I felt compelled to write two juvenile books. They came out of me. I couldn't stop them.

I remember where I was --in the schoolyard, playing handball -- when JFK was assassinated. And I remember where I was when the inspiration hit me to write my first children's book.

I was sitting on my living room floor by the beach in Playa del Rey, California, in 1982. The TV was on -- I was one of the first customers to sign up for Jack Barry Cable TV. (I pulled the salesman into my apartment and told him, "Give me everything you've got.") HBO was an infant; a curiosity. I had a manual cable box with three rows of numbers and had to use levers and push-buttons to change channels. I wish I'd saved that old-fashioned box so I could donate it to the Smithsonian Museum.

Instead of turning in the cable box, I left it in the apartment I was vacating, saving the landladies' son from paying for a deposit. I told the young man to mail me my original deposit when he mailed me the check for my TV, which he was buying. That was over twenty years ago and I still have not received his check.

Anyway, the phone, which was positioned on the coffee table, rang and I answered it eagerly, expecting good news on a movie deal. I remember getting really angry, probably at my first agent, Barbara, because she was delivering the bad news. I was taken advantage of so many times, in 1982 alone, that there is no way to accurately recall which knife-in-the-back was being inserted. I was devastated and justifiably upset. I slammed down the phone.

A wave of calm enveloped me. I smiled and said to myself, "Son, you're taking this all too seriously."

I've since realized that when you address yourself as "Son," you are listening to your higher spirit. You have sent a message to yourself from two hundred years in the future, or some unearthly place. Maybe it's an angel sending you a telepathic email. When this happens, and it doesn't happen often, run right to your computer and start typing.

Since this was 1982, I ran to my electric typewriter.

"You're taking this all too seriously."

Hmm. What if ... a person like me stopped taking all things too seriously. He'd ... what ... he'd go numb, right? He wouldn't care if his house burned down or all his friends moved away ... or if he won the Nobel Peace Prize. He'd have no ups, no downs and no regrets. He'd tell everyone, "Be the best that you can be and say, 'So what?' like me."

The words were rhyming themselves!

Then I decided this person would be a leprechaun. This elf, who was always abused for being too short, too trivial and too much of a loner, finally decided to numb himself to the name-calling. Then, when something great happened, he'd be too numb to enjoy that ... and he'd learn that some things should be taken seriously. There was a fine line between apathy and anguish and he would learn to stay somewhere in the middle of those emotions.

I wrote "A Leprechaun Named Levity" in one night; twenty-eight pages, all in verse. If someone had destroyed those pages, I would not have been able to duplicate them. I looked up and said, "Thank you" to my spirit guides in heaven, who had given me my first children's book.

Unfortunately, my spirit guides didn't give me any inklings about how to market this book. I had taken meetings at Hanna-Barbara and Disney studios. At Hanna-Barbara, I had no success, but I remember they had really neat "Jetsons" wallpaper in the offices. When I met the folks at Disney, it was such a hot day that, while walking to the offices, I had to splatter talcum-powder on myself every few steps so I wouldn't drip sweat on my clothes.

Then, someone gave me directions to my meeting.

"Take Goofy Drive, then turn right on Daffy Way ...."

I felt like it was too hot to mess around. The fellow giving me directions was not being facetious; he was just being accurate.

Southern California is such a strange place that the temperature rose thirty + degrees in the hour or so it took for me to drive from Playa del Rey to Anaheim. I still keep talcum powder in my car.

No one wanted "Levity," my first children's book, so I adapted it into a stage play and teleplay. (A psychic told me that she saw it "Being performed or filmed on a stage.") I gave it to friends, who gave it to their kids and their friends' kids and to people they visited in hospitals. These people would call me after they recovered and tell me how they were uplifted by my twenty-eight page poem. "Levity" had cheered up sick people, just as it had lifted my mood after slamming down the phone and screaming, "Son, you're taking this all too seriously." If I never sold the story, it would be all right.

If I never sold any project, or never saw anything produced or published, it would not be all right.

When I was living in L.A., in the early 1980's, I kept writing children's poems, which were building into a book.

I wrote "Please Don't Wake Up The Raisins" after spending some time at an all-night Laundromat in Marina del Rey. Why did I do my laundry after midnight in a trendy neighborhood? One night, I went next door to the all-night supermarket and crossed paths with Bo Derek. (The film, "10" had just come out.) That's why.

On the night I got the idea for the "Raisins" poem, I brought a sandwich and a container of raisin/carrot salad into the Laundromat. I only did laundry once every six weeks so it took a while and I needed to eat while I cleaned twelve loads. People would look at all the clothes I had to clean and think I had lost a bet or was pledging a particularly tough fraternity. While munching on my sandwich and raisin/carrot salad, "Chuck" entered the Laundromat.

"Chuck" was a Charles Manson clone. He entered with bare feet and a trio of disciples, saying things like, "Insects are gonna inherit the Earth, man" and "trees talk to me, like, all the time."

In California, this was not really an unusual scene. I continued reading my newspaper and eating my sandwich with raisin/carrot salad.

"Chuck" apparently hadn't eaten in a long while. He discontinued his discourse and started staring at my corned beef.

"You gonna eat all that, man?" he asked me.

The other customers all gazed my way to see how I would handle this lunatic.

I said, "Here. You can have half the sandwich."

"Chuck" grabbed the sandwich half and gobbled it down in one bite! Impressive.

Then he started rambling on about aliens and gas stations. I had heard enough.

"Chuck, man, ya gotta be quiet," I scolded.

"Why?" he yelled back. "Why do I have to be quiet, huh?"

His posse was closing in on me, waiting for code words from Chuck to prompt a Laundromat lynching. (I guessed the code words were, "Clockwork Orange" or "Redrum!")

"Why?" I calmly repeated, pointing to the raisin/carrot salad. "Because you're gonna wake up the raisins."

He nodded, in complete understanding and agreement. Then he curled up in the corner of the Laundromat and fell asleep with his disciples.

The other customers gave me creepy looks, thinking that "Chuck" took orders from me or something.

I went home with a half-empty stomach and twelve clean loads of laundry and wrote the following poem:

"Don't Wake Up The Raisins"

Climb out of bed and tip-toe past your toys.

Don't brush your teeth 'cause it makes too much noise.

Say "Shh" to goldfish if they're acting coy.

But, please, don't wake up the raisins.

Your parents are sleeping; they don't rise at dawn.

K.C., the cat, all curled up, starts to yawn.

Is that your best shirt he's curling up on?

It is, but don't wake up the raisins.

Go in the kitchen and open a drawer.

Empty? My goodness, rush right to the store.

Tomorrow you'll probably go back for more.

Unless someone wakes up the raisins.

Walk up the aisle next to the ice cream.

Pass by the soap; you're unusually clean.

Smile at the dried fruit and casually scream:

"Wake up! Time to eat you, you raisins!"

In the following months, I wrote other children's poems, which eventually evolved into a book called, "In Here, Somewhere."

The short version of the book follows.

"In Here, Somewhere"

IN A TOWN, SOMEWHERE ...

(DRAWING: RICH PEOPLE LIVING IT UP)

Witches

The Town That I Live In
Has More Than One Witch.
They Get What They Want
With A Nod Or A Twitch.

They Have All They Need,
But They Need To Have More.
They're Looking For Something,
But What? And What For?

I Felt Kind Of Sorry
For Witches I Knew.
They All Seemed To Like Me
So I Liked Them, Too.

People In Town Asked
If I Were A Witch.
I Just Have A Lot Of
Witch Fwends.

(DRAWING: A YOUNG, NERVOUS MAGICIAN ON STAGE)

Josh, The Young Magician

The Bag Of Magic Tricks Was Full,
But None Were Working Right.
Josh, The Young Magician Feared

A Short Career: One Night!

Less Than Calm, He Prepped A Trick,
He Hadn't Yet Refined It.
The Bag Of Tricks Said, "Josh! Think Quick!
It's In Here, Somewhere, Find It."

IN A DESERT, SOMEWHERE ...

(DRAWING: PROFILE OF A CAMEL)

Extra Effort

"Don't Be Sad Or Somber
Just Because You're In A Slump.
Give That Extra Effort
And You'll Soon Get Past The Hump.

"Set Your Goals Realistically;
Take A Steady Course.
Look At All I Overcame --
I Used To Be A Horse."

(DRAWING: A FLYING HORSE)

Shalom, You Flying Horse

Shalom, You Flying Horse
You're All Alone Up In The Sky.
People In The Middle East
Know You're A Peaceful Guy.

Every Now And Then
When You Spot Fighting Down Below,
You Land On Sand To Lend A Hand
Or Just To Say, "Hello."

But Now, Shalom, You Flying Horse,

You're Joined Up In The Sky

By Radar Planes And Fighter Squads

Who Think You Are A Spy.

They Have Their Anti-airhorse Guns

And Airspace To Enforce.

You've Had Your Fun -- Turn 'round And Run.

Shalom ... You Fleeing Horse.

(DRAWING: A RHINO DRESSED AS A TAXI)

Take An Uncomfy Ride On A Rhino

There Are Lots Of Ways To Get Around.

Up High In An Airplane; A Car Underground.

Neither Compare To A New Way I've Found.

Take An Uncomfy Ride

On A Rhino.

Don't Worry 'bout Traffic. Believe Me There's None.

No Taxis Are Rhinos? You're Lookin' At One.

Getting To School Can Be Easy And Fun.

Take An Uncomfy Ride

On A Rhino.

I Won't Make You Carsick. I Don't Have Five Gears.

Strap On My Seatbelt, You'll Lose All Your Fears.

That Is, If You Realize My Seatbelts Are Ears.

Take An Uncomfy Ride

On A Rhino.

Sit On My Forehead. Hold Onto My Horn.

Now That You're Ready I Just Have To Warn

About All The Stockings And Pants That I've Torn.

Take An Uncomfy Ride

On A Rhino.

(DRAWING: CLOSE UP OF AN ANGRY SNAKE)

The Natural

"I Haven't Got A Resume.
Divorce Forced Me To Work.
They Tell Me I'm A Natural For
Complaint Department Clerk."

(DRAWING: AN ELEPHANT WITH HIS TRUNK IN HIS MOUTH)

Old Habits

"People Say
It's Foolish.
Animals Think
It's Dumb.

My Doctor Says
I'm Better Off --
I Used To Suck My Thumb!"

(DRAWING: A DROOLING, LAUGHING COYOTE)

Zach, The Loveable Coyote

Little Larry Had A Pet
Coyote, He Called "Zach."
Who Ate The Rug And Tv Set
When Larry Turned His Back.

One Day, His Father Asked For His
Report Card And His Grades.
Larry Said, "Zach Ate Them.

You Know He Loves Scrambled A's."

So Larry's Dad Went Down To School
To See If It Were True.
Did Larry Get All A's? Who Knows?
Zach Ate The Classroom, Too.

IN A FOREST, SOMEWHERE ...

(DRAWING: AN ALLIGATOR LURKING IN A SWAMP)

The New Neighbors

I Took My Lifetime Savings
From The Bank To Buy Some Land.
I Noticed A "For Sale" Sign
Sinking Quickly In The Sand.

They Told Me It Was Safe Here
For An Eager Speculator.
I'll Ask This Kindly Gentleman
If He'll Watch Out For 'gators.

(DRAWING: A BEAR STRETCHING HIS ARMS AND LEGS)

And The First Round Draft Pick Is ...

"I'M STRETCHING MY ARMS
AND I'M LIFTING MY LEGS.
I ONCE WAS A VERY GOOD HUNTER.
BUT THIS YEAR I'M TRYING
TO BREAK INTO SPORTS.
DO YOU KNOW IF THE BEARS NEED A PUNTER?"

(DRAWING: A DANCING PELICAN)

Weight Watcher

"FIVE, SIX, SEVEN, EIGHT;
I'M DANCING HERE BECAUSE YOU ATE
ALL THE CRABMEAT ON YOUR PLATE.
ONE OF US SHOULD WATCH OUR WEIGHT!"

(DRAWING: DUCKS SITTING BY A LAKE)

I Wish That It Would Rain

"Sitting by this man-made lake
How much sunshine can I take?
There are no clouds, for goodness sake.
I wish that it would rain.

"I splash around to help stay cool.
Why don't they let us in the pool?
It's stupid but a rule's a rule.
I wish that it would rain.

"Maybe I'll go 'cross the lawn
And turn the sprinkler system on.
If they found out, I'd soon be gone.
I wish that it would rain.

"It's still too hot to eat the food.
I'm really not quite in the mood.
(Be hotter if I wasn't nude.)
I wish that it would rain."

"I dunk my head to look for fish.
Sole would make a tasty dish.

But if I had just one more wish,
I'd wish that it would rain.

"I guess I'm imitating man.
Lying down to get a tan.
This grass feels like a frying pan.
I wish that it would rain.

"I now decide the sun is stuck.
My wife and I are out of luck.
You think it's fun to be a duck?
I wish that it would rain."

In Here, Somewhere

It's In Here, Somewhere, Yes It Is,
A Story That You'll Find
Cheerful And Uplifting.
If You Don't, Well, I Don't Mind …
Much.

Sometimes, People Only Read
Words They Believe Are Right.
To Get Through With New Ideas,
I Need To Use A Light
Touch.

Poetry, It Seems To Me,
Can Make Our Learning Fun
And Help Us Ask More Questions, Like,
"Today, What Have I Done?"

They Say No One Is Out There
Who Cares To Read, It's True.
I Can't Share This With Anyone;
No One, That Is, But You.

Producing Your Own Stories: "Jordi's Place"

I was certain that "In Here, Somewhere" or "A Leprechaun Named Levity" would be published in short order. Well, they weren't. I kept getting rejection letters which read, "There is a lot to like about your book but ...."I adapted "Levity" into a children's stage play (as the psychic had suggested) and tried to get the story some exposure. Maybe I could produce a children's TV show and sell the pilot episode to the networks, which were always hungry for children's programming.

My adventure is described below.

"Jordi's Place"

HE WAS THE WORLD'S ONLY TALKING MIME --

AND THE ONLY ONE WHO COULDN'T REMEMBER HIS LINES.

I was very busy that summer Saturday in Atlantic City. Topping my "Things to Do" list was go to the beach, meet my dad at the race track and cruise the night clubs. Somehow, I found time to stop at an art supply store and copy comic strips I had written.

I started talking to a guy named George, stage name Jordi, who claimed to be the world's only talking mime. He told me Halloween was the only night of the year when he didn't paint his face and approach strangers. We were both young, struggling artists who created works for children so we talked about collaborating on a children's TV pilot. I'd adapt my stage play, "A Leprechaun Named Levity," into a TV script and he'd be the lead actor. We would co-produce and co-direct, shoot on videotape and sell the pilot to local stations.

Chance meetings turn into viable TV projects all the time in Los Angeles so why couldn't it happen in Atlantic City?

"Call me, we'll do lunch at the beach," works well in either town.

A week later, we met at Jordi's apartment in a shabby part of town. (Keep in mind, any time you leave an Atlantic City casino, you're in a shabby part of town.) I couldn't wait to put "Levity" on videotape, if only to get some exposure for my work.

I believed "Levity" was my best children's story; one that was created with the help of automatic writing, inspired by spirits of the night.

Jordi wasn't impressed by it, nor by spirits of the night. He floored me immediately by saying he had a problem with the play. He wanted something simpler; to play Jordi, not Levity. He didn't have limitations as an actor; he just couldn't play any character other than Jordi. He had no confidence in his craft or in his ability to make decisions, but I thought I could compensate with my writing and experience. (I also thought I could turn a few sinners into saints with my trust and compassion, but that's another story.)

Basically, it was a game of, "Bait-and-Switch." When Jordi said "No" to "Levity," I said "OK" because I had written some children's skits and poems, such as, "Please Don't Wake Up The Raisins!"

I asked Jordi to precisely target our age level. He squirmed in his old, tattered lounger, while police sirens wailed outside on the street, and told me a secret about mimes. When children are very young, they like mimes but when they get to be about age seven, they hate them. Even a well behaved second-grader will mouth off to a mime; turn hostile, as if some sort of mime-baiting gene kicks in at age seven.

We needed five-or six-year-olds in the studio audience, unless we wanted to produce a show called, "Kids Gone Wild" or, "When Children Attack!"

We were given permission to tape the show at a day- care center near Atlantic City, in Pleasantville, New Jersey. I adapted my skits and poems into a thirty minute TV script, believing that, "Please Don't Wake Up The Raisins," was going to be a real crowd pleaser, as long as the crowd was very, very young.

On our second meeting, I met Jordi's girlfriend. She scolded him every chance she got. While he barbecued, she yelled, "Don't flip the steaks more than once!" with such rancor, I thought she had to be kidding. She wasn't kidding; she was ready to bury his face in the fiery charcoal pit if he overflipped the steaks.

"Just once!" she repeated through clenched teeth.

Jordi put down his barbecue fork and told me sheepishly that she was going to co-star in, "Jordi's Place."

"She insists," he whispered.

I wasn't about to say no and spend the rest of the night picking charcoal out of my face. I guess I could've said no, if I was standing closer to the barbecue fork, but I wasn't sure the fork offered enough protection from this vampire woman.

Jordi told me he had hired an inexpensive production company. I told him about the company I had formed years earlier in Los Angeles, DPR (which are my initials) Productions.

"Very funny," he said. "I must have told you already."

"Told me what?"

"That's who I hired -- DPR productions."

It was a complete coincidence. This company had the same name as my former company. I wondered; did Spielberg and his partners ever work with a catering company called SKG? What were the odds? Was this a good sign or a portent of more bizarre events?

Pleasantville, New Jersey, is a small town that has an inordinate number of cemeteries -- not cozy little lawns with a few old stones but bizarre, theme-park sized cemeteries, all over town. It's possible that more people are underground than above it. There are more plots than parking meters, more grave-stones than grade-schoolers. When the town was laid out, the founders must have decided that this was the place where everyone was going to get laid out. Every diner and motel had the same view -- of dirt. I've seen auto malls, but this place was the world's only cemetery mall. So many people were buried in Pleasantville, Jimmy Hoffa could've been there, too.

The day-care center was run by a lady who told me to turn at a cemetery and go past another ceme-tery and, before the next one, turn left into her school. She could've said, "Just turn into the one drive-way without any mausoleums." Or, "Look for one of the few signs in town that doesn't have the words "Born" and "Died" on it.

We shot the first scene, using a few of the five-six year-olds in small roles. They were made up to look like lions in the circus. These "lions" agreed that, since they didn't like their trainer, they would eat him at their next opportunity. (The lesson was about how prejudice is wrong). But, surprise, Jordi showed up as their substitute trainer and told the kids not to hate him because, unlike the other trainer, he loved lions. He'd never use a whip on them. Instead, he'd train them with donuts.

To a neutral observer, Jordi was so tense, so distracted by his girlfriend that he deserved to be eaten ... or at least mauled. The kids were better actors than the star of the show! My star mime was fighting constantly with his girlfriend/co-star and couldn't remember one line. I had to resort to hand-printing giant cue cards, the size of windshields. Without them, we could not have taped anything except for

Jordi's blank, frightened expression. In retrospect, that may have been the way to go. Everyone would've looked at the tape, seen him frozen in fear, unable to utter even a syllable, and figured, "Well, he's a mime. He's not supposed to talk."

So there I was, with a lead actor who was completely disoriented and hassled, failing every aspect of acting, sabotaging our work. No exaggeration -- he couldn't be trusted to go out for pizza.

That's when he insisted that he, alone, direct.

Call me an alarmist, but I started to get a bad feeling. I knew why all kids above the age of six hated mimes.

When things looked like they couldn't get worse, the circuits overloaded and the power went out in the day-care center. This happened four or five times until somebody pulled the plugs on a few lights. Something told me the darkness on the set would ultimately be a blessing.

Unexpectedly, we received some good news: Dom DeLuise, who had met Jordi once, agreed to work for free from his Atlantic City hotel suite. All we had to do was bring the equipment up and he would act as a guest star in "Jordi's Place," which I was hoping to rename, "Dom's Place," whether I could get Dom DeLuise's face on tape for thirty minutes or thirty seconds.

After we left the day care center and shot a scene on the beach (where the giant cue cards started blowing away) we pushed all the equipment down the boardwalk, in the pouring rain. It would've made a good scene in a darkly comic film, except that no one would have believed that all these bizarre events were unfolding around one production.

Of course, things got worse. When we finally got to the hotel/casino, the managers wouldn't let us in. They hadn't approved our project nor even heard about it. Jordi called Dom DeLuise from the courtesy phone and told him we were being impeded. DeLuise told management that, if we were not allowed upstairs with our equipment, he wasn't going to perform his New Years' Eve show the next night. So they let us in.

Dom DeLuise hugged Jordi like he was an old war buddy. He soon admitted to me that he hated working with a script and we should just, "Trust in the Lord" (ad-lib). He wouldn't read, "Please Don't Wake Up The Raisins," nor would he read, "Shalom, You Flying Horse," "Zach, The Loveable Coyote" or, "I Wish That It Would Rain" (about a family of vacationing ducks).

He insisted on ad-libbing with the world's only talking mime, who, due to pressure from a surly girlfriend and a lack of experience in front of TV cameras, couldn't ad-lib back!

A week later, it was time to edit the mess. By then, Jordi had vanished! I paid all post-production expenses. The lion scene looked decent (because the kids were good actors) but the Dom DeLuise segment was awkward. Dom and Jordi ad-libbed about bananas, mostly. (The hotel had sent up a fruit basket to apologize for the misunderstanding.) The show aired on a tiny station in New Jersey; luckily, only once.

The next summer, I walked into a casino and there was Jordi, working as a mime.

"We should work together again. Write me some material," he said, like nothing had happened.

He introduced me to his new girlfriend -- who was exactly like his ex-girlfriend.

"I'm engaged," he said, with a sheepish smile.

I later bumped into Dom DeLuise in a New York City theater and we talked like old friends.

"I'm a damaged ego," he revealed to me. "I want everyone to like me."

I learned a few things from my experience, like, when barbecuing, never flip a steak more than once. Also, if you want everyone to like you, don't become a mime. If you do go into the mime game, for your own sake, try not to talk.

Patience And Persistence

Twenty years passed. A hundred publishers rejected "Levity," which was now beautifully illustrated by a Philadelphia artist, Sharon Wakschul. I shortened the story for people who liked it but thought it was too long. No one liked it enough to publish it.

Finally, in 2002, "Levity" was published as a children's stage play by Plays Magazine. It has been performed by children on school stages across the U.S. The psychic was right.

I didn't feel frustrated that it took twenty years to get noticed. I felt grateful that it didn't take fifty years. I'm most grateful that, long before it was published, it cheered up sick people in hospitals.

The short version of the children's picture book, "A Leprechaun Named Levity" appears later in this book, in Appendix "D".

Selling Children's Books Without An Agent

While my first children's book was a gift from a higher spirit and my second was sparked by a nut in a Laundromat, my third children's book was inspired by nature.

It was September of 1991. I had just met my future wife and we were doing what many lovers do in the formative stages of a lifetime affair. We strolled hand-in-hand on the beach at sunset.

In the film, "The Naked Gun," Leslie Nielsen and Pricilla Presley strolled on the beach, rode mechanical bulls, drove bumper cars and took part in a slew of silly antics while Herman's Hermits sang, "Somethin' tells me I'm into somethin' good."

Well, if you add pizza and subtract the mechanical bulls, that was us. Then, all of a sudden, an ocean breeze blew in from the east and a cloud appeared overhead. The cloud was black and orange ... and flapping!

"What's going on?" I wondered.

My future wife, looking straight up with a puzzled expression, asked, "What is that?"

It was fifty-thousand, or more, Monarch butterflies in the midst of their Canada-to-Mexico, late summer migration.

It was as spectacular a scene as you could imagine, akin to watching an alien ride in on a surfboard. Our mouths opened in awe. The butterflies were lined up in perfect formations. Each battalion had a sergeants-at-arms floating off to the side. They landed, all fifty-thousand of them, on the beach near our feet. They looked exhausted.

The butterflies lined up in the sand, still in perfect formation. I tilted my head to see if they were spelling out a message for us. It was a mystical experience; like running with the bulls in Spain or swimming with the whales in Baja. We felt privileged to share the same beach with these magnificent voyagers.

I called people who knew about such natural phenomena. One told me how butterflies, considered to be the greatest navigators in the world, traveled hundreds of miles a day from Canada to their winter homes in South Central Mexico.

"They go right through New Jersey every year at this time," I was told.

A butterfly expert told me how lucky I was to have been standing in the right spot at the right time to witness a butterfly migration. She had never seen one, and she made her living as a butterfly expert!

I learned how butterflies were significantly endangered by illegal logging in Mexico and by poisoned vegetation in the U.S. Their numbers had been dropping each year because they had trouble finding safe food and/or breeding grounds. On Earth for millions of years, the Eastern Monarchs were dangerously close to extinction.

Western Monarchs, who migrate from Kansas to California, are protected by state laws. Years later, residents of Pismo Beach, California, told me that when the Monarchs vibrate on a local tree, it looks like the entire tree is shimmering. I found myself drawn to the Monarchs' breeding grounds and drove miles out of my way to get there, even though it was July and the butterflies were in Kansas.

After my close encounter with the Eastern Monarchs I wrote, "The Traveling Monarchs," about a ten year-old New Jersey girl who helps butterflies migrate safely during a cold snap. (The butterflies communicated with the girl by spelling out messages.)

The easy part was over. Now I had to go sell the middle-grade book without an agent.

The Query Letter

I had completed three children's books but still had no agent to help me sell them to publishers. So I sat down and wrote a query letter.

<u>Before you have an agent, your query letter to publishers is your agent!</u> And it had better be good. It is the only proof to the publishing world that you're not a rank amateur with delusions of grandeur. The one thing you can be reasonably sure of, in a business that treats new writers like they're invisible geeks or carriers of the plague, is that your query letter will get read.

The question is: do you want to impress a publisher or an agent? If apublisher loves your book, the book will be published. if an agent loves your work, it only ensures that the book will get pitched to a publisher. That's why I prefer sending queries to publishers; there is only one green light needed prior to publication, not two. What good is it if one hundred agents love your work, but every publisher in the world rejects it? I believe in contacting children's book publishers first and then, after you've had a few small success, contacting agents.

Of course, I believe in any plan that reduces or eliminates the need for agents. Like drugs and guns, it might not be a bad idea to take them off the street.

How long should it take to realize some success in your publishing career? Oh, ten or twenty years. Thirty, tops.

When I composed my query letter to publishers, I knew I was dealing with busy people who considered me a nuisance. I had to get them to like me; to consider me a writer who might be the one in a thousand who, although agentless, had talent and a clue about how the business worked.

I had two quotes hanging by my computer that were staring at me every day. One was by poet Robert Burns, who wrote, "What a gift it would be to see ourselves as others see us." I was fascinated by the quote and tried to fit it into my query letter.

Instead, I decided to write a short story about someone who actually had that gift, hated it, then old-lang syned it. (Burns, of course, wrote "Old Lang Syne.")

I kept the notion in my head, trying to see myself as publishers saw me. I was still a pest in their eyes. So I had to come across as a seasoned, interesting pest.

The other quote, for possible use in my query letter, was penned by Robert Browning. Browning's wife, Elizabeth Bartlett Browning, was the more famous of the writing couple. Robert Browning, however, was completely undaunted by this or by rejection. He wrote that "A man's reach should exceed his grasp." There's an old Eastern European saying, "He didn't know from borscht," which means he kept on doing his thing, right or wrong, successful or not. He kept plugging, even in the face or constant rejection and humiliation. Any writer can relate to that. If you find Browning's, "A man's reach should exceed his grasp" quote meaningless, you're probably not a writer. You may not even be human. Heck, even lawyers live by those words.

I found a way to include Browning's quote in my query letter to publishers. I also included information about my small publishing successes (children's books, stage plays, museum books, magazine articles; optioned screenplays and other material).

A sample of my query letter follows. I may be more specific in future letters, in case the reader never finds time to read my project list.

Before I write the letter, I write comments to myself. Example: "They publish nonfiction only; hobby books, humor, nature, sports. Send complete books: pigeon, onion, hot peppers."

Date

Name, address, email, etc

Name of Editor

NAME OF PUBLISHER

Street Address

City, State, Zip

Dear (editor's name):

As you probably know, Robert Browning thought a man's reach should exceed his grasp and was known for being undaunted by failure. I felt his spirit inside me today and thought I'd contact you.

Although I've been writing since 1980, when I received an MFA from USC's film school, it's only been recently that I've had my work published on a consistent basis. Whether it's luck meeting preparedness, talent meeting tenacity or a blind squirrel finding a few acorns, I'm happy to experience it.

In January, 2002, shortly after my children's book, "Running Through Kenya" was published, the National Liberty Museum published my book about philanthropist Harry Stern. The next month, Stained Glass Magazine published my profile on artist Maurice Gareau. In March, Plays Magazine published my children's stageplay, "A Leprechaun Named Levity." Plays also published my, "Satchel Paige ... Did What?!" last month.

This Summer, (XYZ) Magazine published, "Where Did The Ball Go?" about my first golf outing (which was as painful as the Inquisition and took almost as long).

Last Spring, Emmy Magazine published an article about a TV commercial I wrote and produced. When Emmy Magazine's check arrived, I shouted, "I'd like to thank the Academy!"

I always wanted to say that.

I would appreciate your consideration of the enclosed stories, all described on the enclosed project list. If you would like to read any other project on the list, please advise me and I would be happy to send it to you.

When I'm not writing on spec, I teach children's book writing and screenwriting at Bucks County Community College near Philadelphia.

I look forward to your reply and to one day saying, "I'd like to thank my publisher!" Until then, I'll remain (for the most part) undaunted.

Best Regards,

Don Rutberg

encls./projlist, sase

Analysis Of The Query Letter

In the first paragraph of my query letter, I let publishers know that I will be undaunted by any rejection. This is the opposite of telling them that, if they brush me off, they will be responsible for my swan dive off a high-rise balcony. I try to put them at ease by acknowledging the notion that my odds of success with them are very low ... but it's OK.

It's like approaching a beautiful woman or dapper man in a nightclub. Hey, they must be looking for something or they wouldn't be standing there, open to solicitations. If you walk up to them with a smile on your face and cheerfully say, "I know you're very picky, but if you like what you see, let's dance," you might acquire a worthwhile friend.

In the following paragraph, I take the advice of screenwriter William Goldman (who wrote "Butch Cassidy and the Sundance Kid" and many others). Goldman suggests that a writer should exude supreme confidence and enthusiasm in combination with total humility. It's a tough union of personality traits; like saying, "I am bigger than Elvis ... and, by the way, I'm also your humble servant."

So I humbly describe my small successes early in the query letter. I adapt these paragraphs for the specific reader. If it's a children's book publisher, I highlight my published juvenile works; if it's a magazine editor, I tell him or her about my published articles. Nonfiction publishers learn that I write books for a local museum. When approaching movie producers, I make things up -- no, I tell about the scripts that I've optioned, sold or written for hire. (I conveniently omit the fact that, so far, none have been produced.)

I inform publishers that I'm a writing instructor, to build on my credibility. Who knows if that means anything to them.

When I mention thanking the Academy after Emmy Magazine's check arrived and how I always wanted to say that, I'm only trying to inject some humor. (My friends all laughed when I told them.)

A few sentences later, I bring back the "Academy" quote by telling them I'd like to thank them someday.

Finally, I bring back the Browning quote; telling them I'm undaunted ... for the most part. I'm admitting that I don't take rejection as well as I claimed but I am working on it.

Example Of A Bad Query Letter

It is not easy to purposely write something bad. That was the problem with the movie, "Ishtar." The writers were trying to show that Warren Beatty and Dustin Hoffman were terrible performers. It played less as ironic comedy and more as a terrible act.

Here are some sentences that will turn an editor or agent against you.
- *My friends all say that I'm a great writer.*
- *My play was performed at my cousin's house.*
- *You are crazy if you don't sign me up right away.*
- *If you don't get back to me within a week, I will show up at your door.*
- *If you teach me what you know, I can be great someday.*
- *I want you to find me a writing partner.*
- *I need money desperately so I wrote something yesterday.*
- *I've written a satire about (name of group) because I hate these people.*

And, of course, my all-time favorite; an actual letter that came to my literary agency's door and read:

- *"I am practically illiterate but I think you'll like my work."*

A bad query letter offends the reader. It makes blanket assertions and unreasonable demands.

Put yourself in editors' shoes. They are busy people and have seen thousands of unsolicited query letters in their careers, most of which were a waste of time.

Try to stand out in a good way. Most of your competitors will stand out in a bad way or blend in with the bland crowd. You must be different, clever, likeable and professional. Before you mail a query letter, ask yourself if you are presenting yourself as all of those things. If not, try again.

Tell them why your story is unique and worth telling; why it will be a commercial success. Don't assume that they will "get it" right away, after reading a paragraph or two. I receive many rejection letters that begin, "Your book is fascinating and deserves to be published" or "It's a story worth telling." So getting a publisher to agree that the story is worth telling is only the first test. You can receive an A+ on the test and still fail the course.

I once received a reply from a query letter that included the sentence, "Your letter was the best piece of writing I have seen in a long time." The woman who sent me that letter was a book publisher. And she still didn't want to work with me!

So, a good query can only open a door slightly. A bad query letter will make it seem as if you don't exist. Then, you'll get all depressed and stop writing, stop improving. It will make you say, "What's the use?"

Although you're a terrific writer, you'll probably wind up saying, "What's the use?" at some point in your career. If you want to have some hope to build on, write professional query letters. They will lead to getting your work read, the biggest step on your journey to publishing success.

You're looking OK but obsessed with success.

Strike it rich; looking good will have you obsessed.

Of course; relax!

The Project List - Children's Books

The most important aspect of my query letter occurs when I refer to my project list. The synopses on that list are the puppies I put in the storefront window. The story ideas must be so appealing that the customer wants to come into my store.

My project list includes one, two or three sentence summaries of my books, articles or scripts. I arrange them logically; for example, nonfiction books, followed by middle-grade fiction books followed by books for younger children.

My magazine article project list, which appears later in this book, includes general interest fiction, humorous nonfiction, historical nonfiction and other genres. My screenplay project list summarizes screenplays, stage plays, novels, nonfiction books and TV series. (Note: Don't call your books for adults "adult books." The reader may think you've written something pornographic.)

Sometimes, this approach works well with publishers who will only read queries. They specifically state, "Don't send any books!" Other times, it is better to send one or two synopses only. I never can tell whether to submit an entire list of twenty-thirty project summaries or push one or two books. I prefer to send one or two complete books to publishers who will read unsolicited material. Some publishers insist on, "Queries only!"

On one occasion, everything in the sales process went smoothly. I sent a book called, "Running Through Kenya" to a publisher called, "Books For Black Children" and received a contract soon after. Boy, was I confused by that series of events.

That sounds easy, doesn't it? To sell a book, send a story about Kenya to a publisher targeting black children. I've submitted appropriate books to logical publishers like this hundreds of times. The best-case scenario -- send the book, receive a contract -- has happened exactly once. I've sold other books, stage plays and articles ... but it never went this smoothly. If selling all my books were that easy, the shock would overwhelm me.

I didn't make a lot of money from "Running Through Kenya," which is described on the project list that follows, but it helped me appear more credible and professional in my query letters. It was a confidence boost that proved I could sell my children's books without an agent.

My children's book project list is below.

Donald Paul Rutberg

DPRinnet@aol.com

USC screenwriting graduate (MFA)

Published book author, comic book author, children's book author.

Published journalist and playwright.

Writer/Producer of children's TV shows and commercials.

"A Writer's First Aid Kit" published September, 2004; Pale Horse Publishing.

CHILDREN'S BOOKS -- NONFICTION

HOT PEPPERS FOR POP: During the Great Depression, a fifteen year-old boy earns enough money in hot-pepper eating contests to attend a major league baseball game, where he sits on the field with Dizzy Dean and drinks from the dugout water fountain.

OUT OF THE WILDERNESS: During WWII, an orphaned, Polish, Jewish youth miraculously eludes the Nazis, joins the Russian army, gets arrested for "Counter Revolutionary Propaganda," nearly starves to death in prison; survives in a wilderness commune, escapes to and from the Polish army, posing as a Greek concentration camp survivor, and finds his family in America.

LIFE AFTER DEATH: Imagine a place where there is total peace, love, knowledge and wonder; where there is no violence, hatred or greed and where no one judges you. Millions of near death survivors claim there is such a place -- and the only way to get there is to die. Do we live many lifetimes, do Beings of Light exist in heaven, do ghosts walk among us ... or are they all just products of our wildest dreams?

HANGIN' WITH HOMELESS OTIS: Tall, lean, black, bug-eyed, drug-free, high-strung Otis is homeless by choice. He survives by applying his intelligence and communicative skills in the city streets, "developing relationships" (not "panhandling") and dodging danger.

WHY HOMING PIGEONS COME HOME: Descendants of the dove, Homing Pigeons are known as war heroes and bad housekeepers ... whose special gift allows them to flow with the Earth's magnetic fields.

CHILDREN'S BOOKS BIOGRAPHICAL FICTION -- THE "DID WHAT?!" (TM) SERIES

BENJAMIN BANNEKER ... DID WHAT?!: Benjamin Banneker was an 18th Century surveyor, astronomer, clockmaker, mathematician, equal rights advocate and protégé of Thomas Jefferson, as well as a free black man. But not everyone believes in his accomplishments -- not even the kids who go to Benjamin Banneker Elementary School in Maryland.

SATCHEL PAIGE ... DID WHAT?!: Satchel Paige was the major league Rookie of the Year at 42, a pitcher for the Atlanta Braves at 62 and the first black baseball player inducted into the Hall of Fame. He was also known for carrying a dozen suitcases at one time and perfecting his aim by throwing rocks at chickens. But not everyone believes in his accomplishments -- not even the kids playing baseball at Satchel Paige Stadium in Kansas City. (Stage play version was published in PLAYS, DRAMA MAGAZINE, 1/03; rights retained by author.)

NEIL ARMSTRONG ... DID WHAT?!: When Neil Armstrong took his historic moonwalk, he weighed only twenty-five pounds yet he retrieved bits of the sun and left footprints that would last a million years. But not everyone believes in his accomplishments -- not even the kids landing at Neil Armstrong Airport in Ohio.

Donald Paul Rutberg

DPRinnet@aol.com

CHILDREN'S BOOKS -- MIDDLE GRADE FICTION

ENDANGERED ANIMAL SERIES:

THE GREAT BEAR AFFAIR: On a hunting trip to Maine, twelve year-old twin boys are overwrought when their father shoots a black bear and deposits her in the back of his truck, with plans to stuff her. But the animal-loving twins are the first to realize the bear isn't dead, just unconscious ... and is being followed by her twin cubs.

THE TRAVELING MONARCHS: A ten year-old New Jersey girl adopts thousands of Eastern Monarch butterflies, the world's greatest navigators, who migrate from Canada to Mexico. With an early freeze coming, their food supply tainted and forests destroyed, the Monarchs seem doomed. When the butterflies reveal their hidden talents, the girl devises a plan to help them survive.

RABBIT-NAPPER!: Witnesses to a rabbit abduction, a ten year-old boy and his nine year-old sister try to influence the bunny's release. But the rabbit-napping cat, and her owner, have other plans.

SAVING SEEFOOD: A ten year-old girl, heartbroken when her horse, Seefood, runs away from home, chases after him to Saratoga Springs, New York. In Saratoga, Seefood's birthplace, the girl learns that her "champion" horse never won a penny on the race course ... yet was an unforgettable character beloved by all for his kindness, intelligence and community service.

WHALE A'SALT!: An eleven year-old boy tries to convince his father not to build a salt processing factory on an inlet in Baja, Mexico -- where endangered California Gray Whales have been breeding for two million years!

THE GOATS WHO ATE FIRE: Because they eat too much, Luis' goats must go out and find second jobs on the night shift. They succeed after Luis, their twelve year-old shepherd, introduces them to a troubled mayor on a dry, grassy hill that's become a fire hazard.

MOSES THE WOLF DOG (GOES TO SCHOOL): Moses, one-quarter wolf, is considered too dangerous to live with people. He's placed on a raft and sent down the Los Angeles river, where he and his new owners must prove he's more of a good little doggie than a big bad wolf.

BED TIME FOR SLOTH BEARS: Saved from jungle fires in Indonesia, sloth bears, also known as honey bears, adapt quickly to U.S. zoos. The question is: can anyone get them to stay awake past ten am?

HOMING PIGEONS AND OTHER HEROES: Modern-day Homing Pigeons travel back in time to save the lives of children in Italy during World War II ... or so claims an Italian boy's grandfather after the family racing pigeons mysteriously disappear in a magnetic storm.

CATS NIGHT OUT: Dozens of cats are in danger when their home, an old stadium, is scheduled for implosion. A cat-loving boy and girl put themselves in danger, too, but have no luck trying to rescue the untamed felines. Magically, they are all given the opportunity to transport themselves to any place on Earth, at any point in time. Where will they choose to go? And is a time portal really a good thing?

Donald Paul Rutberg

DPRinnet@aol.com

CHILDREN'S BOOKS -- MIDDLE GRADE FICTION

COMMUNITY PROPERTY: Children of divorce sue for, and win, custody of the home. In this story about children's rights, the ex-spouses are forced to share the home equally and independently, confronting responsibilities they ignored while married.

TECHNOPHOBIA!: Children of divorce move in with their grandparents; into a test home with a Home Nerve Center -- a computer brain that does all household tasks. The children soon notice that their grandparents have gotten carried away with the new technologies -- and the Home Nerve Center has a mind of its own!

ELIJAH'S BACK!: After a 2,800 year working vacation, Elijah, the Biblical prophet, is returned to Earth, no worse for wear. When he moves in with his black descendants, he finds it difficult to adjust or remain low-key.

ALFREDO CAUGHT A BLUE TOMATO: While fishing with his ailing grandfather, 12 year-old Alfredo catches something unusual on his line - a blue tomato on a vine. Is the blue tomato a freak of nature or a magical gift?

HANGIN' WITH HOMELESS OTIS: In this fictional, middle grade version of the Otis story (see page one for the nonfiction, older version) no one seems to trust the bug-eyed, highstrung homeless man, except for the boy who knows him best.

TILT TOWN: While stopping in one of the windiest towns in Northern California, a boy notices that trees are tilted to one side, as are the flowers, buildings, buses and people. The boy solves the problem, with help from folks who live at the other end of the valley and are tilted the other way.

THE BAR-MITZVAH DEAL: A 13 year-old boy spends most of the day negotiating an internet business deal over his cell phone - but his new partners have no idea that he's an eighth-grader or that today is his bar-mitzvah celebration.

HIDDEN STAR: A dedicated yet under-qualified teenaged astronomer, using his late uncle's telescope, accomplishes what few have done since Galileo's time: he discovers a planet. But will his newfound celebrity impress the girl of his dreams and procure a scholarship?

OUR DAD, SUPERFAN: The Superhero of the future is a sports fan. In the children's version of this story, based on a nationally distributed comic book, we introduce the only superhero who's likely to remind kids of their dads.

TIX: In 1970, a 12 year-old girl must delay the advancing computer age in order to save her grandparents' race track kitchen. Instead, she stumbles upon clusters of winning tickets and a moral dilemma.

RUNNING THROUGH KENYA: The orphaned animals on a Kenyan reserve are no longer endangered. Instead, they're troubled -- like cranky teenagers at summer camp. Giraffes refuse to eat, eagles won't exercise and hippos hog the pond. Their behavior improves when a Kenyan teenager, hoping to earn a spot on the Kenyan Junior Olympic team, runs through the reserve in desperate need of help. (Published 1/00 by Books For Black Children; rights retained by author.)

Don Rutberg

Donald Paul Rutberg

DPRinnet@aol.com

BOOKS FOR YOUNGER CHILDREN

WHAT TIME DO THE SQUIRRELS GO TO WORK?: A nature loving family moves into their dream apartment in the woods near the river, where squirrels seem to know all the ins and outs.

A LEPRECHAUN NAMED LEVITY: The story, written in verse, is about a leprechaun who refuses to take anything in his life seriously. Through a series of adventures with various creatures in the forest (including a piano-playing tree, a vacationing duck and a cash-poor alien) Levity finally learns there is a happy medium between apathy and anguish. (Stage play version was published in PLAYS, DRAMA MAGAZINE, 3/02; book/film rights retained by author)

IN HERE, SOMEWHERE: A book of stories in verse, such as, "Please Don't Wake Up The Raisins!" "Shalom, You Flying Horse," "Zach, The Loveable Coyote," and "Take An Uncomfy Ride On A Rhino."

LUCKY LADY BUG: No one understands why a little girl protects a certain insect - her "Lucky Lady Bug" - until the lady bug proves how lucky she really is.

MY FIRST SNEEZE: A Board Book about an unexpected event.

THE STORY OF ONION: (nonfiction) Onion was a pint-sized racehorse whom everyone thought was too slow, too small and too young, until he defeated the mighty Secretariat, the greatest racehorse of all time.

YOUNG ADULT BOOKS/ SCREENPLAYS:

SUPERFAN: It is 2020 and sports society has gone beyond escapism to insanity ... on its way to the unnatural. A sports nut named Murray joyfully jeopardizes his marriage, his job and his life in order to win the Superfan trophy. He and his eleven year-old protege prove that the heroes are in the cheap seats after the pampered players are kidnapped and forced to play in a "Real" World Series. (Based on a comic book & comic strip)

SUMMER AT SARATOGA: A young man quits his "perfect" job in the family dress business and takes his chances, acquiring two race horses and falling in love with the horses' trainer. In one frantic summer, he's stalked by the trainer's telepathic, telekinetic, terribly jealous ex-boyfriend and discovers the horses are superstar clones, who may be worth millions.

TECHNOBRED: Cloning can eradicate disease and famine or introduce problems even more deadly. It can also bring together an orphaned girl and a loving pet. "TECHNOBRED" is a contemporary "boy and his horse" story about the abandoned and unwanted triumphing through love and courage. The "boy" is an orphaned girl and the "horse" is a secret genetics experiment. When these two team up with a has-been trainer, they win the world's most prestigious race. But when they realize the entrants in the race are all the same horse, all cloned from the same illegal embryo, they decide to expose the conspiracy, even if it means losing their own champion runner.

Good Things Can Happen Without An Agent

It's a good thing when a publisher tells you he or she likes a story on your project list and asks you to send it, "At your convenience." Usually, when this occurs, the publisher will want you to shorten the piece, lengthen it, change its focus or, in the case of "A Leprechaun Named Levity" and "Satchel Paige ... Did What?!" adapt it into a stage play.

When Elizabeth Preston of Plays Magazine said she would seriously consider my stories if they were written as stage plays, I didn't ponder the difficulties of such adaptations. I adapted them, got them into print and felt redeemed, knowing they were being performed in schools across the country.

I was able to retain the rights to the original books. How did I accomplish this? I sent a legal document that was so convoluted that Elizabeth said, "Whatever." The stories were published once in Plays and then were mine again. Legalese worked for me, not against me, for a change.

The trademark office in Washington, DC, seems to be using legalese against me and my lawyers. It's taken years to get a trademark for my "... Did What?!" series. There was a bonus attached to the sale of "Satchel Paige ... Did What?!" When it was published in Plays Magazine, I could prove to the trademark office that the trademark was "in use."

My lawyer said he hoped the trademark office would be satisfied that my trademark was "in use." Could the examiners in the trademark office really claim that the project was not in use, even though it was printed in thousands of magazines?

"The office just laid off 150 examiners," my lawyer advised.

Great.

(Note: The trademark has been approved, after a three-year process.)

A company that produces audiotaped stories for children read my project list, liked the middle grade fiction ideas and asked to read the books. It looks like we'll be working together after I adapt the stories to audiotape format.

(Note: I never heard from these people again.)

In March, 2002, I sent a query letter and project list to Viking Books, part of the Penguin Putnam empire. They ignored me for fourteen months! Then I received a letter asking me to send, "Hot Peppers For Pop" right away. The book "looked interesting" to them.

So, fourteen months after they received my letter, they decided my work was interesting. I submitted the book, waited four more months, then received a nice rejection letter. My book was "fascinating" but not quite right for them. Oh, and it was too mature for very young kids. (I didn't write it for very young kids and they knew it.)

As soon as I read the letter, I sent them another nonfiction book for middle readers. ("I hope you don't mind if I try again," I wrote.)

Viking has a policy that dictates they will not read books from unagented writers. Yet they are reading my books. This is a good thing. (Read more about this scenario later.)

On January 14th, 2004, I read about Delacorte Books For Young Readers in the Society of Children's Book Writers and Illustrators (SCBWI) newsletter. Delacorte is owned by the mighty Random House and will only read books sent through an agency. But the newsletter indicated that one editor, Stephanie Lane, would read unsolicited queries. I started typing the letter within a minute of reading that blurb and sent Stephanie a query and project list.

Eight days later (!) I received this reply:

Dear Mr. Rutberg:

Thank you for your letter and list of projects. I'd be interested in taking a look at "COMMUNITY PROPERTY" if you'd like to send me the full manuscript. I'd also love to see "OUT OF THE WILDERNESS."

Best Wishes,

Stephanie Lane, Delacorte BFYR

I especially liked the "Best Wishes" line.

So, the next day, I sent those two projects to Delacorte, with an SASE, despite the fact she had solicited the work. (Sometimes the editor who requests your work will mail your SASE back to you, unused.) The SCBWI newsletter indicated that she was looking for books of historical fiction and she had asked to read nonfiction but that wasn't my biggest concern. You see, "Community Property" was not yet written as a book, only as a TV movie treatment!

There was no reason to panic. I spent the evening adapting the treatment into a book proposal. I printed it, bound it, put it in a package with "Out Of The Wilderness" and mailed the package ASAP.

Normally, I would've mailed the requested work out within an hour. But I couldn't mail a TV movie treatment to a children's book publisher. The adaptation took twenty-four hours and the U.S. Postal Service took another twenty-four hours. She had my books in her hands before she could forget my name.

Almost four months have passed since I submitted the requested materials yet I have not heard back from Delacorte. It could be that Stephanie lost my books or she could still be considering them. I will call her soon and try to find out what is happening. When I tell her secretary that the books were requested, I should be treated with respect. (If I had sent the books out of the blue, they'd probably tell me to stop bothering them.)

When I went to look for Delacorte's listing in my reference books, I noticed they were only listed under Random House. I looked for Stephanie's letter and couldn't find it. So I went to writersmarket.com, a web site to which I am subscribed. A search on writersmarket.com turned up the phone number for Delacorte, along with a greeting: "Not currently seeking unsolicited mss."

A writer needs to push his/her way into editors' hearts and minds. If you send out a hundred queries and receive five requests, you're doing well. But you have no control over whether or not editors actually read the books they requested. You just have to hope that three out of five read what they requested and one of them offers a contract.

To summarize: a writer can get noticed by sending queries and/or project lists to appropriate publishers (or producers) found in logical sources (Writer's Market, writer's magazines, newsletters, Literary Market Place and others) -- without having an agent.

Bad Things Can Happen Without An Agent

The worst thing occurs when publishers or producers ask to read your work, then, six months later, send you a form rejection letter without one word of constructive criticism. They think enough of you to request your story but don't give you a single clue as to why they can't publish it.

You could get a return package in the mail with your books in it ... and that's all. No letter, no return address, no way to identify who mailed it back to you except for the postmark!

Today, I received my original return SASE with only my "Crimes" article and a two page, screenplay project list. I sent the same package to dozens of producers a few months ago. Most have not yet replied. It could have come from any of them. My only clue was the postmark, from Santa Clarita, California. But, according to my notes, none of those letters were sent to Santa Clarita. It took me a half hour to come to the conclusion that I won't know who rejected me for about a year.

I received a letter today that started,

"Dear :"

Blank! I was Mr. "Blank." They didn't bother to fill in the word "sir" or "author" or "sucker."

The most frequently occurring bad thing is waiting six months to hear from a publisher about your query, then opening a form rejection letter. This gets annoying and is the reason why I ignore publishers who insist on, "No simultaneous submissions."

What exactly does this mean? It means they want the exclusive right to read your unsolicited book, for as long as it takes them to get back to you. That could be many months from now or years from now or just before the Earth's core heats the oceans to a boil in the year 8585 and melts all remaining cyborgs. Refusing to read a simultaneous submission takes unmitigated gall. These publishers, who have little or no respect for your role in the publishing business, demand total respect from you. When you obey their unreasonable demand to send your book exclusively to them, you will wind up despising them.

Like jaywalking on a desolate street to help a lost child, rules like these are made to be broken. Send your book to as many publishers as you like. Give your book a chance to get noticed. If someone wants to publish it, send a letter to the others and tell them the book is off the market. There is a 99.99% chance that those publishers will have no idea who you are or why you are wasting their time. Your book will be in a pile in a closet next to a mop.

By all means, tell the publisher who wants exclusivity that they can have it, with your appreciation. Then send the book to twenty-five other publishers! It sounds sneaky, but I used to be one of the suckers who gave these publishers an exclusive look at my latest books. I always regretted it. The good thing about not having an agent for your children's books is that you don't have to patiently wait while your book is sent to one publisher every three months (while your other books don't get sent anywhere). Submit your books like frisbees; make sure they are landing in logical hands. Don't send a Young Adult book to a picture book publisher.

Sometimes, the publisher brushes you off by advising you to seek other publishers. (That means, "Don't ever contact us again.")

I've gotten form rejection letters from my project list query, tried again, and sold a project to the same publisher. Some folks don't get much from a synopsis; they can only judge you on the merits of a completed book, article or script.

On page one of my project list is a description of a nonfiction book called, "Life After Death." (See Appendix "H".) I wrote the first few chapters and complete outline after developing a relationship with a West Coast publisher. The company's representative was very nice and offered me a choice of subjects to write about for one of their series. I chose life after (and over) death because I felt close to the subject, having written about the only lawyer in heaven. (See Appendices "A" and "B".)

The book practically wrote itself. I studied over a dozen books on the subject, extracted some really interesting anecdotes and theories and broke them down into headings. Case studies, religion-versus-science, mediums, reincarnation, ghosts; it was all good stuff. It was looking well-organized to me and each chapter seemed to be adding up to the same number of pages. The age level, pacing and word count were just what the company wanted. I eagerly sent the first few chapters and outline to the editor so she could give me the go-ahead and send me my first payment. The editor called me four months later (I had written about half the book in one month) and said, "The book is too interesting."

The woman indicated that, in order to have it published, I would have to make the book less interesting! This actually happened to me. I pictured what she must have looked like -- mousy, diminutive, frowning, hunched over, wearing a house dress. I wanted to tell her what an imbecile she was -- and then I remembered all my research from the no-longer-soon-to-be-published book, "Life After Death." We're supposed to love our enemies; pray for them. I began praying for her to be fired that afternoon ... but I knew that wasn't the spiritual road I was supposed to take, either.

All I could do was finish the book and try to sell it elsewhere. I was not willing to extract the interesting parts for a few thousand bucks. If they had offered me $100,000, I would have been advised (by my accountant and my wife, who are the same person) to write a non-interesting book and buy a house with the proceeds. I still would've walked away or made only minor changes; I never would have never given her what she wanted. Why go through all that aggravation to create a book that you wouldn't be proud to show people?

(Note: I am contacting a publisher who specializes in books for funeral homes. I've been told by a friend that this company needs books like "Life After Death" for young children. If they are interested, I will rewrite the book for seven-ten year-olds, for a company that actually wants an interesting book.)

What other bad things can happen when you try to sell your work without an agent? Well, I received some interest in two more nonfiction stories, described on page one of my project list.

A magazine editor told me she would publish both stories, "Out Of The Wilderness" and "Hot Peppers For Pop" if I shortened them. One would go in the March issue; the other in the June issue. That's how it was supposed to work.

I shortened both books by about 75%; adapting them into magazine feature articles. (I still hoped to sell them as children's books.) Then, as requested, I submitted both stories on disk, along with my social security number and recent photo. The woman called me to say she had received all my materials and would contact me when the first story was published, probably in March.

In mid-March, 2003,I called her to ask for my check and a copy of the magazine. The company's 800 number was disconnected. Uh-oh. But wait ... they were still in business. I called another number and asked to speak to the woman who was going to publish my stories.

"She left -- and she took your stuff with her," I was told.

I replied, "You mean, she left and took my social security number and my photo with her?"

There was confusion. I tried to stay calm about the possibility of identity theft. Weeks later, I was told that, yes, they had my stories and would publish one of them soon.

That was months ago. I think they have no idea where my materials went and are stalling until their lawyers can find a way to get rid of me.

Keep in mind, I turned down offers from other magazine editors who asked to read these two stories, because I thought I had already sold them to these clowns.

It rings of fraud to me, but what can a writer do? Spend five thousand dollars to sue a magazine over a two-hundred-and-fifty dollar fee for an article?

The stories were about my father's childhood adventures at a baseball game in 1936 and my cousin's escape from the Holocaust in the 1940's. I told my Dad and my cousin that their stories would be published; then I had to tell them they would not appear. That was the worst part of it all -- at least, until someone actually steals my identity with the social security number and photo I naively provided. (If someone gives you a credit card with my name on it, don't honor it unless the man has gray hair.)

(Note: The company found my articles, finally, and said I would have to rewrite them again. "Uh … no thanks," I told them and then strongly suggested they send back all my materials. Publishers always complain that people like you and I waste their time. They conveniently forget about the instances when they waste our time, lose our work, lie, space-out, stall or perform ignobly in other ways.)

One children's book publisher asked to read a shortened version of, "Hangin' With Homeless Otis." (It is described on the third page of my list.)

"We would certainly be interested in reading a ten-twelve page version of the Otis story," the publisher wrote.

That was a year ago. I have not heard from them. I sent a follow-up letter to them six months ago. Nothing. At least they didn't ask for my social security number, credit card number, driver's license number, recent photo and my mother's maiden name.

More recently, the company that would "certainly be interested" in the shortened "Otis" story rejected my "Life After Death" book -- after seventeen months. I sent them a quick letter, thanking them for reviewing "Life After Death" and asking about the "Otis" book. I didn't browbeat them for being apathetic numbskulls (although they had clearly proven to be such). Instead, I gently reminded them that they had asked me to shorten a book for them, I had complied, yet still had not gotten a response.

I'm guessing they will ignore my latest letter and reject "Otis" about ten months from now. (Note: I never heard back from them.) That would translate to almost two years for them to read the book they had asked me to write. Sounds like they've really got it together.

Today, an outdoor magazine publisher wrote, "I am embarrassed to tell you that a child whose mother works down the hall took your (pigeon pamphlet) from my desk. We have been unable to locate it."

Also today, a movie producer who read my query and requested my screenplay, returned the script, minus the last sixteen pages!

"I liked the twists and turns," she wrote. She may have liked the final twists/turns on pages 106-121, had she not lost them!

I once had trouble reaching a publisher, even though the company agreed to read query letters from unagented writers. The reason I couldn't promote my work to them was because ... they didn't have a mail slot!

The following article describes my real-life dilemma.

"Those Disappearing Mail Slots"

I had mailed the query letter and writing samples certified/return receipt so I'd be certain the publisher received the materials. The U.S. Postal Service lost my little black date book when I was twenty-one -- when it was still worth something, so I'm always skeptical of their abilities. Sure enough, after a two-week wait, the green receipt was not returned through my front door.

This disgruntled postal customer called to complain.

"Did you simply lose the return receipt or did you lose the package, too?"

The postal supervisor promised to ask the postman when he returned. So I called back and waited for a clumsy excuse from a destined-to-be-disgruntled postal employee. Maybe someone had found my little black book from the disco era.

The official excuse was: "The address in question has no mail slot."

I was thrown off-balance.

"You mean, it's not the post office's fault?"

"We warned the people at that address; they must provide a mail slot and they have not done so."

Then it occurred to me; this publisher was all over the internet. The editors depended mainly on computers and fax machines, having mutated into beings-who-live-on-Earth-but-don't-need-mail-slots.

Human beings have always needed mail slots. Cave men would draw stick figures of a buffalo hunt on a piece of slate with a piece of chalk, then toss the work of art into a neighbor's cave. Caves, inherently, have mail slots.

Every inventor throughout history had to patent ideas (sometimes, right after they stole them) and could not have done so without a mail slot.

Vincent Van Gogh needed a mail slot to deliver his severed ear to brother, Theo. What were his options -- Ear Mail?

Everyone we know depends on mail slots but that's about to change. The computer and fax machine will soon render the mail slot obsolete.

So what's next? The umbrella could go quickly -- abandoned by people who never leave their homes. The same could happen to shovels since we won't have to clear a path through the snow for the mailman anymore.

What will happen to forty year-old lost love letters that are found and then sent to their intended mail slots, when there are no mail slots?

How will we receive those free vacation offers in the mail? The ones that read: "Talk to us for ten minutes and then enjoy the mansion near the lake for the rest of the weekend as our guest."

How will we apply anonymously for gun permits?

If mail slots are passé, we won't be able to make fun of the U.S. Postal Service anymore. Disgruntled ex-postal employees will be at an all time high and are sure to make headlines. When they do, they won't be stories about macho mailmen who wear their short pants through rain, sleet, snow or gloom of night.

They'll be stories about gloom.

I don't miss Richard Nixon, our Servel refrigerator or eight-track tapes, but I could miss my mail slot.

Finally, I had to accept that the 20th Century has gone over the horizon. I got rid of my mail slot and telephone/answering machine and replaced them with a computer and fax machine.

Maybe now I'll learn how to use the darn things.

Keeping Track Of Your Submissions

As you've already discovered, an unagented writer must do his/her own market research and yes, it's trivial and repulsive. If somebody's got to do it, why shouldn't the responsibility fall to the person who loves his/her books as a parent loves his children? Why not take the initiative to find your "kids" a good home?

Buy a few reference books (they are easy to find in any book store or library) with publishers' addresses, contact names and current needs and match them up with your work. Someone needs historical nonfiction? Send that company your nonfiction story about a child who attends his first baseball game during the Great Depression. A publisher in the Northwest needs middle grade fiction relating to nature? Send them your whale story. Make sure they are willing to read entire manuscripts (look under the heading, "How to contact" before submitting the book).

Theoretically, you can send the whale book to fifty nature publishers in one day. The following day, you can send out fifty copies of the baseball book. I have done this and stayed in the post office for so long, the post office manager threatened to charge me rent!

The cost to mail each package, containing one fifty page book, is about four dollars. The SASE doubles the cost. Often, I will mail packages 4th class/media/book rate. This rate is much less than eight dollar round-trip, about three dollars ($1.44 each way; if heavier, $1.84 each way).

When you think about it, spending one hundred-fifty dollars to send your book to and from fifty publishers is not a bad deal. (The book may cost another two-three dollars to copy and bind.) If one company decides to publish it, you've leaped over the biggest hurdle of your career -- selling your first book.

Be prepared to hear nasty comments from people standing in line behind you in the post office. I try to buy metered postage for the outside envelopes (I use #10 tyvecs) and buy stamps, which I put on later, for the inside (SASE) envelopes. In this way, I don't tie up the line for more than thirty minutes.

Nasty comments from customers pale in comparison to nasty comments from postal workers. Some of them will loathe you for making them think and work. If you tell them that an eighty-three cent stamp and a one cent stamp add up to eighty-four cents, they will snap at you for telling them how to do their job.

I try to be friendly and polite to postal workers because, without them, I couldn't get my books to industry professionals. (Very few publishers or agents accept emails from unknown writers.) Despite going out of my way to be courteous, one female postal worker didn't like me. How did I know this? She told me!

This is a true story. I brought one package, which needed a SASE, to the window. I couldn't see the monitor and the woman wouldn't tell me the price, so I guessed, "Three-ninety-five, right?"

She snapped, "You know what it costs!"

The only way I could've known for sure what the package costs is if I had mailed a standard envelope with one piece of paper inside. Then, I would've known it required a 37 cent stamp. Otherwise, how could I tell the difference between 1.9 ounces and 2.1?

(One time, I sent one piece of paper, a 37 cent letter, to a publisher owned by Disney and it was "returned to sender" for insufficient funds! I'm still scratching my head over that one.)

I asked the clerk, "Why won't you tell me what the package costs?"

She answered, "Because I don't like you."

She said I "threw things" at her when I came to her window. I had never been to her window before! Her boss said she was justified in withholding the price from me because I had been so "rude" to her in the past. Huh?

Many postal workers help me put stamps on SASE's during their breaks. They either love me or hate me. One clerk snapped at me for using ten cents worth of scotch tape.

"We don't supply tape!" she screamed.

"I spend five grand a year here," I argued.

"No tape!"

That's like going to a restaurant three nights a week, month after month, year after year, and getting scolded for using pepper.

"We don't supply pepper! No pepper!"

So I bring my own tape to the post office.

Some publishers will reply six-eight months after you've mailed them your book -- even if they've requested your book. If you pester them, they will still wait six-eight months before mailing you a form rejection letter. It's not that they're insensitive to your feelings; it's just that they consider you a fly in the restroom. They will ignore you for months; then, when the mood strikes, they'll open the restroom window to let you fly away. This is considered a benevolent act, a much kinder way to get rid of you than using a flyswatter or toxic room deodorizer.

As mundane and non-creative as it may be, it is imperative that you keep track of your submissions. When you receive a positive reply ("Please send us a sample") you will be able to quickly locate your original letter to the company, what they publish, where you found the listing and any other pertinent information.

I keep an "Expect Reply" file in my computer. When "XYZ" Publishers returns my book in my SASE, I ask the computer to search for "XYZ." Then I read my own notes, such as, "Whale book sent to XYZ Pubs 3/21/03, to Jane Doe. They need nature books for middle grades. Re SCBWI newsletter." (More info about SCBWI, the Society of Children's Book Writers and Illustrators, appears later in this section.)

I open the envelope with my memory refreshed about their needs. If their rejection letter states, "We enjoyed reading your whale book and hope you will keep us in mind with other nature stories," I send the information to my "Try Again" file. A few weeks later, I mail them another book, maybe one about butterflies, along with a short letter thanking them for their interest in my work.

If they send me a form rejection letter after six months, which is common, I send the information to my "PUBX.doc" file, which could be called "TRASHEDBYPUBS.doc". If I see the name of a publisher and I'm not sure whether they've rejected me, I go the "PUBX" file or the profoundly dead-end file, called "UR.doc," for "unlikely replies". (The "UR" file has information on publishers and agents who have died, been fired or incarcerated, had nervous breakdowns or who have steamed the stamps off my SASE. Often, it is a combination of these factors.)

Don't waste your time on companies that treat you poorly. Be persistent with companies who seem willing to read more of your work and write back to you with personal, respectful letters.

Deciphering Letters From Agents/Publishers

I received a package in November, 2003, from Lisa Findlay, an editor at Random House. It was uplifting to see the package stuffed in my mailbox because Random House does not, as a rule, read books from unagented writers like myself. I was not competing with thousands of unsolicited submissions, only with a few hundred agented submissions or those from known writers.

First, I checked my notes to see when I had mailed my four children's books to Lisa. OK, it was in January, 2003. That wasn't bad; it had taken only ten months to hear back from her.

The ten month wait, believe it or not, wasn't the worst part.

I had gotten a nice, personalized rejection from Lisa a year earlier. She told me that she liked my Holocaust survival story (about my eighty-three year-old cousin) and suggested I include much more about World War II or much less; in other words, don't leave in a moderate amount. Later, I read in the Society of Children's Book Writers & Illustrators' newsletter that Lisa was "ready to build her own list" and "wanted to develop new talent." I also read that she was looking for middle-grade historical fiction and fantasy.

So I told Lisa in my letter that I appreciated her previous feedback and was enclosing books that I considered to be historical fiction and fantasy.

Ten months later, her letter to me read like this:

"Dear Mr. Rutberg: Thank you for submitting (books) for my consideration. Although I enjoyed your ideas, I do not think they are right for our list at this time."

So far, it was a typical form letter.

"I am returning your materials herewith. Due to an overwhelming volume, I am longer be accepting unagented submissions unless they are conference-related. Thank you for thinking of Random House! Yours Truly, Lisa Findlay, Assistant Editor, Random House Young Readers Group."

"I am longer be accepting..."?

What did that mean? I waited ten months to hear from an editor that had read and complimented my earlier work and who had requested unsolicited books in a SCBWI newsletter, only to receive a sloppy, nonsensical form letter? She didn't omit one word or slightly mess up the syntax - she murdered the whole sentence. It was like a hybrid of "I will no longer be accepting" or "I am no longer accepting" submissions. Didn't anyone proof-read the letter, which, undoubtedly, was being mailed to hundreds, if not thousands of writers?

My feeling is that Lisa Findlay does not want to develop new talent for Random House Children's Books. More likely, she wants unknown writers to leave her alone. If I were her, I'd worry less about what new writers were doing and worry more about the shoddy work that was coming out of the home office.

If a writer butchered a sentence as she did, an editor would sneer and say, "What an idiot. Why would I ever want to work with that person?"

And if she asked to read my work and I waited ten months to respond, do you think she'd still be interested in me? Many publishers have asked to read my books and never responded to my package. Like agents, these editors are more likely to be slobs than thieves.

Generally speaking, you can expect to receive letters from agents and publishers which fall into four categories.

1. "GET LOST!"

The agent/publisher tells you, via form letter, to go away. They may advise you to take a writing course or submit your work to their competitors. Forget about these people. They are positive energy drainers.

2. "NO OFFENSE BUT ... GET LOST!"

The company sends you a form letter that indicates your material is not what they seek -- at this time (or any time between now and the day they retire). Yes, they mean "Get lost" but they don't really insult you. I received one such letter today. It included the message, "I admire your tenacity." You can try again with these people, but the odds of them accepting your work are slim. If a new submissions editor is hired, he or she may like your work more than his or her predecessor.

3. "TRY AGAIN!"

You get a non-form letter that indicates you are a good writer. The agent/editor may actually compliment your work. I've gotten rejections that included the phrases, "Wonderful stories" or "I admire the intent of your story" or "Someone should publish this book." (One agent wrote that I should start my own publishing company.) You must try again with these folks. Study their needs in reference books. If they sell or publish mostly nonfiction, send them your best nonfiction books with a letter that states, "I appreciate your interest and kind words and hope you don't mind if I try again."

4. "GREEN MEANS GO!"

Someone is interested in your work and asks you to send a book or script to their attention. This is a green light. You must put your foot on the accelerator. Submit exactly what they've requested (or as close to it as possible) within a day or two (not three months later).

Recently, an agent asked to read the first hundred pages of my novel about the only lawyer in heaven. The problem was, I had written it as a screenplay and comedy series. I stopped what I was doing (writing the book you are now reading) and adapted the screenplay into a novel, or at least the first hundred pages of the novel. I did not want to wait a few months, then submit the novel to a man who didn't remember who I was or what book I had proposed.

(The agent rejected the sample pages of my novel but he also requested another book, about the woman jockeys. I will try again with a company that flashed a green light at me.)

There is a little known, fifth category. It is called the, "OOOPS! WE SENT YOU ANOTHER WRITER'S MATERIALS!"

This situation has happened to me several times in the last few months. I open the tyvec envelope, look for the company's name, refer to related notes in my "Expect Reply" file and read the form rejection letter. Then, when I check to see if they've mailed back all my books, scripts or articles, I notice a foreign work. Joe Blow's anti-war article or Suzy Q's picture book is mingling with my books. There is no note to Joe or Nancy; their work has simply been lumped together with mine. When the agents or publishers find Joe and Nancy's SASE, and can't find their accompanying work, guess what they do with the SASE's? That's right, they chuck them. I know that some of my submissions are inadvertently returned to other writers, who also chuck them. That's why I have an "Unlikely Reply" file. Some of my work is ignored and some is lost.

The last time this happened, I called the fellow whose rejected work was accidentally sent to me. I wanted to be courteous; to "do unto others" and all that. The guy had a New Jersey address and I have an unlimited long distance plan. (My wife thinks I single-handedly put MCI into bankruptcy.)

Anyway, I called the man, explained what had happened; advised him not to submit handwritten stories, which he had foolishly done. Agents and publishers will brand you an amateur if you send material written in longhand. He was very appreciative and we chatted about writing for ten minutes. I felt as if I had done a good deed, which, I should've known, never goes unpunished.

Today, I received my phone bill from MCI. There was an additional thirteen dollar charge for a call made to Toronto, Ontario, Canada! This non-typist listed an address in New Jersey but a phone number at his home in Canada. What made me angry was that he never told me I was spending $13 on a ten minute call to tell him something that should have only taken thirty seconds. He hid the fact that I was calling him in a foreign country.

My studies regarding "Life After Death" taught me that I should be happy about doing a good deed, and I should forgive this dolt. I'm working on it, I guess.

As far as deciphering contents of your SASE that are returned with no letter whatsoever, all you can do is check the postmark. If the package was mailed from Hawaii and you've only sent one letter to the 50th state, you're in luck. You'll know who rejected you. Otherwise, fuhgetaboutit. In about a year, you'll notice that one publisher never responded to your almost forgotten query. The only reason it's not totally forgotten is because you've kept track of your submissions. Then you'll know for sure which "busy" person disregarded your very existence.

"Busy" people usually say they're busy so they can be excused for cruel, insensitive behavior. In the 1980's, I sent a "Barney Miller" script to the show's producer. I didn't know that my agent, Barbara, had just sent the same script to him. A few weeks later, this "busy co-executive producer" (as he referred to himself) called Barbara and abused her for twenty minutes! He wasn't too busy to intimidate a struggling, female agent. If he were really busy, why would he vault into a twenty minute tantrum?

To recap: forget about those agents and publishers in category one, the "Get Lost" letters. Don't spend too much time contacting the apathetic form letter rejecters in category two, "No Offense But ... Get Lost." Pester the folks in category three, "Try Again," who call you by name and offer encouraging rejections. Respond to requests to read your work (category four, "Green Means Go") as if you're a starving lion who has spotted a limping hyena alone near a pond.

Working With A Children's Book Agent

In the late 1980's, shocked, as we all were, by the death of disco, I solicited agency representation for my children's books. (I had completed three, along with a Young Adult novel.)

I knew, from my experiences with Hollywood agents, that I had to prove to them I was a diamond in the rough. (A few years later, I would name my literary agency "DR" for Diamonds in the Rough.) The best way to ingratiate myself to children's book agents was to inform them that I had been represented by agents in Hollywood, had optioned several screenplays and was now concentrating on writing juvenile books.

I decided to travel ninety miles to New York City and visit selected agents out of the blue. What made this complicated and ill-fated was the reality that agents detest spontaneous visits by unknown writers. The only thing worse than blue-sky phone solicitations are blue-sky visits. To them, unagented writers are mostly psychos and illiterates. How do I know this? Remember, I was an agent. They wrote to me and admitted they were psychos and illiterates! ("But I think you'll like my book," they would add.)

Agents rarely have to deal with new writers in person because few writers have the guts to risk getting a door slammed in their face. I was used to the door-slams and brush-offs. Some I was proud of when I considered the source. Anyway, all I wanted was a face-to-face meeting with one out of twenty agents. I would pitch my books, leave my project list and hope for a return phone call.

I dressed up, took a train to Manhattan and a cab to the agents' offices. In most cases, I couldn't even get inside the buildings! For a moment, I wished I were back in Hollywood, where an unknown writer could walk the streets in sunny, comfortable weather and then return to an apartment near the beach or stop off at Santa Monica Pier, the Getty Museum or some other neat place.

I wondered how many struggling writers were denied entry into office buildings where agents worked ... and then, while wandering around on the streets, became hookers?

I decided against returning to Hollywood, becoming a hooker (often, it's the same thing) or trying some other slimy, desperate maneuver. Instead, I sneaked into the building of a very old, well-established New York literary agency and took the elevator to an upper floor.

What would you do? (Forget the hooker option. It's been done, literally, to death.) There was no way I could get my foot into their office. Even if I did, they would see that my shoe had been ripped open at the toe-line by a very quick-closing elevator. Never let your guard down in New York City, not even in a near-empty elevator.

I went into the bathroom and used it as a War Room, peeking out into the hallway. No man left the office to use the toilet, but a woman did! All I had to do was turn into Richard Gere for a minute and, while hiding my shredded shoe, charm her into telling me how to get an audience with an agent. Maybe she was an agent! While most screenplay agents were men, most juvenile book agents were women.

As it turned out, she was a secretary and she liked my Richard Gere imitation (sport jacket held by two fingers and slung over my shoulder, a la "American Gigolo"). I told her I needed her help and would name my first-born movie after her if she could get me past the door and into her agency's office.

She gave me the name of the most approachable agent in her office.

"Tell Bob that Cindy said you were a friend of Jane's and he should let you in for a minute."

I thanked the young woman, who, for some reason, rushed off to the ladies room. Then I walked into the office to talk to Bob, because Cindy said I was a friend of Jane's.

One thing was certain: there was no throng of struggling writers waiting to get into that office. Who would consciously stoop to this level; who else would humiliate themselves just to talk to an agent whose only real talent was ordering martinis after last call?

I eagerly entered the office. The element of surprise was my only asset. I could read Bob's thoughts: "How the hell did he get up here?"

The other agents surrounded me, as if I were about to pull out an AK-47 in a fit of "Writer's Rage." Other secretaries had dialed 9-1 ... and had their fingertips on the next "1." I pitched my books, left my project list and heard sighs of relief as I left the office a minute or two later. I thanked Cindy as we passed in the hall and told her the name of my latest screenplay -- "How Cindy Got Fired."

Next, I took a twenty dollar cab ride to the end of the island to see an agent who had written a book about getting an agent. He wasn't there, but I was allowed to speak to his secretary in the one room office. Scripts were piled up to the ceiling! There weren't two or three piles but a dozen piles, ten feet high.

"He's got to catch up on his reading," the agent's secretary explained.

The secretary was destined to be an agent -- she had mastered the art of distorting the truth. I knew the truth. The guy would never catch up on his reading. He was more concerned with selling his book on how to get an agent than he was with finding new clients. New writers had purchased his book and sent him their work, thinking he cared about them. They were suckers, but they were better off than I was because I had spent twenty bucks on cab fare, each way, to see him in person and solicit his interest and respect. The only way he'd have interest in me was if I showed him my wallet. The only thing he respected was my wallet's contents.

I got back into a cab and took out another twenty dollar bill. I had learned the truth -- his office was a big, square trash dump for unsolicited scripts. It was a place where embryonic dreams went to die, in ten foot piles. That bit of knowledge cost me forty bucks, plus tip.

But I heard an interesting comment on the cab ride back to midtown Manhattan, one I'll never forget. A guy on a bike was cut off in gridlocked traffic by my cab driver. The bicyclist shouted to the cab driver, "Another asshole in a hurry to go nowhere!"

It was street poetry, authentic and truthful. Now I was going to visit more agents in New York City. The truth-telling portion of my trip, as far as my ears were concerned, was about to end.

I left the cab and knocked on an agent's basement door. He spoke to me through bars on his windows, like I was the Central Park Strangler. Others spoke tersely, nervously, via intercom systems. Basically, I freaked out the people I was trying to put at ease. Spontaneous visits weren't going to procure me an agent.

Children's Book Agents I Have Known

I found agents with the help of the Society of Children's Book Writers and Illustrators (SCBWI), the Children's Book Council (CBC) and the Association of Author's Representatives (AAR), among others. I sent out hundreds of queries at a time.

I had written more books for children, including the nonfiction books, "Out Of The Wilderness" and "Hot Peppers For Pop" (see project list) and added them to my expanding list. One agent who asked to read "Wilderness" said it was too long; another who requested the book said it was too short. At least they gave me some guidance.

One agent, on Broadway, asked to read my butterfly book. Another NYC agent asked to read "Hot Peppers For Pop." When the second agent sent me a contract a few days before the first one did, I asked the first agent to be patient; maybe work with me in the future. She said "OK."

I took a train to New York, feeling better about myself. I arrived early so I went into a department store, Daffy's, and bought a few colorful shirts. I met with the agent and found her to be extremely crotchety. She was in her late 70's. That's why she related to my Depression-era story.

"So, you think you can sell, 'Hot Peppers'? I asked cheerfully.

"How do I know if I can sell it?" she snapped. "I just know I like it! That's enough questions."

Are you sure you want an agent? Wouldn't you rather have a mean, crotchety, old woman snapping at you for no reason? In this case, I had both -- in one ancient, broken-down package.

We spent the remainder of our meeting talking about my new shirts. She liked the colors and suggested I dry-clean the pastels. I took notes. I learned enough to open a laundry service if the writing gig didn't work out.

This woman submitted my book to a handful of publishers in the next six months. I was forbidden from sending out any books on my own. She would have no control over my submissions if I did that. So, instead of me sending out six different books to a total of one hundred publishers, the agent submitted one book to exactly five publishers. After six months, we were done.

Agents, who complain incessantly about having their time wasted by writers, are often a waste of time for writers. It's true that publishers have more faith in books submitted by agents, as opposed to new writers. That doesn't mean agents always help writers sell books. They can slow down your marketing efforts, too.

I called the agent on Broadway and she agreed to represent my butterfly book (only that one book). I received a letter from her agency, declaring an interest in working with me. The letter read, "Congratulations. The verdit is in. We love your book."

"Verdit" -- what the hell was a "verdit?" Did they mean verdict? They couldn't spell verdict? This was a bad sign, a red flag and a tummy-tussler.

I signed up anyway.

I asked if I could visit their office to get acquainted. They reluctantly agreed. When I arrived, the secretary seemed to be dialing 9-1 ... ready to hit the next "1" if I got out of hand. They still didn't like me being there even though they had recruited me as a client!

I pitched more of my projects, hoping they would take on my body of work, not just one book. A few weeks later, they said they liked "A Leprechaun Named Levity" as well as "The Traveling Monarchs." I signed a contract for both. One sub-agent mentioned that "Levity" seemed a bit too long so I handed her two versions of the picture book in verse; one short (fourteen pages) and one long (twenty-eight pages).

Months passed and "Monarchs" did not sell. They were ready to send "Levity" out to publishers. One problem existed, however.

"'Levity' needs to be shortened," the sub-agent told me.

"Huh? It is shortened! I gave you two versions; one long and one short!"

I could' have added the phrase, "You dope!" but didn't.

The "verdit" was in: I didn't want to waste any more time with that agency.

Often, agents will speak at libraries or conferences in a town near your home. I went to a library in Doylestown, PA and noticed that the agent was sitting in front of an oil painting of Pearl S. Buck. In my query letter, I told her how good she looked, in the shadow of such a great woman as Ms. Buck. This agent loved the comparison! She wrote several paragraphs about what it meant to her to be compared, in any way, to Pearl S. Buck. Then she rejected my material.

The Agent / Writer Contract

In most cases, when you agree to work with an agent, you will have to sign a contract. In most of those cases, you will get nauseous reading it. The only contract that I've ever signed that was more one-sided against me was the one recently sent to my apartment by The Philadelphia Eagles, regarding my Stadium Builder's Fund. That contract prohibits me from doing anything besides paying them promptly.

Here is the good news. If you, or the agent, are unhappy with the relationship, either of you can write a letter of termination, which will take effect in ninety days. So, if you decide the agent is a hindrance -- and providing that he or she has not sold anything for you recently -- you can hit the "eject" button. Escape hatches are vital to all contracts and you will have one with any deal you sign with an agent.

You will give your agent the exclusive right to peddle one project for a year (sometimes two years). You will not be allowed to market that project without the agent's approval nor will you be allowed to market your other books/scripts. The agent may charge you for photocopying, long distance phone calls or overnight mailings. If the agent sells your book or script, he or she receives ten-fifteen percent commission.

The money derived from the sale of your project goes to your agent. Then, after the agent takes a cut, you get paid. The agent does not promise to work hard for you forever so you shouldn't promise to stay with him or her forever.

My mentor, writer A.J. (Jack) Langguth, has retained the same agent for decades. They seem to have a wonderful, hand-in-glove relationship; more like friends than partners. Jack has taught me about many aspects of life, especially those related to surviving a writing career. Yet I can't understand how he can be so darn satisfied with this one agent. I lie awake nights wondering what it would be like to have that kind of long-term, respectful relationship. It seems so unattainable to me. Maybe it's a war thing. (In the 1960's, Jack was a New York Times' reporter and Bureau Chief in Vietnam.) Or perhaps it's a freak of business nature.

It could be there are plenty of wonderful agents out there, and I just don't have the track record to allure them. I'd have to earn a ton of money and a trunk full of awards to get them to talk to me.

Why would I want to sign with a front-running agent like that anyway? I'd rather show loyalty toward an agent who believed in me when most agents wouldn't even return my SASE's. (That's why I just signed with novice agent David Freedman. Our contract appears earlier in this book.)

When a contract from an agent arrives in your mailbox, just sign it and hope for the best. You will be at the bottom of the agent's list of priorities. He or she won't spend a lot of time pushing your work. Recognize that fact and stay humble. Don't expect the agent to spread your project around to dozens of publishers and producers in the first week. Expect them to test your project with one or two buyers. This exercise will take up about five minutes of an agent's time, the maximum time they are willing to allot to a new writer.

Why You Need An Agent Or Attorney

I wanted to get my project list to HBO, a cable network that produces many stories for children. The company was listed in one of my reference books (Writer's Market) with an address and the name of the person to contact. However, they would not respond to a letter from me. Any proposal had to come from an agent or entertainment attorney.

I called my close friend, David Rudenstein, and told him, if anyone asked, he was an entertainment attorney. (He's actually a criminal lawyer.) I wrote a query letter to HBO, gave it to him to rewrite on his stationary, and asked him to send it out. Three months later, HBO sent me a form rejection letter (category two - "No Offense, But Get Lost").

If you want a realistic chance to propose your work to a company like HBO, you'd better have an agent.

Why Can't You Depend On Great Contacts?

This story is really depressing, but you should be able to handle it, especially since it didn't happen to you. It involves my children's story about Homing Pigeons.

Not many people appreciate the wild pigeons they see in the park, flying past their eyeballs. But Homing Pigeons, or Homers, who are descendants of the dove, are well-disciplined athletes and heroic animals. That's not my opinion; it has been documented. They have won medals for bravery in wartime.

Of course, I didn't know this when I read a newspaper article about Homers who had mysteriously disappeared during a race. The article explained how they rarely disappeared; they usually flew back to their coops no matter what the conditions, navigating through the Earth's magnetic fields in ways we could not understand.

My first thought was, "They time traveled! Those sunovaguns did it!"

I don't know why I thought that but wouldn't it translate into a good children's book?

"Time-traveling Homing Pigeons save lives during World War II!"

I set out to research my fictional, middle-grade book.

My Dad suggested I visit his cousin, who had a feed store near downtown Philadelphia. This cousin told me to visit a pigeon expert named Ben Garberman (more on him later in the book) and to contact the American Pigeon Racing Association.

The man at the APRA loved my idea for a nonfiction pamphlet on Homing Pigeons, aimed at their new members. (They had 50,000 members.) I sent him the first draft and he liked it a lot. He asked for rewrites, which I gave him. Then he asked for more rewrites, to appease the board of directors. I rewrote the pamphlet to please everyone on the board. I made plans with a graphic artist to produce thousands of these pamphlets, based on promises from the APRA that they would purchase them for their new members and include them in their information packets.

Then, the man I was dealing with at the APRA left the association. His replacement had never heard of me or my pamphlet and told me to get lost! I explained to her that I had worked on the rewrites, at her predecessors request, for over six months. Click.

An agent would have secured a deal for me before I did any of the rewrites. My "great contact" at the APRA turned out to be a depressing tease. Like my "Life After Death" book, however, I hope to sell the pigeon pamphlet to someone else, in the next decade or two.

Should You Send An Agent Money?

One agent asked me to pay him five-thousand dollars for a budget breakdown and his help in marketing my screenplay. He actually asked how much money I had in the bank, how much my wife earned per year and if I had any outside sources of income. (I was tempted to tell him, "No, except for that big hotel/casino I own on the Strip in Las Vegas.") I declined his kind offer to work together. Recently, I read a web article written by this same agent. He came across as the most helpful, open-minded, money-isn't-everything kind of guy you could imagine. I was laughing out loud at my computer. It's possible that he takes five grand from dozens of suckers or trust-fund kids each year, then works with two of them, trying to promote those two scripts. He's less of an agent and more of a trust-fund raider.

This agent did write something interesting, though. He reported that agents who work for big companies must bring in over a hundred thousand dollars in commissions each year just to pay their own expenses. If an agent like that has twenty clients and only earns fifty-thousand dollars in commissions, based on five-hundred thousand dollars in sales, he or she will probably get fired.

Another agent asked me for six-hundred dollars to market my "Life After Death" book to publishers of spiritual texts. I declined, even though she worked in a town called Joshua Tree and it sure sounded like a spiritual place.

Generally speaking, only unscrupulous agents ask for money to review the work of unknown writers. If you insist on spending money to promote your work, try some of the shortcuts to success described earlier in this book (evapeel@earthlink.net, THE INSIDER'S SYSTEM, etc.).

Attending Children's Books Conferences

Do you want to stand out in a crowd? One sure-fire way for any man to stand out is to show up at a children's book writing conference. For me, attending such a conference is like wandering into a N.O.W. meeting and mingling among smart, determined women. The ladies look at me like I'm an oddity; as if I made a wrong turn out of a Sci-Fi conference. They think it's sweet that I have an interest in children's books. I get many pats on the head.

A Writer's First Aid Kit

As a male writer trying to break into the Girls' Club, I'm a bit like female jockey Diane Crump trying to break into the Boys' Club. Happily, they do have restrooms for both genders at these conferences. Unlike a football stadium, the men's room is usually the less crowded place.

No matter your gender, these meetings are good for the soul. Everyone there is trying to write something to help children. There is little ego involved. Someone is trying to help kids deal with dyslexia, another writer is trying to help kids deal with grief, another is helping kids understand the importance of the natural world while another helps children overcome the threats of bullies. I've noticed a similar pattern in my children's book writing classes at Bucks County Community College. Everybody's intentions are beautiful. All the students want to help kids. That is not true in my TV/film writing classes. Many of those writers want to get rich quick and satisfy their egos.

That is why I consider writing children's books preferable to writing screenplays. Sensitive, unselfish people are drawn to the former. In many cases, selfish people are drawn to the latter.

To digress for a moment, I always felt that many aspiring screenwriters landed in Los Angeles from towns all over the world, where they were hated by everyone from the grocery clerks to the mayor. Yet, when they arrived in L.A., they expected to be loved by their new neighbors. Many were jerks and outcasts; they weren't labeled as such because no one bothered to get to know them.

"I've got a bad reputation here at home; I'll move to L.A. and develop a great reputation in a few weeks," seemed to be their approach. It didn't work. If people hated them in Des Moines or Dublin, they also hated them when they settled in California.

I attended a large children's book conference in New York City in February, 2002. If you were there, you would've had no trouble finding me in the crowd. I was the guy. I don't mean "The Guy," as in "The Man." I mean, I was the only man there. OK, I exaggerate slightly. I would guess the men were outnumbered 100-1.

There were no pitch sessions with publishers, editors or agents. I sat in the throng and took notes. What were the panel members seeking? Did they want picture books, middle-grade books; fiction or nonfiction? I jotted down anything that could make them laugh in the letter I would send. In a way, I was like talk show host, ready to remind them of something interesting they said and tack on a joke about it. If they said that they were inundated with books about turtles, for example, and never wanted to see another turtle story the rest of their lives, I wrote that I spoke to my attorney, who was a turtle, and he said he was offended but not surprised by the slanderous remarks.

I knew I would have an advantage if I made them smile and if I sent them books based on what they needed. They could reject me, but at least they would appreciate the fact that I wasn't wasting their time. I was someone who paid attention, a professional.

When I got home, I sent appropriate books to all the companies who seemed like a good fit for my stories. I put "NY Conference" on the outside label so they knew I had attended and was serious about marketing my work.

After that conference, at which I sold exactly zero books to publishers and acquired zero agents, I took some liberties. I located a list of speakers for the next conference and wrote to them, "At the last minute, I realized I couldn't attend the conference. If I had been there, I would have tried to get you to read my book, entitled ...." and so on.

That didn't get me published either, but I saved the one thousand dollars I would've spent in New York City. Lately, I don't keep up the façade that I had "planned to attend, then I was called away, but if I had been there ...." I just refer to the New York conference and mail them my books. If they love my work, will they really care that I faked my intention to attend a conference? No, they'll be happy I submitted to them.

Keep in mind that, as of November, 2003, there are one-hundred-sixty publishers or producers reading my work. A large percentage of them will never reply, despite my providing them with self-addressed stamped envelopes. So let's take off the gloves, shall we? Let's roll around in the dirt and admit that following all the rules doesn't make sense. Be clever, intuitive, sneaky and pester when you must … as long as you remember to submit to appropriate publishers.

Think back to the Random House story. The syntax-challenged assistant editor revealed that she wouldn't read any more of my work because I didn't have an agent. She wrote that she would read my work if it was sent after a conference.

What would you do?

1. You could tuck your tail between your legs and crawl away forever, like a rodent.

2. You could travel to a conference, hope the editor is a guest speaker and then submit something appropriate to her.

3. You could say that you attended the conference and then submit something appropriate to the editor, with a label on the outside of the envelope reading, "Conference-related."

4. You could forget about her because she showed you zero respect by making you wait ten months and writing you a letter that didn't make sense.

The only wrong answer is #1.

The Society of Children's Book Writers & Illustrators (contact SCBWI at www.scbwi.org or join for about sixty dollars) mailed me a brochure announcing its February, 2004 Mid-Year Conference. It is their fifth annual conference and takes place at The Roosevelt Hotel, Madison at 45th Street, in New York City.

The Roosevelt boasts about having the longest bar in Manhattan, but I thought it looked about as long as every other bar I'd seen in the city. A shot of good vodka costs almost ten dollars. I advise hanging out at the bar to meet industry professionals but staying sober.

Let me take you through the process of analyzing the SCBWI brochure and making marketing decisions.

First of all, the faculty consists of a half-dozen children's book authors. Forget about sending a book to them. They're your competition. Listen to them speak if you go to the conference. Next.

Executive editors from Hyperion Books for Children, Little, Brown & Co., Harcourt Inc., Scholastic, Dial Books and HarperCollins will be there. They are the ones you should try to contact. They will probably tell the audience to write "SCBWI Conference" on the outside of the envelope and send certain types of children's books. Some will say they want nonfiction, some will want only picture books.

Of the names on the conference faculty, I only recognize one editor who has rejected me in the past, Tara Weikum, at HarperCollins. (Every one of the companies has rejected me, but only one specific editor on the faculty has done it.) Let's go to my "PUBX" file and see what Ms. Weikum rejected and when she did so. Here it is, from my PUBX 5/02 file:

xRN, xWHALE, xGOATS: TARA WEIKUM, HARPERCOLLINS 3/22/02. XX 5/4/02. "TOO SHORT." (SCBWI NL)

Translation: I read about Tara in the SCBWI newsletter in May of 2002 and sent her three books, "Rabbit-Napper!", "Whale A'Salt" and "The Goats Who Ate Fire." Six weeks later, she rejected them, calling the books, "Too short."

Is she worth contacting again, with longer books? Probably. She didn't send a form rejection letter, which is a positive sign. I'll send her my project list.

The editors at the other five companies don't know me, although their predecessors have all rejected my books at one time or another.

What would you do if you were in my position?

Here's what I will do: I'll tell them I'm going to attend the SCBWI conference in February and I'm trying to get a head start by sending my books ahead of time. I will be careful not to re-send "Rabbit-Napper!", "Whale A'Salt" and "The Goats Who Ate Fire" to Tara, who has already rejected them as "too short."

What will I send these other editors? I'll look them all up in reference books with publisher listings and send appropriate materials.

HarperCollins claims they don't read books from unagented writers. Well, the good news is: it's not totally true. They've read many of my books. The bad news is: they've treated me like a leper for over a decade.

I do not want to deal with them anymore.

On the other hand, I can work around the minor problems; tell them they've read my work in the past, I'll be going to the SCBWI conference, I'm a published writer of children's books and stage plays.

Sometimes, being a SCBWI member is the only credential you need to get your work read!

Now, let's consider Scholastic Books. They only read query letters. Manuscripts will be viciously shredded and burned, then stomped on, or something like that. This executive editor, Kate Waters, has never rejected me. (If an assistant editor rejects your work, you will never know if the executive editor loves it. If you can somehow reach the boss, you will only have to please one person, not two or three.) I'll send a query to Ms. Waters with my children's book project list. A message in a bottle has a better chance of receiving a positive reply.

Little, Brown & Co. has rejected me twelve times. How much abuse can one writer take? I'll pass.

I'll take a chance and send Dial samples of my nonfiction books, "Out of the Wilderness," "Hot Peppers For Pop" and "Why Homing Pigeons Come Home." They may not ask to read the entire books ("no unsolicited submissions") but they claim they will read ten page samples. They may also give me a break because I've been published.

Harcourt takes nine months to send me form rejection letters. Forget 'em -- and this time I mean it.

Let's consider the final editor at Hyperion Books For Children. Looking through Ellen Shapiro's "Guide To Children's Books," I see that the company is owned by Disney Publishing Worldwide and publishes one-hundred-fifty books per year. Hmm. Do they publish first time authors? Yes, at a 5% clip - that's not bad. Do they accept unsolicited books from unagented authors? No - that's not good. They recently published, "No More Dead Dogs." I like that title. I'll give them a shot; tell them I'm attending the conference.

The final tally is: three editors will get query letters and project lists, Dial will get those two items plus some short, nonfiction samples, and the other two will "Get nothing and they'll like it!" I am quoting from the film, "Caddyshack" but in this case, I mean it quite literally. They'll be happy to have only 999 unknown writers contacting them today, instead of 1,000.

"Get anything in the slush pile today?" an editor will ask her assistant.

"I got nothing and I like it," she'll reply.

Here is the letter I sent out to Dial Books For Young Readers. It is similar to the others.

Sample Letter To Attending Editors

Donald Paul Rutberg

(Address, phone number) DPRinnet@aol.com

· USC screenwriting graduate (MFA)

· Published book author, comic book author, children's book author.

· Published journalist and playwright.

· Writer/Producer of children's TV shows and commercials.

· "Writer's First Aid Kit" published September, 2004; Pale Horse Publishing.

November 24, 2003

Ms. Rebecca Waugh

Dial BFYR

(address)

Dear Ms. Waugh:

I will be attending the SCBWI Mid-Year Conference in New York this coming February and thought I would get a head start on my marketing. I look forward to hearing you speak but would also appreciate a chance to submit my work to you for consideration.

I am enclosing my project list, along with short samples of middle grade nonfiction books. If you see a synopsis or sample that appeals to you, please let me know in the enclosed SASE and I will gladly send the complete book(s) right out.

Until me meet in February, please have a wonderful holiday season.

Best Regards,

Donald Paul Rutberg

Encl./juv proj, hp, wilderness, pign nf samples

Instant Feedback From Hyperion Books

Less than a month after I mailed my query letter and project list to Donna Bray at Hyperion, I received a reply. The Disney Company mailed me back a big envelope and supplied its own postage! This can be a very good sign. The editor can like your work so much that he or she doesn't want you to spend money on a SASE.

Once, an editor Federal Expressed my work back to me; it was waiting at the Fed Ex center in Bristol, PA. I was going on vacation the next day so I drove to Bristol to pick up this very important package. I had sent the editor my pigeon pamphlet, "Why Homing Pigeons Come Home." I reasoned that if she didn't like it, she would've simply returned it to me in the SASE I had provided. By sending it via Federal Express, that meant, quite possibly, she was sending me a contract!

After I ripped open the envelope, I read a lovely rejection letter. She enjoyed the book immensely but couldn't publish it for some vague reason. She didn't want me to spend money on SASE's whenever I submitted to her in the future. She included my original SASE in the package, so I could use it again. She was trying to save me money and show respect and gratitude for my submission.

I wanted to scream! Why did she get my hopes up so high if she knew she was going to disappoint me? Why ruin my vacation? It was August; didn't she know that my wife and I vacation in Saratoga Springs, NY, every August? (We go twice if I'm allowed to have my way.)

I've been rejected one thousand times by publishers. This was the first and only time that I was rejected via Federal Express. Usually, an editor won't spend a penny of the company's money to reject an unknown writer. This woman spent twelve dollars, and it made me sick.

Anyway, I was curious to see that Disney had spent eighty-three cents of its own money, plus the cost of a large envelope, to reply to my query. I opened the envelope and saw that the letter was signed by Kathryn E. Williams, Senior Legal Assistant at the Walt Disney Company.

First of all, what is a "Senior Legal Assistant"? How can an assistant be called "Senior"? A partner can be a senior partner; a District Attorney can be an assistant District Attorney but what the hell was she? I knew this was going to be a bad letter. Here it is, with my notes in italics:

Dear Mr. Rutberg:

Your recent submission was received by one of our Company's business units. However, while we appreciate your writing to us, our Company's policy prevents consideration of your submission. (*Why would they appreciate my going against company policy?*)

As a matter of long-standing policy, The Walt Disney Company does not accept unsolicited creative submissions.   (*Hyperion has considered my unsolicited work in the past.*)

Please understand that the policy's purpose is to prevent any confusion over the ownership of ideas that the Company is working on or considering.   (*This is a nice way of saying they think you will sue them if they publish a book similar to yours.*)

Compliance with this policy on unsolicited submissions is the Legal Department's responsibility, and that is why your submission was given to us for response. We are returning it to you without having reviewed it or retaining any copies of it in our files.   (*I guess they did a memory wipe on the person who opened the letter, like in the film, "Paycheck."*)

Thank you very much for your interest in the Walt Disney Company.

Sincerely,

Kathryn E. Williams

The reality is, if I attend the SCBWI Conference in New York, Donna Bray, of Hyperion (the lady who sent my query to the legal department) will tell me and everyone else there that it's OK to send her unsolicited queries and/or books. I guess sometimes you have to follow the rules. Darn.

Persisting With Hyperion Books For Children

The letter from a senior legal assistant was bothering me. Why would Hyperion read my unsolicited work and then, a few months later, refuse to read more work and instead send me a "Stay Away!" letter from high-priced attorneys? It was like a baseball umpire calling a pitch below my knees a ball, then, three innings later, calling the same pitch a strike. Where was the consistency?

Months later, after I had signed with agent David Freedman, I asked David to send two of my books to the same editor (Donna Bray) at Hyperion. She read the books and rejected them. But she also included a brochure to help David understand the company's needs. She was leaving the door open for him to send more of my books.

This can be considered a small victory. Ever hear the expression, "No salesman will visit your home"? Submitting through an agent was more like hearing, "No lawyer will send nasty, confusing letters to your mailbox."

More About A Children's Book Conference

I've been writing more than I've been marketing lately. I like it that way. I'd have to be crazy not to like it. Now that I have a screenplay agent in Los Angeles, perhaps I can talk him into submitting more of my children's books. (Update: I talked him into it but he required me to prepare the packages and buy the stamps. In April, 2004, I sent him a box with 15 bound copies of "Hot Peppers ..." and "Wilderness" in 15 stamped envelopes. My agent then wrote 15 letters and submitted the material to publishers.)That will make it incredibly easier to sell a book. My work will go into the good pile instead of the slush pile. The slush pile gets ignored about 99% of the time. The theory is, if the writer doesn't have an agent, his or her work can't be good.

I once heard how the children's book publishers review unsolicited, unagented material. Every third or fourth Friday, the staff has a meeting to discuss these books. No one wants to go to these staff meetings - it's Friday, for goodness sake. The bosses order pizzas and everyone talks about what they've read in the slush pile. If it weren't for those pizzas, there would be no mention of the unsolicited manuscripts. It would be as if they never existed, like they were not mailed at great expense but launched into a giant, galactic black hole. If you sell an unsolicited book to a major company, you owe much to Mario over at the pizza joint on East 23rd Street. (I don't know for sure if there's a Mario or a pizza parlor on East 23rd Street, but there has to be one within a block or two.)

I'm also thinking about Viking Children's Books. If Ann Rivers Gunton, whom you'll read about in the next chapter, goes ahead and publishes "The Goats Who Ate Fire," I will have access to publishers who never wanted to hear from me. If I have an agent and a current contract with a company like Viking, I won't have to scrounge around, begging editors to look at my work. I admit, however, that I'm a scrounger. I'm also a schmoozer. If I have to scrounge and schmooze the rest of my career, I can handle that.

Back to the SCBWI brochure. You can't contact other authors and we've already covered the editors. Who else will attend?

Agents! Rosemary Stimola, Scott Treimel and Melissa Turk have all rejected me within the past year. I won't bother them again. You, however, should try to impress them with your work. Don't tell them you know me.

A few of the faculty are public relations and promotional experts. They usually will work with published books and charge a fee. I sent my pigeon book, "Why Homing Pigeons Come Home" to Susan Raab a few years ago. She sent it right back to me.

Sara Rutenberg is an entertainment attorney. I like her name! It is very close to my last name. My grandmother was Sarah Rutberg. I don't think she can help me get published, though.

Debbie Hochman Turvey is the founder of an agency that sends authors out on public appearances. She will not want to deal with me until sales from this book, or others, reach the tens of thousands. By then, I probably won't need her services.

Have you noticed that virtually everyone related to this conference is female?

The conference begins on Saturday, February 7th, 2004, with registration, coffee and muffins. The following day, they will serve coffee and bagels. Why the discrepancy? Why is Saturday a muffin morning and Sunday a bagel bash? I must ask someone connected to SCBWI. If you email me, I will let you know what the real deal is, with regard to the muffin/bagel situation. I know there has to be a story there. My antennae are twitching.

On Saturday and Sunday, the editors will tell the attendees what they are hoping to publish. There are lectures/Workshops On Writing for appropriate age levels, marketing strategies, negotiating and other subjects of interest.

Then there is a live pitch session. This is something new for 2004.

Before you get too excited about the prospect of pitching your book ideas, one-on-one, to interested editors, let me relay to you the brochure's fine print:

"The live pitch session will be a continuation of the morning Editors/Art Directors Workshops (you choose to attend one workshop with an editor) so you will stay in your assigned workshop rooms. Here's how it works … For Writers: Attendees may write a two-to-three-line summary (synopsis) of their book idea. A Regional Advisor (sounds impressive) in each session will collect the pitches, select several at random, and read the ideas to the editor leading the workshop. The editor will then respond to the pitch."

Whoa! What the hell do they mean by "at random"? I'll tell you what they mean - they're suggesting you travel thousands of miles to hear, in all likelihood, an evaluation of someone else's story idea! That is a terrible way to hold a pitch session. Why don't they guarantee us five minutes alone with these six editors? (I'd look forward to meeting Donna Bray of Hyperion. I'd spend five minutes asking her why she dumped me on the legal department at Disney.) If they must charge more for the service, so be it. If I had five minutes to pitch to editors, I'm confident I could get half of them to request one or two of my books. At the Los Angeles screenplay pitch sessions, that's exactly what happened; fifty percent of the producers asked to read my work.

If you are just starting out, I recommend that you attend SCBWI conferences. There is also a conference scheduled for Los Angeles every summer and in different regions throughout the year, although regional conferences are on a smaller scale.

Finally, if you are a lonely man seeking a sensitive, creative woman, by all means, get yourself to the Roosevelt Hotel every February for the Mid-Year Conference! You'll have about two thousand wonderful ladies to choose from. Maybe one will agree to illustrate your children's book!

If you are a married man, try to concentrate on the speakers, not the two thousand excited women surrounding you. Better yet, bring your wife.

Gleaning Information About Publishers

The SCBWI (www.scbwi.org) publishes a newsletter that includes market news and interviews with publishers. The organization also sponsors conferences and getaways.

What I noticed from the November-December, 2003 issue of the SCBWI Bulletin:

- Agent Warning! The San Angelo, Texas police department is investigating the Janet Kay Literary Agency. (Submit to that agency at your own risk.)
- Congress wants to change the term of a copyright from the life of the creator plus seventy years to a straight fifty years from the creation of the work. Some members want to shorten the term to seven years from the time the work was created. (Ouch! It takes some writers seven years to mail out query letters.) To learn more about the Bill (H.R. 2601, the public domain enhancement act) go to http://news.com.com/2008-1082_3-1013830.html.
- The 32nd SCBWI Summer Conference, held in Los Angeles in August, 2003, attracted one thousand conferees.
- If you are an illustrator, check out a book on contracts called, "Business and Legal Forms for Illustrators" by Tad Crawford.
- The Bulletin includes a listing of upcoming regional children's book conferences and lectures. This promotes conferences in various U.S. cities as well as Workshops Held In Taiwan, Sweden, Greece And France.
- Needed subjects, requested by teachers, students, parents and librarians include biographies, the history of street racing, the history of bad teen behavior, multi-cultural role models, deep-sea vents (perhaps you are familiar with these), company-built towns across America (such as Hershey, PA and Pullman, IL).
- The Bulletin is packed with all kinds of publishing news and submission requirements. That is perhaps the most valuable, useable aspect of the newsletter.

Another helpful organization is the Children's Book Council. (www.cbcbooks.org).

I subscribe to two other newsletters: Children's Book Insider (www.write4kids.com) and Children's Book Writer. I recommend these publications to anyone who is ready to submit their books to children's book publishers.

Other periodicals include Publishers' Weekly (www.publishersWeekly.com) and The Horn Book.

Each month, I open up the envelopes and go to the market segment of the newsletters. I may find that a new editor at a big company is open to unsolicited nonfiction submissions. Or else I discover that an assistant editor who complimented my work at company Z is now the executive editor at company Y. I learn about which magazines are interested in stories about endangered animals and other useful information.

After I've finished marking up these newsletters, I make notes to submit to all logical candidates. I might try to submit to four or five of these publishers listed in each of the newsletters. When I add them to the SCBWI newsletter, I have a whole bunch of letters to write.

After I write the ten or so letters each month (sometimes it's more like twenty-five letters) I "pick the order." In other words, I make a list of which books I must print and bind in order to make my submissions. Some publishers only get project lists. Most get two-three books. So I need to produce about twenty books; for example, three "Levity," two "Monarch" and five "Hot Peppers."

I rush over to the old but trusty bureau in the living room and open the middle drawer. The drawer won't open. Why? It is crammed with children's books. (The middle drawer holds my children's books; the top drawer contains screenplays.)Very gently, I manage to open it and take out what I need. If I don't have five "Hot Peppers," for example, I print the rest, then put the books in binders. (These three-hole binders cost seventy-five cents a piece and have clear, plastic covers.)

I shove my letters and books into the #10 tyvec envelopes. Then I adhere the labels to the outside. Next, I place return labels on the other tyvec envelopes, fold them in half so they fit into the outgoing tyvec, and I'm ready to go to the post office.

At the post office, I have to weigh the envelopes, add the metered postage, then write down how many stamps I will have to buy for the SASE's. Yes, it is time consuming.

If I didn't subscribe to the newsletters, though, I wouldn't have any current information as to the needs of juvenile publishers.

Setbacks Can Be Your Friends

If I hadn't had so many horrific, unpleasantly surprising setbacks when I lived in L.A., my life, almost certainly, would have been less joyful. I would have never met my wife. I would have been away from my family, kept falling in love with the wrong women, grinding my teeth, fighting with partners and other messy things. Lately I have realized that all those setbacks actually helped me in the long run.

Because I was traveling in July, 2003, I couldn't interview for a university teaching job. That freed me up to travel to Los Angeles, attract an agent, and get my work into the hands of two dozen producers.

An editor who worked for a publisher in New Jersey, Troll Books, wanted to publish my Holocaust survival story, "Out of the Wilderness" in June, 2003. When she wrote to tell me how much she loved the story, she also explained that they were in Chapter 11 bankruptcy. I laughed out loud when I read the letter. It would be impossible to get any closer to a publishing contract without actually having one.

During my pitch sessions at the L.A. Expo in October, 2003, a producer from Twilight Pictures asked to read the "Wilderness" screenplay. (I had only written it as a book for teenagers so I sent them a three-page synopsis.) If they like it, I will adapt the book into a screenplay. If they choose to option the screenplay, I will be better off not having to deal with a financially-strapped publisher like Troll.

In November, 2003, I read that Troll had been absorbed by a publishing giant, Scholastic Books. So now all I have to do is hope that the woman who liked my book still has a job with the parent company, still has some say as to what gets published, still remembers my book and, after moving around, still knows how to contact me. I need four green lights. In all probability, one of those lights has turned red on me.

Put it this way: When I return from shopping or from the hockey court, I don't rush to my caller ID box and check out whether or not that editor called me while I was gone. I just hope the setback will turn out to be my friend.

The worries, the burdens, the doubts and the fear

Abate when the plane lands and loved ones appear.

Of course; relax!

When Bad Letters Are Good And Vice-Versa

Just like setbacks can help you, bad letters can be good things.

I have received letters that offer nothing but criticism. The publisher lectures me that he only works with picture books and I sent a middle-grade book. Or he only wants fiction and I sent nonfiction. Or he wants books with less than seven hundred words and I sent a book with twenty-five hundred. Or he wants single titles and I sent a series concept.

Somewhere in the letter, however, he tells me that if I send single title picture books, especially about animals, he will gladly read them. Often, I have to read the letters three times to realize the letter is an invitation to submit to a specific editor at a company that normally does not read unagented submissions.

Read your rejection letters carefully and repeatedly. (The form rejections can be tossed without reading more than five words.) If you see an opening, any opening, jump through it and try again with the company.

When you get a promotion at work, it can, on occasion, turn out badly, can't it? Well, sometimes an upbeat, complimentary letter is really instructing you to work for free. That's not exactly the deal of the millennium. If you want to write something for no guaranteed financial gain, write what you want, not what others want.

I once received what appeared to be a good letter from a publisher. After I read it a few times, I found myself cursing out loud. It was really a stinker.

The letter came from Bloodhorse Publications, which publishes a magazine and books for horse owners and horse lovers. Their magazine is mentioned in my screenplay, "The Jockettes," because, in 1969, Bloodhorse took a public stand in support of equal rights for female jockeys.

After a few letters back and forth, I sent the editor a fifty page screen treatment and asked if she would be interested in publishing a book, set in the late 1960's, about the original female jockeys. The editor wrote, "I am very interested in the subject matter and would be eager to read a nonfiction sample."

I had already sent her a nonfiction sample, in the form of a treatment. She knew where I was going with the story, what I would cover in the book. If she liked it half as much as she said she did, she could have easily given me an advance to start the book version. All she did was say, in effect, "If you research for another year, and then write a whole bunch of chapters on spec, we'll be glad to take a no-obligation look at your book."

That was a terribly back-handed expression of interest. They wanted to take a look but wanted to take zero chances. If the book turned out great, I was instructed to send it to them. After years of researching and writing, maybe they would've offered me one thousand dollars, if I gave them a couple of extensive rewrites. Who needed that kind of one-way interest? The letter was full of encouraging phrases and it meant simply, "We'll get behind the project only after it's a surefire money-maker."

I started to understand why Diane Crump's ex-husband, Don Divine, used to send his pit bulls after reporters and magazine editors. These people can be annoying. If they were any more annoying, they could pass as agents. (I haven't ridiculed agents for many pages and want to be consistent in that regard.)

Once, in October, 2003, I made a terrible mistake in a letter but that mistake could turn out to very fortunate for me.

I meant to send "Out of the Wilderness" to Ann Rivers Gunton, at Viking Children's Books. Ann had read "Hot Peppers For Pop" and rejected it with some encouraging words. So I sent her another nonfiction, middle-grade family story. It was the sensible thing to do.

On the same day, I sent a letter to Randi Rivers, of Charlesbridge Press. I asked her to review my books for younger readers, including, "The Goats Who Ate Fire."

I must have printed two labels to Viking, mixing up the names Anne Rivers Gunton and Randi Rivers. Ann Rivers Gunton received both of my packages.

A few weeks later, Ann wrote to tell me she thought "Goats" was "enticing and original." If I made a few changes, she could be interested in publishing it!

"Wait a minute," I said out loud, checking my notes. "I didn't send her that book."

I did send her the "Goats" book -- by mistake. In the process of sending out a thousand packages and query letters over the last few years (I have receipts to prove it) I made this one mistake. Go figure that it could actually help me get a book published with a giant company like Viking. (Penguin Putnam owns Viking).

By the way, make sure you keep track of your copying and Post Office expenses. It could help you at tax time if you manage to sell enough of your writing.

I don't recommend making mistakes on purpose, but this episode proves that it's better to be lucky than smart.

A guy asked his friend, "Would you rather be smart or lucky?"

The friend answers, "I'd choose to be lucky."

The first guy says, "You have to be smart to choose lucky."

The smartest person isn't always the most successful, in case you didn't know.

A man asks his friend, an old timer and an immigrant, "How did you do so well in your lifetime? You came to this country as a boy, you hardly spoke the language, you only went to the seventh grade, never learned to read or write that well; barely studied science or math …."

The old, wealthy immigrant said, "It was easy. I bought something for a dollar, and I sold it for ten dollars. As long as I made my ten percent, I was all right."

Setbacks, accidents, stupid luck … embrace them all. They are your friends.

A few months after I rewrote "Goats" for Viking, Ms. Gunton took the story to her executive board. The board thought my book, about a little kid who helps his herd of goats, was "too journalistic; not enough like a picture book."

Was I disappointed? You know I was. The editor at Viking genuinely liked the book. But if "Goats" wasn't appropriate for little kids, then what is? Trust me, it does not read like a farm journal or a college zoology textbook. It's about how little Luis takes his goats into the valley! Does that sound too mature for children?

OK, so her very nice letter, telling me how she liked my book, was really a bad event in my career because her co-workers said "No." I regrouped and sent Ms. Rivers a nice thank you note. While I was sending her the note, I thought I'd submit more books. This lead to more teeth-gnashing.

Penguin Putnam, Viking's parent, owns so many imprints that almost every book I submitted in the next package was "too similar to what we're already doing." The company publishes hundreds of children's books a year. They have every animal covered. They've published books on every schoolyard, every emotion, every star in the universe.

Think of a book subject. OK, here's the first thing that popped into my mind - winter. Penguin Putnam, in all likelihood, has published a children's book on early winter, mid-winter, late winter; snow, snow days, the winter solstice, ice, slush, shoveling, dogs lost in the snow while shoveling, sledding, sledding with dogs, etc. - in the past few years alone. Why even try again with these people?

Why? Because I had one of their editor's respect and attention. As long as Ms. Gunton would consider my books, I would be mailing them to her, cheerfully.

I sent her "Hangin' With Homeless Otis," the fictional version of my Otis story. (I have also written an older, nonfiction version.) I believe that I'm am one of the few people in the world who took the time to sit with a homeless man (once a week, for years) and get to know about him and his lifestyle. To me, it was a fascinating street education. I was exposed to the sadness of bigotry and mental illness. I also saw the beauty of human generosity. I laughed a lot with my buddy, Otis. When my girlfriend (now wife) approached us, Otis would hug her. That's how close we were to this intelligent, yet unstable street person.

So what did Ms. Gunton say about my "Otis" book? She called the title and the story "unintentionally belittling." Why in the world would I belittle Otis? I admired him. I wrote about his clear-cut strengths and weaknesses while we sat shoulder to shoulder on a downtown crate. Yet the editor, who liked my other work, thought I was tearing Otis down.

That was the final straw, right? You're thinking that was when I gave up on Viking. Uh-uh. I sent five more books to them recently. Here are my current notes about my dealings with Viking. I am not a naturally organized person but, when it comes to keeping track of submissions, I have no choice. I must be precise.

expect reply, try again. Elijah, bear, bf, rn, pignnf 4/16 to anne rivers gunton, viking books. Later?: whale, moses? Plutojuv?, supjuv?, Prev: xSf (too similar), xonion, xsquirrel (too similar), xsneeze, xotisfic (unintentionally belittling), xsatchbk (too similar) x'd 4/5 (3/1). Prev: she x'd goats, lev, ihs, sb, hp, life. xx 2/2: "goats too journalistic, not enough like a pic bk." Goats rr sent to anne rivers gunton, 10/28 as per her comments! On 1/21 she said she liked revision & brought it to ed meeting x'd1/31. thanku letr to anne 3/1. "thanks for going to bat for my goats!" try again! prev: xHP BK x'd 8/30/03, sent 5/6/03 at her request. Prev: x'd lifeintro, 1 pg nf proj x'd 5/5/03, orig snt 3/11/02! took 14 months to reply! "hp very interesting." prev: letr re goats rr soon 10/13. See pubs sep oct 03: prev: xlev, xihs, xsb x'd 10/9. prev: chaim bk 9/2. x'd 10/15. I accidentally sent her goats, lev, ihs, sb 9/2.all x'd.

In my letter to Ms. Gunton, I tried to convey the notion that my latest batch of books, including "Elijah's Back!" and "The Great Bear Affair," would not be similar to anything that Penguin Putnam had recently published. Here is an excerpt from that letter:

Dear Ms. Gunton:

I hope you will find time to consider the enclosed books. I'm enclosing a page of synopses to help familiarize you with the material. It's a safe bet that your company hasn't published anything similar to my stories about a time-traveling Biblical prophet or bear-hunting twins.

If they have recently released books about time-traveling Biblical prophets or bear-hunting twins, I may have to accept the fact that I'm not Viking material; that there is no Don Rutberg-Penguin Putnam partnership pending. I just hope they don't accuse me of unintentionally belittling Biblical prophets or bears.

I received a letter recently from a prestigious company in New York City, Abrams Books For Young Readers. This company published over one million copies of one book. They've been in business for a long, long time.

As you can tell from my notes below, they have rejected me on numerous occasions.

expect reply, life bk, Elijah, pignfc 4/27 to Ms. Abbey Barrett, Amulet books (Abrams bfyr). later: moses?, sb?, sup? Tix? Kenya? -- prev: xgoats, xwhale, xbear, xonion xx'd 4/23, sent 3/30 to Susan Van Metre, On 4/23, Abbey said unique real life events made for charming children's stories. But they need more excitement; need to grab reader's attention. Good story hook alone not enough. Prev: xrn, xbann (again), xbf xx'd 3/29. (sent 3/16/04 at her request after I sent her juvproj 1/14/04) Midgrades. from scbwi nl. prev: x6/25/03. xotisjuv, xpignpam, ?xbann??(yet she requested it later!), xsf, xsquirl, xihs, juvproj sent 2/19/03 to Susan Van Metre, harry n. abrams bfyr. mid gr, ya novels. also pic bks & nf. prev: xlev, xhp, xchaim, xjuvproj. x'd 2/6/03. (sent 1/9/03).

Their ongoing rejection letters, which, on the surface, seem terrible, are actually very good. No, I'm not crazy and I'll explain why. (Or, at least, if I am crazy, it's not because of Abrams BFYR.)

Reading from the bottom of my paragraph, Susan van Metre rejected my first batch of books (with a form letter) in February, 2003, four weeks after I sent them. That's a speedy reply. Two weeks later, I sent another batch. Ms. Van Metre took four months to send me her next form rejection. Seven months later, I tried again with my project list. That tactic worked -- despite the fact she had ignored my project list a year earlier. She asked me to send three books, including "Benjamin Banneker ... Did What?!" which she had read and rejected the year before. (I guess she hadn't read it very carefully.) She rejected all three in less than two weeks.

The very next day, I sent her some more books, along with the following letter:

Dear Ms. Van Metre:

Thank you for requesting my middle grade books last month and for your quick review.

The voice inside my head, which claims to be Robert Browning, suggests that my reach exceed my grasp and I stay undaunted by rejection.

"Submit some different books to that classy company on West 18th Street," the voice commands.

And so I'm enclosing a few of my favorites.

We both appreciate your consideration and look forward to your reply.

Best Regards,

Don Rutberg

Encl./goats, whale, bear, onion, sase

Although I had sent this letter and fresh batch of books to Ms. Van Metre, I was rejected, three weeks later, by her assistant, Abbey Barrett. Ms. Barrett wrote that, "Unique real life events made for charming children's stories. But they need more excitement; need to grab the reader's attention. A good story hook alone is not enough."

I tried again, sending more books to Ms. Barrett, along with this letter:

Dear Abbey:

Thank you for calling my books "charming" and for reviewing them so thoughtfully.

The voice inside my head, which claims to be Robert Browning, suggests that I remain undaunted by rejection.

"Submit some different books to that classy company on West 18th Street," the voice commands. "It's just a matter of time until you click."

(Did Browning use the word "click" or am I channeling a dead poet from the 1990's?)

I'm enclosing a few books that you may find more exciting and attention-grabbing than my most recently submitted stories. They are longer books, written for older children.

We all appreciate your consideration and look forward to your reply.

Best Regards,

Don Rutberg

Encl./Elijah, pignfic, life, sase

Viking and Abrams send me a steady stream of rejections. Still, I consider their letters good ones. They are working with me until I can provide them with a book they can use.

Now I'd like to tell you about a really bad rejection letter. (I've been saving this story.) This letter was stunningly irritating at first sight - before I even opened the envelope.

A few months ago, I received a rejection letter from Sky Magazine. The envelope was one of those peel-and-seal types; you know, there is a strip on a gluey surface and when you want to seal the envelope, you peel off the strip and press it down.

Well, someone at Sky Magazine, probably the same person who decided that my articles were not good enough for their pages, licked the paper strip! That's right, he or she slobbered all over the strip, not realizing that the strip was designed to be pulled off and pressed down. I think a baby monkey would have been able to figure out the peel-and-seal system. This magazine editor, however, did not understand how it worked. The saliva-stained envelope was opened when it returned to me. There was no way it could be sealed with the strip in place.

I am thinking about taking the envelope to a local lab for a DNA test. Who's saliva is on the envelope? (No one signed the letter.) Was it a combo-slobber from two people?

The slobber-not-seal affair begs more questions. Did the culprits lick everything they saw? Did they push when the sign on the door said "pull"? Did they try to put food in their ears?

If an editor can't figure out the peel-and-seal system, he or she doesn't deserve your story. He or she doesn't know right from wrong or good from bad. If that editor dismisses you … that's a good sign. If he or she thinks you're a great writer … that's very bad.

What About Children's Magazines?

In the children's book writing class I teach at Bucks County Community College, many beginning writers want to develop juvenile books when it's obvious they only have enough material for magazine articles. That's like trying to make one Klondike bar last for a month. It sort of ruins the fun.

Here are two examples.

A woman was writing about pioneering female journalists; Nellie Blye, Margaret B. White and others. Since I'm currently writing about pioneering female jockeys, I loved the idea. When she handed in sample chapters, she had only written a page on each woman. She hadn't found much information about these women's lives. She would've needed to write about the life stories of seventy female journalists to fill a book. She had only heard of ten.

Another student was writing about how dreams impacted the careers of famous writers and inventors. I had already known about Robert Louis Stevenson dreaming the ending of his famous "... Jekyll and Hyde" book. Other greats, like Albert Einstein, had also solved their problems subconsciously in dreams and went on to make shattering breakthroughs in science, art or other fields. One woman, Madam C.J. Walker, dreamt about the ingredients for a hair product. This solution, which prevented hair loss, made Ms. Walker the United States' first African-American millionairess.

The writer had only compiled a few of these stories, each a few pages long. She was writing a magazine article, not a book.

The children's magazine market is much easier to break into than the juvenile book market. After you sell a children's article, you can tell book publishers that you are published in your field. They will read your query letters with more interest.

I was able to adapt two of my children's books into stage plays and sell them to a children's magazine, called Plays Magazine. (Remember to retain the book rights if you do this.) Often, as in "Life After Death" and "Why Homing Pigeons Come Home," I will break down certain chapters of my book and try to sell the chapters as magazine articles. My cousin's Holocaust story and my Dad's baseball story were shortened and sold as articles -- or so I thought. The editor left the company and the deal fell through. For months, I waited to see if the magazine editors were going to live up to their word or try to steal my identity; it could've gone either way. As it turned out, they did neither and I told them to forget it.

My story about Homeless Otis is a nonfiction juvenile book, a fiction juvenile book and two nonfiction magazine articles, one for children, one for adults. That makes it a 4-1 marketing opportunity.

My shortest books of children's fiction (under two thousand words) are also targeted to children's magazines. Try sending query letters to book publishers and magazine editors. Take an objective look at the book you are writing and ask yourself: is this really a book or is it better suited for a children's magazine? Stories over fifty pages are probably book projects.

The age levels your stories are intended for must also be considered. We will discuss that important factor in the next chapter.

Writing For Appropriate Age Levels

When writing for adults, you may, on occasion, whip out a thesaurus to find fancy words for your stories. When you write for children, you must do the opposite. The perfect word may not be perfect for children. For example, when writing a picture book for children ages four-eight, don't use words like misanthropic and petulant to reveal a character trait of a grumpy neighbor.

When writing chapter books, you will have to find the sixth grade word for incorrigible or transient, for example. If this proves to be a hopeless or temporary task, then you're not cut out for writing children's books.

The fastest, cruelest way to kill your chances of selling a children's book, other than submitting a handwritten, unfocused query letter, is to write for an inappropriate age level. If you are serious about selling your children's book, whether it's about a mouse or a firehouse, it must be consistent in subject matter and vocabulary with the age of your readers.

Here are some categories and age levels:

- A board book must be for and about children four years old or younger. Often, they are about physical senses, sounds or natural images. Parents read board books to their kids.
- A picture book is written for children four-eight years old. It employs only one main character, who solves the problem him/herself. The main character changes in some way by the story's end.
- An easy reader book is written for six-nine year-olds. The main characters are better developed and often have humorous flaws. They solve the problem without help from adults.
- A chapter book is written for eight-eleven year-olds. The main characters' emotions are more apparent. They have a more complex set of character traits and stronger opinions about the world. They socialize in larger groups.
- A middle grade book is written for nine-thirteen year-olds. The main characters have clearer roles in societal groups. They care about issues beyond their immediate needs. Secondary characters may be introduced.
- A Young Adult (YA) book is written for thirteen-seventeen year-olds. The main characters are complex and are coming of age. They are aware of adult society and how they fit in (or don't fit in). They often rebel against society's rules.

Before you do anything, analyze your idea and decide on an age group. Children like to read about characters slightly older than themselves. So aim your story about a sixth grade bully at fourth or fifth graders. Don't create a bulky three-hundred page book or flimsy two-page book for these nine and ten year-olds. Get a feel for how children view the world at different ages. Ask questions of your kids or your friends' kids. Think like a child!

As a college senior, I took a class in language acquisition, never dreaming that it would help me in my career. (Taking the algebra course hasn't helped at all.) I had been accepted to graduate school and was traveling back and forth from Philadelphia to Los Angeles, making arrangements as to where I'd live. Who had time to study or write papers? All I needed were a couple of C's so I could graduate and move out West. The surf was up, dude (although, back in 1977, I think they said "man" instead of "dude").

For my term paper, I wanted to write about children at various ages and discover how quickly or slowly they acquired language. Would a six year old understand a certain word? Would a ten year old know that word? What were the factors involved?

This was a perfect assignment for a future children's book writer. Ascertaining the approximate vocabulary of all age levels, from six-sixteen, would make it easier for me to identify and cater to my target audience.

The distractions, however, were formidable. You see, there were all those graduation parties, end of summer parties and going away parties to attend. I needed to acquire more of a warm weather wardrobe. I had to pack up my stereo and hundreds of records. (I still have the records.) The car needed an oil change. Girlfriends needed goodbye kisses.

These last-minute details demanded much of my time and attention. Besides, all I needed were a couple of C's in those final courses, whatever they were. What were they? Oh, right, language acquisition and ... something else.

So, in addition to scientifically examining the language skills of children, ages six-sixteen, I sat and imagined what words I had learned at age six, seven, eight, etc.

"Did I know the word terrify at age six?" I asked myself.

"Nah, probably not. I think I knew it by age nine."

I do not recommend this type of "scientific" study -- combining solid research with a good imagination. I won't tell you about all the other hair-brained schemes I concocted as a college student because you'll be amused and may want to try them yourselves.

Warning! Do Not Try This In Your College Career!

I sound like Ted Kennedy, don't I?

(OK, I will relay some amusing college stories, later in this book, in an article called, "New Kid In Town.")

If you only imagine what kind of vocabulary your intended readers possess, you will still be on the right track. Although your words are properly targeted, you must develop age-appropriate themes. Don't scare little kids half to death (as the "Harry Potter" books did) and don't write down to kids in elementary, middle school or high school. Young people are more sophisticated (thanks to TV) than ever. They've seen terrorist attacks and wars and their favorite athletes stricken by AIDS. If MTV were available when I was a pre-teen, I would've grown up twice as quickly; maybe even traded in my goalie stick for drum sticks and been the subject of a "True Hollywood Story" by now (on MTV's sister station, VH1).

There is also something called a "Hi-Lo" book. This is aimed at older kids who read at a lower level. They're old enough to know about mature themes but can't read a book at that age level. So, you can write a book about school violence, for example, for fourteen year-olds, using a ten year-old child's vocabulary. That's a tricky maneuver; one I've never tried.

The more children's books that you write, the more sensitive you will become with regard to appropriate age levels. If you aren't sure that your story is aimed at the proper the age level, give your rough draft to friends who are raising young children. They will probably know if you've hit or missed your target audience.

I've been told that Alijandra Magilner's "Children's Writer's Word Book," published by Writer's Digest Books (ISBN # 0-89879-511-7) has lists of age-appropriate words. The book will give you a fifth-grade synonym for appropriate, for example, as well as other tips for word usage.

Remember that your characters, not your plot, drive the story. Everything in the plot must evolve from the character's specific situation. For example, a girl is an animal lover, so when she discovers an endangered animal ... or a boy loves sports, so when he decides to attend a baseball game.... Do not decide on the story's ending before creating the characters. Do not make your characters come across as predictable. Understand what makes them tick before writing the book.

Writing Children's Picture Books

Picture books are only a few pages long and are aimed at young readers, ages four-eight. Illustrations are vital and used throughout the books.

Here are some Warnings Regarding Picture Books.

If you utilize rhyme schemes, you had better make them smooth-sounding. Many writers fall in love with rhymes (probably because they loved reading rhyming books as children) but can not execute them. The verses come off as choppy and stuttered. This will ruin your chances of getting the book published, even if the story itself is charming and delightful.

I like to start with the chorus, the repeated verse. This may comprise one-third of your book. In "Levity," the chorus was:

"I don't take it seriously,"

He said to folks he met.

"You have highs and you have lows

But I have no regret.

What's so darn important, Tree?

Why take it so seriously?

Be the best that you can be

And say 'So What?' like me."

In another verse, when Levity addresses a vain ghost, I changed it slightly to:

"What's so darn important, Guy?

Looks can kill and looks can lie.

You know when you're looking good

So smile often, as you should."

You must be careful to avoid forced rhymes as well as gratuitously talking animals. You may think that talking animals are cute, but most publishers will disagree. It's not that they want to club your love-able, loquacious panda across the head. They just don't want to read about a sibling rivalry between two cocker spaniels, narrated by the spaniels' birth mother.

Beginning writers often over-employ talking animals. The overuse causes children's book publishers to blanch at the idea. In their minds, the odds of your submitting a terrific talking animal story are very low. Some publishers will tell you in their "tips" section of a reference book: "No talking animal stories!"

One of my students recently told me, "Animals talk! They can communicate. I don't care what publishers say."

Well, of course they talk. When I looked into the eyes of a cat who was kidnapping a baby rabbit, those eyes said to me, "You must know I'm a cat and this is what I do."

The sea lions at Fisherman's Wharf in San Francisco were telling each other, "Don't try to sit on my dock. This is my spot!"

The migrating butterflies told me, "We are tired from an all-day flight."

I admit that animals talk. Yet publishers want to "shush" them.

I've read this warning from a certain publisher, then gone to a book store and read a talking animal story published by that same company! So let me translate for you: they don't want talking animal stories from you, a new writer.

That said, if you feel compelled to write about a pair of talking zoo apes who break out of their cages and see for themselves how humans live in the "outside" world, as one of my students recently did, go ahead and write it. Be prepared to prove that your talking apes story is different from the 6,842 others that annoyed the editor no end.

When my wife and I moved into this apartment by the Delaware river, we were delighted to find wild geese, squirrels, ground hogs and other wild creatures running up trees and through open spaces. We were less delighted to learn that squirrels had moved into the open spaces in our walls!

To me, this was the genesis of my next children's book. To my wife, this was going to be genocide for a bunch of "Rats with bushy tails."

The squirrels kept outsmarting the squirrel-chasing handymen sent by our apartment managers. They laughed at barbed-wire and duct tape blockades and ignored peanut butter traps. They liked climbing on Vaseline-lined trees and may have thought they were in an amusement park. The rainspout was their stairway; branches were their swings. The young squirrels seemed to enjoy living in crawl spaces between our walls.

Every morning, at about five or six am, they would scurry around, as if they were getting ready for work. I imagined them cleaning up, getting dressed and reading the paper while preparing for a busy day of foraging.

My wife, however, was imagining them in cages on a firing range. The trouble was, even if we trapped them, the county would only accept twenty squirrels at a time and would charge us for each squirrel collected. It was obvious that, if we booted out twenty of the varmints, fifty other squirrels would be in our walls by daybreak.

Handymen eventually hack-sawed through our walls and enticed the little guys to come out and play. When the squirrels saw us staring at them, they wore expressions that conveyed their inner feelings.

"Hey, it's a party!"

They had absolutely no fear of humans. I believed they knew they were smarter than our handymen. When the squirrels were all out foraging one afternoon, the men managed to seal all the entrances.

Now, how was I going to write this story, which was titled, "What Time Do The Squirrels Go To Work?" I wanted to avoid talking animals, but I wanted to include the squirrels', "It's a party" attitude and clever antics.

I aimed the book at eight year olds and made the main character an animal-loving, ten year-old girl whose family had just moved into an apartment near the river and woods. Through this child, young readers could relate to the problem of animals infringing on human dwellings. I tried to make it an amusing story, a problem-solving story (which publishers prefer) and give the animals intelligence without turning them into talky cartoon characters. I let the animals win at the end. The squirrels, along with the geese and ground hog, are cuddled around the fireplace, like dogs or cats, part of the family.

Another animal, a racehorse named Onion, is the subject of one of my other picture books. Onion was a real racehorse, a stubby, average runner, who once defeated the great Secretariat. It was the biggest upset since a horse named Upset defeated the mighty Man O' War and coined a new word in the English language.

I wanted to impart to children that they shouldn't accept negativity; that they should reject the notion they are too small, too young, too slow, too anything. Hey, if Onion could beat the greatest horse of all time, they could rise up and do the unexpected, too.

I wrote most of it unrhymed, narrated by a fan or a child's history teacher, not the horse.

But I did include a chorus:

"I'M STRETCHING MY LEGS AND I'M PULLING AWAY

BECAUSE MY NAME IS ONION AND TODAY IS MY DAY!"

I believe the theme of never giving up is an important one for children. When you're told that you can't do something, work even harder to prove you can. Tell them, "MY NAME IS (WHATEVER YOUR NAME IS) AND TODAY IS MY DAY!"

This advice is also relevant for unknown writers.

Writing Board Books --"My First Sneeze"

There are songs that I sing in my head for no reason

And they're always in synch with my mood and the season.

Of course; relax!

When you write a board book, for children up to age four, you are writing for people who cannot read. Sounds funny, doesn't it? Actually, you're writing for Mommy and Daddy, who will read the book to their little ones and show them the pictures.

Board books deal with very basic themes. "War And Peace," for example, was not intended to be a board book. Think about issues which consume infants, like burping, grabbing a cat's tail, pulling out a blade of grass, throwing a rattle. If you like, see an age-regression therapist and learn what issues deeply affected you as an infant. If your biggest concern in those formative years was concocting a plan to get rid of your older brother, then you probably should not write board books. Take a stab at gothic horror stories. Or at least aim for the middle grades.

I decided that one of my most interesting experiences as an infant was probably my first sneeze. So I wrote about what it must have been like, sitting there, in my crib, feeling my nose explode.

The book is printed next in this text. I offer two pages; one with just the text and one with the text and proposed illustrations.

"My First Sneeze"

Light Shines Through.
I Can Do
Something New.

Ah-ah-choo!

Look Around.
Spin Around.
What's That Sound?

From The Trees,
Springtime Breeze --
My First Sneeze.

Ah-ah-choo!
That Makes Two.

"My First Sneeze"

(Proposed Illustration -- We See A Baby In A Crib Near An Open Window)

Light Shines Through.
I Can Do
Something New.
Ah-ah-choo!

Look Around.

(Proposed Illustration -- The Baby Looks Dazzled; Looks Around For Clues In All Directions)

Spin Around.

(Proposed Illustration -- The Baby Spins Around Like A Dog Chasing His Own Tail)

(Proposed Illustration -- The Baby Now Has A Different View Through The Open Window; He Sees And Hears Rustling Leaves)

What's That Sound?

From The Trees,
Springtime Breeze --
My First Sneeze.
Ah-ah-choo!
That Makes Two.

Common Mistakes To Avoid

One of my students wrote a board book for children in nontraditional families. Since there are millions of children in the U.S. who are raised by single parents, grandparents, same sex parents or other arrangements, I thought it was a fine idea.

The book was written for children up to two years old. It was one hundred words in length. The only problem was -- I couldn't understand it! There were so many characters in the hundred word book that I got lost. I kept thinking, "Who is that? What is her relationship to the child? Wait. That's a woman named Jo? Her partner is a woman named Louie? Jo and Louie are the parents. Or are they sisters?"

If you've written a board book that confuses adults, you've done something wrong.

Another student wrote about mouse siblings. When the owl swooped in to grab them for his next meal, one mouse went scampering to the right, another went angling to the right ....

"And what about the third mouse?" I asked.

"He stops right before the tree stump; sort of freezes there so the owl won't catch him."

The other students let out a nervous giggle.

"Then you've got one dead mouse!" I screamed. "If he just stands there, frozen, the owl will bite his little head off. The second part of your book will be about his funeral! What's the title of this book: "The Mouse Who Stopped Running"?

Maybe the sequels would be called, "The Fish Who Stopped Swimming" and "This Bird Won't Flap." Disaster stories worked well for Irwin Allen, but he did not produce films for children.

Another student wrote about the hard feelings between a black cat and a bulldog. I mean, this was like a Sicilian vendetta; totally inappropriate for young kids.

"What happens at the end?" I wondered.

The student laughed devilishly.

Finally, I asked him, "Is there a contract killing?"

The student got my point. He rewrote his children's story depicting circumstances in which the cat and dog learned to respect each other, despite their differences.

A common misconception about picture books and all children's books is that you must submit them with illustrations. This can do more harm than good. Why? Because publishers are already paying their staff illustrators. Why would they want to pay your artist, too?

Submitting just the text of a picture book or board book is preferable. If they want to publish your work, they'll hand over the text to their graphics department, which will whip up the illustrations. They will probably be grateful that they don't have to pay an outside artist. Or they may like your book but dislike your artist's work. Then you'll have to break the bad news to your partner. Who needs that aggravation?

However, if you think an artist has greatly improved the overall quality of your book; that he or she deserves half the credit and half the money when your book sells, go ahead and have your book illustrated. I did that with "Levity" and was happy with the outcome. While only one of the drawings was published alongside my "Levity" stage play in Plays Magazine, perhaps they will all be included in the published book version.

In some cases, a publisher will solicit illustrations. If one says, "Illustrations must accompany all books," then make sure you comply. Most publishers, however, prefer to receive text only.

Sample Contracts Between Writer And Artist

Make sure you have a letter agreement with your artist, indicating who owns the book rights, how you plan to proceed with submissions and other considerations. Samples of my contracts with artists are printed on the following pages.

The first contract was sent to Al Weisner, the artist who sketched my nationally distributed comic book, "SUPERFAN 1999." The second contract was sent to the proposed artist for my trademarked children's book series, "... Did What?!" but never signed.

The second book in that series, "Satchel Paige ... Did What?!" was published as a stage play by Plays Magazine but Plays supplied the only drawing that was used. I later hired the comic book artist to draw the cover page of "Benjamin Banneker ... Did What?!" The book is unpublished so far, and I have no obligation to use the same artist when it is published. The cover drawing, however, helped me get a trademark and could help me sell it next year.

Again, these contracts are meant to be guides, not ironclad legal documents. I've always believed that it's better to have a handshake agreement with someone you really trust than a signed contract with someone you don't know. I have entered into an agreement with the first woman jockey to ever win a thoroughbred horse race in North America. (My dealings with Diane Crump appear earlier in this book.) I knew going in that she was a kind, decent woman, motivated by forces other than money. Although we signed a letter agreement in May, 2003, I knew in my heart that I didn't really need one. The feeling of trust was better than knowing I had a signed contract with her.

Date

Donald Paul Rutberg

Artists' name & address

RE: "SUPERFAN 1999" COMIC BOOK -- LETTER AGREEMENT

Dear (Artist):

This agreement is being sent to you to solidify our working arrangement on "SUPERFAN 1999," a comic book, to be published in August, 1990. This agreement may be amended by mutual consent in writing at a later date.

We are equal co-owners in regard to the creation and publication of a "SUPERFAN 1999" comic book. Your fifty percent (50%) interest will be earned through your comic book art work. My fifty percent (50%) will be earned through my comic book writing. These obligations cannot be assigned. The rights to receive income relative to this agreement can be assigned.

At this time, this venture will be considered a co-proprietorship. Subsequent to the publication of the first issue of "SUPERFAN 1999", however, we both agree to create a corporation. We will each own fifty percent (50%) of non-transferable stock in this corporation, which must be established before the publication of the second issue of SUPERFAN 1999, should we decide to publish such an issue.

Although the first issue of "SUPERFAN 1999" will be published by (your company), "SUPERFAN 1999," once a corporation is formed by you and I, will be a totally separate entity from any and all other publications of (your company). All profits or losses created by the "SUPERFAN 1999" comic book that we publish together will be shared equally by us and cannot be affected by profits or losses created by other publications or entities of (your company).

Since our working arrangement concerns only the "SUPERFAN 1999" comic book, you have no rights to share monies I may earn in a SUPERFAN movie, novel or TV series/feature, all of which were written and registered/copyrighted by myself before you and I met. Any art work done in conjunction with the sale of a movie, novel or TV series/feature could include you, but that decision would be at the discretion of the producers or publishers. Should we both be sued and lose a law suit because of my story line, I will reimburse you for any legal expenses or claims against the co-proprietorship.

Starting January 1, 1990, all essential expenses pertaining to this project such as printing, production, marketing, distribution, art and computer supplies will be shared by you and I equally. All other agreed upon expenses will be shared equally. If agreement is not reached on any expense, one partner may pay that expense. Meetings to pay or repay monthly expenses will be held at reasonable intervals. If we agree on an expense, both of us must sign the check or checks. We will each have individual access to our published P.O. Box until January 31, 1991, even if our working arrangement has terminated.

Either co-owner may work on other projects during the course of this contract, but each of us will complete his work on this comic book within a reasonable period of time. If you are unable, due to illness or death, or unwilling to complete any issue(s) of the "SUPERFAN 1999" comic book during the course of this agreement, I have the right to replace you as the artist/co-owner. You are not entitled to receive any profits from such issues you are unable or unwilling to complete. You are entitled to half the net profits from the issue(s) you have completed. You may keep all original story pages from the comic book(s) that we publish together.

If the first issue of "SUPERFAN 1999" (August, 1990) does not attract an initial order from distributors of 1,500 comic books, then neither one of us has any obligation to continue working on future issues of "SUPERFAN 1999" and either one of us can terminate this agreement, by notice in writing to the other, at that time. "SUPERFAN 1999" may be published by another entity starting with the second issue, whether we have terminated our co-proprietorship in order to continue working together as a corporation or if we have simply terminated our co-proprietorship in order to end our working arrangement. All debts, including accounting debts, must be paid off no later than one month after any dissolution of co-proprietorship.

This agreement is valid until September 30, 1990, at which time either one of us can terminate, by notice in writing to the other, our working arrangement. During the course of this agreement, you and I will share equally in the comic book rights to "SUPERFAN 1999" and we will both continue to share comic book rights in any comic book we work on and publish together. If we choose to terminate or not renew this agreement, all future rights, including comic book rights, revert to me. If, after our working relationship has been terminated, I publish a "SUPERFAN 1999" comic book with another artist, I agree to give you ten percent (10%) of my net profits from the comic book starting October 1, 1990 and ending September 30, 1991. All unsold issues of any comic book we publish together will be divided equally between you and I.

We may extend the term of this agreement by mutual consent in writing. If there is a dispute between us, we each agree to designate a representative and those representatives must agree on a third party who will arbitrate our dispute. We both agree that the arbitrators decision will be binding.

If you consent to this agreement, please indicate your approval by signing below. I hope this will be the beginning of a long and fruitful working relationship between us.

Signed and Agreed by:

(Artist) _____

Donald Paul Rutberg _____

Date

Donald Paul Rutberg

Artist's name & address

RE: "DID WHAT?!" Book Series -- Letter Agreement

Dear (Artist):

This agreement is being sent to you to solidify our working arrangement on a series of trademarked books I've written called, "DID WHAT?!" I am retaining your services to illustrate these books. The first book in the series is called, "BENJAMIN BANNEKER ... DID WHAT?!"

For supplying the artwork on the cover and within the pages of the first five (5) "DID WHAT?!" books (not to exceed ten drawings per book or ten books per year), you will receive a $400 advance versus a 13% royalty of the net profits from the book(s). That is, you will receive four hundred dollars ($400) upon receipt of finished and approved artwork, then start to receive thirteen percent (13%) of the net profits only after your thirteen percent (13%) is equal to the amount of four hundred ($400). If thirteen percent (13%) of the net profits from the sale of this book(s) falls below four hundred dollars ($400), then you are not entitled to anything more than the original payment of four hundred dollars ($400) per book.

You agree to the terms of this agreement and to supply the artwork for the first ten (10) "DID WHAT?!" books. For books six through ten (6-10), all conditions will remain the same as stated in this letter, except you will receive a five hundred and twenty-five dollar ($525) advance versus a thirteen percent (13%) royalty of the net profits from the book(s). I am not obligated to use you as an artist after ten books have been published.

Your name will appear on the book(s) covers, although the size of the font used on the covers will be completely my decision.

You agree to allow me to promote your artwork in any way I deem suitable, including the use of web-sites and published advertisements.

Your interest will be earned through your art work. Your obligations can not be assigned. The rights to receive income relative to this agreement can be assigned.

Since our working arrangement concerns only the "DID WHAT?!" book(s), you have no rights to share monies I may earn in a "DID WHAT?!" movie or TV series/feature or any other medium. You recognize that the concept was trademarked and copyrighted by myself before you and I met.

You are not obligated to pay for any essential expenses pertaining to this project such as printing, pro-duction, marketing and distribution. You do agree to supply art work and appropriate computer layouts.

Either of us may work on other projects during the course of this contract but each of us will complete his work on this book(s) within a reasonable period of time. If you are unable, due to illness or death, to complete any book(s) during the course of this agreement, I have the right to replace you as the artist. You are not entitled to receive any monies from such book(s) you are unable or unwilling to complete. If, without good cause, you do not supply the required artwork for the first ten books, you agree to pay me five thousand dollars ($5,000).

You will be paid only for the books I decide to publish, ranging from one to ten books.

We may terminate this agreement, by notice in writing, at any time after the first ten books are published.

All rights to this series belong to me. All rights to the series format also belong to me.

This agreement may be amended by mutual consent in writing at a later date. We may extend the term of this agreement by mutual consent in writing. If there is a dispute between us, we each agree that the jurisdiction of any dispute will be in the city and county of Philadelphia, PA.

If you consent to this agreement, please indicate your approval by signing below. I hope this will be the beginning of a long and fruitful working relationship between us.

Signed and Agreed by, in the city and county of Philadelphia, PA, on (date):

(Artist) _____

Donald Paul Rutberg _____

Children's Middle Grade Fiction Book

Middle grade fiction is my favorite type of children's book. I know this because almost half of my children's books are written for this age group. I can joke with nine-thirteen year old kids, make fun of adults (we're not always right, you know) and teach them, in a fictional setting, about important issues like nature, homelessness, other cultures and astronomy. I try to entertain them while sneaking in a lot of information that will help them understand the world around them.

I bet some of you feel the same way. So let me tell you how I go about writing these middle grade books. Maybe it will help you get published.

The main group of middle grade fiction books is a series about children helping endangered animals during the kids' summer vacations. (I originally called the series, "Summer Help" but decided to just call it, "Endangered Animals Series.") One of these books, "Running through Kenya," has been published. The original, "The Traveling Monarchs," is still unpublished. The main characters in "Monarchs" and "Bed Time For Sloth Bears" are motivated to do something important before the summer ends. The summer, to me, has always been a time to recharge my batteries and make personal changes. The thought of a year-round school year terrifies me, although I mostly pick my own hours to teach at Rosemont College's MFA program and at Bucks County Community College and I haven't been a student since Jimmy Carter's brother was making headlines.

Personal experiences, like witnessing the butterfly migration, have motivated me to write many of these books. For example, I once walked out my front door and found myself in step with a neighborhood cat, who had a baby rabbit in her mouth. The cat was giving me a proud look, like, "Look what I caught. Pretty neat, huh?" and I was saying, "Stop! Rabbit-Napper!"

The cat didn't run away; she kept walking with me side-by-side. She didn't show any remorse. The baby rabbit, meanwhile, was terrified.

The cat with the mouthful of rabbit turned with me as I approached my car and gained eye contact. I swear I could read her mind: "You must know I'm a cat and this is what I do."

So I wrote "Rabbit-Napper!" about two children, a brother and a sister, who try to extricate the baby bunny from the ferocious feline. It's a problem-solving story, where the kids, not the adults, eventually solve the problem.

I had written a Young Adult novel about a girl and her horse (see "Technobred" treatment in Appendix "C") and had an idea for a middle grade book on a similar subject. In "Saving Seafood," the girl's horse runs away from home. She follows this rascal to Saratoga Springs, NY, the horse's birthplace, where she learns he wasn't the champion runner she thought he was. In fact, he never earned a dime on the race track, yet everybody loved this horse.

He was gentle with handicapped kids, calming to high-strung horses before a race; a great tour-giving horse, a museum horse and police horse. He had done everything people demanded of him and became a community-service legend. He was also smarter than many of the people who loved him. He knew how to take mints from people's pockets, open the gate to his stall with his teeth, turn on radios and other tricks. He wasn't successful in his racing career; he was just loveable.

Years later, I learned there actually was a loveable rascal like Seafood in Kentucky. When he died, people across the state cried. I wrote this story to let kids know that they needn't be fabulously successful to be mightily loved.

I've also written about children saving endangered whales, goats, wolf dogs, sloth bears and black bears. In the black bear story, twin cubs form a bond with twin boys on their father's bear hunting trip. The boys are the only ones who realize that Mama Bear is not dead, only unconscious in Dad's truck. They help Mama Bear survive so she can return to her frightened twin cubs.

Before writing, "Elijah's Back!" I read that the Biblical prophet, Elijah, never died. He was allegedly sucked up in a whirlwind, into a chariot of fire in the sky.

A wave of recognition swept over me.

"He was abducted by aliens!"

Hey, if pigeons could time travel and lawyers could be recruited by angels to work in heaven, then Biblical prophets could be abducted by aliens. (If you think these theories are incorrect, go ahead and prove it!)

So I wrote about the return of Elijah, centuries later, to modern day America. It was little bit like "The 2,000 Year Old Man" skit done decades earlier by Mel Brooks and Carl Reiner. I mean, if Elijah never died, why couldn't he come back to Earth? If he was sucked up in a whirlwind, what is the most likely explanation for his disappearance? He was transported into a spacecraft, right? It seemed like the best answer to me.

In this book, I was able to tell children the story of Elijah's life. He was quite a fanatic, known as G-d's warrior. If he could learn tolerance, anybody could.

All in all, I have received hundreds of rejection letters regarding these books. The number may be higher. Yet "Running Through Kenya" sold in one week. It went one-for-one, while the other middle grade fiction books, combined, have gone zero-for-five-hundred.

I am including "The Traveling Monarchs" in this book, in Appendix "E", as an example of a middle-grade fiction book.

Common Mistakes To Avoid

One of my best students was writing a middle grade dream story. His protagonists, brothers aged eleven and thirteen, had lost their mother. They escaped from their grief through lucid dreaming. They could actually meet in their lucid dreams and have adventures.

What kind of adventures? They' would meet up with characters from "The Wizard Of Oz," "Treasure Island" and other classic children's books.

Stop right there! Do you know how many beginning writers use characters from "The Wizard Of Oz" to tell their stories? Scrillions! If I were an editor and read a query letter explaining how the book borrows characters from that book, I'd tear up the letter.

Use your own characters! Can't you think up a villain like the wicked witch of the ... wherever. (The direction of her home always confused me.) Why not write about a wicked politician? That's hardly a stretch. Instead of the cowardly lion, create a surly warthog and team him up with his sullen cousin, the hippo. Don't use well-loved characters from books you read as children. Use your imagination!

Also in this dream story, the writer created many different situations, none of which featured the boys' late mother. I kept waiting for their mom to be introduced, but she never appeared.

It was a dream story. The kids could dream up any character in or out of this world, real or imagined, permanent or temporary. Anything! Don't you think that, in the subconscious minds of these two boys, their late mother's image was alive and vivid?

Don't be afraid to expose the inner feelings of your characters. One student actually expressed to me, "I thought we weren't supposed to dig too deeply into a character's personality." Rely on your instincts instead of trying to appeal to a publisher's current needs. Those needs will have changed by the time you write and submit that book.

Also, if you write about a frog that gets lost, make sure that your child characters, not adults, help return the frog to his home. Do not have the frog turn into a prince. That's been done.

Suppose You Can't Find A Good Premise?

Make believe you're writing a TV show or a screenplay or a novel. Develop a treatment, similar to the outlines described earlier in this book.

Start with a concept. Do you want to write about the environment, family or moral issues, sports, countries that you've visited or events that you've witnessed? One of my students took a trip to Europe and was locked inside her old hotel room. (The lock on the door broke.) The problem was, the bathroom was down the hall and she hadn't made a pit stop since she left the airport. So her husband climbed out the window, onto the street, at night, in a foreign city neither had previously visited, to find a locksmith or a hatchet. Oh, and they didn't speak the local language.

This was a unique situation for her to exploit in a book. It had an urgent problem which needed solving. I told her to change the woman in the story to a little girl; locked in a room by herself, frightened, with a full bladder. Editors could relate to the problem, as would all other humans. Plus, the story had plenty of inherent, unsophisticated comedy, which kids love.

Your characters in a children's fiction book can be based on yourself as a child, your own children or their friends. The story revolves around them, not adults. Your book should encourage children to act independently and solve problems on their own. These characters, as in any good story, should change in some way by story's end. Their predicament should teach them how to confront the challenges of childhood and build self-confidence. If they fail, they should emerge from the experience knowing that failure has the potential to be a great learning tool if it doesn't grind you down. (See the chapter, "Setbacks Can Be Our Friends.")

You can take historical characters or settings and create fictional stories based on them. Or take an exciting, well-known situation and throw your characters right into the mix. (Don't throw them into "The Wizard Of Oz" story. That was fiction, not real-life, although some of my students don't seem to get it.)

In my "... Did What?!" books, my characters, Bo and Hank, reenact what life was like after the Revolutionary War, during the Great Depression and during the space race. They impart historical information in a fictional setting. The setting is always a comfortable one; a walk to school, a baseball field, a cardboard spacecraft in a backyard.

Bo and Hank are typical kids who describe the lives of extraordinary heroes. Bo is always telling Hank what these heroes accomplished and Hank is always retorting, "He did what? He did not!"

Regarding the book, "Neil Armstrong ... Did What?!" I exchanged several letters with the first man to walk on the moon. He was and is a very private person and difficult to approach. When I wrote to him and asked if he would read my book about his career, as a favor to a fellow USC graduate, he agreed.

In that book, I mentioned his website, where children could write to him. I also mentioned how he took only a comb and a pack of lifesavers with him on his historic Apollo 11 voyage.

As it turned out, the website was run by others without his full support. He said my research was wrong; he did not bring a comb and lifesavers to the moon. Since the book was inaccurate, he could not lend his support to it. He understood it was historical fiction and I was free to write anything I wanted in a fictional context.

I offered to take out the segment about the comb and lifesavers. He wasn't interested. Astronauts, even retired ones, are tough guys. My research indicated he had quite a sense of humor, but he never showed that side of his personality to me. Guess it was a "moon thing" and I didn't understand, having never played golf on the moon's surface, with one-sixth the gravity of earth, nor collected tiny bits of the sun, as he had.

Are you skeptical about Armstrong having a sense of humor? My research unearthed (sorry) that, when he returned from the moon and was placed in quarantine, he toyed with the idea of painting his face with India ink, like he had "space spots" or some freaky, alien condition! Hey, the man rejected me, but I have to admit, that would've been funny. Of course, had he gone through with the prank, he would've been in quarantine until he was ninety. NASA honchos aren't known for their sense of humor, which is probably a good thing.

Still searching for a good children's book idea? Here's one from my "Projects To Write" file. (Any time I get an idea, I send it to this computer file.) It's called, "Tilt Town."

I was driving through a California town, on my way from Lake Tahoe, Nevada to San Francisco. My wife and her aunt and uncle were in the car with me. I noticed that the trees, bushes and flowers were all tilted to one side.

"The wind blows from one direction," Uncle Irving said. "Like crazy. It's because of the mountain passes."

"Are the buildings tilted, too?" I wondered. "The school buses? The people?"

I was blown away by an idea about a child who solves the town's tilting problem by making a deal with people who lived on the other side of the valley, who were tilted the other way.

I read that there were hundreds of stray cats living in Veteran's Stadium in Philadelphia. By the time you read this, the "Vet" will have been demolished to make room for more parking lots. (It has been obsolete since Philadelphia built two new stadiums.) What will become of those cats? Who will remove them from the stadium to save their lives? How will they get them to leave?

Why are ladybugs considered lucky? Why is it that we swat flies and murder spiders but, when we see a ladybug, we smile and say, "Oh, look. It's a cute, lucky, little ladybug. Don't hurt her."

Your mind should work in similar, quirky ways. When you get an idea, jot down a sentence or two and wait for the idea to develop subconsciously. A few months later, like magic, the story will be better focused in your head, although you haven't given it any conscious thought.

Once you have your premise for a picture book, think about the characters in your story. Who is your hero and your villain? What motivates them to act? Where does the story take them and how does the action change them? Break it all down into three acts and, when you're comfortable with the structure, start writing.

If you're still unable to write, go to the library or book store and read children's books on similar subjects. If you can't find anything similar to your story, that could mean you have a unique idea … or a story that nobody wants to read. Most probably, it means that publishers don't yet know if the idea is worth publishing and they are not willing, as usual, to take any chances.

Final Thoughts On Children's Fiction

How will you know if your story is on the right track?

Well, when I wrote the bear-hunting story, I attended a trade show for hunters. Everyone there owned a truck and a gun and wasn't afraid to use either to kill animals or anti-gun activists. I was a sheep at a wolves' convention, as much out of step with my surroundings as Hunter S. Thompson was at a D.E.A. convention.

I thought to myself, "This is perfect."

I was able to see and feel the joy of bear hunters as they scurried around, buying tree stands and holsters. I shopped for camouflage clothes, patted stuffed elk heads; watched videos where hunters shot arrows at terrorized elk. The hunters gathered around the dying animals and posed for pictures, like they had captured the world's worst terrorist or something. Hunters explained how they did it, why they did it; why it was good for the environment.

As I watched an elk scream in pain or a bear belt out his death shriek, I knew that, while hunting may be good for the environment, it was not good for the animals' health. No way.

Bear hunting has been described as ninety-nine percent boredom and one percent pure terror. Hunters live for that one percent terror.

After attending the trade show, escorted by my friend, Stuart, who told everyone I was "OK to talk to," I was able to write a balanced story about bear hunting. I didn't know I was on the right track until later.

In "The Great Bear Affair," a grandfather (based on my friend, Stuart) takes his twelve year-old twin grandsons on a hunting trip to Maine. The twins are horrified when they see Mama Bear shot and tossed into the back of a truck, especially when they notice that Mama Bear is being followed by her twin cubs. (I learned that a Mama Bear will often send her cubs into dangerous areas first, to protect herself.)

About six months after I wrote the book about Stuart and his fictional twin grandsons, he told me that his daughter was pregnant -- with twins! She later delivered twin boys. That was how I knew I was on the right track.

As mentioned earlier, my book about a loveable rascal of a race horse was already written when I read about a horse who did all the things my fictional horse did in the story.

In my "Our Dad, Superfan" children's book, adapted from my comic book and screenplay, many of my predictions about a futuristic sports society have come true.

As far as my Young Adult book, "Technobred," is concerned, everybody seems to be writing cloning stories these days. In 2003, scientists were finally able to clone a horse. I wrote my book about a cloned race horse in 1982!

Being on the right track is a good omen. Being lucky is preferable. Try to be both and then submit your books with precise timing. Don't be discouraged if you are twenty years ahead of your time because in twenty years, you'll be first in line to sell a "hot" property.

Writing/Researching Children's Nonfiction

After receiving a spec assignment to write "Life After Death," I read every book I could on the subject. These books were written for adults, which was great because I would be writing for a different age group -- teenagers.

Why aim for teenagers and not younger kids? Because I didn't think a story about a man lying on a gurney in the morgue, blowing on a sheet to show he was still alive, was really a picture book. Similarly, I didn't feel that the tale of a man who claimed he died, was barbequed and basted by hungry devils, then saved by Jesus and returned to Earth, was well-suited for middle grade readers. Teenagers would think those stories, among others, were neat. Teenagers could understand the concept of loving their enemies; younger children (and most adults, for that matter) could not.

I proceeded to take notes from all the books in my possession on this subject. Many books were about reincarnation. Some were about Near Death Experiences and life in heaven. (According to a Gallup Poll, among those who believed in the afterlife, almost no one thought they'd be sent to hell. Being a student of human nature, I found that point comical. In my screenplay/novel about the only lawyer in heaven, "When Angels Speak ..." the devil's boss mentions the results of that poll and laughs hysterically.)

Other chapters in my book were about contact with the dead (ghosts, mediums and others) religion versus science, pro versus con ... the chapters were well-defined, all related to my main theme. When I found an interesting story about mediums, for example, I sent the tidbit to the "Mediums" chapter. A good Near Death Experience tale went to the NDE chapter. A detailed report on what heaven looks like (it's a crystal city; always dusk and seventy-eight degrees) went to the "Life in Heaven" chapter.

When I studied my notes, I estimated that each chapter was about fifteen pages long. I expanded my notes into sections within each chapter (as I did while prepping this book) carefully keeping track of where the information came from, and wrote a six-chapter, one hundred page book.

When publishers reject this book, they tell me how well-organized it is. No one repeats the annoying phrase I heard from the California publisher who asked me to write the book on spec: "This is too interesting for us to publish."

After I finished "Life After Death," I realized what I had to do. I took much of the information and weaved it into my screenplay about the only lawyer in heaven. Despite the fact that "When Angels Speak ..." was a fictional movie script and a comedy, I improved it dramatically by adding details from the books I had read and the one I had written.

At one point in the script, Dominic, the messenger who delivers the bad news to Charley, sees that the lawyer doesn't want to accept reality.

Dominic asks Charley, "See any beautiful gardens, with flowers dancing in the breeze, like they've got an intelligence all their own?"

"No," Charley answers.

"See any of your favorite deceased relatives, dressed in shimmering robes, composed of tiny diamonds?"

"Uh-uh."

"Then ya ain't in heaven!"

I was able to write this scene in the screenplay and novel because of the research I had done for my nonfiction book.

Whether you are writing a children's book, screenplay, whatever; structure is the key element to success.

Homing Pigeons -- Who Are They, Really?

No, I didn't say to myself, "Son, write a book on time-traveling pigeons." It went nothing like that. If it had, I wouldn't have told anyone, including you, about it; with the possible exception of the psychiatrist I would've been obliged to consult.

Like many of my projects, "Why Homing Pigeons Come Home" was sparked by a newspaper article. The more I read about Homing Pigeons, who were lost in a magnetic storm, the more intrigued I became. They rarely got lost? They remembered every landmark they ever saw? I couldn't do those things. They were given medals during World War II for saving the lives of hundreds of soldiers? Huh?

It was time to research. I started at my cousin's feed store downtown. He told me about Homing Pigeons and told me to talk to his friend, Ben Garberman, if I wanted to learn more.

"How long has Ben been raising Homers?" I asked my seventy-five year-old cousin.

"About seventy years," I was told. "The only years when Ben didn't raise pigeons were in the early 1940's when he was in Auschwitz."

I called Ben Garberman, the "Pigeon Man." He turned me away.

"Vat do I know about peegins?" he asked.

"Uh, more than I do," I answered.

He told me he wasn't feeling well, and I should call back in the spring.

When I called back, he was feeling better and invited me to his home in southern New Jersey. In his backyard, I was introduced to hundreds of beautiful birds.

Have you ever walked into a dog owner's home, where the dogs inspect you; sniff you, run to you or from you? It was exactly the same way with these pigeons. They flew from perch to perch, squawking, landing on each other's heads and feet.

"They don't recognize you," Ben explained. "Strangers make them nervous."

He told me stories about ancient pigeons, war-time pigeons, famous pigeons and his pigeons. He revealed that, in the early 20th Century, it was common for Europeans, emigrating to the U.S., to bring pigeons with them. People would buy houses near rivers because the birds liked to navigate over landmarks like rivers.

He explained that they are one-way fliers. You take them to another location and they circle around, sense the magnetic flow, and head home.

Why do they always come home? So they can be reunited with their loved ones. That's why they are considered a reliable way to send messages to their home base. Before modern devices like the radio were invented, pigeons were the only reliable carriers of information. They were FedEx without the trucks, UPS without the Brown (unless they happened to be brown). They brought results home from the very first Olympic Games! Their ancestors, doves, brought back sticks to Noah on his ark, proving that land was nearby and the flood waters had receded. How could you not love these feathered helpers?

Although Homing Pigeons descended from the dove, a symbol of peace, they fight viciously amongst themselves. I loved the duality. They are athletes who race through the air in competitions like horses race on the track. I wanted to take one home to show to my wife.

As it turned out, I brought my wife to Ben's home a week later. She was going to help me take photos of the birds in flight during a training race. When we got inside one of Ben's trailers, pigeons started scooting around in the air, near my wife's head. She said something about not wanting to get her eyes clawed and vacated the trailer. It was up to me to photograph these graceful athletes in very tight quarters.

"Come on, little birdies," I cooed. "Fly into my camera lens. Land on my head, my ears; just give me a good angle. A nice close-up. Look heroic. Flap over here. Show me the medals you've won."

I was excited. Not only was I surrounded by nature, I quickly realized that I didn't have to hire an artist. I was the artist (photographer). I didn't have to write a contract or split the proceeds with a temperamental partner.

My full-time partner, my bird-phobic wife, stayed in the car with the windows closed, wearing oversized yellow sunglasses that looked like goggles -- sort of a cross between Jamie Lee Curtis and Elton John.

Again, I broke the research into logical chapters. Pigeon evolution, history, heroics; who were they, really? They were not the annoying, brazen, wild pigeons who congregate on downtown street corners, eating stones on ten degree days. (Their digestive systems actually need gravel; it's like us eating a salad.) Much like butterflies, they were navigational geniuses. They were bred by humans for speed and endurance, like race horses. A fast Homer can sell for ten thousand dollars. I was tempted to try to breed a few myself. I wondered what a lightening-quick butterfly would bring on the open market.

After the Pigeon Racing Association replaced its president and withdrew its offer to buy thousands of my pigeon pamphlets, I made a few samples, with the help of a graphic artist, and tried to sell them on my own. The last nonfiction book (published in the U.S.) that I could find about Homing Pigeons was written in 1949!

Could it be that American children would be interested in reading about these brave, athletic birds? There are currently tens of thousands of pigeon fan club members in the U.S. Could children in Europe, where pigeon racing is as popular as baseball is here, be the target audience for my pamphlet?

I had no clear idea how to sell the pamphlet. I just felt I should write it.

The nonfiction book, "Why Homing Pigeons Come Home," appears later in this book, in Appendix "F".

Introducing "Homeless Otis"

What do children really know about the issue of homelessness? I guessed very little, so I wrote about my experiences with a crafty homeless man, named Otis.

A sample from my nonfiction book, "Hangin' With Homeless Otis," is printed below.

"HANGIN' WITH HOMELESS OTIS"

(Nonfiction for ages 11-15)

LIFE ON THE STREET

Otis is a homeless man who lives on the sidewalk of a Philadelphia street.

On most days, Otis sits on a blue milk crate in front of a convenience store and watches the people. He encourages office workers and tourists to put spare change into his plastic cup. He doesn't call this begging for money or panhandling. He calls it, "developing relationships."

Otis has a great vocabulary. When people walk by, he'll say to them, "You are ideally situated for today's endeavors," which means they are perfectly prepared for the day ahead. Or he'll say, "You dignify us all," which means they are looking elegant and setting a fine example for the rest of us.

He'll kiss a well-dressed woman's hand one minute, then turn abruptly to salute a marine in uniform.

Otis collects coins from generous people who enjoy his compliments and feel sorry for him. He trades his dimes and nickels for quarters, then sells the quarters to strangers who park their cars at curb side meters. He always makes money on the deal and uses this approach to build a customer base. "Would you be kind enough to sell me four quarters for ten dimes?" is a great icebreaker.

He puts some of the quarters in parking meters so his friends won't get parking tickets. He is always arguing with the meter maid, who has little to do all day because the meters are full.

Sometimes, a grateful person will repay Otis for his meter-watching by buying him a cup of coffee in the convenience store. Otis will only drink the coffee if it is loaded with sugar. (He prefers eight packets.) He is always arguing with the store manager, who refuses to let him inside.

The store manager and meter maid both think Otis is up to no good. Otis says they don't like him because of the way he looks -- he is a shabbily dressed, tall, lean, black man with bulging bug-eyes and rattling false teeth. Otis says he is always getting in trouble because of "mistaken identity."

"I was there but I didn't do it," is one of Otis' favorite sayings.

A shiny van stops near his crate and a city official steps out to talk to him. The official is a young, well-dressed black woman who clearly cares about Otis.

When he sees her, Otis hides everything of value that he owns. He warns her not to "castigate or denigrate" (criticize) him.

But she is only here to offer him a free ride from his regular spot on the crate to a homeless shelter, and back again. All he has to do in return is talk to her about getting a J-O-B.

"Can I sit up front in the shiny van?" Otis asks.

"Free ride in the captain's chair," she replies.

"Nothing is ever free," Otis says. "Especially from you."

"How about this spot of yours; isn't it rent-free?"

"Because there's no renting the outdoors."

"But it's dangerous. Look, you're not some drug abuser or drunk or psychotic who can't cope with the world," the woman tells him. "Maybe you're a little unbalanced, but if you take your medicine, you're capable of working and living on your own."

He tells her, "I will take your proposal to heart, most assuredly, although I must pass on it at this time."

In other words, "No thanks. The shelter is too dangerous."

"Why do you always turn me down?"

"Too many rules at your shelter. Too many rules I don't like."

Homeless shelters offer meals and beds to the needy. Otis insists that other homeless men steal from him and hit him whenever he sleeps there, so he stays away from shelters, even on the coldest winter nights.

"Besides, I'd be a feather in your cap," he tells the city official.

That means she will be given extra credit, a gold star, for rounding up Otis and bringing him into the shelter. Her bosses and co-workers will be impressed, knowing that Otis does not like to be told what to do, where to go or when to leave. If anyone takes him for granted or forces him to do something, he'll do the opposite. For example, if someone tells Otis that he has to stay in the United States, he'll probably take the next bus to Mexico.

Of all the important things we are taught to do as children -- go to college, get a job, get married, have children and buy a house -- Otis has done none of them! Surviving without any of these things, especially a job and a place to live, is quite remarkable.

It's as if he's living in society without being a part of it. In some ways, he's invisible. The rules of our government don't apply to him, except when they work in his favor; for example, when he collects his welfare check or food stamps. He makes a profit buying and selling food stamps. These are some of the reasons why he chooses to live on the street.

He tells the lady in the shiny van that, if she sweetens the offer, he'll think about going with her to the shelter. She tells him not to freeze to death while he's thinking about it.

"Stubborn fool. I don't know why you stay. Must be a death wish," she mumbles as she drives away.

The owner of the restaurant next door to the convenience store also offers Otis a J-O-B. Otis smiles and tells the man, "No thanks."

The truth is, Otis makes more money sitting on his crate with a plastic cup than he would make working in the restaurant or with the van lady.

(End nonfiction sample)

Writing A Story As Fiction And Nonfiction

I had originally planned to write both the Homing Pigeon story and the Otis story as works of fiction, but after interviewing Ben in the coop and Otis on the crate, I knew I had to write nonfiction books first, while they were fresh in my mind. When they were finished, I told myself, "Son, it's time to adapt these stories into fiction, as originally planned."

When you refer to yourself as "Son," it is time to get serious. Far be it from me to ignore my higher spirit.

The research for the Homing Pigeon fiction book was already done. I took what I had learned from Ben and other sources and applied it to this new book.

In this story, a child with a disability decides to become a trainer of Homing Pigeons. He is motivated by his desire to please his grandfather (a fictionalized version of Ben) and compete in a sport because his bad foot won't allow him to compete in more popular sports.

When the grandfather's beloved pigeons disappear in a magnetic storm, the boy feels like he did something wrong. What if his crazy grandfather is right when he tells everyone in town that the pigeons time-traveled to save GI's in 1943 Italy?

The book is about a boy who defends his grandfather's wild ideas. The boy is the real hero; not the grandfather or the pigeons.

With Otis, I wanted to make the main character, the person who is drawn into Otis' world, a ten-year-old-boy, not an adult. I knew that if I were a child and I told my parents about a new friend I had made, a homeless man, they would have locked me in my room.

That's exactly the problem my main character faces in this story. His instincts and one-on-one experiences with Otis tell him that it's OK to have this new friend but society tells him that it's wrong. What does a child do when his gut tells him one thing and figures of authority tell him another? While respecting your elders is usually a good thing, it isn't always the right thing.

I attended a party in the late 1970's and was amazed to find the sixty year old host barbequing ribs on outdoor grills at three am and indulging in nitrous oxide, called "whippets." Inhaling this gas, used primarily by dentists, made him high and happy, ready for another rib.

I told him, "I heard this stuff kills brain cells and should only be administered by a doctor or dentist."

He turned to me and said, "Respect your elders."

This being the 1970's, I replied, "Nixon's my elder."

I'm sure he considered me a buzz-kill or appetite suppressor but I knew that following his lead, showing respect for my self-destructive elders, was the dumbest thing I could have done (although I did enjoy a few ribs).

My Otis fiction book almost didn't get written because my agent in 1992 advised against writing it, claiming it was, "Too mature for kids." I'm glad I ignored her. (That was the same agent who said, "The verdit (sic) is in.") In the book, the child is told by adults to avoid Otis, a kind, generous, protective, homeless man. It is the popular opinion of well-intentioned adults ... but it is wrong.

Often, a publisher will seem like a perfect match for your story, but the company publishes only fiction or only nonfiction. If you write a story both ways, your problem will be solved and you'll have a book to submit.

Before I wrote Otis both ways, I was limited to nonfiction book publishers who wanted books on social issues, like homelessness. I couldn't submit my Otis story to publishers of fiction/social issues.

The same principle held true with my pigeon story. It's like covering both red and black on the roulette wheel. If someone wanted a nature book, fiction or nonfiction, I could send them a pigeon book.

Usually, the nonfiction versions are longer than the fiction. Also, I believe the nonfiction books are easier to sell because there is always a need for information. So it's a good idea to write the nonfiction version first.

A sample of my fiction book about Otis, for younger readers, is printed below.

Hangin' With Homeless Otis

(Fiction for ages 8-10)

Chuck had just turned ten and was finally old enough to go to work with his father,

or at least follow him around. On this late August morning, Chuck's father pulled his car up to a parking meter on a city street.

Here's a dollar," Dad said to Chuck. "Go into the mini-market and exchange it for four quarters. Then put the quarters in the meter. I'll meet you inside the office. Don't talk to any strangers."

Dad dashed inside the office building while Chuck walked over to the mini-market with a dollar bill in his hand. Suddenly, a homeless person was at his side.

"Hey, man, I need that dollar more than you. How many dollars do you have?"

"One," Chuck answered.

"I haven't got any money and I haven't eaten all week. Did you eat breakfast this morning?"

"Yes," Chuck said, still clutching the dollar bill.

"What did you eat?"

Chuck started to say "cereal" but the man went right on talking.

"Give me the dollar so I can eat. Do a good deed. I'll pay you back some day, I mean it. I don't lie."

"I'm sorry," Chuck said, "but I need this dollar. It's all I have."

The homeless man turned around and asked someone else the same questions.

Chuck noticed a middle-aged man sitting on a crate near the front door of the mini-market. Tall, lean, black, bug-eyed Otis shook the change in his plastic cup.

"Another beggar," Chuck thought so he took a wide turn toward the door to avoid Otis. Chuck kept his eyes on the teen-aged skateboarders skating around the pavilion.

The mini-market was packed. Chuck waited in line, then asked the cashier to break his dollar into four quarters.

"We don't give change. Next!"

"But our meter will expire and we'll get a ticket."

"We don't give change unless you buy something. Next!"

Slowly, Chuck realized he would have to get his quarters somewhere else. He walked out of the mini-market.

Otis saw the boy standing still and called out, "That's why I won't spend my money in that store. They won't even give you change unless you buy something."

Chuck nodded, still bewildered.

"But if you buy something, it will cost you a dollar and then you can't get the quarters you need. Am I right?"

"Where can I get quarters around here?" Chuck asked.

"Right here. Want me to help you get some?"

"Sure."

As if the curtain in a theater had just been raised, Otis whirled around and approached people on the street. A well-dressed woman smiled when she saw Otis' face.

"Madam, you are the best dressed woman I've seen all month."

"Oh, come on, Otis," she said, giggling.

"Would you be so kind as to grant one, small request? Could you, please, exchange my dimes and nickels for quarters?" Otis asked as he held up his cup.

"Of course. Here are four quarters ...."

Otis started fumbling with his dimes, trying to count them.

"You can have the quarters, Otis. Just keep smiling," the woman said as she rushed into the mini-market.

Otis waved for Chuck to follow him.

"Let's feed your Dad's meter," Otis said.

"How did you know --"

"I saw where your Dad parked. It's my job to notice."

"But I haven't given you my dollar, yet."

"We'll get to that later. I trust you."

Otis put the four quarters in the meter, then looked inside Chuck's family car.

"What's that in the back?" he asked the boy.

"My skateboard."

"Well, if you like your skateboard, and want to keep it, you'd better put it in the trunk of the car when you come downtown. That way, no one will steal it."

"I'll tell my Dad. I should get back now. Thanks. By the way, I'm Chuck. What's your name?"

"Just call me the guy you owe a dollar."

"That's right. I almost forgot. I still have the dollar."

"Go tell your Dad you took care of the meter so he doesn't worry. Then tell him you're working on a deal for more quarters. Meet me at my crate."

In the office, Dad was punching numbers into a computer. Chuck explained what had happened.

"Don't make any deals with homeless men. They're all desperate and dangerous. Pay him one dollar, thank him and come right back," Dad instructed.

Otis would not accept the dollar.

"Although I would appreciate a coffee and lemon pie," he told Chuck. "Total cost, ninety-nine cents."

"Sure."

"Thank you so very much. I am grateful to you, Chuck. Oh, make the coffee black, with eight sugars."

Moments later, in the mini-mart, Chuck lost count of how many sugars he had used. He counted the empty packs, noticed a few had fallen on the floor and wondered if Otis would be able to tell the difference between coffee with seven packs of sugar and coffee with eight or nine packs.

After Chuck had paid for the coffee and lemon pie, he left the market. Otis had already exchanged his nickels and dimes for quarters.

"Thank you, my man," Otis said, before sipping the coffee. "Eight sugars. Perfect."

"How did you get those quarters?" Chuck asked. "Begging? Panhandling?"

"I don't beg or panhandle. I develop relationships. I got these quarters through the fair trade of my nickels and dimes. Would you like to buy these quarters so you can feed your meter for the whole day?"

"I only have one penny on me. It's your penny, really."

Otis told Chuck, "In that case, I'll watch your meter and make sure you don't get a parking ticket. I'll use my own coins, if necessary. Now you can go skateboarding with those kids."

"I'd love to, but I have to ask Dad first."

Dad told Chuck it was OK to skateboard so Chuck took his board out of the car and joined some teenagers in the pavilion area.

"You can't skate here," one teenaged boy said.

"Why not? I've got a skateboard."

"Your parents have to work in the tower to skateboard in the pavilion."

"Which tower?"

"The phone company tower! Right next to you."

The other teenagers laughed at Chuck and began pushing him away.

Otis glared at the boys, his bug-eyes bulging.

"This is my friend, and I told him he could skateboard!"

"Sorry, Otis. We didn't know," a second teenager said.

"Don't let them pick on you," Otis told Chuck.

The boys skated together until the work day was over.

Chuck waved goodbye to Otis and followed his father, who walked quickly past the crates.

The next day, Dad found another parking spot near the office and near Otis' crate. Chuck was looking forward to seeing Otis and to skateboarding. As Chuck and Dad approached the crate, they could see policemen questioning Otis and kicking him.

"Why did you sneak on the subway when we warned you not to do it again?" a policeman asked Otis, while poking a nightstick into his armpit.

"As usual, it is a case of mistaken identity. However, I will not hold a grudge against you because I love this city and its people."

"Stay away from the subway station or we'll throw you back in jail!" the policeman warned.

Dad told his son, "The police know he's a criminal. See, you can't trust him."

(End fiction sample)

(For those of you who are curious about how this story ends, Otis gets arrested for helping a psychotic drifter. When Chuck's dad sees how unselfish Otis can be, he finds a job for him in a local deli, delivering food trays to offices. Otis makes plenty of money on tips and, although I didn't tell this to the young readers, gives none of it to the IRS. Chuck, meanwhile, decides he wants to be a lawyer and help homeless people like Otis.)

Writing Family Stories

If you have a family, you've heard family stories.

You have listened, with declining degrees of alacrity, to parents or grandparents talk about how, as youths, they had to walk twenty miles through the snow every day to get to school. (So what if Pa or

Grandpa grew up in San Diego?) Their stories needed an audience and you were stuck in the living room, waiting for the turkey to be served. Whatever.

My dad often retells his favorite stories, most of which deal with his poor but loving childhood during the Great Depression. He ran with dead-end kids, in sneakers lined with cardboard, and played catcher in baseball games without any equipment. He hopped on freight trains, sneaked into theaters; went to a day camp for the underweight and underprivileged, where he got into seven fights in seven days.

His parents, my grandparents, worked non-stop in a grocery store. They couldn't afford to buy him much of anything. One night, my grandfather took my dad to a prize fight, but only my dad could go inside because two tickets were too expensive. My grandparents didn't consider taking my dad to a baseball game because they knew nothing about the sport. They were still learning to speak English.

So my dad, after listening to the 1933 All-Star Game on a friends' radio (participants in that game included Babe Ruth, Lou Gehrig and other greats) vowed to save enough money to attend his first major league ballgame. He was not yet thirteen years old.

For Baby Boomers or their kids, going to a ballgame was a normal routine: a birthright. Dad would buy the tickets, gas up the car, pay for parking; it was easily done. Tickets only cost a few bucks when I was a child in the '60's. (My article on the subject, "The '64 Series," appears later in this section.)

For a Depression-era child, saving fifty-seven cents (the price of admission) was more like a year-round challenge. It took planning, trickery, timing and luck. Salaries in those days, for trained adults, were a few dollars a week.

My dad ran telephone messages from his parents' store (it was the only phone in the neighborhood) and earned two dollars in tips (all nickels). Then he got hit by a car and the ensuing hospital visit cost two dollars. He was broke again. Every time he saved enough money to go to a game, his sneakers would rip in half or some other problem would arise.

Then, while running a phone message next door to a customer in Shuky's cafe, Shuky, the owner, told my dad, "Kid, if you eat this hot pepper, I'll give everyone in here a beer and give you a dime!"

So my dad became the hot pepper eating champ of North Philadelphia at age fifteen. He used the money he earned in the summer of 1936 to attend his first ballgame, a double-header between the Phillies and the St. Louis Cardinals, dubbed the "Gashouse Gang," which featured Dizzy Dean.

If my dad had been elected President of the United States or won the Nobel Prize, he would never tell strangers about those achievements. Instead, he'd tell them how he managed to attend his first ballgame in 1936 and got to sit right on the field and drink from the dugout water fountain.

I had heard the story so many times that I finally checked out the newspaper article about the games on microfilm. Sure enough, the photograph showed kids sitting right on the field. (It was an overflow crowd.) It really was one hundred degrees that day. Dizzy Dean really did get rocked by the sad-sack Phillies.

I decided to write his story as a middle grade children's book. I believed that eleven-thirteen year-old boys would want to read about a fifteen year-old boy (children enjoy reading about slightly older kids) in a frantic situation, in a sports-related setting, in a different time period.

How would I go about re-telling this story? I had heard it so many times I could almost recite in from memory, as could my brother, mother, wife and a few cousins and neighbors. I gave Dad a tape recorder and he put the story on tape for posterity.

My choices were to tell it in the first person, in Dad's voice, or retell it from a semi-fictional point of view, in his fictional grandson's voice.

I don't know how many times I changed the voice of the narrator in "Hot Peppers For Pop." I went from first person/Dad's voice to third person/grandson's voice every time I heard from a publisher or agent. Finally, I decided that it would be totally authentic, with no fictional grandson involved. I shortened the ending and finished with Dad getting home from the game and collapsing in his room from heat exhaustion.

"When I got back, I barely made it to the bedroom. The pot belly stove, with the thin, worn-out, iron-plated exterior in the middle of my bedroom, may not have been glowing red ... but I was."

I was led to believe that this story, in a shorter format, was going to be published in early 2003. The magazine editor who liked it and told me to send it on disk, along with my social security number and photo, stopped returning my calls but this book got me my first children's book agent. Publishers and editors who grew up during the Depression seem to like it best.

Another relative had a much harsher childhood. I wrote about my eighty-four year-old cousin's escape from the Holocaust and called it, "Out Of The Wilderness."

(This was supposed to be published as a magazine article in early 2003, as well. Wait, let me check my messages to see if the editor has called to tell me the good news; that she's found my lost disk and social security number and photo. Nope. I guess they lost my phone number, too.)

I always knew that my dad's cousin, Herman, had lived through an incredible adventure in Europe in the 1930's and '40's. I went to interview him with my mini-tape recorder. His story was vivid and dramatic. I couldn't understand how he was still alive!

Herman's father, my great-uncle, was the only member of his immediate family not to leave Vilnius -- a town in Poland; now it's in Lithuania -- in the early 1900's. So, while my dad and his first cousin, Herman, were both born in 1920, my dad was born in Philadelphia and Herman was born in hell.

Herman's parents died by 1925. He was sent to a Jewish orphanage and grew up in an anti-Semitic country with World War II brewing. He worked in a flour mill, earned a few zloty -- dimes -- a week and slept on a bench with some straw bedding. He called those years, "The best years of my youth" so you know what's coming.

He was one step ahead of the Nazis. Invariably, just after he left a town, the people would be arrested or killed. He finally joined the Russian army, where he made a comment that landed him in a gulag. ("Back home in Poland, if you had money, at least you could buy things. Here, money is worthless," he had said.)

His comment was considered anti-Communist propaganda and he was sentenced to ten years in prison. (His lawyer, who was hired by the same people who were prosecuting him, thought it wasn't a bad deal, considering the "gravity" of his crime.) He was about to starve to death when he was released by a doctor, who was also from Vilnius. In the winter of 1943, he walked out into the Russian wilderness.

The farmers along the trail gave him food and shelter.

"Weren't they afraid to let an ex-con into their homes?" I asked Herman.

"No, they were more afraid of the Russian police," he answered.

The saying in Russia at the time was, "You're either in jail, just out of jail or going to jail soon."

After working in an agricultural commune, with old men and women, he was redrafted, then re-arrested for walking around without his papers. He hopped a train to Tashkent (then in Central Asia, now in Uzbekistan) and hid. He finally joined a Polish division of the Russian army.

His remaining family, meanwhile, was being killed in Auschwitz. His single sister didn't want to survive alone so she lied and said she was the mother of her sister's second child. (The Nazis let single men and women live to perform slave labor.) The Nazis killed both of Herman's sisters and all of his nephews.

In the army, driving to Warsaw, Herman was nearly killed by shrapnel twice. Just before he was to cross the river on a suicide mission, his commanders called off the attack and decided to wait for the river to freeze. His life was miraculously spared again. This pattern continued for years.

After the war, my great-aunts noticed an ad he had placed in the Forward newspaper and brought him to America.

Herman's story is a unique Holocaust survival story. He was never in a concentration camp and his problems were not caused by his being Jewish; they were related to his being Polish. I saw this story as a screenplay but I wrote it first as a middle grade book. I could ask children, "Hey, do you think that you have a rough childhood because someone stole your scooter or drank your last Yoo-Hoo? Wait until you read about Herman's childhood."

Suppose You Can't Find A Good Premise?

If you can't find a good premise, take a look at events described in newspapers, events from your day-to-day life or, better yet, from your own childhood.

The following story was written as an article but I will eventually adapt it into a book for children.

The '64 Series

It was October, 1964, and I remember being excited, not only because I was going to be nine in a month, but also because the Philadelphia Phillies were in the World Series and I was going to see them play at Connie Mack Stadium.

We were driving down Roosevelt Boulevard: my parents, my older brother and me -- the middle child of the baby boomer generation -- and I was staring out the back window at the fins on the 1962 Caddy. Why were they there? What did they do for the car? One thing was clear to me -- they weren't in place to improve the car's appearance.

"Sit down. I can't see out the back window," my dad called to me from his bucket seat. I was thinking, since the speedometer read fifty mph, he should have been looking out the front windshield, not monitoring my actions behind him. I didn't want to jeopardize my first World Series game, so I sat back and looked out the side window instead.

I watched the local kids playing football on the grassy island separating lanes of the boulevard. A kid would make a nice sideline catch inches from a slew of cars traveling over fifty mph. The real trick was not letting his momentum carry him out of bounds, into traffic. Fencing barefoot on ice would've been a safer activity. I thought how unfair it was that these kids, who would've been my neighbors if my family hadn't moved in 1955, could play tackle football and dodge the cars and I wasn't even allowed to ride my bike in the street.

The weather that day was better suited for football than baseball. Football games were different, though; more of a fan-bonding experience. My favorite fan was the guy who sat next to me on the benches they called reserve seats in Franklin Field. He was so large that he blocked every gust of wind that entered the stadium. I would tell him to take care of himself after every game, especially in December, because I wanted him there next time, blocking the wind.

I noticed that, besides the football weather, everyone in my family was dressed in Eagles' green. We weren't anywhere near Connie Mack Stadium. Pretty soon, I saw a familiar mob walking to Franklin Field.

"Wait!" I screamed. "We're at the wrong stadium!"

I was the only one who noticed.

"Baseball season's over, dummy," my brother reported.

Impossible. The Phillies would've had to lose, what, nine games in a row to blow the pennant.

Officially, they lost ten games in a row those last few weeks of the 1964 season. Chico Ruiz of the Reds stealing home in the tenth inning and nine other catastrophes were, perceptibly, too painful a subject for my family to discuss in public or in private. So I never found out about it until that Sunday in October, when my World Series dreams were shot down.

It was my version of the missiles of October.

Q & A

Q: How many children's books are published in the U.S. every year?

A: Five thousand!

Q: Why so many?

A: Baby Boomers have produced a lot of children who enjoy reading.

Q: What are the main age groups for children's books?

A: Board books are written for toddlers. Their parents read them the books until they can read for themselves. Picture books are written for four-eight year olds and rely heavily on illustrations. Easy Readers are aimed at ages six-nine. Next come chapter books, for ages eight-eleven. Middle grade books are for nine-twelve (or thirteen) year-olds. Young Adult books are aimed at teens, thirteen-seventeen.

An aspiring children's book writer, Tracy, wrote this to me:

"I am still working on marketing, 'A Yellow Rose For Savvi.' I finally completed my list of publishers to contact - that took forever! I came up with nineteen potential publishers after searching through one-hundred-fifty on the Internet. I printed out their guidelines and put them in a binder so I am organized."

Tracy is doing fine, so far.

"I need to put the finishing touches on the book and start working on the query letter. Should I bother to break the book into page numbers? Some guides say I don't have to include page numbers. Do I need to lay out the picture book in exactly twenty-six pages? Do I double space for a page break and then make a note of it? Thanks, Tracy."

Tracy started to wobble a little there, late in her letter. The answers are: yes, put page numbers on your book. No, you don't have to lay out the book in exactly twenty-six pages, like it would look in the final draft, sitting at the printing shop. You can double space to indicate a break but don't include notes to the editor within the pages of the text.

If your book is approximately the word count they are looking for, submit it in a convenient format. The editor will know it's a picture book that can be arranged in twenty-six pages. The less you worry about the layout, the better.

A writer should concentrate on the story and how it is told. No one will reject you because you handed in a picture book that was something other than twenty-six pages in length. Concentrate on the heart and soul of the story.

Here is the first draft of Tracy's Query Letter to publishers:

Dear Don,

I came up with this cover letter for the publishers that accept full manuscripts. Let me know what you think. Thanks!

Dear Editor:

I am submitting my picture book, A Yellow Rose for Savvi, for your consideration. It is a touching story about friendship, loss, change and renewal. It is written with the intent of bringing pleasure to the child as well as providing an opportunity to enhance understanding of the value of relationship.

Of course, as you can imagine, I believe this to be a book worth publishing. I hope that you will agree.

I thank you for your time and attention, and I look forward to hearing from you.

Sincerely,

Tracy

SASE enclosed

Here is my reply to Tracy:

Dear Tracy,

In the first paragraph, underline or put quotes around your book's title. Cut out the word "touching".' A story about friendship, loss and renewal has to be touching or it wouldn't make any sense. Don't make the publisher think that you state the obvious in your writing. It will be a turn-off. Also, change "relationship" to "relationships."

In the second paragraph, cut out, "of course, as you can imagine." Change the rest of the sentence to: "I believe this is a book worth publishing. I hope you agree."

In the third paragraph, write, "I thank you for your time and attention and look forward to hearing from you."

Sincerely,

Tracy

encl./ A Yellow Rose For Savvi, sase

Tracy should also advise the publishers how many words are in the book and the age group for which it is written.

Here is an update on Tracy's progress. She sold a children's story to Hopscotch Magazine. That's great news, right? There is a catch, however. The story won't be published until 2009!

Q: Should I submit to Canadian children's book publishers?

A: No, they are a very low percentage group. They rarely get back to me, although I always

enclose an International Reply Coupon. These IRCs are harder to find than Chinese rum.

Q: Should I knock on the doors of children's book publishers and agents?

A: If you do, there won't be much competition. It is rarely done, as I discovered first-hand.

Q: Why don't more aspiring writers go knocking on doors?

A: Because it is a sure way to get a door slammed in your face. The only reason why a publisher or agent would be happy to see a new writer at their door is if they were looking for new writers to sign. The overwhelming majority are not looking.

Q: Why aren't they looking for new writers?

A: Because they consider unagented writers to be amateurs, unless proven otherwise.

Q: How do you prove to them that you are really good, despite a lack of experience and publishing credits?

A: Send them a beautifully written book out of the blue. Or send them a clever query letter, wait for them to request a book, then send them a masterpiece.

Q: Will I be better off submitting my children's books without an agent?

A: It's possible. When an agent signs you, it is usually to represent one of your books. The agent will most likely submit that book to five or six publishers in the course of many months. When you work by yourself, there is no limit on how many publishers you can reach or how many different books you can submit. I've sent to fifty publishers in one week. Some, say thirty, got query letters; the other twenty got completed (yet short) books.

Q: How long does it take to prepare fifty packages?

A: At least a week. I research "logical candidates" for my books, type in their names and addresses, then decide what to send each publisher. Next, I type two letters; one is simply a query asking them to review my project list, the other is a letter describing what books are enclosed for their consideration. So, one set of letters asks them if they want to read anything, the other set thanks them in advance for reading the enclosed books. I personalize each one of the fifty letters, then print them, along with fifty labels. Then I stuff the envelopes with the proper materials and I'm off to the post office.

Q: When I prepare the SASE, with my return address on the front of the envelope (the one that is returning to me) whose address do I put in the upper left corner? Do I put the publisher's return address, my own return address (so it returns to me either way) or leave it blank?

A: I usually leave it blank or write the publisher's initials ("RH" for Random House) in the upper left corner of the SASE so I know who is returning my work before I open the envelope. Publishers will often put their address stamp in that upper corner. A few times, when I didn't bother to put a code word or initial ID in that area, I received rejections with no written return addresses and no notes. I wasn't even sure who had rejected me! So, to avoid that scenario, I recommend jotting down the name of the publisher, or at least the initials, in the return address area of the returning SASEs.

Q: How much does it cost to reach fifty publishers?

A: The thirty query letters cost less than a dollar each, including the stamps on the inside (SASE) and outside envelopes. The other twenty packages, with books inside, can cost about five dollars each, including the SASE. Total cost is about one-hundred-thirty dollars. If I'm low on funds, I send the packages via book rate, bringing the total cost to under a hundred dollars.

Q: Can I always mail my books via book rate?

A: No. If the package is very light, say only twelve pages, the book rate doesn't apply.

Q: What happens next? What's the likely outcome of this extravagant marketing plan?

A: You wait. After a few weeks, you'll receive a handful of form letter rejections. Then, you may receive a positive reply. A publisher who received only a query letter/project list and reviewed your list may want to read your bear story. You send it out right away, not two months later. Then, after six-eight weeks, you'll hear from the publishers who received your books. Some will send form letter rejections; some will reject your work for a legitimate reason and compliment your writing skills. "Please keep us in mind for future submissions," they'll write and include a smiley face symbol somewhere on the page. You must try again, quickly, with those people. Several months later, you may still be waiting for twenty-two of the fifty to reply. Then, one day, one of the stragglers may write to advise you that their company is interested in publishing your book if you make a few changes or shorten it in certain spots.

Q: What if I don't really want to shorten my book; the one that took me twelve years to write?

A: You shorten it anyway!

Q: Suppose they only want to pay me a few thousand dollars for the book that I shorten, against my better judgment?

A: Rock star Steve Miller and screenwriter Woody Allen wrote, "Take The Money And Run." They both can't be wrong!

Final Thoughts: Children's Nonfiction Books

"Hot Peppers For Pop," "Out Of The Wilderness" and almost all of my juvenile nonfiction books were written for children ages twelve and up. My aim is to get at least one of the books published and re-sell it as a screenplay. The Oscars won by "The Pianist" and, before that, "Schindler's List" should attract interest to my cousin's real-life, death-defying Holocaust story.

A writer is supposed to know the characters in his or her story. Well, many of the characters in "Hot Peppers For Pop" and "Out Of The Wilderness" are my relatives. I know them well. I know their stories well, also, after listening to them repeatedly on audio tape.

In fiction, you, the writer, must invent interesting characters, dramatic situations and clever twists and turns. Your imagination can run wild. Your character can eat nothing but clams and have seven girlfriends, all named Eureka. It is a challenge to your creative abilities, but there are hardly any limits.

In a good nonfiction story, however, you are limited by what actually happened. You can't invent a convenient plot point. Since everything is already prepared for you, you don't have to wrack your brain to devise a solution to a problem. Your job is not to mess it up. You must squeeze the drama out of the true story and present it to the reader without wasting a drop.

Part Three - Novels And Nonfiction Books

Novels And Nonfiction For Adults

If you want to write for adults but don't feel comfortable with the screenplay format, show some fortitude and take a stab at writing novels or nonfiction books. If you're thinking, "Wait, that sounds complicated," try to approach them as extended short stories or articles.

For instance, suppose you've written a short story about a lawyer who died and accepted a job as heavenly counsel. After you've completed the twenty page story about the lawyer and his buddy, the messenger who erroneously delivered the bad news, you could expand it to include details of an entirely new world, where there is no violence, hatred or greed. You could explore conflicts within heaven, conflicts between heaven and hell and between the angels and those left behind on Earth.

If you've written a short story about your experiences in the dress business, for example, expand it into a novel that starts in the dress business, then takes off in another direction. That's what I did with "Summer At Saratoga." The main character, disillusioned with the life of a traveling salesman, quits his cushy job to manage a stable of race horses. The horses turn out to be clones, who could be worth millions or could be ineligible to race. The conflicts take a few hundred pages to resolve.

Maybe you have written a nonfiction article about the first woman jockey to ever ride in a thoroughbred race. You've got twenty great pages without mentioning the other female jockeys who were vying for that honor. Expand the article into a full-length nonfiction book by writing about the other jockeys, the men who barred women from applying for jockey licenses, the court battle that ensued, the women attorneys who worked on the case for free, the race track managers and trainers who were caught in the middle.

The key is choosing an idea for a novel or full-length nonfiction book that will hold up for three hundred or more pages. You must create/report on more of a conflict than a cat getting stuck in a tree. (The cat tale is not likely to remain interesting past page two. That doesn't make me a cat-hater.)

Your novel characters and subplots must be better developed than those in a short story. Your story arcs (a story arc happens at the end of acts one, two and three, with act three being the end of the book) must be spread out evenly.

It is important for you to hook the reader early in your novel or nonfiction book. Don't wait until page one-hundred-fifty to make the book "really good." An editor is going to read the first ten pages and, by then, he or she had better be hooked. You must give them a reason to keep reading by drawing them into your story.

My publisher, Charlotte Hardwick, told me that book buyers often read the front cover of a book for fifteen seconds, flip it over and read the back cover for forty-five seconds. If they're still interested, they'll scan the index. They must see three things they need, three points of interest in the index in order for them to purchase the book.

I laughed when I heard that. Why? Because in the film business, especially in the video rental side of the film industry, all you need to get the buyer's cash is a trailer, a poster of the film, featuring a beautiful woman or man. If videos were offered when I was a teenager, and I saw Raquel Welch in her little cavewoman bikini on the cover of the video box, I would have rented it, no questions asked. Apparently, movie producers and romance novel publishers are aware of this selling point. It is a very, very old sales angle.

I've always believed that my novel/movie about the only lawyer in heaven, if it were ever published/produced, would do well in stores because the covers would feature the lawyer with a gorgeous blonde angel and a voluptuous brunette devil. (I wouldn't be inventing the women after the book/film was finished - those characters are really in my story.) Maybe we could dress those women in cave-women bikinis. So what if that idea makes no sense? It would make plenty of dollars.

Therefore, if you are thinking of self-publishing a book (more information about self-published books appears later in this book) make sure you put a photo of a beautiful, sexy person on the cover, even if your book is about trigonometry.

Adapting Your Novel Into Screenplay Format

By now, you should know the basics of screenplay format.

Adaptations, from novel to screenplay or vice-versa, are not really hard to do. Some novels will not adapt well into screenplays (such as "Hotel New Hampshire," the only movie I ever walked out on) but many will. It's like writing a skit and adapting it into a short story (or vice-versa) on the same subject.

In the first course I took in television writing, I was assigned a "Star Trek" short story and told to adapt it into a teleplay. Writing that teleplay, about Kirk and Spock and McCoy -- well, McCoy's character was probably drinking in the med-lab much of the time -- was really a treat. I felt like I was writing about my old college buddies. (The power of television is frightening.) Adapting a favorite short story into teleplay is a great way to experience the differences between a novel and a screenplay. After a few tries, you'll be adept at writing in either format.

Below is a two-page sample from the middle of my "Summer At Saratoga" novel, followed by a two-page sample from the screenplay adaptation. (I wrote the novel first.)

Novel Sample To Be Adapted

("Summer At Saratoga")

We watched through binoculars and listened on the walkie-talkies from the makeshift finish line. Janice said into the walkie-talkie, "We're almost ready for Labratt to work."

Ben was puzzled by the concept of the starting gate.

He asked Grace, "Suppose that contraption has a power failure during a real race? The horses would never get outta there."

Grace answered, "The gates open when the power switch is turned off."

Willie whistled in amazement.

"That is pure genius," Willie said. "That's wizardry; Thomas Edison kinda stuff."

"Edison was a thief," Otis barked.

"What?!"

"He stole most of his so-called inventions."

"No way," Willie said.

"He didn't want people like you and me to watch 'Life Motion Pictures,' as they used to call movies. He only wanted the upper-class to watch films."

"How 'bout that," Willie said with a shrug, before he turned to attention to Labratt entering the starting gate a few hundred yards away.

I was confused by all this civility.

"Aren't you gonna argue with him, Willie?" I asked with some suspicion.

"Why?"

"Because you always argue with Otis. If he says Edison was a snob, you say he was a man of the people. If he says Elvis was abducted by aliens, you say you've got forensic evidence that proves he died in a Vegas bathroom in '77."

"I'm givin' him the benefit of the doubt."

"Did you two bond or something last night?"

"We got along."

"Really?"

"Grace and I also bonded," Ben said romantically.

"I was listening politely, ya big lug," Grace replied.

Ben gave me the double "thumbs-up" sign.

I spotted Labratt in my binoculars. He exploded from the starting gate and ran effortlessly for a quarter-mile, which I timed in just over twenty-three seconds. Janice was screaming something into her walkie-talkie, but I was too excited to listen.

Labratt took the turn well and raced toward us at the finish line. Alfredo was sitting on the colt, motionless.

"I've got twenty-three and change for the quarter," Grace told me.

"Me, too."

Labratt ran the next quarter mile in another twenty-three + seconds. Grace and I looked at each other, trying not to get the other too excited.

"Forty-seven?"

She nodded.

"Maybe a shade under."

"We know which horse is gonna be the star," Grace said.

"Is he fast?" Ben asked.

"Yes ... he ... is!"

"Maybe the other one is faster," Ben suggested.

"Don't be greedy, Ben," I snapped.

"Why not?"

Screenplay Adaptation of Novel Sample

("Summer At Saratoga")

ANGLE on gang at the finish line

> JANICE
> (on walkie-talkie)
> We're almost ready for Labratt to work.

> BEN
> Grace, suppose that contraption has a power failure during a real race? The horses would never get outta there.

> GRACE
> The gates open when the power switch is turned off.

> WILLIE
> (whistles)
> That is pure genius. That's wizardry; Thomas Edison kinda stuff.

> OTIS
> Edison was a thief.

> WILLIE
> What?!

> OTIS
> He stole most of his inventions. He didn't want people like you and me to watch "Life Motion Pictures," as they used to call movies. He only wanted the upper-class to watch films.

> WILLIE
> How 'bout that.

> DANNY
> Aren't you gonna argue with him, Willie?

> WILLIE
> Why?

                    DANNY
Because you always argue with Otis. If he
says Edison was a snob, you say he was a
man of the people. If he says Elvis was
abducted by aliens, you say you've got
forensic evidence that proves he died in a
Vegas bathroom in '77.

                    WILLIE
I'm givin' him the benefit of the doubt.

                    DANNY
     (suspicious)
Did you two bond or something last night?

                    WILLIE
We got along.

                    BEN
Grace and I also bonded.

                    GRACE
I was listening politely, ya big lug.

Ben gives Danny the double "thumbs-up" sign.

ANGLE on Labratt running around the track. He explodes from the starting gate and runs effortlessly for a quarter-mile. Janice screams into her walkie-talkie. Labratt takes the turn well and races toward the gang standing at the finish line. Alfredo is just sitting on the colt, motionless.

                    GRACE
I've got twenty-three and change for the
quarter.

                    DANNY
Me, too.

Labratt runs the next quarter mile swiftly.

ANGLE on Grace and Danny, exchanging hopeful looks.

                    DANNY
Forty-seven?

                    GRACE
     (nods)
Maybe a shade under. We know which horse
is gonna be the star.

> BEN
> Is he fast?

> DANNY
> Yes ... he ... is!

> BEN
> Maybe the other one is faster.

> DANNY
> Don't be greedy, Ben!

> BEN
> Why not?

Researching Novels And Nonfiction Books

The best way to research a novel is to live in the characters' world. When I wrote the novel, "Summer At Saratoga," I relied on my experiences as a traveling dress salesman and as a regular Saratoga visitor. I knew the people and places that appeared in my novel. They were real to me. Even when I was holding up dresses in little stores in Reading, PA or Wilmington, DE, I was mining stories for my novel. When my sales partner, Ben, was lying unconscious in the passenger seat of the van, waking up only to remind me not to take him to a hospital (he didn't trust doctors; "Why should I make them rich?" he often barked at me) I knew the scene would be included in my novel. Here is an example of novel research that was derived from real life.

I was selling dresses in the Mid-Atlantic states with my seventy-five year-old partner, Ben. We stopped for the night at an inexpensive motel that Ben recommended.

By the time I had parked the van and entered the lobby, Ben, a veteran traveler, was involved in a terrible argument with the young motel clerk.

"Forty dollars a night? In this dump?"

The clerk looked like he was about to cry.

I said, "Ben, I thought you stayed here before and you liked it."

"Sure, because it was only twenty-nine dollars a night."

"What year was that?"

Ben answered, "1974!"

While researching a book about an undercover IRS agent, I simply interviewed the man about his life story. When I researched a screenplay about the first movie mogul, I read the notes of an historian who had spent many years digging up the information. Both stories involved separating the good material from the mundane.

I was inspired to write "The Money Machine" screenplay after reading, in 1980, a Los Angeles Times article about a real-life crime from 1970. I wrote the script by filling in the blanks. I invented the characters and story lines The Times didn't know about or didn't publish and plugged them into my script. It is technically "based on a true story" despite my adding dramatic characters and scenes.

The stage play/screenplay, "Hangin' With Homeless Otis" is based on my real-life conversations with the homeless man on a crate in front of a convenience store. I hung out with Otis every Monday for years. Maybe I should call the project, "Mondays With Otis."

I was able to write "Life After Death" after reading more than a dozen books on the subject. I've always believed this project crossed over (pun intended) from Young Adult to adult readerships. I also watched all the psychics on TV, except for Ms. Cleo. I re-read, "The Reincarnation Of Peter Proud," of course.

The film version of "The Reincarnation Of Peter Proud" starred Michael Sarrazin, who turned down the lead role in "The Graduate." The second dumbest thing an actor ever did was when Donald Sutherland chose to take took a modest sum of up-front money to appear in "Animal House." Sutherland turned down a percentage of the profits, which would've earned him millions.

In order to write "The Jockettes," I had to interview Diane Crump and dozens of other people who "were there" in 1969. It was a complex, time-consuming assignment. The key was listening to the interviews on audiotape and structuring the outline in an organized fashion.

No matter how you research, via interviews, the Internet or by personal experience, the success of your book will depend on your personal style. Don't try to imitate someone else's style. Whether you want to be detached from the action or immersed in it, rely on the style that comes from deep inside you, no matter what anybody says.

Samples of "Summer At Saratoga" (novel, Appendix "G") and "Life After Death" (nonfiction, Appendix "H") appear later in this book.

Death Of A "Ghetto Princess" Deal

Sometimes, others can do your research for you. That was the case with "Ghetto Princess." A student of mine wrote the first draft of this nice-guy-meets-bad-girl novel. It was uneven and amateurish, but, plot-wise, extremely compelling. He asked me to Rewrite The Story For Him, For A Fee. I agreed to work with him and finished the first draft in about six weeks.

I didn't have to hang around in "The Badlands" to rewrite this story. The student had spent most of the previous two years there (chasing the "bad girl" main character in real life). I didn't have to interview the crack-heads and dope fiends. He had seen them almost every day for years. He knew what made them tick.

"Come on, we'll go down to K & A and take a look around," my writing partner suggested.

K & A, the corner of Kensington and Allegheny Avenues in North Philadelphia, is probably the most dangerous place in the U.S. It's the place where police refused to patrol a few years ago, citing safety concerns. It has the highest rate of juvenile homicide in the country. I could list a dozen other factors relating to the dangers of driving around K & A. My partner had to go there; he owned several houses in the area. I didn't have to visit. I told him to do some more research without me. I just didn't feel like getting shot over a twenty dollar bill that someone thought I might have on me. I didn't want my final words to be, "But it's not dope. It's a box of Altoids, wintergreen flavor!"

My work on the second draft of this project stopped abruptly however, after I asked my partner on the "Ghetto Princess" story to sign a contract so I would be assured that my name appeared on the book. I also wanted to be compensated in the event the book sold more than three thousand copies. (The book was likely to be self-published by this guy; most self-published books never reach the three thousand-sold plateau.) I was already being paid an hourly fee but I felt that I deserved a bonus if the book sold better than expected. This guy agreed to my terms in a meeting in April, 2004, and I prepared to re-write this book.

A week later, I received the following contract in my email box:

Don Rutberg

GENERAL AGREEMENT

THIS AGREEMENT made this _____ day of _____, 2004

By and between _____ (First Party)

And _____Donald Paul Rutberg _____ (Second Party)

WITNESSETH: That in consideration of the mutual covenants and agreements to be kept and performed on the part of said parties hereto, respectively as herein stated, the said party of the first part does hereby covenant and agree that it shall:

1. I (his name) agree to pay Donald Paul Rutberg Twenty five percent (25%) of all Profits from the book called Ghetto Princess after (his name) has paid all promotional materials, expenses and advertising costs in association with from the book called Ghetto Princess. Providing Donald Paul Rutberg agrees to do all of the following statements stated after the number 2 below. (His name) agrees to allow Donald Paul Rutberg's name to be on the cover of said book, promotional materials and advertising materials associated with the said book. The name Donald Paul Rutberg shall always appear under the name (his name) and 25% smaller on the said book and on all other materials associated with the media, promotional materials, and advertising materials

2. And said party of the second part covenants and agrees that it shall:

Write, rewrite and edit to completion, until the final draft of the book called Ghetto Princess is complete and (his name) agrees that it is complete and fully completed and ready to go to a publisher of (his name's) choice.

This is the end of number 2.

3. Other terms to be coserved by and between the parties:

Donald Paul Rutberg agrees to return all hourly rate monies he received from (his name) as an hourly rate to aid in the writing of the book called Ghetto Princess before he receives any or all of his 25% of the profits from the book called Ghetto Princess. Donald Paul Rutberg will receive Twenty Five Percent (25%) of the profits from said book only by agreeing to this entire agreement.

This agreement shall be binding upon all parties, their successors, assigns and personal representatives. Time is of the essence on all undertakings. This agreement shall be enforced under the laws of the state of Pennsylvania (U.S.A.)

This is the entire agreement.

First Party_____ (his name)_____ Date_____

Second Party____Donald Paul Rutberg_____Date_____

Translation

Basically, this guy wanted to give me only minor credit, even though I wrote the book, and then take back all the money he paid me as an hourly wage for a chance to eventually earn some of it back. He could've sold a million copies, then claimed he never made a profit after promotional fees were paid. He was trying to con me into working for free and accepting almost no credit. I sent him this letter:

Dear (name):

I got a laugh out of that agreement.

Do I look like a guy who just fell out of a turnip truck?

I don't know what to say.

You want your name first. Fine. I agree and give you my blessing. But you can't minimize my name. We'll have the same size names. Where do you want to put my mini-sized name? On the inside cover, next to a cola commercial? Same sized names!

Why don't you put a line through my name or a big X through it? Spell my name (just like your name). Then it can be written by (you) and (you).

If I returned all monies paid when you started to pay me twenty-five percent, I could lose a lot of money! I'd have to return your money, (XXX amount of dollars) in order for you to generously pay me maybe a few hundred?! Are you playing with me? This is a joke, right? I hope so.

Come on. The money paid is spent or will be spent. That doesn't go back to you and neither does my car or my shoes. If things go great, then give me a percentage of the profits. Also, No One In The World Gets Unlimited rewrites. No one. Not even the movie or publishing moguls. There is a rewrite and a polish, that's it. You would have me contractually obligated to rewrite for years and could sue me if I ever stopped. I won't turn in a bad book and then say I'm finished and forget it. But I won't rewrite until you say you're happy. That's just not realistic. You sound like the greedy cop in our story except this stuff is getting pulled on me. It's not so entertaining when it's me.

I've always told you I sign deals I can live with but I have never signed a deal I can't live with. It is insulting to tell me that you want me to return (money) so I can get a few hundred dollars, after all the time I have invested in the book. Wouldn't you feel like a heel doing that? I know I would.

Get it straight or I won't agree to anything. No hard feelings. I can live with walking away. I can't live with giving back money for a chance at getting a small percentage back. I'm not a lawyer but I know right from wrong. My gut knows. You're destroying my enthusiasm for the project. You don't want to do that to a creative person. It's like I'm babysitting your story. Do you want to antagonize the babysitter? I could be working on the story now instead of writing this complaint letter.

You once told me that you don't screw anyone who hasn't tried to screw you. The agreement you sent me contradicts that statement, sorry to say.

Sincerely,

Don

Then he wrote the following letter back to me. This is his unedited text, honest:

Don:

your e mail was too long to read intyrly (sic). (I have ADD) but you really miss read (sic) it if your (sic) that upset. you didn't understand the math. we'll have to talk. your (sic) not thinking, it's a good contract on both sides. don't such lond (sic) e mails, and then i'll read all of them.

P.S. you either miss read (sic) it , or just jumped to conclosions (sic) right away!

(His name)

So I wrote back to him:

I've got other projects that are really important to me; that I must do now.

After reading your contract, and the letter you sent, telling me I misread the contract and I wasn't think-ing, I realize you don't want to give me credit or a percentage or much of anything. So a contract won't mean anything. I'd have to settle for my hourly wage and that's all, with or without a contract.

So, I've lost my incentive to re-write your book. I need to work on my stuff now. Producers and publish-ers are waiting to read them.

Send me your address and I'll mail your check back to you. Maybe in a few months, I can pick up again at an hourly rate, when I'm finished my other projects.

You said you have ADD so I'll end this here. Funny, when I would send you twenty pages of the book to read, you read them all in a few minutes. But my one page email was too long for you to read. I guess you just got ADD last week.

Tell me if you want to wait for my schedule to clear.

Don

His reply (unedited) was:

no i'v (sic) been waiting 4 yr scedual (sic) to clear too long. please mail a check to

(his address) Thank you

I hadn't felt this good about quitting something since I dropped biology in college. If you can't live with a deal, as the James Gang sang thirty years ago, "Just turn your pretty head and walk away."

Sample Contracts For Writing A Life Story

In order to protect you and the person you are writing about, you should both sign a letter agreement, stating simply that you are working together for a certain period of time. By doing so, you are prevented from writing the story and selling it without the subject's permission and he or she is prevented from cutting you out to work with another writer who jumps in and promises to generate big bucks in a jiffy.

All the letter agreement does is allow you, the writer, the exclusive right, for a year or two, to develop and promote the project. If you find a deal that you both like, you can go to the next round of contracts. If the subject doesn't like the deal, he or she does not have to accept it, nor do you.

The following letter agreements, meant as guides, are between a writer and subject of a life story and a writer and researcher of a life story. Their purpose is to show both parties' intentions and provide a form of arbitration if there is a disagreement. Usually, there are no problems until money is bandied about. Then everyone starts grabbing and pushing and screaming, "We had a deal!"

So the letter agreement had better be clear.

Date _____

Your name and address _____

Subject's name and address _____

RE: PROPOSED BOOK/FILM PROJECT

Dear (Subject):

This letter agreement shall act to confirm our discussions and act to legally bind us relative to your life story. Our intent is to create and sell a book, screenplay, article and/or similar entity based on your life story.

By signing below, you agree to tender to me the exclusive right to market your life story to publishers, producers, agents and similar entities from March 15, 2003 until March 15, 2004. If/when we receive an offer to sell this project, we must both agree to the terms before we accept any offer. We may amend and/or extend this agreement by mutual consent.

If you are unable for any reason to execute this agreement, your rights will be assigned to your daughter, (daughter's name).

Please sign and return to me the enclosed copy of this letter to signify your confirmation of the foregoing terms. I look forward to working with you to get this worthy story published and/or produced.

Sincerely,

Your name _____

Agreed to By: _____

(Subject)

Date

Your name and address

Researcher's name and address

RE: "THE 'LUBIN' PROJECT"

Dear (Researcher):

This letter agreement shall act to confirm our discussions and act to legally bind us relative to the above project, The "Lubin" Project, the true story of an early filmmaker whom you have researched for many years. Our intent is to create a premise, story treatment and screenplay based on Mr. Lubin's life, to be produced as a feature film, television film, TV series or similar entity.

Your role in this project will be as technical advisor and you will assist in the research and development of the script and proposed film. You will be paid an amount consistent with the usual rate for a technical advisor, an amount not less than $10,000, and receive screen credit as technical advisor.

My role in this project will be as writer of the story treatment, screenplay and rewritten screenplay.

Each of us shall have exclusive control, which control can not be assigned without agreement in writing by both of us, over the marketing of this project. We shall each be responsible to keep the other one closely informed as to marketing developments, and to promptly notify the other of any viable offers or serious interests. Only you or I, and no one else, may send the treatment(s) or script(s) out.

If my script(s) are not acceptable to the producers of the proposed film or entity, I will receive associate producer credit and be paid an amount consistent with the usual rate for an associate producer, not to be less than $10,000.

This agreement shall be valid for one (1) year from the time the first draft of the screenplay is completed, or one (1) year from (date), whichever date is earlier. We may extend our agreement after the one year is over by mutual consent. Also, you agree to give me a fair opportunity to match any offer you might receive in the first year after our agreement ends, if it ends before we can make a sale.

If circumstances warrant, you may be entitled to receive credit on the project as, "Associate Producer", and if circumstances warrant, I may be entitled to receive credit as both writer and associate producer.

Since you continue to do academic work on Mr. Lubin, no articles or books that you write or publish on the subject of Lubin shall be considered as being infringements on the material that we produce, such as a screenplay, however, such other articles or books shall not utilize the screenplay, or excerpts therefrom, therein, without our mutual consent. To the best of your knowledge, the information you are providing is original research material, except where you specify otherwise at a reasonable time, before production has commenced.

The fact that the screenplay will be registered exclusively by me does not negate the fact that you exert co-ownership over this project with me.

As a method of arbitrating any disputes that may arise during the course of this project, we agree that we shall each choose a legal representative who must agree upon a neutral third party to reach a settlement.

This shall also confirm that by entering into this agreement, I understand that you have a full-time job, and that you are not compelled to be available to travel and/or take off a substantial time should a production company or other entity desire assistance in producing this project, however, you do agree to make reasonable efforts to work with prospective entities by telephone and/or letter.

By signing below, you agree to tender to me the right to proceed with you on the sale of this project. Please sign and return to me the enclosed copy of this letter to signify your confirmation of the foregoing terms. I look forward to working with you to get this worthy idea produced.

Sincerely,

Your name _____

Agreed to By:

Researcher _____

Acquiring Film Rights - Existing Books

If you read a book, love it, and want to write a screenplay based on that book, make sure you follow the proper procedure. Even that doesn't always work, if you recall my story about getting the rights to the "Pluto" book. (I just typed "fights" instead of "rights" and that was no accident.)

You must contact the publisher and its sub-rights department to ascertain who owns the rights and if they are available. With the Pluto story, the company representative said the rights were theirs, free and clear -- when they were really in the process of reverting back to the author. If the rights belong to the author and are available, you may have to get a hold of the author's agent.

In some cases, you will have to pay thousands or more to acquire the rights to the book. In others, you can sign a contract for a dollar a day option or even a free one. Then you must write the script or at least a treatment and go peddle the project. That will make you a producer/writer. You may wind up being some sort of producer who helps coordinate the project and not the credited writer. That's OK, if you're just starting out.

I received a call from a family friend years ago.

"You have to read this book called, 'Ishi.'"

"What's an 'Ishi?'" I asked.

"He was the last Yahi Indian in Northern California. They killed everyone in his tribe except for him because he was able to hide in a meat packing plant."

I had all sorts of questions. Why was the book so good? Who killed the Yahi Indians? Was Ishi a vegetarian? (I was looking for an ironic aspect in the story.)

I read the book, written by the anthropologist who had discovered Ishi. It was fascinating and bittersweet. It would make a great movie.

Why? Because it depicted man's inhumanity to his fellow man. When white settlers wiped out practically all of the Indians in Northern California after the Gold Rush, they turned some into circus performers; curiosities, freaks. Ishi went on tour, much to his chagrin, working for the people who had killed everyone he ever knew or loved. He called the white man "Smart but not wise."

I called Berkeley Press to get the rights to this wonderful book.

"It's in litigation," I was told.

The widow of the anthropologist was fighting with the publisher for the rights to the book.

"Well, when will it be un-litigated?" I asked, sounding much like my own character in "When Angels Speak ...," the only lawyer in heaven, Charley Merriweather.

"Give us a call in a year," the publisher said.

About a year later, I received a message from my father on my answering machine.

"Your story is on HBO tonight."

"What's he talking about?" I wondered. "What did HBO do to me now?"

I don't mean to imply that HBO acted unscrupulously. It's just that I couldn't pitch them anything until I had an agent and they repeatedly produced projects similar to my own. The cable giant and I were on the same page, but I couldn't get them to read any of my pages.

Instead of the slogan, "It's not TV, it's HBO" they should change it for my sake to, "You can watch but not participate in our fine programming."

I checked the TV listings and saw that Jon Voight was starring in an HBO original movie, "Last Of His Tribe." It was based on the book, "Ishi."

"Shit!"

I didn't mean "Store High In Transit." (That was how shit got its name. Manure/fertilizer would explode on ships unless it was stored on one of the upper decks. How did the middle finger salute originate? In the fifteenth Century, the English vowed to cut off the middle fingers of the French soldiers, so they couldn't shoot any more arrows at them. When the French won unexpectedly, they "flipped them the bird," their middle fingers, to show they still had them attached to their hands. The "bird" was in reference to the fact that they could still shoot pheasant feathers; they could still "pluck yew.")

Back to the Ishi story. If I had offered fifty thousand dollars to the anthropologist's widow or Berkeley Press, maybe I would've come away with the rights to the book. I don't know how I would've gotten the project to HBO. I was not meant to write that screenplay, I guess. I learned that, when someone tells you that they read a book that would make a great movie, pay attention. When someone tells you they have a personal experience that would make a great movie, listen to what they have to say.

You don't want to be thought of as smart but not wise, do you?

Here is a recent example. A guy approached me at my thirtieth high school reunion. I remembered him from creative writing class. He was more of an artist than a writer. He said he had a story that would make a great movie and asked me if I had ever written a war story. I told him about "Out Of The Wilderness."

"My father has been fighting deportation for twelve years," he told me.

"What was he -- a Nazi guard or something?" I wondered.

"Yeah."

It seems that his father, at age 17, was kidnapped from his home in Slovakia in 1943 and forced to work as a guard at a concentration camp. He stood on the perimeter of the camp and helped form a human chain. According to my classmate, his father hardly ever set foot in the camp. He was a human shield; the first to die if the Allies invaded the area.

His father would not sign a document and admit that he was a war criminal. He would lose his social security by doing so. He didn't think he had done anything wrong. So the U.S. government took him to court and the battle was still raging after twelve years. My classmates' father declared bankruptcy at age seventy-nine. It was like an ongoing nightmare for the family.

In all likelihood, his father's story would make a compelling movie.

As far as getting the rights to a song to include in your proposed movie, don't do what I once did.

I thought the song, "We're The Kids In America" by Kim Wilde (does anybody remember her?) would be a perfect fit for my "Superfan" movie. The script was then called "America's Team." There is a party scene where the players, after they are kidnapped and forced to play in a "real" World Series, dance in a conga line. (What dopes!) The song, "We're The Kids In America" was ideal in both spirit and style.

So, being the inexperienced knucklehead that I was, I wrote to an executive at the record label.

"Dear (Record Company Executive): I am not a famous writer or anything, but I think a song by Kim Wilde would fit perfectly into my movie. Is there any chance I can get the rights to that song? How exactly does it work? Sincerely, Don Rutberg."

I never heard from them and I bashed myself for being so amateurish. Why would anyone respond to a letter like that? It was like a third grader writing to them about a business deal. I should have waited until I had a deal to sell the screenplay, then tell the producers or the studio that a particular song would really spice up a key scene. Or call the record company and ask what it would cost to acquire the rights to the song for a movie.

Acquiring rights to a successful book will minimize the fact that you have little or no track record. If you somehow acquired the rights to Mario Puzo's "Mafia" (the original title of "The Godfather") in 1970, do you think anyone would have cared that they had never heard of you? They could have tried to underpay you, but they would not have shooed you away and passed on a great project.

Acquiring Film Rights - Unpublished Books

Is it easier to acquire rights to an unpublished book? Yes and no. You won't have to deal with lawyers at a mega-media company and you probably won't have to pay much for the rights. But you'll have to deal with some geek who thinks his research is so perfect that it can not be changed in any way. You'll have to make him/her understand how the business works.

I once heard about an historian/teacher who had spent his adult life researching the first movie mogul, Sigmund Lubin. (The contract for "The Lubin Project" appears earlier in this book.) When I went to his house to discuss the story, the researcher told me it was, "An embarrassment of riches."

Believe it or not, he was right! The concept from my film treatment follows.

Concept - "Twenty Million Nickels"

The major architects of the movie industry were mere children of impoverished immigrants when Sigmund Lubin, a peddler of optical wares, came to America in 1876. By 1915, Lubin had helped evolve a flash-in-the-pan sideshow act called "Life Motion Pictures" from a lower-class amusement into a worldwide industry.

He was the first to commercialize the movie business and the first to simultaneously produce, distribute and exhibit films. He was also the first to make millions; amassing eleven million.

By 1916, Lubin was the first to lose millions in the movie business. The industry which he had pioneered forgot him. In his final years, he peddled optical wares.

"Twenty Million Nickels" depicts the true life story of Sigmund Lubin, the original movie mogul. In 1897, long before the term "mogul" was introduced, Lubin used his

ophthalmology background to manufacture movie cameras and improve on Thomas Edison's Vitascope machines. Whereas Edison wanted to restrict and control movie production/distribution and cultivate a wealthy clientele, Lubin relied on his technical resources, commercial instincts and promotional skills to heighten the demand and cultivate a mass appeal. Lubin catered to the growing number of immigrants, like himself, who were eager to embrace an undemanding form of entertainment. Viewing a modern wonder -- a picture that moved -- required no clean clothes, knowledge of English or sobriety. All one needed was a nickel and ten minutes.

(Edison didn't want the immigrants' nickels. Lubin did, claiming that "Twenty million nickels equals a million dollars!")

For ten years, Lubin battled in the courtroom with Edison, eventually becoming his partner in the Patents Company. But the pirate and chameleon in Lubin felt frustrated in the role

of establishment fat-cat. His newfound wealth couldn't squelch his desire to take risks. Also, he knew that because he was an immigrant and a Jew, he would never be fully accepted by his new partners. When Samuel Goldwyn, Jesse Lasky and Cecil B. DeMille came to Lubin, their competitor, and admitted they were about to lose everything because their film, "The Squaw Man" was a technical disaster, Lubin saved the film and possibly their careers. By helping independents (mostly Jewish immigrants) gain a foothold in the industry, Lubin weakened his own Patents Company, which was later ruled to be in violation of Antitrust laws and disbanded. When World War I prevented foreign distribution and a fire destroyed his entire film library, his expansive empire did more than collapse. It was erased from history.

"Twenty Million Nickels" is a character study of a complex man who assimilates in America by pioneering an entire industry. Sigmund Lubin is an inventor, optician, carnival barker, theater owner ... pirate and patriarch, business tycoon and labor leader, philanthropist, medical researcher and peep show peddler. Through Lubin, we begin to understand the Hollywood moguls who follow, as well as the industry which, incredibly, allows, even nurtures this type of personality.

Sigmund Lubin's name does not compare in stature to Edison, DeMille or Carl Laemmle. But, in 1915, Laemmle's Universal City was a miniature version of Lubin's Betzwood Studio. More intriguing than his staggering rise and fall or his shaping of an industry which continues to shape society itself, is the fact that no one remembers Lubin's enormous contribution.

(End concept from treatment)

As it turned out, the researcher had spent twenty years digging up facts about Lubin and jotting them down and I had read his notes and written a treatment in three weeks. The man resented me for manipulating his meticulous research so quickly -- like I cared.

As soon as I registered the treatment (the title page read: written by me, researched by him) I sent the treatment to my agent, the lady in Minnesota. (This was in 1990.) When the researcher called me a few days later to see what was happening, I told him that nothing was happening; the agent only had the treatment for a few days. I told him he had to be patient.

That was it, as far as he was concerned. He thought that I was fooling with him because no producer had received and reviewed the treatment after a few days!

"You're just a BS artist," he told me.

The truth was, he didn't want anyone else touching his research. He wanted it all for himself. I didn't try to change his mind. If producers really wanted to develop the story at some point, they would probably demand changes throughout. This guy would have never allowed that. I'd have been caught in the middle of a fight between an unreasonable producer and an irrational historian. The agent would get involved in the fight, creating, no doubt, "An embarrassment of bitches."

If you pursue the rights to an unpublished book, make sure the author/researcher is rational and willing to be flexible down the road.

Selling Novels And Nonfiction Books

Either way, this task is not easy. Try to ingratiate yourself and your book to an industry professional. Start by sending a fabulous query letter, with a list of tightly written, crisp synopses, to publishers and agents (names and addresses can be found in reference books). Then you have to hope that the submissions editor or agent asks to see your work. One out of twenty might ask you to send the first hundred pages on spec.

It is very unlikely that a publisher or agent will ask you, an unknown writer, to submit more than one sample. There is a good chance that your letter will be ignored completely. That's nothing to worry about; it's the nature of the business.

I recently submitted my three page, novel/ screenplay/ TV/ nonfiction book project list to agents. That version is printed earlier in this book, in part one, and the book-only version appears next in this text.

This project list combines synopses from all my lists. Some projects cross over from screenplay to novel or from nonfiction book to juvenile book. I adapt it for the "customer." If I'm submitting to a publisher of nonfiction books, for example, I remove the novel and TV series synopses. When submitting to an agent who will only consider novels, I remove the nonfiction book synopses.

Some industry professionals will be overwhelmed by the amount of projects I propose on this list and consider me a fraud. Others will be impressed and consider me industrious. My motto is: "Pester them either way!"

Project List -- Novels/ Books/Screenplays

Donald Paul Rutberg

Email: DPRinnet@aol.com

NOVELS/ SCREENPLAYS

"THE JOCKETTES": In the late 1960's, no female jockey had ever ridden in a thoroughbred horse race. The men who controlled the "Sport of Kings" considered women too weak to control an 1,100 pound animal running at 35 miles an hour. That didn't stop women from seeking out jockeys' licenses. Men barred them from applying. They went to court and got their licenses. Men boycotted the racetracks. They began to ride horses in actual races. Men threw stones at their trailers. Finally, in 1969, female jockeys started winning races at North American race tracks. This is the inspirational true story of Diane Crump, the first female jockey to ride in the U.S., and the other pioneering women who overcame incredible obstacles to win equal rights on the racetrack. (The exclusive rights to Diane Crump's life story are attached to this project.)

THE MONEY MACHINE: In 2002, computer hackers altered "Pick 6" tickets worth $3 million. But in 1970, there were no computers to hack. Crooks had to use a more hands-on approach ... so they stole a tote machine, hand-cranked it and printed winning tickets after the races were over! For several months, the race track was giving money away to its patrons and it didn't know why! When the crooks were finally caught due to their own error, they exchanged the money machine -- for freedom. In essence, the advancing computer age was delayed just long enough to ensure this "Sting"-like perfect crime. (Based on a true story)

WHEN ANGELS SPEAK ... (THEY ARGUE): An outgoing, arbitration lawyer dies and is disap-pointed to learn that he's been assigned a similar job in a dull, sterile world known as heaven. With no chance to enjoy the Earthly pleasures his spirit craves, the only lawyer in heaven enters the game of angelic politics, hoping to add some life to his death. (Also a TV series)

SUPERFAN 2020: It is 2020 and sports society has gone beyond escapism to insanity ... on its way to the unnatural. A sports nut named Murray joyfully jeopardizes his marriage, his job and his life in order to win the Superfan trophy. He and his 11 year-old protégé prove that the heroes are in the cheap seats after the pampered players are forced to play in a "Real" World Series. (Also a comic book -- nationally distributed)

SUMMER AT SARATOGA: A young man quits his "perfect" job in the family dress business and takes his chances, acquiring two race horses and falling in love with the horses' trainer. In one frantic summer, he's stalked by the trainer's telepathic, telekinetic, terribly jealous ex-boyfriend and discovers the horses are superstar clones, who may be worth millions.

HANGIN' WITH HOMELESS OTIS: Tall, lean, black, 50'ish, bug-eyed, drug-free, high-strung Otis is homeless by choice. He applies his intelligence and communicative skills in the city streets, "develop-ing relationships" (not "panhandling") and dodging death. Otis is considered a nuisance by everyone in the street, except for the young man who knows him best. (Based on a true story; also a stage play)

PROJECT LIST

Donald Paul Rutberg
Email: DPRinnet@aol.com

NONFICTION BOOKS

A WRITER'S FIRST AID KIT: A writer-turned-literary agent discovers unsettling truths about each profession and, from a dual perspective, offers advice for unagented writers. (Includes chapters on how to write and market TV/film treatments, children's books, magazine articles, etc.)

(Published by Pale Horse Publishing, 2004)

WHEN BABY BOOMERS WERE YOUNG: A collection of stories and poems from Baby Boomers' childhoods; while we can still remember them.

OUT OF THE WILDERNESS: During WWII, an orphaned, Polish, Jewish teenager miraculously eludes the Nazis, joins the Russian army, gets arrested for "Counter Revolutionary Propaganda," nearly starves to death in prison; survives in a wilderness commune, escapes to and from the Polish army posing as a Greek concentration camp survivor and finds his family in America.

HOT PEPPERS FOR POP: During the Great Depression, a 15 year-old boy earns enough money in hot-pepper eating contests to attend a major league baseball game, where he sits on the field with Dizzy Dean and drinks from the dugout water fountain.

TWENTY MILLION NICKELS: The true story of Sigmund Lubin, an immigrant optician who transforms a flash-in-the-pan sideshow act called "Life Motion Pictures" from a lower-class amusement into a world-wide industry. Competitors with Thomas Edison, partners with Samuel Goldwyn -- then vice-versa! -- Lubin is the first to make millions in the movie business ... and the first to lose millions.

LIFE AFTER DEATH: Imagine a place where there is total peace, love, knowledge and wonder; where there is no violence, hatred or greed and where no one judges you. Millions of near death survivors claim there is such a place -- and the only way to get there is to die. Do we live many lifetimes, do Beings of Light exist in heaven, do ghosts walk among us ... or are they all just products of our wildest dreams?

EXTERNAL REVENUE SERVICE: Like any organization which loses billions to delinquent accounts, yet survives, the IRS has its share of heroes and victims. In this, the biggest corruption case in IRS history, an honest-yet-flashy agent is pressured to work undercover for the IRS' internal investigation of corruption. With no undercover training, he must deal with an alarming abundance of bribery-minded accountants, businessmen and respected civic leaders as well as elite IRS supervisors with hidden agendas.

WHY HOMING PIGEONS COME HOME: Descendants of the dove, Homing Pigeons are known as war heroes and bad housekeepers ... who have a special gift that allows them to flow with the Earth's magnetic fields.

PROJECT LIST

Donald Paul Rutberg

Email: DPRinnet@aol.com

YOUNG ADULT FICTION

TECHNOBRED: Cloning can eradicate disease and famine or introduce problems even more deadly. It can also bring together an orphaned girl and a loving pet. "TECHNOBRED" is a contemporary "boy and his horse" story about the abandoned and unwanted triumphing through love and courage. The "boy" is an orphaned girl and the "horse" is a secret genetics experiment. When these two team up with a down-on-his-luck trainer, they win the most prestigious race in the world. But there is some concern when they realize the entrants in the race are all the same horse; all cloned from the same illegal embryo. The heroes decide to stop the conspiracy, even if it means losing their own champion runner.

COMMUNITY PROPERTY: Children of divorce sue for, and win, custody of the home. In this story about children's rights, the ex-spouses are forced to share the home equally and independently, confronting responsibilities they ignored while married.

OVER-ACHIEVEMENT: Reform-schoolers run their own "Young Achievers" business and do so well that nervous city officials halt the program.

TECHNOPHOBIA!: Children of divorce move in with their grandparents; into a test home with a Home Nerve Center -- a computer brain that does all household tasks. The children soon notice that their grandparents have gotten carried away with the new technologies -- and the Home Nerve Center has a mind of its own!

HIDDEN STAR: A dedicated yet under-qualified teenaged astronomer, using his late uncle's telescope, accomplishes what few have done since Galileo's time: he discovers a planet. But will his newfound celebrity impress the girl of his dreams and procure a scholarship?

ELIJAH'S BACK!: After 2,800 years as an alien abductee, Elijah, the Biblical prophet, is returned to Earth for the new millennium, no worse for wear. When he moves in with his black descendants in New York City, he finds it difficult to adjust or remain even remotely low-key.

BREAKIN' NEW GROUND: An innovative real estate developer pioneers a self-contained community built underneath New York City, where social deviants form their own society -- with a very different set of ground rules.

About The Project List

When I claim that certain projects are completed novels/screenplays, sometimes I mean they are both completed and other times I mean they are one or the other. (In the hope of reaching all interested parties, I list them as both.) They are all destined to be both. Not all of them, at this point, are screenplays and novels.

So, when I sent out this project list recently, I was hopeful that agents would ask to read one of my novels. I was also hopeful that they wouldn't ask to read the novel versions of "The Money Machine" or "When Angels Speak" ... because they weren't yet written as novels, only as screenplays!

Several producers asked to read the screenplay for "The Money Machine." That was great news. One agent asked to read "When Angels Speak," the novel! I had to adapt it (the first one hundred pages only) in a few weeks.

I don't recommend this kind of shotgun marketing, unless you are the type that thrives under pressure.

I don't expect to sell a novel until I've had some success selling screenplays. My experience tells me that I will see one of my screenplays produced before I see a novel in print. The reason, in part, is because I've been able to attract screenplay agents but have never been offered a contract from a novel agent.

The irony is that, without an agent, I can pitch my novels to publishers more easily than I can pitch my scripts to producers. My gut tells me to push the screenplays hardest. Who am I to ignore my gut (higher spirit)?

It is interesting to note that no agent ever asked to read this book. Charlotte Hardwick, of Pale Horse Publishing, liked my query letter and asked to read some of my stories about children of divorce. She complimented my writing but didn't think she could successfully publish those books. So I pestered her. (Remember, pestering is a good thing.) Eventually, I told her about this guide book and she replied that she had enjoyed more publishing success with guide books than with any other books.

I never sent the book you are currently reading to an agent. (If I had, it would not have been because they wanted to read it.) Now it is published. What's up with that? I'll tell you what's up -- I "developed a relationship" (Homeless Otis' favorite term, though it referred to panhandling) with an approachable publisher and stumbled upon a mutual interest (guide books). In other words, I got lucky in the marketing department.

With regard to my nonfiction book (and screenplay) about pioneering female jockeys, "The Jockettes" (see project list above) I sent many query letters to industry professionals. An agent, publisher and magazine editor all asked to read this true story. Like my "Pluto" story from the 1980's, that was how I knew the project had appeal and was worth developing. In April, 2003, I went to Virginia and met the first woman jockey to ride in a thoroughbred race, Dianne Crump. That was twelve years after I spoke to the first female jockey to win a race, Barbara Jo Rubin, so don't expect these nonfiction book projects to evolve quickly.

As you know by now, I couldn't reach Barbara Jo. I suspect she ignored my calls and letters for months. Serendipity must have sprayed its secret dust on me because, in trying unsuccessfully to reach Ms. Rubin, I spoke to dozens of people who told me fabulous stories about the women jockeys of that era -- late 1960's. By failing to find Rubin, I found wonderful material for my book/film.

Dianne Crump, on the other hand, was easy to find and easier to like. After I met with her and recorded her stories, I wrote a movie treatment, screenplay and will soon, possibly, write a few chapters of a nonfiction book. With the success of the mega-budgeted "Seabiscuit" film in 2003, I believe producers will be anxious to produce more period pieces set at the race track.

I've been working on female jockey projects, on and off, for over twenty years. (Details appear earlier in this book.) The last thing I want to see now is a TV ad promoting a new movie called, "The Barbara Jo Rubin Story." If I happened to see that ad, I would laugh, I would cry and then I would get back to work on another project.

Bob Dylan wrote, "In Paterson, that's just the way things go." Well, it's the same deal in your writing career.

It's best to follow Randy Newman's advice: "You got to roll with the punches. That's what you got to do."

Other Ways To Get Your Book Published

I answered an ad from the National Liberty Museum, the only museum that depends solely on art to diffuse bigotry and hatred. The founder needed a writer to work on museum copy, speeches, newsletters, magazine articles and books. I've been writing freelance for them for years.

The founder gives me writing assignments, then I interview interesting subjects in person or over the phone.

One such assignment concerned a local philanthropist, Harry Stern. This man was so wonderful that, after two meetings, I was calling him "Uncle Harry." He saluted me, military style, whenever I left his office.

During our third meeting, his sister, Blanche, was called in to help me understand Harry's life as a child. He was from a poor family and, at age four, was sent to live with his grandparents on their chicken farm in Vineland, New Jersey.

As Blanche revealed her family history, she unconsciously and repeatedly scraped the buttons on her suit against the table. I knew that later, when I listened to the tape recording, I was going to hear ear-splitting screeches, like fingernails on a blackboard, only worse. I was hoping she'd leave quickly.

I felt so comfortable with Harry that I snapped at Blanche, "If you don't stop scraping those buttons against the table, I'm going to get your brother and me some earplugs."

Blanche stopped the button-scraping and told me how her brother, at age six, used to bury his grandmother's jewelry in the ground, expecting it to grow!

I wanted to kiss Blanche. She had given me the first paragraph of my book. Her story explained Harry's entire life; how he was always planning for the future.

The book was published by the museum. I had to plead to get my name printed at the beginning of the story. (Getting credit is often more problematic than getting paid.) Now, when I write query letters, I tell agents and publishers that I'm a published author of nonfiction books.

The best part of working on that project was I got to know Harry Stern. You know how I often complain about people in Los Angeles, who think they're important and act like creeps?

Well, Harry is the antithesis; a genuinely important, philanthropic man who acts like a prince.

Q & A

Q: How do I market my novel or nonfiction book after it's completed?

A: Write a synopsis of the novel project and a proposal for the Nonfiction project.

Q: How do I do that?

A: A synopsis is a catchy one-paragraph description of your novel. To write a proposal, read books by proposal writing experts. A proposal is basically an outline of the book and an explanation of why the book will be embraced by readers. ("This book is unique because ..." or ... "other books on this subject have sold well.")

Q: Once I have written a synopsis or proposal, then what?

A: Then you find logical candidates for your book. Maybe it's an agent who handles your type of novel. Or perhaps it's a publisher who handles books on similar themes (wildlife, for example).

Q: OK, I've found those logical candidates. Now what?

A: Send them letters or emails. Tell them about your background and what you have written. Ask them if they would be willing to take a look at a sample.

Q: Why not ask to send the entire book?

A: Because they won't want to read the entire book. If they are interested, they will only want to see a sample.

Q: Is it easier to sell a book than a screenplay?

A: Theoretically, yes. There are many more books published than screenplays produced every year. It is easier to get agents to read your book sample than your screenplay sample.

Q: Do I have to sign with an agent to have any chance of success?

A: It's not imperative. You must really impress publishers with your synopsis if you want to motivate them to ask you for a writing sample.

Q: If I tell publishers that I've written a novel and a screenplay on the same subject, will they be impressed?

A: Not really. You'll still be an unagented writer and therefore a nobody and a tough sell. If you've optioned the screenplay and are trying to sell the novel, the answer is "yes." Or if the novel is already published and has sold well, and now you're peddling the screenplay, then the answer is also "yes."

Q: When is the best time to write?

A: Some people like to get up at dawn and start writing. Others, like myself, are most creative late at night. I feel as if there is less interference in the air late at night. It isn't a logical assessment, but I believe the lines of communication to "universal truths" are more open when most people are sleeping. Determine when you are at your best and try to find time to write during that highly creative period. I've noticed that the period between ten pm and four am is very quiet. I receive no phone calls, faxes or emails. My wife is sleeping. The football or baseball games on TV have all ended. There are no distractions. I've always been at my best late at night. It may have something to do with biorhythms and biological clocks. If you know any scientists, ask them about it. Since this is "Ask the Poet" and not "Ask the Scientist,"

I see it this way:

I live at night 'cause I'm havin' too much fun, To go to sleep when I'm still full of run. Of course; relax!

Part Four - Magazine Articles

Writing Magazine Articles

While writing freelance for the National Liberty Museum, I noticed that many of the exhibits were rather gloomy; Anne Frank hiding in her room, Nelson Mandela locked in a prison Cell and other exhibits. The art, while important, was often depressing.

I had an idea about a funny interview with Attila the Hun. We could videotape a two character scene and have one of the actors dress up like a Hun, take a bigotry test and fail to answer one question correctly. It was sure to lighten up the mood and drive home the point that, if Attila could work on his bigoted attitudes, anyone could.

The museum's founder looked at me as if I were crazy. He waved me away. This wasn't a comedy club; it was a museum.

I wrote the scene anyway. Then I adapted it into a magazine article, which appears below.

"A Bigotry Test"

Maybe you've heard of me. I'm the guy who had his genetic map posted on the Internet -- a bad idea for anyone who had a blind great-grandmother and crazy great uncle. No one who had seen my genetic map would hire me, let me drive, vote or play hockey. So I applied for a job at a museum which existed to promote liberty and diffuse bigotry. It was a natural fit for me since the museum was inherently non-discriminating and was within walking distance of my apartment.

Happily, I was hired and assigned to stand near the Dead Sea Scrolls' exhibit, where I would administer a videotaped bigotry test to museum guests. I acted like a game show host; asking questions, marking down the answers and talking to patrons about how our society can eradicate bigotry by spreading good values to children when they are very, very young. After all, parents with hatred in their hearts teach their children to hate certain ethnic or racial groups by the time the kids are six years old.

The job promised to be inspiring and fun ... until I met my first contestant. As the video camera rolled, I shook hands with a large fellow dressed like a Viking. His name tag read, "Attila".

"Hello," I said, reading from my script, "and welcome to the museum's bigotry exam. This test is different from all others because you don't have to study for it, you don't have to take it if you don't want to ... and it allows you to learn something about yourself and your innermost feelings toward bigotry."

The big guy smiled. He hadn't understood a word I'd said.

"Helping us sort things out today on our journey of self-discovery is ... Attila. Attila, welcome to the museum."

"Thanks for having me. I was afraid my reputation -- you know, being a Hun and everything -- might scare you away."

"Not at all," I answered. "We accept you as a decent human being with an open mind. We look forward to having you take this test so you can share your analysis and philosophies."

"I promise one thing," Attila said. "I'll be honest."

"Great. Here's the first question. Push buttons one, two, three or four on your computer screen -- that's the machine right in front of you -- indicating which best describes your parents' attitude toward other cultures:

1. Treat all people equally.

2. Treat your own people better than others.

3. Treat one particular group as an enemy.

4. Hate anyone different from yourself."

Attila quickly responded, "That's easy. Four."

Attila smiled, as if he had won something.

"So your parents were bigoted?"

"I don't know about that. My dad hated anyone who wasn't a Hun. He had some real inflammatory words for our neighbors, who always moved away sooner or later. I was more open-minded than Dad. Want me to call him so he can join us?"

"Uh, no, that's all right. Next question: If everyone around me expresses their hatred, then it's OK for me to hate, also."

"1. Agree strongly.

2. It depends.

3. Not usually.

4. Never."

"I think I'll go with number one," Attila said.

"You agree strongly that it's OK to hate?"

"Go with popular opinion," he said with a shrug. "It's gotta be popular for a reason. Right?"

I thought the guy was pulling my leg; he wasn't.

Attila looked over my shoulder and tried to read the remaining questions, to get an edge.

"Third question."

"How am I doing, so far?"

"We'll find out later. Question: If your neighbor had a brick thrown through his window, you would:

1. Move.

2. Tell him, in a nice way, that he should move.

3. Buy some bricks and join the mob.

4. Show support for your neighbor in a tangible way."

"My answer is two. Tell him to move for his own good," the Hun/museum guest said.

"So you wouldn't throw bricks at his window?"

"And have to deal with all that broken glass? No way. We Huns didn't damage our own villages. We were civilized."

"And highly respected, no doubt, by other cultures... which leads to my next question: How interested are you in learning about other cultures?"

1. Not at all interested.

2. Slightly interested if that culture affects my life.

3. Willing to learn.

4. Very interested."

"I'd say two," Attila uttered.

"So you're slightly interested. Explain."

"Well, a few times we went over to burn down villages -- "

"Excuse me, did you say burn down villages?"

"Yeah."

"Why?"

"Because they weren't Huns. They were different."

Attila seemed surprised by my silence and stunned look. He went over and tapped the microphone on the video camera.

"Is this thing working?"

"Yes, we can hear you. Go on."

"So, while we burned the villages, I would ask a few questions about the people. You know, where they came from, where they were going."

I shouted, "Where they were going? They were getting as far away from you as they could! Because you destroyed everything they had built!"

"I took an interest in their culture. Was that so wrong?"

"Uh, next question, and I hope everybody is doing better than our guest here. OK, when you're angry at someone, do you attack their race or religion and scapegoat someone who's not involved in your argument?

1. Yes, if I'm really angry.

2. Yes, even if I'm just joking.

3. Sometimes, even if I feel badly later.

4. Never."

His answer was, "One and two."

"So you would attack someone's ethnic or racial background if you thought he was a bad driver?"

I was still sensitive about being denied a driver's license renewal because of my genetic map; remember, my blind great-grandmother.

"Heck," Attila admitted, "I'd even attack the horse he was driving."

"What do you think causes bigotry?

1. Self-hatred.

2. Common sense.

3. Parental teachings.

4. Minorities taking away our jobs."

He answered, "All of the above."

"That wasn't an option."

"Then I'll pick any three of 'em."

"You must choose one."

"Ok, I'll choose number one."

"So you admit to self-hatred!"

"No, you told me to choose one so I chose it."

"We'll leave that one blank, to match your expression."

"If you think it will help my score."

"I don't think you're going to have a score. I do know you need help."

"Hey, I'm being honest."

"That's true. We appreciate it. Next: If you were working on a project and it all fell apart, you would most likely:

1. Blame the boss or teacher.

2. Blame it on the bossa-nova.

3. Blame it on bad luck.

4. Patiently rebuild it."

"Well, it wouldn't be two because the bossa-nova dance craze wasn't around fifteen hundred years ago. So I'd have to blame it on the boss or the teacher or probably the Romans, number one."

Attila happened to glance across the room at the maps of ancient Rome.

I put down the script and said, "You know, history records that you spared Rome after the Pope pleaded with you for mercy."

"Well, I liked Rome and I liked the Pope. I didn't like the Romans. Chasing me up the mountains, down the mountains ...."

Attila pointed to the map and the mountain passes on which he was chased. "Like they hated me from the old neighborhood or somethin'. All because of one little war."

"Speaking of war, we've lost more youngsters in the last eleven years through street violence than we lost in the entire Vietnam War. What does that mean to you?"

1. The war wasn't that big.

2. There are too many kids anyway.

3. Too many guns are on the street.

4. There's too much hatred in the street."

Attila turned to look at the map of Southeast Asia.

"One. Small war."

"You surprised me. I thought you would say, `Too many kids.'"

"No, I love children ... if they're Huns."

"Speaking of children, where do you think they should be taught about bigotry?

1. In school by the teacher

2. At home by the parents.

3. In a house of worship by the clergy.

4. All of the above."

Attila answered, "Two. At home, by parents. Period."

"Suppose the parents are members of a hate group?"

"They're still the parents."

"In that case, tell me, if the parents teach kids to hate, should teachers explain about historical exploitation?"

The big guy was completely confused.

He asked, "What happened to the multiple choice questions?"

I phrased it another way.

"Have we heard enough about slavery and the Holocaust and should we now try to put it behind us since so much time has passed?"

1. Strongly agree.

2. Strongly disagree.

3. We need to hear a little more.

4. We need to hear more if the exploitation affects my people."

"Three. I'd need to hear more because ... I never heard about slavery and the Holocaust. Happened long after my time. Never read about them. Never learned to read. I'm being honest."

"True to your word. Keep it up. Do you think `average' people -- "

"By average, do you mean the average Hun?"

"Yes, the average Hun; should he or she be offended by bigoted remarks and actions aimed at minorities?

1. Never get offended or involved.

2. Only get offended if you're in the middle of it.

3. Yes, then report the offender to authorities.

4. Yes, realizing that bigoted remarks destroy the fabric of society."

Attila revealed, "I'd kill everyone who wasn't a Hun."

"You have to choose one, two, three or four."

"Two. Only if I was in the middle of it, and I couldn't get my lunch on time because of all the arguing."

"Are you proud of your heritage?" I wondered.

"Absolutely."

"How many heroes of liberty can you name?"

"One. Me."

"Speaking of heroes, which hero in the fight for liberty said the following: `I hate that person, therefore I must get to know him better'?

1. Martin Luther King.

2. George Washington.

3. Nelson Mandela.

4. Abraham Lincoln."

"You've got me at a disadvantage, being out of step with the times. It doesn't sound like an old Hun proverb ...."

"No it isn't," I said. "Take a guess."

"Four."

"Terrific guess!" I screamed. "It was Lincoln!"

Attila celebrated by pumping his fist in victory. He announced, "I'm goin' to the bonus round!"

"Not yet. Here's another question: `An eye for an eye and a tooth for a tooth':

1. Is an old Hun proverb.

2. Is a good philosophy.

3. Is a good start.

4. Will make us all blind and toothless."

"One," a now confident Attila answered. "It's an old Hun favorite. We set in to music. I'll be glad to sing it --"

"Maybe later. Meanwhile, do you have a basic distrust of any race or religion that will be with you forever?

1. Yes, in a major way.

2. Yes, in a minor way.

3. Not at all.

4. Never thought about it."

"My gut reaction is to say `One'. I have a basic distrust of all non-Huns. It's worked for me."

"If it's worked so well, why are you the last living Hun on Earth?"

The Hun said, with regret, "Intermarriage."

"Only a few more questions. Are you willing to strengthen your efforts to stand up against bigotry and violence?

1. Very much so.

2. A little bit.

3. It depends on the situations I encounter.

4. No, not at all."

"Three. It depends," he said while nodding.

"How would you feel standing up to a hate group in your area?

1. Afraid.

2. Ready to fight.

3. Proud.

4. Confused."

"Two. I'm always ready to fight. I'm not a `smoother-over.'"

"Finally, when you leave here, what will you tell your friends?

1. Make a contract with yourself to fight bigotry throughout your life.

2. Hate crimes are unacceptable, period.

3. Join together to form a stand-up group.

4. All of the above."

"Wow, that's a hard one. Eh, four! All of the above. I'm guessing, though."

I was shocked. He had actually gotten two right.

"That's a great way to end the test, Attila!" I told him as I patted him on his fur-covered back.

With much hope, he asked me, "Did I get 'em all right?"

"Uh, we'll see in the next segment. There are people waiting in line to take their bigotry tests. So, for now, thank you for joining us and, next time, bring your wife, Hilda."

"You know," Attila said wistfully, "I died on my wedding night and I always wanted to tell her that I loved her."

"I see you're a compassionate man. As a matter of fact, history records that you were considered fair and decent by some of your enemies. If you had to do it all over again, would you be less bigoted?"

"Yes, I would. If I can change, so can everyone else who visits your museum. All you men and women in line over there, teach your children tolerance instead of hatred!"

The folks in line ran out of the room in fear -- Attila's delivery was a bit confrontational -- but I smiled.

"That's a nice thought, buddy. Come on, I'll take you on a tour of the museum."

As I turned off the camera and showed him the awesome stained-glass panels of Biblical figures, Attila asked, "What about my bonus round?"

"Maybe next time."

Developing Fiction And Nonfiction Articles

Many of my magazine articles are inspired by newspaper articles that seem to leave out the interesting aspects. My imagination fills in the blanks. Here is an example.

"Peyote For The Kids"

I once had a college professor who advised me to read the newspaper every day, cover to cover.

"That's where you'll find all your good stories," he insisted.

Much to my surprise, he was right. Where else could I have discovered the following stories? One thing's for sure -- I never could have invented them.

Headline: "By 3000, Genetics Will Put IQS At 180"

In this news item, I learned that futurists believe our IQs will rise to 180, thanks to genetic engineering. We'll eat protein powders instead of meat and give up religion. After some global warming, the East Coast will eventually be underwater.

Also in the future, humans will be faster, stronger and taller, as will their legal clones. What will your work day be like? Put it this way; you'll be able to take the rest of your life off. Work won't exist. You'll stay home and tinker with artistic endeavors (like reading the newspaper cover to cover, then writing an article about it).

Crime and drug abuse will be eliminated. Prostitution will be legalized. The English language will become so fragmented that you probably won't be able to understand your cross-country cousin's dialect. Natural people, like you and me, will be outnumbered by artificial or enhanced humans. You'll be able to see more colors with ultraviolet vision. A "total recall" gene will enable some people to remember everything; a trait that will drive them insane (and probably their clones, as well).

Headline: "Pentagon Project: Guided Rats"

The Pentagon is currently developing live, remote-controlled rats to detect land mines and find people trapped in collapsed buildings. The rats have their brains wired so they can be prompted to turn right or left. They can smell people who are trapped and explosives. The rats work in teams of twenty or thirty. All wear microchips and data links on their backs.

Why do the rats follow orders? They think the signal is coming from their whiskers, which they use to navigate. Also, if they make the right choice, their brains' pleasure centers are stimulated. They feel as if they have eaten a great meal or enjoyed a fresh drink of water.

Zap -- "Aah."

Basically, the rats turn into intelligent robots, toy trucks with whiskers. Anybody have an ethical problem with that? You probably will when they start using cocker spaniels.

Headline: "The Tiniest Phone Yet: It Fits In Your Fillings"

A "telephone tooth," installed in one of your molars, will allow you to receive phone calls, listen to music and connect to verbal Internet sites without anyone else hearing a thing.

"It felt strange," said an eight year-old, who added he would be happy to hear from his friends in bed without his parents knowing about it.

Spies could secretly receive instructions; athletes could hear the coach's new play selection. A tiny device outside the body allows the user to turn the "telephone tooth" on and off. This may be the futuristic version of selective hearing.

"Sorry, honey, I had my tooth turned off and didn't hear you when you asked me to stop watching the game and take out the trash."

Headline: "Women's Brains May Recall More Emotions"

Here's a shocker -- women's brains are wired to feel and recall emotions more keenly than the brains of men. Women are better at recognizing highly evocative photographs weeks after first seeing them. Their neural responses to emotional scenes are much more active than men's; their brains are better organized to perceive and remember emotions. Women have a better auto-biographical memory than men -- for everything, not just emotional moments.

Magnetic resonance imaging measures neural blood flow through the brain. Women's brains go wild when they see pictures of a gun or a dirty toilet. Most men's brains consider these pictures neutral.

Women dwell on marital infidelity more than men. Not surprisingly, clinical depression is more common in women, possibly indicating that a selective memory is a healthy thing.

Headline: "Scientists Stumped As Earth Takes On A Slightly New Shape"

The Earth is less round than it used to be; fatter around the middle and flatter at the poles. (The Earth and I are getting a middle age belly at the same time! I feel so in touch!) NASA and other groups measured the Earth's shape shift by monitoring tiny changes in the orbits of nine satellites.

Our planet has always been a little thick around the middle. The bulge is caused by its rotation. Sir Isaac Newton, in 1687, said he thought it was shaped like a turnip or a pumpkin. Actually, the Earth is twenty-six miles longer through the equator than it is from pole to pole.

The problem can be blamed on postglacial rebound. (The last Ice Age ended 10,000 years ago so no one from that era is around to protest.) Scientists believe that the vast weight of the glaciers distorted the Earth's shape. Now that they are mostly gone, the planet is springing back to form, like a once-flattened sponge ball.

It may be that sloshing in the Earth's liquid core, called "geomagnetic jerks" is causing the shape shift. (At one time or another, many of us have come across such a jerk.) Or the change could be connected to "El Nino." The only thing we know for sure is that the changes are affecting our Earth, not the "Other Earth."

Headline: "Another Earth May Be Out There"

I told you no one could invent these stories. In this newspaper article, astronomers say they've found an alien planetary system that resembles our own. It has a Jupiter-like gas giant orbiting a sun about as old as ours, at a similar distance. The system has been described as a "first cousin" to our solar system. That could mean Earth's cousin is orbiting the other sun.

"An Earth-mass planet could exist ... and such a planet would be stable," said Geoffrey Marcy, a Cal-Berkeley astronomer. So far, "We simply can't detect them."

We could, "Get a direct picture of this planet" in the next ten years, said astrophysicist David Spergel, of Princeton University.

I'd recommend buying a ticket on E-BAY to this other Earth now. The grass there is probably greener.

The aforementioned stories, while printed in a respectable newspaper, are not very plausible; not likely to affect our lives in the near future. The next newspaper story is the most implausible.

Headline: "Father Wants To Give Peyote To Son, 4, In A Church Ritual"

An American Indian says the court system is infringing on his religious freedom by prohibiting him from giving his four year-old son peyote during spiritual ceremonies.

Peyote, a hallucinogenic plant which has mescaline as its active chemical ingredient, is considered a sacrament in the Indian church where the father, thirty-five year-old Jonathan Fowler, attends. Fowler credits peyote with helping him overcome alcoholism and "come into contact with G-d as I know him."

How can he know anyone or anything when he's high on peyote? Did the crack pipe help him know his landlord better? Did LSD help him quit chewing tobacco?

Indians have been ingesting the bitter-tasting cactus plant for thousands of years, believing it enlightens and heals them. The U.S. criminal code states that anyone caught with more than four ounces of peyote can be judiciously enlightened in prison for twenty years.

Fowler's ex-wife opposes the idea of their four year-old son taking peyote for any reason. Fowler, who is suing for the right to give peyote to his son, thinks it's up to the child.

"If he says next week that he feels ready to take it, then OK," he said.

Who, besides a geomagnetic jerk, would sue for the right to give mescaline to a four-year-old?

Is it possible that the boy's first full sentence will be, "I'm ready to try some peyote, Pop"?

If I could go forward in time, I would seek out a sensitive woman with an IQ of 180 and ask her to make a phone call to the other Earth, using the phone in her tooth. I'd tell her to instruct the guided rats to stop delivering peyote to parents who want to give it to their four-year-old kids. Then, I'd make plans to travel back to the present time, stopping only to pick up a newspaper.

Adapting Magazine Articles Into Sketches

When my agent asked me if I had any comedy sketches that he could submit to his contact at Saturday Night Live, I said, "Sure."

I didn't actually have sketches. I had written articles that would adapt to comedy sketches. They were written for magazines because I didn't have an agent when I wrote them and knew I would not be able to get my sketches read by TV producers.

I stopped what I was doing (re-writing this book) and adapted a few articles into sketches. The article above, "Peyote For The Kids And Other Newspaper Headlines" appears as a sketch below.

FADE IN:

INT. SET OF "UPDATE" - NIGHT

JIM and TINA sit at the anchor desk, smile for the cameras.

                    ANNOUNCER (V.O.)
          And now it's time for "Update."

                    TINA
          In the news tonight, scientists are stumped at
          images which prove the Earth has taken on a
          slightly new shape. It's less round than it
          used to be; fatter around the middle and flat-
          ter at the poles. The bulge may be due to its
          rotation. Sir Isaac Newton, in 1687, thought
          the Earth was shaped like a turnip or a
          pumpkin.

GRAPHIC IN BG SHOWS THREE PHOTOS SIDE-BY-SIDE: A TURNIP, A PUMPKIN AND THE EARTH.

                    TINA
          You decide. (beat) The problem may be
          caused by sloshing in the Earth's liquid core,
          called "geomagnetic jerks." Fortunately, the
          changes are only affecting our Earth, not the
          "Other Earth," right Jim?

                    JIM
          Nice segue, Tina, because another Earth
          may be out there. Astronomers say they've
          found an alien planetary system that resem-
          bles our own. It has a Jupiter-like gas giant
          orbiting a sun about as old as ours, at a simi-
          lar distance. We could get a direct picture of
          this planet in the next ten years, according to
          a Princeton University astrophysicist, who
          told our staff, "I'd recommend buying a
          ticket to this other Earth now. The grass
          there is probably greener."

                    TINA
          In other scientific news, geneticists believe
          that, by the year 3000, our IQs will rise to
          180, thanks to genetic engineering. We'll eat
          protein powders instead of meat and give up
          religion. After some global warming, the
          East Coast will eventually be underwater.

JIM

Also in the future, humans will be faster, stronger and taller, as will their legal clones. What will your work day be like? Put it this way; you'll be able to take the rest of your life off. Work won't exist.

You'll stay home and tinker with artistic endeavors, like writing comedy sketches. Crime and drug abuse will be eliminated. Prostitution will be legalized. The English language will become so fragmented that you probably won't be able to understand your cross-country cousin's dialect.

TINA

Uh, Jim. I've just been told that we have your cousin, Bosco, on the video phone from Louisiana.

JIM

(pleasantly surprised)

Is that right? Bosco?

GRAPHIC IN BACKGROUND SHOWS US A LIVE FEED OF A MAN, BOSCO, DRESSED LIKE A WITCH DOCTOR.

BOSCO

Hello, Jimbalaya.

Bosco speaks in a Cajun dialect that we can not understand. He keeps talking, as Jim and Tina exchange curious shrugs. finally, the screen goes blank.

TINA

(forced smile)

Looks like the future is now.

(recovering; reading notes)

In other news, the Pentagon has recently revealed that it is developing live, remote-control-guided rats to detect land mines and find people trapped in collapsed buildings. The rats have their brains wired so they can be prompted to turn right or left. They can smell people who are trapped as well as explosives. The rats work in teams of 20 or 30. All wear microchips and data links on their backs.

JIM

You may be wondering -- why do the rats
follow orders?
It's because they think the signal is coming
from their whiskers, which they use to navigate. Also, if they make the right choice,
their brains' pleasure centers are stimulated.
They feel as if they have just eaten a great
meal or enjoyed a fresh drink of water. Basically, the rats turn into intelligent robots; toy
trucks with whiskers. Anybody have an ethical problem with that? You probably will
when they start using cocker spaniels.

GRAPHIC IN BG SHOWS A PICTURE OF A COCKER SPANIEL WITH FOOT-LONG WHISKERS.

TINA

The tiniest phone yet: it fits in your fillings.
Yes, a "telephone tooth," installed in one of
your molars, will soon allow you to receive
phone calls, listen to music and connect to
verbal Internet sites without anyone else
hearing a thing. Spies could secretly receive
instructions; athletes could hear the coach's
new play selection. A tiny device outside the
body allows the user to turn the "telephone
tooth" on and off. This may be the futuristic
version of selective hearing. Jim?

JIM

Sorry, honey, I had my tooth turned off and
didn't hear you when you asked me to turn
off the game and take out the trash.

TINA

And I thought I'd heard it all.

JIM

This just in: Women's brains are wired to
feel and recall emotions more keenly than
the brains of men. Women are better at recognizing highly evocative photographs
weeks after first seeing them. Their neural
responses to emotional scenes are much
more active than men's; their brains better
organized to perceive and remember emotions. Women have a better auto-biographical memory than men; for everything, not
just emotional moments.

                    TINA
Magnetic resonance imaging measures neural blood flow through the brain. Women's
brains go wild when they see certain pictures ... let's take a look.

GRAPHIC IN BG SHOWS US AN IMAGE OF A GUN. TINA GASPS.

NEXT, WE SEE AN IMAGE OF A SPILLED BOTTLE OF BEER. JIM GASPS.

NEXT, WE SEE AN IMAGE OF A DIRTY TOILET. TINA GASPS.

NEXT, WE AN IMAGE OF A MAN BEING PHOTOGRAPHED WITH A HOOKER IN A MOTEL ROOM. JIM GASPS.

NEXT, WE SEE AN IMAGE OF "CLOSED" SIGN AT A MALL ENTRANCE. TINA GASPS.

NEXT, WE SEE AN IMAGE OF A BROKEN TV SET. JIM GASPS.

                    JIM
             (composing himself)
Women dwell on marital infidelity more so
than men. Not surprisingly, clinical depression is more common in women, possibly
indicating that a selective memory and hearing are healthy things.

                    TINA
And now for our most implausible story.
Headline: "Father wants to give peyote to
son, age four, in a church ritual."

                    JIM
An American Indian says the court system is
infringing on his religious freedom by prohibiting him from giving his four year-old
son peyote during spiritual ceremonies.

                    TINA
Peyote, a hallucinogenic plant which has
mescaline as its active chemical ingredient,
is considered a sacrament in the Indian
church where the thirty-five year-old father
worships. The man credits peyote with helping him overcome alcoholism and "Come
into contact with G-d as I know him."

JIM
The man also claims that LSD helped him quit biting his nails and the crack pipe helped him know his landlord better.

GRAPHIC IN BG SHOWS US BOSCO AGAIN. HE'S RAISING HIS HAND.

BOSCO
If it's inherent to his religious practices, I say let the man do what he wants.

TINA
Oh, all of a sudden you speak English!

Bosco abruptly disappears from the screen.

JIM
All I know, Tina, is that if I could go forward in time ...
(speaks very, very quickly)
I would seek out a sensitive woman with an IQ of 180 and ask her to make a phone call to the other Earth, using the phone in her tooth. I'd tell her to instruct the guided rats to stop delivering peyote to parents who want to give it to their four year-old kids.
(takes a deep breath)
Say goodnight, Bosco.

Bosco Waves And Sends Regards In A Dialect We Can Not Understand.

FADE OUT

The Project List - Magazine Articles

Many of my magazine articles are inspired by little things I see or hear. For example, I see senior citizens lining up their pills before they eat. Will that be me someday? I see Pete Rose excluded from the Hall of Fame and I ask, "Did he bet on little league games?"

My first game of golf was embarrassing. Why not share the experience with other bad golfers? I receive "lovely perfume samplers" in the mail that prevent me from breathing. Am I alone or are there others with perfume allergies? How many innocent people are killed each year by perfume samplers, lovely as they are?

I've written many nostalgia pieces. I guess I've always been the sentimental sort. In college, my roommates would limit me, honestly, to one reminiscence per day. My nostalgia pieces have added up to a series, called, "When Baby Boomers Were Young." Those stories, as well as the rest of my magazine articles, are described on following pages.

Donald Paul Rutberg

DPRinnet@aol.com

USC screenwriting graduate (MFA)

Published book author, comic book author, children's book author.

Published journalist and playwright.

Writer/Producer of children's TV shows and commercials.

"A Writer's First Aid Kit" published September, 2004; Pale Horse Publishing.

MAGAZINE ARTICLES -- FICTION

CONTEMPORARY CULTURE/ SOCIAL ISSUES/ HUMOR

GENETICALLY MAPPED: What happens to the "genetically less fortunate" after they've had their human genome mapped, other than losing their jobs, insurance policies, leisure activities, dignity, human rights and fundamental freedoms?

BOYS NIGHT OUT: What do you do when food is your only vice and you can't properly digest cheese, beans, garlic, tomato sauce, chocolate and other treats? You take a pill or two or three....

FILL 'ER UP WITH BORAX: In ten years, cars will be fueled by soapy water instead of gasoline. That idea may need a test-drive.

THE GIFT: Robert Burns wrote, "What a gift it would be to see ourselves as others see us." Obviously, Burns never received that sort of gift because, if he had, he would've made plans to auld laung syne it the next morning. That was what I hoped to do -- but you know what they say about the best laid plans of mice and men....

OSAMA'S LITTLE PROBLEM: A journalist learns that bin Laden is still sore about a tabloid story which exposes his lovemaking failures.

HISTORICAL FICTION

A BIGOTRY TEST: Readers can take this test and compare their innermost feelings on bigotry with special guest, Attila the Hun. (Published by Messenger Magazine, January, 2003)

ABRAHAM'S NEW WORDS: About 5,000 years ago, Abraham tried to teach his people new words ("hope," "progress," "justice" and "freedom") as G-d had commanded. Unfortunately for Abraham, no one had the faintest idea what he was talking about, except for his son, Isaac.

SPORTS/HUMOR-FICTION

CODE WORD: "INTERVIEW": Pete Rose's influential Little League manager believes Pete will enter the Hall of Fame; in fact, he'll bet on it.

SUPERFAN 2020: The Superhero of the future is a sports fan in this comic strip, based on a nationally distributed comic book.

OPTIONAL QUIZ: A series of multiple choice quizzes which test readers' knowledge of various sports, one joke at a time.

THE PUCK STOPS HERE: When this 48 year-old goaltender donned the "tools of ignorance" and returned to the hockey nets, I learned that my muscles, at least, had a good memory. (nonfiction)

Donald Paul Rutberg

DPRinnet@aol.com

MAGAZINE ARTICLES -- NONFICTION

CONTEMPORARY CULTURE/ SOCIAL ISSUES/ HUMOR

IN AND OUT OF THE NIELSEN FAMILY: We were selected to represent the viewing habits of 28,100 homes (98,50 people). We didn't mind the responsibility or loss of privacy, just the tearing up of our carpets and TV's, the five hour installation, rewiring and auto dialing.

EAT MY VOLTAGE: Our rental car was a Hybrid Vehicle, which ran on gas and electricity. I don't recommend driving this type of car if you're colorblind, prone to lead poisoning of if you've never seen a turtle.

PEYOTE FOR THE KIDS (AND OTHER NEWSPAPER HEADLINES): Stories about guided rats, tooth phones, other Earths and peyote for kids have all been printed in my newspaper. Talk about stranger than fiction ....

HANGIN' WITH HOMELESS OTIS: Tall, lean, black, fifty-ish, bug-eyed, drug-free, high-strung Otis is homeless by choice. He survives by applying his intelligence and communicative skills in city streets, "developing relationships" (not "panhandling") and dodging death.

LIFE AFTER DEATH: Imagine a place where there is total peace, love, knowledge and wonder; where there is no violence, hatred or greed and where no one judges you. Millions of near death survivors claim there is such a place -- and the only way to get there is to die. Do we live many lifetimes, do Beings of Light exist in heaven, do ghosts walk among us ... or are they all just products of our wildest dreams?

HOW ANDREA READS: Andrea was a special eighth grader; sweet, angelic and boy-crazy. She was also fourteen and could barely read.

NEW KID IN TOWN: A "problem student"-turned-college professor discovers unsettling truths about each station and, from a dual perspective, offers advice to college-bound students.

THOSE DISAPPEARING MAIL SLOTS: The return receipt I had filled out never returned. The surprise was: it wasn't the post office's fault!

ALLERGIC TO JUNK MAIL: Have you ever been rendered unconscious by an unsolicited perfume sampler in the mail? Consumer advocates need to go on an anti-perfume crusade before someone invents perfumed e-mail.

PARKING METERS AND THE PRESIDENCY: A candidate's pledge to improve the downtown parking situation would have procured my vote forever.

"JORDI'S PLACE": Our children's TV show featured Jordi, the world's only talking mime -- and the only one who couldn't remember his lines!

THE PROBLEM WITH VIDEOPHONES: My girlfriend and I desired to see each other when we talked on the phone every night. With incompatible brands of videophones, it was like buying a lawn mower and toaster and expecting them to work well together.

Donald Paul Rutberg

DPRinnet@aol.com

MAGAZINE ARTICLES

NONFICTION / NOSTALGIA SERIES

"WHEN BABY BOOMERS WERE YOUNG"

WHEN BABY BOOMERS WERE YOUNG: "IT'S A GREEN THING": Memories of our first baseball games almost always include an unreal shade of green. Why is it that we recall "Green grass, green walls, green seats, pillars and posts" but hardly ever remember "All that white ice" or "All that perfectly brown dirt"? What are the grounds for all this green loving? Why does it evoke such joy?

WHEN BABY BOOMERS WERE YOUNG: "THE '64 SERIES": In October, 1964, this nine year-old boy had tickets for his first World Series game. Unfortunately, no one told me that the hometown Phillies had collapsed in spectacular fashion and would not be playing.

WHEN BABY BOOMERS WERE YOUNG: "JFK": The JFK assassination seemed kind of strange to this third-grader in 1963. Forty years later, I feel justified in mocking the adult explanations.

WHEN BABY BOOMERS WERE YOUNG: "THE JOCKETTES": In the late 1960's, no female jockey had ever won a thoroughbred horse race. The men who ruled the "Sport of Kings" considered women too weak to control an eleven-hundred pound animal running at thirty-five miles per hour. That didn't stop women from seeking out jockeys' licenses. Men barred them from applying. They went to court and got their licenses. Men boycotted the racetracks. They began to ride horses in actual races. Men threw stones at their trailers. Finally, in 1969, female jockeys started winning races at North American race tracks. This is the inspirational true story of Diane Crump and the other pioneering women who overcame incredible obstacles and won equal rights on the racetrack.

WHEN BABY BOOMERS WERE YOUNG: "HOW CRIMES HAVE CHANGED": In 2002, computer hackers altered "Pick 6" tickets worth three million dollars. But in 1970, there were no computers to hack. Crooks had to use a more hands-on approach ... so they stole a tote machine and printed winning tickets after each race was declared official.

WHEN BABY BOOMERS WERE YOUNG: TO PROTECT AND (OVER 1 BILLION) SERVED: Some police cars now carry advertising slogans for car dealers. What's next: ads for fast food chains and Internet gambling? Has law enforcement changed that much since we were young or have we?

WHEN BABY BOOMERS WERE YOUNG: KISSES AND HANDCUFFS: I was trying to comfort a young woman going through a divorce and ended up crawling on my living room floor to stay hidden from the sheriff serving the bench warrant. How could I have known that a private investigator was following us or that "serial kissing" was a crime?

<u>WHEN BABY BOOMERS WERE YOUNG: "THE NON-PLANET PLUTO"</u>: Everybody in the sixth grade wanted to write their astronomy reports on the big planets, Jupiter and Saturn. So I became an expert on Pluto, which never resembled any of the other planets and was always looked upon as an outsider, hanger-on-er or one half of an orbiting, frozen marble set. Now, Pluto is no longer considered a planet! (Published by Horizon Air Magazine, December, 2003)

<u>WHEN BABY BOOMERS WERE YOUNG: SILVER YEARS LIKE GOLD</u>: Why is middle age the best? Because it's a buffer between very young and very old; the only time when our parents or kids don't make decisions for us.

Donald Paul Rutberg
DPRinnet@aol.com

MAGAZINE ARTICLES

HISTORICAL NONFICTION

OUT OF THE WILDERNESS: During WWII, an orphaned, Polish, Jewish youth miraculously eludes the Nazis, joins the Russian army, gets arrested for "Counter Revolutionary Propaganda," nearly starves to death in prison; survives in a wilderness commune, escapes to and from the Polish army posing as a Greek concentration camp survivor and finds his family in America.

HOT PEPPERS FOR POP: During the Great Depression, a fifteen-year-old boy earns enough money in hot-pepper eating contests to attend a major league baseball game, where he sits on the field with Dizzy Dean and drinks from the dugout water fountain.

TWENTY MILLION NICKELS: The true story of Sigmund Lubin, an immigrant optician who transformed a 19th Century, flash-in-the-pan sideshow act called "Life Motion Pictures" from a lower-class amusement into a worldwide industry. Competitors with Thomas Edison, partners with Samuel Goldwyn -- then vice-versa -- Lubin was the first to make millions in the movie business ... and the first to lose millions.

A HERO'S THEME: While writing about heroic men and women for the National Liberty Museum, a common theme emerged: their greatness was derived from the great respect they held for all human life.

FUZZY GOES TO PARIS: Louis Feldman, nicknamed "Fuzzy" because of his thick, black hair, bought his first harmonica in 1917, at age six, for ten cents. Two years later, he was hired by a Philadelphia harmonica band. At age fourteen, Fuzzy was whisked away from school and his struggling family to join the prestigious Borrah Minevitch Harmonica Rascals on a world tour, playing for kings and queens and later appearing on "The Ed Sullivan Show" and in twelve films.

CHILDREN'S MAGAZINE STORIES

NONFICTION

WHY HOMING PIGEONS COME HOME: Descendants of the dove, Homing Pigeons are known as war heroes and bad housekeepers ... who have a special gift that allows them to flow with the Earth's magnetic fields.

THE STORY OF ONION: Onion was a pint-sized racehorse whom everyone thought was too slow, too small and too young -- until he defeated the mighty Secretariat, the greatest racehorse of all time.

Don Rutberg

Donald Paul Rutberg

DPRinnet@aol.com

CHILDREN'S MAGAZINE STORIES

FICTION

SAVING SEEFOOD: A ten year-old girl, heartbroken when her horse, Seefood, runs away from home, chases after him to Saratoga Springs, New York. In Saratoga, Seefood's birthplace, the girl learns that her "champion" horse never won a penny on the race course ... yet was an unforgettable character beloved by all for his kindness, intelligence and community service.

WHAT TIME DO THE SQUIRRELS GO TO WORK?: A nature loving family moves into their dream apartment in the woods near a river, where squirrels seem to know all the ins and outs.

MOSES THE WOLF DOG (GOES TO SCHOOL): Moses, one-quarter wolf, is considered too danger-ous to live with people. He's placed on a raft and sent down the Los Angeles river, where he and his new owners must prove he's more of a good little doggie than a big bad wolf.

THE GOATS WHO ATE FIRE: Because they eat too much, Luis' goats must go out and find second jobs on the night shift. They succeed after Luis, their twelve-year-old shepherd, introduces them to a troubled mayor on a dry, grassy hill that's become a fire hazard.

A LEPRECHAUN NAMED LEVITY: The story, written in verse, is about a leprechaun who refuses to take anything in his life seriously. Through a series of adventures with various creatures in the forest (including a piano-playing tree, a vacationing duck and a cash-poor alien) Levity finally learns there is a happy medium between apathy and anguish. (Stage play version published in PLAYS, DRAMA MAG-AZINE, March, 2002; rights retained by author.)

MY FIRST SNEEZE: A story for young readers about an unexpected event.

THE "DID WHAT?!" (TM) SERIES-- BIOGRAPHICAL FICTION

BENJAMIN BANNEKER ... DID WHAT?!: Benjamin Banneker was an 18th Century surveyor, astron-omer, clockmaker, mathematician, equal rights advocate and associate of Thomas Jefferson, as well as a free, black man. But not everyone believes in his accomplishments -- not even the folks who live across from the Benjamin Banneker School.

SATCHEL PAIGE ... DID WHAT?!: Satchel Paige was the major league Rookie of the Year at forty-two, a pitcher for the Atlanta Braves at sixty-two and the first black baseball player inducted into the Hall of Fame. But not everyone believes in his accomplishments -- not even the folks playing baseball at

Satchel Paige Stadium. (Stage play version was published in PLAYS, DRAMA MAGAZINE, 1/03; rights retained by author.)

NEIL ARMSTRONG... DID WHAT?!: When Neil Armstrong took his historic moonwalk, he weighed only 25 pounds yet he retrieved bits of the sun and left footprints that will last a million years.

Don Rutberg

Donald Paul Rutberg

DPRinnet@aol.com

PUBLISHED MAGAZINE ARTICLES

(Rights retained by author)

CONTEMPORARY CULTURE/ SOCIAL ISSUES/ HUMOR

NONFICTION

TRICK OR TREAT?: My longtime friend, for religious reasons, would not allow his daughter out for Halloween. Then I remembered something from our childhood: I went trick-or-treating with him!

(Published by The Jewish Journal, October, 2003)

WHERE DID THE BALL GO?: My first-ever round of golf was as painful as the Inquisition and lasted almost as long. Even worse, it was my idea to bring the video camera. The game gets easier ... doesn't it?
(Published by Horizon Air Magazine, August, 2003)

THERE'S A LIGHT SHINING THROUGH: A profile of French-Canadian stained-glass artist Maurice Gareau, who creates religious figures in free-standing glass and plenty of positive energy.

(Published by Stained-Glass Quarterly Magazine, January, 2002)

GIVE AND LET GIVE: Harry Stern began his life as a philanthropist at age ten, when he sent Indian Head pennies to starving cousins in Poland. At the time, during the Depression, Harry was so poor that he had to leave his family to work on a chicken farm. Now a retired weapons manufacturer who contributed much to Israel's self-reliance and survival, Stern's inspiring story of success and philanthropy was published by the National Liberty Museum, January, 2002.

"DON POOCH": Our TV commercial was supposed to be a parody of "The Godfather" and attract new customers. When we used real wiseguys to portray "Don Pooch's" bodyguards, "shooting" the commercial took on a double meaning. Instead of airing on the TV news, we came close to landing there, as the lead story.

(Published by Emmy Magazine, April, 2002)

Marketing Fiction And Nonfiction Articles

One of the first articles I had published was a "Guest Opinion" in the Philadelphia Daily News. The story was about the assassination of JFK and how, as a child, I didn't believe a word of the official investigation. Decades later, I still didn't believe a word. I kept waiting to understand the intricacies and let my brain grow into the explanation. I'm still waiting. Maybe my senator, Arlen Spector, will explain it all to me when he campaigns for his 109th term in 2004. (He won the primary election in April, 2004. I'm wondering if one of his voters did an about-face and voted for him three times -- the magic ballot theory or some such twist.)

Start by writing about a subject which stirs your passion. Maybe you are a "Save the Planet" enthusiast or a music buff. If you are, write about the poisoning of the oceans or the greatest band you ever heard. Then send the article to a local newspaper.

"A Bigotry Test" was published by Messenger Magazine in early 2003. The unusual part of that deal was that the editor claimed he didn't have money to pay me for the story, which he clearly enjoyed.

I said, "You have to pay me something."

He reiterated that, while he regretted it, he didn't have the cash in his budget.

This probably won't happen again; to me or to you but that's the way the article got published.

Publishing credits, even minor ones, add to a writer's credibility. When you're starting your career, take whatever you can get in the way of credits. As you move forward, take steps to make what you can "live with," then as much as possible. Always try to retain the rights to your articles so you can sell them later to other Magazines.

I also wrote an article about the heroes that the National Liberty Museum had honored. I studied the lives of these great people so I could complete my assignment of writing display copy for the museum walls. Once I had examined their lives side by side, I realized why they were so great.

I wrote a poem about it.

"Their Greatness, Derived From The Great Respect,

They Held For Human Life As A Whole,

Turned On The Light That Turned Back The Tyrant

With Weapons Of Spirit And Soul

The article was never published. But the poem was published. (I slipped it into this book!)

This reminds me of a story about author Mario Puzo. In the 1970's, after "The Godfather" had made Puzo famous, a studio commissioned him to write the first draft of the movie, "Earthquake." We studied the script in film school. It was a disaster. I don't mean a disaster film; an actual disaster.

The studio fired him and brought in another writer to work on an entirely new version of "Earthquake." Years later, Puzo wrote the screenplay for one of the "Superman" films. As I watched the movie, I laughed as Lois Lane was swept up and nearly killed by ... an earthquake! Puzo had thumbed his nose at the "Earthquake" producers and written an earthquake scene for his next film. Maybe he already had the scene written and inserted a superhero and changed the name of the damsel in distress to "Lois."

Don Rutberg

In 2002, I sent my article about how I almost sold my "Pluto" movie to Emmy Magazine. The editor wanted to publish it but claimed he didn't have room. He actually thanked me by name in the editorial section (for sending the story). "The Non-Planet Pluto" was published a year later by Horizon Air Magazine.

Horizon also published my article about my first golf outing, "Where Did The Ball Go?" I mention in the article that my first round of golf was as painful as the Inquisition and took almost as long. (Rat-a-tat-tat, boom! Thank you. You're a great audience. Don't forget to tip your server. I'm here every Saturday night. Try the veal.)

Once editors like your work, you can keep trying to sell them stuff. Pester them until they do.

Since I came so close to selling one article to Emmy Magazine, I tried again. The rejection letter went to my "Pubx02" file and then right back to my "Try Again" file.

I called the editor, Larry Gerber, and pitched another article for Emmy's next issue, on TV commercials. (Magazine editors are approachable -- not like agents, producers or book publishers.) He laughed as I explained my idea. I knew he would enjoy the article because he enjoyed the pitch. A few months later, "Don Pooch" was published in Emmy.

I pitched another idea to Larry for a future issue on children's programming. He liked the pitch, liked the article and said he would publish it. Then, allegedly to appease the day-time Emmy readers, he said he had to cut the article, "Jordi's Place," which appears earlier in this book.

I pitched another idea to Larry. He always seemed to laugh at my stories so I thought, "Why not try again?"

In 2003, he considered my article called, "In And Out Of The Nielsen Family" for his catch-all issue. In May, 2004, I pitched an excerpt from this book (a few pages about attending writer's conferences) and he said he'd like to read it. The point is, if you develop a good relationship with a magazine editor, you can call him personally, ask what he's looking for and pitch your next story. That's right, pester him until he publishes your work again and again. As you know by now, pestering is good.

Update on Emmy Magazine: I noticed this in my agenda file:

By 7/1/04, call Larry Gerber, Emmy Magazine re tentative assignment to write article about Expo pitch sessions. If he approves, get go-ahead to write 750 word article for October issue, deadline 8/12/04. On 5/12/04, Larry wrote: "The story you described re your humorous pitching adventures sounds like a good possibility for the October issue. I'd like to future your note and get back to you, since we have a ton a projects to deal with before we can get to October assignments. Thanks in advance for your patience and for keeping us in mind." Prev: he likes Nielsen art sent 3/7/03 but he needs companion straight piece on Nielsen. Prev: xjordi. Xcrimesart 3/03. His assistant is Gail Polevoi.

On July 13th, 2004, I called Larry Gerber and learned that he was no longer working at the company! His calls were forwarded to Gail Polevoi's answering machine.

This could still work out fine. I became friendly with Gail when my "Don Pooch" article was published in Emmy Magazine. She and I both had the same professor at USC, Jack Langguth, the writer who provided the foreword to this book. I left a message for Gail and told her how Larry had given me a tentative assignment. If she doesn't want that article about the writers' pitch sessions, I will pitch articles to her that Larry previously rejected. They are fresh ideas to her.

Emmy Magazine has not published my articles for the following reasons: no room ("Pluto") the daytime Emmy folks overruled the editor ("Crimes") and the editor left the company ("Pitch Sessions"). There are a million stories like these in the naked city. If you are going to have a deal evaporate on you, it's preferable to have it happen on an article assignment and not a six-figure screenwriting assignment.

Another article I'd written, about Jews and Halloween, was rejected by dozens of Judaica magazines. It concerned my religious friend who wouldn't allow his kids to go trick or treating. Then I reminded him that, as a child, I went trick or treating with him!

"I didn't know it was wrong then," he explained.

Whatever. I wrote about the origins of Halloween and wondered whether or not trick or treating was kosher. When I sent the story to The Jewish Journal of Los Angeles, the editor liked it and said she'd consider publishing it in October, 2002. In September, 2003, they sent me an email, asking for my photo to put alongside my article. "Trick or Treat" was published, about fifteen years after I had written it.

The Robb Report publishes articles for the luxury lifestyle.

"We're about 'things,'" the editor admitted.

So I started to wonder, "What kinds of things have I written about? I must have an article about things."

I don't own a new home, a new boat, a Rolls Royce or a fancy watch. My computer was ten years old until I purchased a new, modestly priced one in April, 2003.

The list of things I don't have is frighteningly long but I kept thinking of ways to please the editor of The Robb Report because he kept writing how my work was "Clever ... like going home, if that makes any sense ... I'd love to run it but it doesn't fit."

He sent several copies of his magazine, hoping I would catch on to its intentions and spirit. (Its spirit was whispering, "Write about expensive toys for rich folks.")

I sent him my article about a hybrid car that was loaned to me by a car dealer. The theory was that, in a few years car companies will be making expensive hybrids for rich folks.

I wrote to the editor of The Robb Report, "I envision a day when Hummer hybrids will cost $150,000 and get fifty miles to a gallon. Of course, I also envision a day when bulldozers crush the statue of J. Edgar Hoover in front of the FBI building."

He rejected the article but wrote, "I'm with you on the statue."

I will keep trying until I sell an article to this kindred spirit. After all, I have experienced "things" in my life. I co-owned a race horse, traveled to exotic locales ... I'll think of some "thing" that will appeal to him, even if I have to rent a Rolls Royce or a French chateau for a day.

If you know where I can rent a Rolls Royce for less than two-hundred-fifty dollars per day, please send me an email with the information. As a matter of fact, if you know how I can experience any luxury item or service for under two-hundred-fifty dollars, let me know about it. Then I'll write the following letter:

Dear Editor at The Robb Report:

I have just experienced (insert luxury item or service) and believe your readers will want to learn more about it. May I send you my article on the subject?

Sincerely,

Don "Rolls Royce" Rutberg

More About "Great" Contacts

If you've read every word of this book so far, you'll know that I am not a big fan of Reader's Digest. Over the years, I have sent them a dozen stories and they respond by ignoring me every time. They won't even send me a form rejection letter in the SASE I always provide.

I suspect that, for every cuddly, feel-good story they publish, there are dozens of feel-bad stories about how they treat unknown writers. If you are a hip writer, you probably don't want to appear in their magazine anyway. Do you really want to write an article about how nice a person Martha Stewart really is and how she was framed by "jealous" competitors? I don't.

Once, I had a great contact who worked for Reader's Digest. I was recommended to him by my (former) friend's wife, who worked at a giant media company.

I sent this RD executive a wholesome, feel-good story ("Hot Peppers For Pop"). That's when the "feel good" aspect disappeared. Instead of savoring the opportunity to help his friend's friend, he acted like he was being tortured. He clearly hated doing favors for anyone but was obligated/coerced into doing one for the woman who recommended me.

I told the man, "If this doesn't work out, maybe I could send you something else that would be perfect -"

"No, no, no, no, no," the guy told me.

"Excuse me?" I said, almost laughing.

"After this, I'm finished."

"What does that mean - 'finished?'"

"No more favors, recommendations; whatevers."

"Oh, so this is the last time we'll ever speak."

"That is correct."

What a humanitarian. He was spoiling the fun of getting a project to the right editor. I hung up and started screaming at the walls.

If you have a great contact, and that person is loathe to help you, don't ask for any favors!

If you write an article about a discourteous organization that passes itself off as America's feel-good sweetheart, send it to me. I'll definitely want to read it.

What Else Can You Write For Magazines?

If you've written longer pieces, like screenplays, novels or investigative articles, write an article about those pieces; sort of a "Making of" story. This type of article could help you sell the longer projects. I've done that with "How Crimes Have Changed" (related to my screenplay, "The Money Machine") and "The Non-Planet Pluto" (related to my doomed screenplay, "Hidden Star"). As the list indicates, I create my magazine stories by reading newspapers and noticing things. Then I apply my style to the idea. The editor of The Robb Report said it was "Like going home." Maybe your style will be, "Like you're fighting mad." Whatever your style, stick to it. It will make you successful or, at the very least, come across as honest.

When I saw that some police forces were renting out advertising space on their police cruisers, I had to write about it. "What's next -- an ad on a cop car for a fast food chain: 'To Protect ... And (Over One Billion) Served?'"

Recently, a representative of the Nielsen Ratings company asked us to join the Nielsen family. In my style that felt like "going home," I described how the Nielsen people wanted to

tear up my home! "In And Out Of The Nielsen Family" appears later in this book, in Appendix "J".

In some cases, I've shortened longer works and adapted them into magazine articles. This seemed to work with two of my family stories, "Out Of The Wilderness" and "Hot Peppers For Pop" until someone lost my disk, social security number and photograph!

Samples of my fiction (Appendix "I") and nonfiction (Appendix "J") magazine articles appear in the appendices of this book.

How To Create Interest In Your Work

If you've had your work published, call bookstores and ask if you can sign books in their store. Call for permission to speak to your target audience. The store will probably buy a few of your books.

When I speak to young children in book stores, the kids show their appreciation afterward by hugging my kneecaps. These are some of the sweetest experiences of my life. (I discourage this type of behavior from my college students, however.) We talk about all the animals in "Running Through Kenya" and some animals that the kids invent. I still have the poster board promoting my "appearances."

Once, I went to a recital where writers could read excerpts from their books. I figured I could get some exposure for my work; create some interest. Well, one writer exceeded his five minute limit by an hour! He felt it was his right to read from his book, about an imbecile (the author) trying to romance a stewardess. There was almost no time left for anyone else to read his work.

It's a good idea to attend book fairs. At one such fair, I sold some books, met some people and then, when I went to buy a soda, discovered that my books had been swiped from the table. It was flattering, in a way.

Sometimes, I speak to children in their classrooms. In one visit to a middle school, I spoke to emotionally disturbed students about my books. They were fighting, sleeping, screaming -- you name it -- during my presentation. One angelic-looking fifteen-year-old child offered to read her report on a man I was familiar with -- Benjamin Banneker. The problem was, she could barely read. It was one of the most disturbing experiences of my life.

Attending General Writers' Conferences

You should consider attending any kind of writing conference. At many of these events, you can talk to an agent or publisher. Usually, you can talk to only a few. I try to talk to them all. I sign up to meet one, the legal limit, then I slide into a seat at all of their tables. If I'm kicked out of the table, so what? I look like I know what I'm doing, like I'm supposed to be at that table, and I don't get hassled. I like to hang out near the ladies' room and strike up conversations with female agents and publishers, after they've left the ladies' room, of course. This has never actually led to a contract but the shocked industry professional is always impressed by my tenacity.

At the Philadelphia Writer's Conference, I met a screenwriting expert, Jim Breckinridge. Jim is a professional screenplay evaluator. I didn't ask him to critique my script; I asked him to be my writing partner. He said if he liked my work and decided to co-write something with me, he would have to get paid or receive a co-writing credit on the title page. I said, "Sure" (to the co-writing credit).

The keynote speaker at the Philly conference (held every June) was a woman who had labored at a local newspaper until her book got published and sold really well. The book was about how, as a fat woman, she was treated poorly by men. She gave a speech that was less than flattering to men who had dated her, men who had employed her, men who had worked with her and men who were living on planet Earth. I was happy that she had gone from rags to riches, but I wanted her to berate men somewhere else.

When other people get a lucky break, though, try to be happy for them.

Can't resent someone's good fortune, there's got

To be a good reason … or maybe there's not.

Of course; relax!

When you get a lucky break, only your dearest friends will be happy for you. Some of the people you thought were your friends will resent you.

I know this because, when I sell an article, I feel resentment from people I thought were my friends. If I ever sell a screenplay, these people will probably file a protest with the Writer's Guild.

We're all human, but don't let your ego run your life. In every field, stone-cold losers climb to the top and bright minds flounder. If you're the cream, you'll eventually reach the top levels. Don't resent others who rise above you, although they may be fat, miserable, gloating man-bashers.

I have no plans, by the way, to gain one-hundred-fifty pounds, pull out my hair, pour acid on my face and then write a best-selling book about how women can be painfully cruel.

If you go from unknown writer to best-selling author, email me and tell me how you did it. I promise I will be happy for your success. You all seem like wonderful people.

Finally, when attending these conferences, spend a lot of time and money at the bar. That's where agents and editors go to relax. Buy them each a drink or two. Tell them about your work.

At the Philadelphia Writers' Conference, I overheard a book agent who was watching the national news on a TV in the hotel bar say, "The world is coming to an end. I know it."

I saw my opening and said to her, "I agree with you. Before the world does come to an end, I'd like to find a good agent."

She laughed with approval and invited me to send my best novel.

A month later, she rejected it. The good news is that the world is still here. That scenario is better than the other way around.

Other Ways To Make Money Writing

When I moved back from California in the mid-1980's, I temporarily stopped writing screenplays, but I didn't stop writing. I wrote poems, skits and roasts for family and friends. Regarding a steak-loving friend, on his fortieth birthday, I wrote, "Here's a guy whose favorite condiment is fat."

These skits went over well. I was advised to write them professionally.

"The Write Moment" was born.

I put ads in local papers, soliciting the business of anyone who needed a roast for their retiring boss, anniversary poem for their wife, poignant speech for their father's eightieth birthday or other occasion.

It was ironic that my first business card read:

· Writer …

· Screenplays

· Novels

· Stage Plays

· Desperate Poems

· Threatening Memos

· Letters to Unwelcome Relatives

Ten years after my first business card was printed, I really was writing anything a customer wanted me to write.

I wrote many tender poems and biting roasts. The problem was: everybody wanted me to write twenty pages for them and only charge for one hour, maybe two, at twenty-five dollars per hour. Most of my clients thought that paying more than fifty dollars for a roast was excessive. They tried to squeeze thousands of words out me for twenty-five bucks. It became intolerable.

After about a year, I was hoping that no one would answer my ads. I was rooting against the advertising copy I had created. I briefly considered getting a job in advertising.

Have you paid close attention to ads these days? Friends don't let friends go into the advertising business. I realized I must have been losing my mind to consider working for an advertising company. I quickly talked myself out of it. If I hadn't, I would've been forced to lock myself in a car trunk until I came to my senses. My role models do not include the character of Darren Stevens, Samantha's advertising executive husband on the 1960's sitcom, "Bewitched." I mean, this character had a wife with magical powers, who could help him through any problem with a nod or a twitch, and he still looked like he needed a double-martini after every work day.

Years later, I did make some money writing copy for TV commercials. My friend had a clothing store and asked me to write copy for his TV commercial, starring NFL star Reggie White, then with the Philadelphia Eagles.

The problem was, Reggie couldn't pronounce the name of the store, and I wasn't about to criticize him. He was six foot five and weighed three hundred pounds. I didn't want to upset him.

Also, he was a gentleman and an ordained minister. Why be negative? I asked him about scripture, since he signed an autograph for my friend (Mobil Mike asked me to get the autograph for his daughter) with a passage from the New Testament.

Reggie posed for the ad in a gigantic leather parka that was the size of a bedspread. About thirty cows had to die to provide the leather for this XXX-sized parka, complete with leather hood. I got the same parka that day --- and still have it, ten years later.

I was paid to write a TV commercial in the mid-1990's and, to my surprise, it turned out great. Usually, I think the script turned out great but feel a sense of disappointment when I view the finished product, like with "Jordi's Place." This TV ad was well-produced and actually got better after I handed in the script.

It was an ad for a production company that produced commercials. In it, the businessman asks the Godfather, "Don Pooch," if it would be all right for our company to produce commercials for his olive oil business. "Don Pooch" has misgivings and the businessman tells him that everything will be fine as long as he uses the best company, Eagle Films.

"You speak of film or video?" the wise old man asks.

"Either one."

"What are they using now, paisan?"

The Godfather knows he's being filmed!

"Film, Don Pooch. We're on film."

They were on film, and it looked as clear and bright as a movie. It was a little movie.

The Godfather says he'll think about it and the businessman leaves. When he gets to the parking lot, the businessman asks his bodyguard, "Think he's mad at me?"

The bodyguard shrugs.

"I'll wait here," the businessman says nervously. "Y-You start the car."

Everyone laughed at the ending. Now the commercial had to bring in some business so I could make a steady income from future commercials.

The actor who played the businessman bought air-time on the highest rated local TV news program. The commercial aired on a Monday night, after a fantastic Monday Night Football game, in the hours before a blizzard hit the area. Millions of people saw our commercial. Hundreds called, asking us to produce commercials for them.

Unfortunately, the actor who played the businessman changed his mind.

"I want to act in films, not produce commercials," he said.

He didn't return any of the calls. Hundreds of customers were left holding their money. (The article I wrote about this experience was published in Emmy Magazine.)

So, yes, there are many ways to earn a living with your writing. I only recommend an endeavor that will bring you joy.

As Jerry Stiller once said in a movie, "If there's money involved, it ain't love."

In another movie, Richard E. Grant's character said to his unborn child, "This is the only advice I will ever give you. If there's no money involved, it will probably be all right."

In that film, Grant was playing a poet who had been forced to work in the advertising business. It inspired me to write this passage in my novel, "Summer At Saratoga": "Everyone said there were worse things out there than easy money and I believed them."

If you try to make a lot of money writing what you love to write, you'll be happy even if you fail. Remember, if you fail at hard work, you've succeeded in working hard.

By the way, as an undergraduate, I was an advertising major. It was the most non-creative environment I have ever been around. I should have taken the hint and steered clear of writing TV ads

You've read my first business card, from 1979. The following was printed on my second business card, in 1980:

Commerciality.

I've got Commerciality.

Don't rhyme with originality but it sounds like opportunity.

If it reads just like "M*A*S*H"

Then it could bring some cash.

When my villain gets killed

They'll put me (name, address, phone number) in the guild.

Oh, Commerciality. Where's my marketability?

How about a man and his horse?

No, that's too creative. I'll be imitative.

Let the loves scenes pay for my Porsche.

'Cause Commerciality, undeniably, is coming to the tube and a theater near you.

Think you can control it? Your idea, well, they just stole it,

And it ended with a scene you saw in "Rocky II," yeah.

But it lacked integrity, evoked antipathy;

Reminded some of "Star Wars" -- It was written in a bar,

Took place in a planetarium and made some punk a star.

Without commerciality, you'll be a casualty;

Your work won't get to network chiefs

If you're Proctor or Gamble or both.

So remember Commerciality, move up in the industry,

Forget all the misery, you used to feel …

Along with passion and growth.

Self-Publishing Options For Writers

I saw a quote from a publisher recently, in the Philadelphia Inquirer's Consumer Watch, about unpublished writers.

"The vast majority of unpublished material is terrible - it's unpublished because it's unpublishable," the publisher said.

I read that quote and thought, "What an arrogant jackass." This "expert" claimed that most of you, even the twenty-year-olds, are terrible and unpublishable simply because you haven't yet achieved recognition. That really makes me angry. These publishers avoid good, young writers like the plague. The new talent never gets nurtured, and then they say, "See? Point proven. I told you they were no good."

That's like saying certain people make terrible spouses and then making sure that those people don't get dates. They wind up living alone for a hundred years, thus proving they were never marriage material.

This bonehead is saying that I was terrible for twenty years, writing unpublishable books. My answer to him is -- then why are those same books now getting published?

Sometimes I think that, if movie scripts weren't written for young cast members, none of us would see a young actor or actress on screen. If old artists didn't die, we might never see a painting from a young man or woman.

The motto of publishers, producers and agents is: "If you're not currently successful, you never will be."

They are so close-minded that their motto even applies to babies!

"Sorry, kid. You haven't proven a damn thing to me or anyone else. I doubt you ever will, even when they do let ya outta that incubator."

Of course, if you have been successful but hit a two year slump, you're out on your ear, too. You'll be lucky if you can get a seat by the kitchen and have a shrimp shell thrown your way. I heard about one writer who sold a script for mid-six figures when he was 26 years-old. A top agent represented him on the deal. The young writer failed to sell another script for six months and was dropped by his agent!

It wouldn't be such a hideous process if the publishers/producers/agents had talent of their own and commanded respect. Most do not, unless you consider back-slapping a talent.

There's a guy who took the easiest path and the easiest wife,

Making thousands a week and hating his life.

Of course; relax!

The truth is that some new writers don't have much talent or don't know what they're doing. Many young writers, however, deserve to be published and lack the opportunity. The system is at fault. Yet the decision-makers say it's because there is no new talent. Bankers are more open-minded than publishers. Lawyers are kinder; doctors less arrogant.

The truth is, publishers and producers have been saying I was no good for more than twenty years. I am more certain that they are wrong about me having no talent than I'm certain of my talent. It is the deep-seated notion that these front-running clowns are wrong that has kept me going.

A recent survey estimated that eighty percent of all Americans have thought about writing a book. So, what are the alternatives to traditional publishing?

Vanity publishers of years past have been replaced by "print-on-demand" publishers. The advantage to this type of publishing is that the author doesn't have to spend thousands of dollars to typeset and print a large number of books which usually wind up in a box in the author's garage.

Companies such as Xlibris and 1st Books (who send me brochures every other week, it seems) will produce your book in electronic form for a few hundred dollars and wait for you to place an order. You can go about promoting your book and, when you receive two-hundred-fifty orders, call them and order two-hundred-fifty books. The more books you get at one time, the cheaper they cost per copy.

Before we parted company, the co-author of "Ghetto Princess" (the inner-city story outlined by a student) told me that he wanted to self-publish the book. I told him that he must get distribution and marketing or he'd have trouble selling more than a few copies.

"I'm going to rent a billboard on I-95 and promote the book that way," he advised me.

The guy is a promotional sharpie and a self-professed con-man so maybe he will drum up thousands of orders. If he does, he can approach a traditional publisher with the book and say, "See? I sold thousands of copies of this book myself, in only a couple of months!"

I approached Xlibris once, in downtown Philadelphia, to talk about publishing my "… Did What?!" trademarked children's book series. I had spent so much time and money getting the trademark, I felt like I should do something with the book series. In 2002, I managed to get "Satchel Paige … Did What?!" published as a stage play in Plays Magazine. I retained the rights to the series.

At that time, in 2002, Xlibris admitted that they would have trouble distributing a short picture book through their distributor, Ingram. By the time you read this, maybe these self-publishing companies will have worked out the kinks in their distribution process. If you are interested in publishing your book, to have a product to show people, contact these companies and ask what they can do for you.

Check out www.Xlibris.com, www.1stbooks.com and www.iUniverse.com.

For books over one-hundred-fifty pages in length, Xlibris and 1st Books claim that many people will become aware of your book's existence. The book will be available online at their websites and also at amazon.com and barnesandnoble.com. They claim you can also order the books through regular bookstores.

The books typically retail for twenty-two dollars. You, the author, receive a forty percent discount. The set-up costs amount to about $500. They may ask for $500 on Monday, then call you back on Friday and drop the price to $350. They will try to take your money for proof-reading, copyrighting, artwork and other services.

These companies sign up a few hundred new authors per month. They publish several thousand books per year. Very few of these books sell more than a few hundred copies! Once in a while, a traditional publisher will take on the project so there is a glimmer of hope.

Here Are Some More Reasons To Embrace E-books:

- Retail sales of e-books rose forty percent in 2003, to 660,000 copies.
- Retail e-book revenues rose by thirty percent, one percent more than traditional publishers.
- The total number of e-book titles available rose by one-hundred-forty-four percent.

Here Are Some Reasons To Steer Clear Of E-books:

* Forty percent of all e-publishers have gone out of business. Another eighteen percent have stopped taking submissions.
* Time Warner's iPublish folded in 2001, and Random House scaled back its program in 2002.
* Steven King cancelled his serialized e-book, "The Plant" because of sagging sales.
* It is often difficult to get e-books listed on Internet bookstore sites.

For more information about electronic publishing, check out Moira Allen's FAQ at www.writing-world.com/publish/FAQ.shtml. She has published writer's guides, including a book on writing proposals. Contact her at moira@writing-world.com.

Why am I giving you the address of a competitor? Because I'm here to distill the truth, not maximize income (see page one). Besides, you've already purchased this book.

An Instructor's Perspective

In 2002, I began teaching writing courses at Bucks County Community College near Philadelphia. I now teach screenwriting, children's book writing and magazine writing.

In 2004, I began teaching in Rosemont College's MFA in Creative Writing program. The students there are wonderful; bright, talented and attractive. I figured I'd throw that in since they are likely to be reading this far into the book. (It's required reading.)

Holy Family University may hire me soon to teach English to their undergraduates. I hope they do since I can walk to their campus. (The campus is in Philadelphia county and I live in Bucks County but it's only a few blocks away.)

I doubt I will be teaching at all three institutions for decades because I'm kind of a loose cannon and have trouble dealing with authority. Like the undercover IRS agent I wrote about, I'm brash. That often rubs people the wrong way -- like I care. I can never be dismissed from my primary profession -- writing books and scripts on spec.

Anyway, in these classes (go to www.rosemont.edu or www.bucks@edu) I am asked some of the same questions that could be on your mind right now. I have tried to predict some of those questions and answer them effectively. Remember, there are no dumb questions ... and if there were, I would answer them, too, because they provide humor in this otherwise serious text. If you laughed at any point in this book, it proves that humor can be derived from very serious situations. The men in the gallows, preparing for their deaths - now, those guys were funny.

Here is an example of "gallows humor." An old vaudevillian was on his death bed. His protégé held his hand and asked the man, "Is dying hard?"

"No, dying is easy," the old man replied. "Comedy is hard!"

Before we get into the next Q & A chapter, here is some background information about how I got my first teaching gig.

"New Kid In Town"

This first-time college instructor stared at the students and thought, "If they only knew."

Hiring me to teach, anywhere, was like employing a fox to educate the chickens, enlisting an AWOL soldier to command the ROTC program or permitting a lead-foot with one hundred speeding tickets to tutor student drivers. After all, I was a "problem student" (college administrators' term, not mine) at Penn State, Temple (B.A.), Cal State Northridge and USC (MFA). I was like a guy who couldn't get along with women yet had intimate dates every night of the week, year in and year out.

It wasn't as if I disliked my college experience or dwelled longer than normal; I just wasn't there to follow other people's procedures. Heck, I didn't even listen to my well-intentioned, unconditionally loving parents at that age so why listen to strangers claiming to be "advisors"? I knew by their attitude that I was just a number to them. To be frank, the concept of taking their advice never occurred to me.

My first visit to a college campus occurred when I was fourteen. My parents took my older brother to visit Temple University, in North Philadelphia. We parked in a run-down neighborhood near campus and then paid someone to watch our car.

Some local kid called out, "Hey, mister, watch your cahr for a quawrter!" and Dad actually went along with the scam and paid him a quarter just to ... watch our car. I was tempted to get a similar job -- waiting for people to park their cars and then demanding a nickel to watch the paucity of action. After that, maybe I could charge a dime to keep an eye on someone's lawn.

I knew these tricks wouldn't work in my middle-class neighborhood -- the neighbors would probably pat me on the head and keep walking. They only worked in the mean streets near Temple and may have worked in a real fancy neighborhood but I wasn't sure why that was the case.

As a senior in high school, I was a B student. I never actually received a B; I earned A's if I paid attention in class or C's if I flirted with girls from buzzer to bell. I took the SAT's after a late-night party, getting, maybe, two hours of sleep. I did OK and was accepted at Penn State, main campus, starting that summer. I missed being at the beach in the summer and dropped every class except for English and softball, both of which I happened to enjoy. My GPA was terrific that semester. (I had excelled at all physical education courses. One semester, I needed a spare in the tenth frame of my last game to earn an A. "Ka-knock!" I called that course, "Bowling for Grade Points.")

Within a few months, I had transferred to the closest Penn State campus, near Philadelphia. Actually, I went from the main campus in State College (summer) to Delaware County campus (fall) to Abington Campus (winter) all by December first of my freshman year!

For two years, I got mostly A's, a few C's and absolutely no B's.

As a junior, majoring in advertising, I returned to PSU's main campus, where a horrible man told me, "You must take Spanish this semester or transfer to another school. Take your time," he said, "I'll give you thirty seconds." Then he put on a motorcycle helmet, like he was cool or something.

I seethed but stayed and was soon assigned to an annoying advisor. He told me, "You haven't yet taken Spanish or the history of the Russian Revolution. You must --"

"Look, stupid," I said. "I'm not here to listen to your 'sage' advice. It's my life, my education so I'll take what I want. Are we on the same page here?"

He threw a form at me.

"You're now a self-advisor. Congratulations. Get out of my office!"

I took whatever courses I desired during my junior year. When I walked into an advertising class-room, the "stupid" advisor was my teacher! I told him I was having a bad day and didn't mean anything by my "stupid" comment.

I wrote an ad for a bank which read: "More Than Just Money!" The teacher who disliked me was now calling me a "whiz kid." He photocopied my bank ad and distributed it to other advertising classes. I hated the ad -- thought it was boring. As the semester continued, I wrote more creative ads, which the teacher rejected. By the time I wrote my final project, I had gotten so creative that my roommate, who typed for me, asked if I was using LSD.

Sober and serious, I ordered him, "Just type!"

The episode with my advertising teacher reminds me of a scene in "The Doors" movie, where Jim Morrison, played by Val Kilmer, listens incredulously while his UCLA professor, played by Martin Scorsese, lauds his project. When the professor asks him to comment on his brilliant student film, which even his classmates love, Morrison/Kilmer says, "I quit" and walks out.

Uninspired by the PSU advertising major, I walked out; I transferred to Temple University for my senior year after my summer courses at Penn State were cancelled. My roommates had all graduated anyway and I didn't want to break in new ones at PSU.

While at Temple, a teaching assistant gave me a D for a term paper. I told him I had never received any grade lower than an A- for my papers, dating back to the sixth grade. He said my paper was fine; he didn't like my style. I shook an umbrella at him, pointed it at his chest and told the guy, who was one year older than I was, that he wasn't qualified to grade a first grade spelling test. We worked it out without anyone landing in the hospital (him) or prison (me).

In March of my senior year, I took the GRE's, a few hours after attending a Grateful Dead concert, getting, maybe, 45 minutes of sleep. My father is still mad at me for that all-nighter. The dean at Rose-mont College, where I now teach, told me she was the administrator of the GRE test at Temple University in March, 1977. I asked if she remembered me leaning so heavily against the coffee vending machine that it actually prevented me from collapsing onto the floor.

(Here's a quick SAT/GRE tip. I discovered that the test will reward students for reaching the very end of each section. When I got stuck in the middle of a section, I would jump to the last question and work backwards. The final three or four questions, to me at least, were the easiest. If you get bogged down in the middle of a section and don't get to the final questions, you'll miss a few "gimmes".)

I remember drinking about a gallon of vending machine coffee right before the test. (The vending machine really did keep me from toppling over.) Somehow, I improved my score from the SAT's and made plans to attend Cal State Northridge, as a theater arts graduate student.

Then, a horrible woman at Temple told me that since I had taken some doctoral level courses in speech communication, she wouldn't recommend my graduation. (No undergraduate courses were offered my final semester, so I got approval from individual professors to take courses at the graduate level. Where was the crime?)

"I'm done," I said. "Are you going to stop me from graduating because I earned good grades in doc-toral level courses?"

"I would if I could," she said with a sneer.

"In other words, we have nothing more to discuss," I announced before exiting her office, trusty umbrella in hand. Days later, I went to California with a liberal arts degree, not a speech communication degree. (I've had to live with worse.)

While at Cal State, I loved my writing courses more than acting or directing so I decided to seek an MFA in writing at either UCLA or USC. UCLA said I had to have previous success for any chance of acceptance. (I told them I was the twenty-two-year-old assistant director of "Star Wars" but they didn't believe me.)

USC said they'd enjoy having me, if I wanted to write a novel for four credits, a screenplay for four credits, and so on, until I earned thirty-two credits at the post-graduate level.

I finished the 32 credits in nine months. I advised USC administrators of that fact and they admitted they had me down as a provisional student.

"I'm done," I said. "When you figure it out, send the MFA to Mom and Dad in Philadelphia."

Seven months later, they did. Honestly, I had almost forgotten about it. If you think your college graduation will be the most exciting event in the history of civilization, forget it. You'll already be thinking about the next chapter in your life. I've been through it twice and found both to be thoroughly anti-climactic. (My wedding day - now that was exciting.)

What I learned from all that moving around is that I enjoyed my graduate school years much more than my undergraduate years. In graduate school, I was treated like an adult. I was expected to think and develop, not just regurgitate information on test day. If you consider the first four years of college uninspiring, at best, rely on the notion that you may cherish your graduate school experience.

So, here I am, decades later, a professor, shaping the minds and creative writing skills of students. After my first class, though, I had a problem.

One student writer said she wasn't going to talk about her proposed book because she thought someone in the class would steal her idea. The class snapped at her, calling her names, asking what made her so damn special. ("Your work is worth stealing and ours isn't?")

I kindly explained that her work was completely safe. With respect and compassion, I assured her there were no thieves in class. To ease her mind, I told her how to copyright her work with the Library of Congress. If I were her classmate, not her instructor, I would have told her to buy a psychopathology book and pay special attention to the chapter on paranoia. She was one of my first students so I was gentle.

What did she do? She wrote a nasty letter to the college dean, claiming I belittled her! I had gone unpunished as a "problem student" but, decades later, had received a black mark for being a compassionate professor. I felt the same way after my transformation from camper to camp counselor. I was living in a parallel universe. The feeling is best explained by the old song, "Won't Get Fooled Again" by "The Who," which goes, "And their team on the left, is now our team on the right."

Finally, here is my favorite college story. I was on USC's campus in 1980 when a stunning woman parked her fancy jeep in a clearly-marked tow-away zone and proceeded quickly, purposefully, toward a high rise building. Everyone stared at her like she was a movie star -- and she probably was -- but nobody had the guts to say a word, except for me, who shouted, in my best/worst Philadelphia accent, "Hey, lady, watch your cahr for a quawrter!"

She patted me on the head and kept walking.

The actress' gesture sums up my advice to present and future college students. Get your undergraduate degree, no matter how crass it seems, so you can find out what you really want to do with your life. Then pursue those interests in graduate school, where you'll be treated like an adult, not a farm animal with an ID number.

When they give you that advanced degree, don't expect fireworks and a presidential citation. Just pat them on their heads ... and keep walking.

What Kind Of Writer Do You Want To Be?

By now, you have read what it's like to spend time and energy in pursuit of a writing career. If you have any common sense, you'll marry that wealthy guy or girl in your history class and go to work for your industrialist father-in-law. Buy a mansion and yacht and forget about the dreams you had as an idealistic undergraduate. Paul Simon once advised us to pretend that we can build those dreams again.

If you choose financial security over your labor of love, you'll be falling into a trap! You'll be denying the existence of your higher spirit. If you have read this far, you probably have your heart set on being a writer, which is a blessing and a curse.

Feast or famine, feast or famine, I don't know what's worse.

Feast or famine, feast or famine, The blessing is the curse.

You'll be blessed with having enthusiasm for work every day of your life but you'll be cursed with economic hardship for a few decades.

On the other hand, you might be cursed with having to write nonsense for an advertising firm but be blessed with fame and fortune.

I don't know which is worse - the blessing or the curse. I do know I like the sound of the poem. I don't quite understand it (although I wrote it) but that will come with time; sort of like the government's JFK assassination theories.

Here is a Poem About The Writing Life:

There off in the distance,

My apprenticeship,

Driven off by this salesman

More than workmanship.

But when a challenge seems done,

Another one has begun

And the last took a decade

before it was done.

There were times I could have hid.

Some times I really cried.

When they asked me what I did,

I could just say what I tried.

So I've taken a step.

It wasn't for free.

I believe in my plan,

Though it didn't come from me.

I will stick to this writing life

Because there's so much to be won.

Won't it all seem so easy

Right after it's done?

So what kind of writer do you want to be? When people ask, do you want to tell them that you're a struggling screenwriter, struggling novelist, struggling journalist, struggling children's book writer; what?

Forget about what you're going to tell people. As a matter of fact, forget about people altogether. Make believe you're in a pyramid scheme; set your goals and ignore the critics.

Will you apply to graduate school? That is a good place to test yourself, to see if you really want to get up every day and write. I attended USC's graduate school and stayed up every night to write. I would sleep on the beach when the sun came up. When I woke up from my beach nap, I would feel as if someone had hit me in the head with a hammer. I'd take a shower and type another class assignment. I knew I wanted to do the same thing for the rest of my life (minus the dehydrating naps on the beach).

At first, I was a playwriting major. I had some plays published in college and enjoyed every theater class I had taken. When I got to Cal State Northridge as a graduate student, I worked in many theaters that were just plain drafty. I never minded standing around on a movie set in the cold and snow, but I hated those drafty theaters. That was part of the reason why I transferred to a screenwriting program.

There were three terrific programs: USC, UCLA and NYU. I knew I wanted to stay near the center of the movie business so I chose USC, which was fortunate because I didn't bother applying to NYU and UCLA didn't want me. (Like Groucho Marx, I wasn't sure that I wanted entry into a group that would have me as a member. I did know that I wanted to move into the Playa del Rey, California, beachfront apartment that rented for only $350 per month; sealing the deal at USC.)

Don't expect an advanced degree to help you sell your work or impress producers, publishers, editors or agents. I can tell you with certainty that very few people will ask about your degree. Fewer will care. The good news is that an advanced degree can help you in unexpected ways. The only people who asked about my MFA were college administrators; the people who decided if I was worth hiring as a professor. The irony is that I never set out to be a college professor. I did, however, have a recurring dream set on a snowy, Eastern, college campus. When I lived in Playa del Rey, I must have had the same dream -- in which I was in my car, smiling and waving to pretty co-eds waiting at a snowy bus stop -- once a month for seven years. I now believe the college in my dream was Rosemont. Cue the music from "The Shining."

One time, a college administrator, the head of an undergraduate English Department, told me he couldn't consider my resume because I didn't have a master's degree.

"Sure I do. It's right there in the resume."

"Well, it's not in creative writing."

"What are you saying?" I wondered. "That screenwriting is not creative writing? What is it then? Technical writing? Business writing? Medical research writing?"

We argued for a while, evoking fond memories of arguments I had with administrators as an undergraduate.

Even Eva Peel, the woman who helps writers promote their work to producers, told me to drop any reference to my master's degree on my project list. She said producers wouldn't care.

"Why wouldn't they care?" I asked.

"Because it's not the right degree," she barked.

"It's a screenwriting degree from a world-famous film school!" I insisted.

"It is? Oh, that's OK, then."

It's as if the words "MFA, USC" are invisible on the pages of my resume and project lists. Or people read it as "BYOB" or "NO PETS ALLOWED."

The graduate program was invaluable to me for one reason: it allowed me to prove to myself that I wanted to get up every day -- or in my case, every night -- and write. I knew I was cut out for the career.

One magazine writing professor began his class most weeks with, "At the risk of swelling Rutberg's head, I want to read you his lead paragraph."

Another professor, my mentor, Jack Langguth, recommended me to his friend, a producer who worked at the late billionaire Armand Hammer's production company. I sold my first screen treatment a month after finishing my master's degree. It was about the city which hosted the Super Bowl that year.

So, by earning a graduate degree, I gained confidence doing the work, not just talking about it. I got off to a running start. Sure, I stalled for a couple of decades, but that period is over now. As my dad says, "What was, was." As Satchel Paige said, "Don't look back."

In the paragraph describing the college courses I now teach, I tell prospective students, "This course is about doing it, not talking about it."

You will meet many students in your writing courses who talk a good game. They know all the cinematic theories and approaches to novel outlines and plots but they can't write a decent script or book to save their lives! That is why Jim Morrison, played by Val Kilmer in "The Doors" movie, walked out of his classroom. His peers loved his film and he knew that his peers were incompetent.

I don't, however, recommend quitting school and joining a rock and roll band. Roll your eyes when you receive unfair criticism from your classmates.

Maybe you prefer writing magazine articles. In that case, find a college that specializes in journalism. (Northwestern has a great reputation.) Push yourself to be the best student at the best journalism school in the country. Get a great job after graduation and rise to national prominence. After you've established a reputation, write anything you want. You'll probably sell it all.

Also, get to know your instructors. Talk to them after class is over. Drive them home if they don't have a car. You can learn more after class than during class.

In 1978, I drove my instructor, Stephen Longstreet, from his home to his novel writing class at USC, and back again, almost every session. He was in Paris in the 1920's with Ernest Hemingway, Gertrude Stein and other literary giants. He was an artist who earned ten dollars a drawing from The New York Times. When he heard that the Times was paying fifteen dollars for short stories, he became a writer.

"No one influenced my writing," he told me. "I was an artist."

I liked the sound of that.

Longstreet told me that he was responsible for keeping William Faulkner sober when Faulkner moved to Los Angeles in the 1940's or '50's. He said that he had written "Stallion Road," a film which starred Ronald Reagan. A critic wrote in a major newspaper, "If you're a horse, you'll like this movie." Longstreet sent Reagan a telegram: "Our horse saw the movie and didn't like it!"

Longstreet told me in the car, "Life is for living, not for creating great art or making a lot of money. Those are by-products of living. Our lives are filled mainly with failures, with a few minor successes mixed in."

When Jack Langguth, my magazine writing professor (and now one of my dearest friends) asked the class to write an article about someone famous, I wrote about Longstreet. It was called, "Stephen Good; Stephen Bad." (That's what Longstreet said he would call his autobiography.) When speaking about my work, Longstreet said, "It was the only time in my life where I recognized myself in an article." I was filled with pride.

No one bought the article. Editors told me that, "Longstreet hasn't done anything in a while." He wasn't the latest rage. The reality was, he was one of the most interesting men I had ever met in my life. His Hemingway stories alone were worth publishing.

Longstreet said that Hemingway had no sense left at the end of his life because he had been hit in the head too many times. He had been a boxer and absorbed many head blows. Then he had a skylight or roof cave in on his head in Paris. He was also in a plane crash, where he hit his head. When a rescue plane came and picked him up, it crashed!

That reminds me of an older man in Atlantic City whose doctor told him to stop riding a bicycle because he kept getting into bicycle accidents on the boardwalk. The guy stopped riding his bike. One day, later that summer, while walking on the boardwalk, he got run over by a bike!

What are the odds that you'll give up bicycling and get hit by a bike or that just after you've been in a plane crash, you'll be involved in another plane crash?

Hemingway's mother sent him the gun that his father had used to kill himself. That was the same gun Hemingway used to blow his brains out.

"Life is for living."

I never would have known that if I didn't volunteer to drive Stephen Longstreet back and forth to class at USC.

Want a good reason to attend graduate school? I disliked many of my professors as an undergraduate and adored most of my professors as a graduate student. Maybe it was because I had matured. Maybe it was because, at the undergraduate level, they treated students like cattle and motivated them with electronic prods. It was probably both reasons.

If you can't attend undergraduate school ("Moo"), take continuing education courses. Join a writing group in your area. Go to writers' conferences. Believe that the cream will rise to the top and a lucky break will find you.

It is a lot easier to apply first aid to your writing career if you know exactly what medium you want to pursue. People told me to go into sports writing. But I took my own advice about ignoring what people tried to tell me. I wrote what I wanted to write that day, with mixed results and delayed rewards. In the USA, at this point, I would hardly be considered successful. In the Japanese culture, however, where the most successful people are the ones who have freedom to do whatever they want each day, I would probably be asked to sign autographs.

I've been lucky to enjoy so much creative freedom. If freedom is what you need, too, remember that the freest always bleed. Be aware that while you're free but struggling, you will get carved up by the people who took the easiest paths to success. Deal with it, brothers and sisters.

Can I have an "Amen" from the congregation?

Q & A

Q: Will magazine editors read my query letters and reply more consistently than film producers or book publishers?

A: Yes! Just be sure to target appropriate editors. Send a query about bird migrations to a bird-watching magazine, queries about roulette tournaments to a gambling magazine, and so forth.

Here is a question from Stephen (formerly known as "Steve") in my magazine writing class:

Q: How much can I expect to make for writing an ongoing -- every two months -- column on wine for a local magazine? The magazine is flashy looking, glossy, nice.

A: Steve, it sounds like the magazine is expensive to print so the editor should have money to pay you for an ongoing column. I've been paid thousands and I've been paid as little as twenty-five dollars for my articles. You should expect something between those figures, probably closer to the smaller number. If they pay you one-hundred-fifty dollars for every article, take it. In the future, you could send samples of your wine column to a larger publication, and they could hire you away from the local magazine and pay you ten times more for the same work.

Q: Should I be familiar with the magazines I query?

A: In a perfect world, you would have read the magazine every month since the 1980's. When I send out a hundred queries, I do not have time to become familiar with every one of those magazines. If I did, I wouldn't have time to write the queries … or the articles! Research each magazine the best you can in order to submit appropriate material.

Q: Should I submit complete articles, as opposed to query letters, to magazine editors?

A: Yes, unless the magazine specifically indicates, "No unsolicited articles." Think about it. If you have a charming, humorous, interesting five page article -- about 1,250 words -- won't you be better off having an editor read the five pages rather than a two sentence synopsis? I sent the "Pluto" article synopsis to over a hundred magazine editors over a fifteen-year period. No one bought it. Then I sent the article to Emmy Magazine and the editor liked it but couldn't use it. He actually thanked me within the pages of the magazine for sending it to him for consideration, which was unexpected. A year later, I emailed the article -- not just the synopsis -- to Horizon Magazine and they published it a month or two later. So, if a magazine is willing to read an entire article, send your best one to that editor. Better yet, send two.

Q: It's OK to send two articles at the same time?

A: If they are both appropriate for that magazine, sure. Why shoot once at the bear if you have three or four bullets in the chamber? For you animal lovers, think of it like this: at Westminster, why show one dog that you've bred when you can show several beautiful dogs?

Q: Can I submit ten articles at once?

A: No! Unless you send two each to five different editors. That is a good idea because you can get widespread feedback and discover which article has the best chance of selling. When you learn which has the most appeal, send that article out most often.

Q: What are trade Magazines?

A: They are published for plumbers, caterers, morticians, and other trades. They seek stories that will appeal to a certain group of people who work in those fields.

Q: Once I sell an article to an editor, should I keep trying to sell other articles to the same person or move on?

A: Keep trying! Once they have published your work, they feel better about you as a writer. You will be seen as a proven entity; someone who can produce what they need. You should take advantage of that status. It is easier to sell an editor a second and third piece than it is to sell them the first piece.

If you have other questions about how to apply first aid to your writing career, or if you would like me to help you write or rewrite (for a fee) one of your projects (I'll only work with you if I love the story) please feel free to email me from my web site at: www.awritersfirstaidkit.com.

I look forward to answering your emails as quickly as possible.

Final Thoughts On Everything -- Part Two

To further inspire you to persevere with your writing career, take a look at how well it's worked out for me. I'll soon be driving around (for one day) in a (rented) Rolls Royce!

As you get older, it will matter less if your projects bring success, fame and fortune. It's like having your own children. You brought them into the world; does it really matter if they're modestly successful or industry leaders? The correct answer is "No!" You have to love them and do the right thing for them.

Find your writing niche and crank out material until they peel your moribund fingers off the computer keyboard.

I once described my birthday in Hollywood this way:

I'll tell you how my 29th was spent,

Walking streets engraved with hints

Of Hollywood celebrities.

I left no footprints in cement --

All I left were fingerprints

Embedded on these typing keys.

I always write a poem on my birthday. It is like a time capsule, capturing my mood and self-image every November. I recommend that you start doing it, too. In twenty years, I predict you'll read the poem you wrote this year and say, "I was right on target. How did I know what was really going on under the surface?"

I don't share these poems with everyone. No one, that is, but you. Maybe I show them to my wife and parents but that's all. It's as if I'm writing them for another person -- the man I will become in twenty years. I hope that the man in his sixties will look at the old birthday poems, shrug and say, "Look how much I've grown since then."

When things are rough, when you can't sell so much as a thirty-word article to a toddler's magazine, imagine yourself twenty years in the future. Do you think it will seem like such a big deal then? It will probably be a fond memory of your most challenging years.

I just sold a story

And shouted, "Hooray!"

Someday I'll ask myself,

"That made my day?"

Of course; relax!

Like the man said in the film, "Things To Do In Denver When You're Dead": "A person's life is like a mustard burp - momentarily tangy but quickly forgotten."

Try to be like my "Leprechaun Named Levity" and not take things too seriously. I try to break down everything to its simplest form - nothingness! Why worry about nothing?

I just read about a guy who is developing artificial organs -- at age ninety-two. That's what we should be doing at age ninety-two -- developing important projects. This fellow recently received a $500,000 grant to keep working. With inflation, imagine the kind of grant money that should be available to writers by the time we're ninety-two. We could still be in our primes, writing away, happily and healthily, especially if this scientist perfects artificial organs.

I don't know whether writers can make the world a better place, like medical researchers or philanthropists. If your higher spirit tells you, "This is what you must do," then accept it as your fate. There are worse fates, as you know by now if you've read the chapters on agents. (That is my final shot at agents, in this book, anyway.)

Consider the approach taken by Dannion Brinkley, who died (twice) and met his spirit guides in heaven.

"This is what you must do," they instructed before returning him to Earth.

Dannion said, "I was going to spend all of eternity with these beings. I couldn't tell them, 'No.'"

Dannion had to die (twice) to reach the conclusion that he should follow his higher spirit. We, as writers, can reach the same conclusion ... and, with a little first aid, survive!

Resources

Agent Research & Evaluation

www.agentresearch.com/agent_ver.html

American Screenwriters Association

269 S. Beverly Drive, Ste. 2600, Beverly Hills, CA 90212

866-265-9091

asa@goasa.com

Association of Author's Representatives

www.aar-online.org

Canadian Screenwriter

800-567-9974

info@wga.ca

Creative Screenwriting (*highly recommended)

323-957-1406

www.creativescreenwriting.com

Fade In Magazine

fadeinmag@aol.com

Film Threat

818-248-4549

input@filmthreat.com

Hollywood Reporter

323-525-2150

subscriptions@hollywoodreporter.com

Hollywood Scriptwriter

866-HSWRITER

editor@hollywoodscriptwriter.com

Indienews.com

310-288-1882

films@indienews.com

Indiewire.com

contact@indiewire.com

Moviemaker Magazine

310-234-9234

staff@moviemaker.com

Premiere Magazine

212-767-5400

premiere@neodata.com

Publishers Lunch

www.caderbooks.com

Publishers Marketplace

www.publishersmarketplace.com

Publisher's Weekly

publishersweekly.reviewsnews.com

Screentalk Magazine

www.screentalk.org

Screenwriter Magazine

800-418-5637

info@nyscreenwriter.com

Variety

800-323-4345

variety@espcomp.com

Writer Beware

www.sfwa.org/beware

Writers' Guild of America

www.wga.org

Writer's Market

www.writersmarket.com

Written By (Writers' Guild of America, West)

888-974-8629

writtenBy@wga.org

Internet Sites

Alaska Screenwriters

www.asascreenwriters.com/alaskascreenwriters.shtml

Arizona Screenwriters

www.asascreenwriters.com/arizonascreenwriters.shtml

and so on for Cincinnati, Dallas, Hawaii, lawritersgroup, nassaucounty, northernnewjersey, ad infinitum.

Organization of Black Screenwriters (Los Angeles, CA)

www.asascreenwriters.com/orgblackscreen.shtml

Scriptwriters Network (Los Angeles, CA)

www.asascreenwriters.com/scriptwritersnetwork.shtml

Glossary

Above-the-Line Costs: Portion of the budget that covers major creative participants (writer, director, actors and producer) including script and story development costs.

Action: In a script, action is your description of what is happening. Be as visual as possible but don't exceed three lines of action at a time. In a court of law, action is a law suit.

Adaptations: Derivative works. When a motion picture is based on a book, the movie has been adapted from the book.

Adjusted Gross Participation: Gross participation minus certain costs, such as cost of advertising and duplication. Also called "Rolling Gross." If many deductions are allowed, the participant is essentially getting a "net profit" deal.

Advance: Up-front payment against monies that may be payable at some time in the future. Advance payments that are not refundable even if future monies are never due.

AFMA: Is the abbreviation for the American Film Marketing Association, an association for film distributors.

Agency Clause: Is usually added to contracts by agents to contracts that they negotiate, requiring that money owing to the writer under the agreement will be paid to the writer's agent on the writer's behalf. The agent then passes on the royalties or fees to the writer, minus the agent's commission.

Answer Print: The first composite of sound and picture of a motion picture print from the laboratory with editing, score and mixing completed. Usually color values will need to be corrected before a release print is made.

Art Theater: Movie houses that specialize in art films, generally in exclusive engagements, rather than mass-market studio films.

Back End: Writers, producers and actors' profit participation in a film after distribution and/or production costs have been recouped. This can greatly reduce the up front costs of getting a project done.

Below-The-Line Costs: The technical expenses and labor including set construction, crew, camera equipment, film stock, developing and printing.

Box Office Receipts: What the theater owner takes in from ticket sales to customers at the box office. A portion of this revenue is remitted to the studio/distributor in the form of rental payments. These monies are part of the "Back End" profits.

Character Name: element above dialogue in your script. It indicates who is talking.

Completion Bond: A form of insurance, which guarantees financing to complete a film in the event that the producer exceeds the budget. Completion bonds are sometimes required by banks and investors to secure loans and investments in a production. Should a bond be invoked, the completion guarantor may assume control over the production and be in a recoupment position superior to all investors.

Consideration: The reason or inducement for a party to contract with another. Usually money, but can be anything of value such as the obligation to write another screenplay. The right, interest or benefit to one party, or the loss or forbearance of another. A necessary element for a contract to be binding.

Concept: The general idea behind your script.

Context: The world in which your story takes place.

Cross Collateralization: Practice by which distributors off-set financial losses in one medium or market against revenue derived from others. For example, the sales of action figures are combined with those from books, and after the expenses for both are deducted, the remainder, if any, is net revenue. Filmmakers don't like to have revenues and expenses pooled because it may reduce the amount of money they receive.

Crossover: A story, book or film that is initially targeted to a narrow specialty market but achieves acceptance in a wider market.

Dailies (Rushes): Usually an untimed one-light print, made without regard to color balance, from which the action is checked and the best takes selected. The need for rewrites are often determined by producers/directors opinions of the dailies.

Deal Memo: A letter or short contract.

Defamation: A statement that may be false and that injures another's reputation in the community.

Default: Failure to perform. Example: If a writer misses a rewrite during production of a film.

Deferred Payment: When writers, directors, cast, crew or others accept some or all of their compensation later in order to reduce production costs. A deferred fee is generally paid from revenues generated from a completed motion picture, and if a movie is not finished, or it does not generate significant revenue, then the deferred payment holder may not be paid for his contribution.

Development: The process by which an initial idea is turned into a finished screenplay. Includes optioning the rights to an underlying literary property, and commissioning writer(s) to create a treatment, first draft, second draft, rewrite, and polish.

Dialogue: It is every word we hear on screen.

Dissolve: An optical or camera effect in which one scene gradually fades out at the same time that another scene fades in.

Distributor: A company that distributes a motion picture, placing it in theaters and any media, and advertising and promoting it. The major studios nowadays are mostly in the business of financing and distributing films, leaving production to smaller independent companies.

Distribution Expenses: May include taxes, residuals, trade association dues, conversion/transmission costs, collection costs, checking costs, advertising and publicity costs, re-editing costs, print duplication, foreign version costs, transportation and shipping costs, and insurance. Expenses that may effect the Back End participants.

Domestic Rights: Usually defined as U.S. and English-speaking Canada.

Double Distribution Fees: Occurs when a distributor uses a sub-distributor to sell a film. If multiple distributors are allowed to deduct their full fees, the filmmaker and others on the Back End are less likely to see any money.

Exterior (EXT.): This means your scene takes place outside.

Final Cut: The last stage in the editing process. The right to final cut is the right to determine the final version of the picture.

First-Dollar Gross: The most favorable form of gross participation for the participants. Only a few deductions, such as checking fees, taxes and trade association dues are deductible.

First Monies: From the producer's point-of-view, the first revenue received from the distribution of a movie. Not to be confused with profits, first monies are generally allocated to investors until recoupment, but may be allocated in part or in whole to deferred salaries owed to talent or deferred fees owed a film laboratory.

Foreign Sales: Licensing a film in various territories and media outside the U.S. and Canada. Although Canada is a foreign country, American Distributors Typically Acquire English-speaking Canadian Rights when they license U.S. rights.

Front Office: The top executives, the people who control the money.

Genres: A category for your film. It can be comedy, romance, horror, mystery, Sci-fi, and others.

General Partners: Management side of a limited partnership (the position usually occupied by the film's producers) which structures a motion picture investment and raises money from investors who become limited partners. General partners make the business decisions regarding the partnership.

Gross After Break-Even: The participant shares in the gross after the break-even point has been reached. The break-even point can be a set amount or determined by a formula.

Gross Participation: A piece of gross receipts without any deductions for distribution fees or expenses or production costs. However, deductions for checking and collection costs, residuals and taxes are usually deductible. A "piece of the gross" is the most advantageous type of participation from the participant's point of view. In an audit, it is the most easily verified form of participation.

Gross Receipts: Studio/distributor revenues derived from all media, including film rentals, television and home video licenses, merchandising and ancillary sales.

High Concept: An inherently funny or provocative situation. Two men have to dress as women to get accepted to a college, that kind of thing.

Hyphenates: Persons who fulfill two or more major roles such as producer-director, writer-director or actor-director.

Interior (INT.): This means your scene takes place inside.

Libel: The written form of defamation. Slander is the spoken form of defamation.

Licensee: Person who is given a license or permission to do something.

Licensor: The person who gives or grants a license.

Limited Partnership: Form of business enterprise commonly used to finance movies. General partners initiate and control the partnership; limited partners are the investors and have no control of the running of the partnership business and no legal or financial liabilities beyond the amount they have invested.

Master: The final edited and complete film or videotape from which subsequent copies are made.

Merchandising Rights: Right to license, manufacture and distribute merchandise based on characters, names or events in a picture.

Multi-Tiered Audience: An audience of different types of people who find the film attractive for different reasons, and who must be reached by different publicity, promotion or ads.

Negative Cost: Actual cost of producing a film including the manufacture of a completed negative (does not include costs of prints or advertising). It may be defined to include overhead expenses, interest and other expenses, which may inflate the amount way beyond what was actually spent to make the film.

Net Profit: What is left, if anything, after all allowable deductions are taken. This usually amounts to zero. Typically expressed in terms of a portion of 100% of net profits, such as 5% of 100%.

Novelization: A book adapted from a motion picture.

Off-Hollywood: American independent films made outside the studio system.

On Spec: Working for nothing on the hope and speculation that something will come of it.

Original Material: Not derived or adapted from another work.

Pan: A horizontal movement of the camera.

Pan & Scan: Used to transfer a film to video for use on standard television because of the different image aspect ratio (the ratio of the width versus the height of the image).

Parenthetical: A direction to the actor about how to read dialogue. These are being used less, unless it goes against the character's emotion.

Premise: The foundation of your story.

Pro Rata: Proportionately.

Remake: A new production of a previously produced film.

Revision: What most writers have to do after they've finished writing the first draft.

Right of Privacy: The right to be left alone, and to be protected against a variety of intrusive behavior such as unjustified appropriation of one's name, image or likeness; the publicizing of intimate details of one's life without justification and unlawful eavesdropping or surveillance.

Right of Publicity: The right to control the commercial value and use of one's name, likeness and image.

SASE: This means you are expected to supply the proper Self Addressed Stamped Envelope to return anything you expect to get back. This is by no means a guarentee that you will get it or your materials back.

Scene Headings: This tells the reader where the scene takes place; what we are seeing.

Sequel: A book or film that tells a related story that occurs later than the original. A continuation of an earlier story, usually with the same characters.

Shooting Script: A later version of the screenplay in which each separate shot is numbered and camera directions are indicated.

Sitcom: A situation comedy for TV.

Spec: A work done on speculation. A work done in hope of finding a buyer for the finished work.

Story Analyst or Reader: A person employed to read submitted scripts and properties, synopsize and evaluate them. Often the people who have this job don't know a great deal about the subject of the script or filmmaking.

Story Conference: A meeting at which the writer receives suggestions about how to improve his/her script.

Talent: The word used to describe those involved in the artistic aspects of filmmaking such as the writers, actors and directors as opposed to the business people.

Target market: The defined audience segment a distributor seeks to reach with its advertising and promotion campaign, such as teens, women over 30, yuppies, etc.

Television Distribution Fee: Typically 10-25% for U.S. Network broadcast sales, 30-40% for domestic syndication and 45-50% for foreign distribution.

Television Spin-Off: A television series or mini-series based on characters or other elements in a film.

Theme: A unifying idea in your story. Example: Endangered animals should be protected.

Trades: The daily and weekly periodicals of the industry, such as "Variety" and "The Hollywood Reporter."

Translation: The reproduction of a book, movie or other work into another language.

Unagented: A person not represented by an agent.

Work-for-Hire or Work-made-for-hire: Under the Copyright Act this is either 1) a work prepared by an employee within the scope of employment; or 2) a specially ordered or commissioned work of a certain type, such as a motion picture, a contribution to a collective work if the parties expressly agree so in a writing signed by both before work begins.

Appendices

Appendix A: TV Series Treatment

"When Angels Speak ... (They Argue)"

Television Comedy Series
Treatment

Created and Written
by
Donald Paul Rutberg

© 2004

CONCEPT

An outgoing, hedonistic, arbitration lawyer dies and is disappointed to learn that he's been assigned a similar job in a dull, sterile world known as heaven. With no chance to enjoy the Earthly pleasures his spirit craves, the only lawyer in heaven enters the game of angelic politics, hoping to add some life to his death.

"When Angels Speak ... (They Argue)" is a comedy series about characters coping with death -- their own. It's the afterlife story of Charley Merriweather, the only lawyer in heaven, where debate is the only vice. He's called upon to arbitrate differences between argumentative angels and negotiate deals with the devilishly unscrupulous opposition. The folks in hell, it seems, have been taking advantage of angels since the two sides split up.

The series derives its comedy from the characters' personalities clashing with their surroundings. The angels want excitement but not sin. The devils want redemption but not the sterility of heaven. Charley's job is to help turn hell into a rugged version of heaven, without behaving in such a way that will get him banished there forever. He learns that the decisions we make after we die help determine where we belong.

FORMAT

The story unfolds in heaven and hell. Occasionally, Charley will invent reasons to visit his longtime companion, Wanda, on Earth. (He can't get permission to visit Earth from executive angels so he solicits favors from high ranking devils.)

While on negotiating trips, literally, to hell, Charley procures a love interest -- an ex-vampire woman named Karla -- and befriends an inadvertent devil named Dominic. These three find they share the same values, even though they are worlds apart; separated by what we learn is a very fine line.

While he operates a one-angel law office in heaven, Charley meets the religious leader of the angels, Muck, the Caveman Messiah. Through Muck, Charley learns the wisdom of the ages; passages such as, "Go forth to wherest thou climate suits thy clothes."

Charley has a home in heaven but he rarely visits because he must share the place with his ex-wife, Ginger (whom he married for six weeks when he was 18 years old) and her family, all parolees from hell. Although Charley's own family also exists in this home, he doesn't recognize anyone, claiming wistfully, "I used to think all the good relatives were dead. Now I'm dead and they'll all alive!"

The format underscores Charley's need to exist just as he did in his most recent life -- which he can not fully accept as being over.

MAIN CHARACTERS

CHARLEY MERRIWEATHER is the fun-loving attorney whose life changes drastically after he dies. He can no longer earn money as a personal injury lawyer and enjoy an affluent lifestyle, such as he had on Earth. He can, however, apply his arbitration skills in heaven, where even the minor cases hold deep meaning in the grand scheme of existence.

As the only lawyer to gain admission into heaven, Charley feels a responsibility to do a good job. Although he has some moments of weakness while on negotiating trips, his firsthand knowledge of vice, deceit and corruption more than qualifies him to represent heaven in dealings with hell.

Charley's goal is to be reincarnated so he can be reunited with his loved ones on Earth.

DOMINIC is Charley's best friend, a likeable devil who's been unjustly sent to hell.

The reluctant demon acts as tour guide for Charley, enabling the bored angel to let off a little steam in hell. Dominic's one goal in the afterlife is to gain angel status.

MUCK is the cave man messiah just as Muckism is the official religion in heaven. Born too soon (before history) to be revered on Earth, he has just one regret: he could've been Elvis.

THE BOSS is the leader of the devils; a single parent who loves where he lives and has a genuine zest for the afterlife.

#1 & #2 are trans-gendered executive angels who finally decide they need a cagey negotiator like Charley on their side.

WANDA is Charley's loyal ex-secretary on Earth who struggles to take over his law practice. Charley is disturbed when he learns she's engaged to an ambitious medical student. (Charley warns her, "If you're a lawyer and a doctor's wife, they'll never let you in heaven!") Charley misses Wanda, his long-time companion, and invents reasons to visit her on Earth.

KARLA is the kindly vampire woman from hell who falls in love with Charley. She'll do anything for the heavenly lawyer and tries to improve herself to merit his affection.

GINGER was Charley's wife for six weeks -- 25 years ago. Accordingly, he must exist with her in the afterlife. Ginger, who's better suited for hell, will stay in heaven only until Charley can exchange her and her family for angels held hostage down below. Charley gives Ginger's case the highest priority.

LEO is Ginger's brother, also on parole from hell. He's not exactly a great influence on the angels.

HORACE is a very serious, stuffy angel; a buffer between Charley and the decision- makers in heaven.

THE YOUNG POET is mocked by the other angels for being too sensitive. Charley puts him under his wing, literally.

THE WARRIOR ANGEL is a gentle giant; a heavenly "bouncer" who acts as a glorified doorman. Charley offers him a more rewarding job as his executive assistant and law clerk.

MISHA is a psychic on Earth who can communicate with Charley whenever she indulges in peyote, which is often.

PILOT EPISODE STORY OUTLINE: (SEE Pilot Script Which Follows)

FUTURE STORY IDEAS

- Charley, heavily recruited by the other side, cleverly leaves hints that he can be bought. When the Boss bribes Charley with a trip to Earth, the heavenly counselor accepts. Charley sneaks off to visit Wanda but learns that the only thing he can do is get revenge on his former Earthly enemies.

- Charley learns that the official religion of heaven is Muckism, a religion he's never encountered. Charley consults with Muck, the cave man messiah whose image was painted on exactly one cave wall (and never discovered). After receiving an inspirational "Muckstory" lesson, Charley volunteers to lead a bunch of angels, none with combat training, on a mission of mercy to hell. The only lawyer in heaven is also the only angel who knows sneaky tricks to confuse the enemy and he manages to rescue angelic hostages.

- Dominic's son, at age 75 looking more like Dominic's grandfather, arrives in heaven. Dominic wants his son to think of his dad as an angel so he asks Charley to help him fake it.

- Charley has domestic problems with Ginger and her family right before an important meeting. But will his conscience allow him to ship her and her relatives to hell, where they belong?

- The Boss and his devilish cohorts take a bus tour of heaven, made possible through a deal The Boss made with Charley. The devils turn out to be real tourists, clicking away with their cameras, carrying on like kids. Now that they've been to heaven, they privately admit they're jealous of the angels. The devils promise to make hell a rugged version of heaven. The promise is immediately broken.

- Charley returns to Earth when Wanda, his longtime companion, starts her dating life. Her new boyfriend, Charley learns from his contacts in hell, is a con man who victimizes women in mourning.

- Dominic is offered a prestigious position in hell and must decide if he wants to be a big fish in a hellish pond or just a humble angel.

- Charley can help institute a social worker's office in hell if he accepts Karla, the vampire woman, into his heavenly home. Karla, who's got a sweet tooth for the heavenly counselor, moves in with Charley, Ginger and the gang. Charley figures his domestic life can't get any worse ... but it does.

- Charley is nominated for the "Rookie Angel Award". He's the only eligible candidate who doesn't want this award from his community. He wins anyway, infuriating a spurned Horace and bringing internal conflict to the heavenly council.

- Charley, owning a reputation for objectivity, is asked to arbitrate an internal conflict in heaven. The new angels want revised guidelines and dress codes, as well as a revamped admission test for heaven. The old guard angels object, out of respect for tradition.

- Charley is chosen as the starting quarterback in the Thanksgiving day football game pitting heaven against hell. The home field is located in hell and Charley gets advice from some of his heroes from past eras.

- Charley is promised a one on one conference with God, rare for any angel. Charley's nerves, which he thought he left back on Earth, get on edge.

- #1 decides to reincarnate and, due to his/her great record as an angel, has his/her choice of families and situations. Charley helps him/her decide on a certain noble family but, just before birth, Charley discovers this family is less than noble. Can he save #1 from a life of decadence and moral destruction?

- Misha, the psychic on Earth, taps into Charley's consciousness once too often. The only lawyer in heaven visits Earth to dissuade the eccentric psychic from turning his spirit into a carnival act.

Appendix B: TV Series Pilot Script

"When Angels Speak ... (They Argue)"

Television Comedy Series

Pilot Script

"Just Like Starting Over"

Created and Written

by

Donald Paul Rutberg

© 2004

FADE IN:

INT. LAW OFFICE - DAY

CHARLEY MERRIWEATHER, AGE 40, BALDING AND NATTILY DRESSED, LEANS BACK IN HIS CHAIR BEHIND A DESK. SITTING ACROSS FROM HIM IS HIS CLIENT, MRS. MONTEFUSCO, AN ELEGANT LOOKING WOMAN DRESSED UP WITH DIAMONDS. WE SEE AN "ATTORNEY AT LAW" SIGN.

> MRS. MONTEFUSCO
> My husband finally came out and said it - he wants a divorce.

> CHARLEY
> Wait. Are you sure that's what you really want?

> MRS. MONTEFUSCO
> He handed me a briefcase with a lot of money, and told me to just … go away.

> CHARLEY
> (QUICKLY) Maybe it is for the best. We can get started right away … eh, do you have the briefcase with you?

> MRS. MONTEFUSCO
> No. I was so upset, I forgot it.

> CHARLEY
> Here's what I want you to do. Go home and think about it. Then, if you still want to go through with the divorce, bring the money to my office tomorrow.

CHARLEY WALKS HER TO THE DOOR.

> MRS. MONTEFUSCO
> I don't know what I'd do without you, Charley. Could I stay and just … talk?

> CHARLEY
> I wish I could, Mrs. Montefusco, but I coach Little League today.

> MRS. MONTEFUSCO
> It's so sweet that you volunteer your services to the community.

> CHARLEY
> It's more fun than picking up trash from the
> highway.

INT. RECEPTION AREA -- CONTINUOUS ACTION

CHARLEY WAVES GOODBYE TO MRS. MONTEFUSCO, WHO EXITS. ANOTHER CLIENT, EDGAR, SITS WITH HIS FACE AND HANDS WRAPPED IN BANDAGES. EDGAR WAVES HIS BANDAGED HAND AT CHARLEY.

> CHARLEY
> How's the jaw doing, Edgar?

EDGAR MUMBLES SOMETHING THROUGH HIS FACIAL BANDAGES AS CHARLEY PUTS ON HIS COAT.

> CHARLEY
> All your teeth! Beautiful. Hold onto 'em.
> They're worth $500 a piece. And we've got
> witnesses this time.

EDGAR NODS HAPPILY, GRUNTS. CHARLEY APPROACHES HIS SECRETARY, WANDA.

> CHARLEY
> I'll be back. Entertain the troops for me.

> WANDA
> How about if I entertain you tonight?

> CHARLEY
> Before dinner. It's a date.

> WANDA
> And then, afterwards, maybe we could get
> married.

> CHARLEY
> (WHISPERS) Wanda, you know I love you.
> But I'm still recovering from my divorce.

> WANDA
> The 1984 divorce?

> CHARLEY
> I'm a slow healer.

> WANDA
> I guess I'll just wait here and manage your
> office ... until you're all healed.

> CHARLEY
> We can negotiate this point of contention later, in good faith.

> WANDA
> Oh, great. More negotiations.

> CHARLEY
> It's my favorite sport!

EXT. BASEBALL FIELD - LATER THAT DAY

Charley stands at home plate with the opposing manager, WALT.

> CHARLEY
> OK, I'll take first pick.

> WALT
> It's just a practice game. Besides, you had first pick last week.

> CHARLEY
> It was raining. That doesn't count. I'll take Billy.

> WALT
> I'll take Freddy.

> CHARLEY
> He's not coming today.

> WALT
> OK, I'll take Joey.

> CHARLEY
> (Waves to a child) Hey, there's Freddy! I've got him.

> WALT
> (SNEERS) What a lucky break for your team.

> CHARLEY
> There are other good players on the field.

WALT LOOKS AROUND; FROWNS.

> FREDDY
> Mr. Merriweather, Timmy wants to know
> how long he has to hide behind the tree.

> WALT
> You're cheating again!

> CHARLEY
> Hey, I have nothing to do with Timmy's shy-
> ness. I'm not his father. I'm just a manager,
> giving my players a chance to win. Don't be
> a baby. It's only a practice game.

> WALT
> Take your best nine, I'll take the rest.

> CHARLEY
> Agreed. (TO FREDDY) OK, we're gonna
> win this game and then celebrate with pizza.

> FREDDY
> You're the best manager we ever had.

> CHARLEY
> (SHOUTS TOWARD TREE) Timmy, get
> over here! You're pitching today.

TIMMY EMERGES FROM HIS HIDING SPOT.

> TIMMY
> Can I hide somewhere else next time? A dog
> tried to bite me over by that tree.

> CHARLEY
> He did? Well, I'm gonna sue the dog's
> owner, get you some college money. Hey,
> how were you throwing in warm-ups?

> TIMMY
> I was wild; didn't throw a lot of strikes.

> CHARLEY
> (SHOUTS TO WALT)I'll be the home plate
> umpire. Ya mind?

INT. LAW OFFICE - NEXT DAY

CHARLEY LEANS BACK IN HIS CHAIR BEHIND A DESK, ACROSS FROM HIS CLIENT, MRS. KLINGER. THIS CLIENT LOOKS MORE SHABBY THAN WEALTHY.

CHARLEY LEANS FORWARD, ADJUSTS THE "ATTORNEY AT LAW" SIGN.

> MRS. KLINGER
> But I can't fib to the jury.

> CHARLEY
> I'm happy to hear that. After all, you'll be
> under oath.

> MRS. KLINGER
> I'm just not that kind of person. (PAUSES)
> Are we talking about a lot of money?

> CHARLEY
> Hey, I'll be honest. I understand your fears.
> If you're frightened by large sums of money;
> if diamonds make your hands shake --

> MRS. KLINGER
> I could use the money. That's for sure.

> CHARLEY
> But you won't get what you deserve unless
> you build up your credibility.

WE HEAR A BEEP. CHARLEY REACHES FOR THE INTERCOM.

> CHARLEY
> (TO MRS. KLINGER) No one's calling you
> a coward. (INTO THE INTERCOM) What
> is it?

> WANDA (V.O.)
> Your four o'clock is getting impatient.

> CHARLEY
> It's only three. And how do you know she's
> impatient?

> WANDA (V.O.)
> She's standing on the window ledge.

> CHARLEY
> (ALARMED) What? Mrs. Montefusco! (TO
> MRS. KLINGER) Excuse me one moment.

MRS. KLINGER
(EXAMINES HER OWN
RING FINGER) I'll do it. I'll
fib to the jury.

CHARLEY
You're a brave woman.

INT. RECEPTION AREA -- CONTINUOUS ACTION

CHARLEY RUSHES INTO RECEPTION AREA AND APPROACHES WANDA. EDGAR IS STILL WRAPPED IN BANDAGES; STILL WAITING.

CHARLEY
Wanda, where is she?

WANDA
Try looking outside. There aren't many
indoor window ledges.

WANDA LOOKS SURPRISED AS CHARLEY GRABS HIS COAT AND FLIES OUT OF THE OFFICE. WANDA STIFLES A GASP, POINTS AT EDGAR.

WANDA
See that? The knock on lawyers is that they
never save lives. And now he's risking his
own life to save a client.

EDGAR
(MUFFLED; THROUGH BANDAGES)
Why?

WANDA
(QUICKLY) Because she's holding a suitcase full of cash. (BEAT; TILTS HEAD) I
hope he gets a receipt.

INT. HALLWAY IN OFFICE BUILDING --CONTINUOUS ACTION

CHARLEY WALKS TO AN OPEN WINDOW AND LEDGE, WHERE HE'S JOINED BY A CURIOUS, GANGLY, UNKEMPT JANITOR. THEY BOTH LOOK OUT ONTO THE WINDOW LEDGE.

CHARLEY
I have a crazed client out there who's worth
millions. They hear a loud thump, then a
woman screaming from the ledge.

JANITOR
Not doin' her much good, is it?

CHARLEY
If you help me save her, I'll cut you in for a thousand.

JANITOR
(QUICKLY OPENS BAG, REVEALS HEAVY ROPE) I'll tie a rope around ya and hold onto it from in here.

CHARLEY
Wait, that sounds dangerous.

JANITOR
Risk versus reward. I deal with it all the time in the janitorial business.

CHARLEY
Alright, lasso me up. The janitor ties a rope around charley's waist, helps him climbout.

CHARLEY
Mrs. Montefusco. Our meeting was supposed to be inside my office, not out here.

MRS. MONTEFUSCO (V.O.)
I saw my husband with a younger woman!

CHARLEY
I ... I'm as shocked as you are. But I want you to come off the ledge so we can talk about your case. (HOLDING A RECEIPT BOOK) And I can give you a receipt for the cash.

MRS. MONTEFUSCO (V.O.)
I don't want his millions. I just want to ... jump!

CHARLEY
Get in here -- now! Or find yourself another lawyer; one who can fly.Charley helps Mrs. Montefusco through the window, back inside.

CHARLEY
Where's the briefcase with the money? (LOOKS ON THE LEDGE) I'll get it.

CHARLEY CLIMBS OUT ON THE LEDGE AGAIN. MRS. MONTEFUSCO FALLS INTO THE ARMS OF THE JANITOR.

> MRS. MONTEFUSCO
> I'm so confused, so ... desperate.

> JANITOR
> (DROPS ROPE; CHARMINGLY) Ya can
> trust me.

AS THEY EMBRACE, THEY HEAR A WILD SCREAM FROM CHARLEY AS HE AND THE ROPE FALL OUT THE WIN-
DOW. WE HEAR A DULL THUD, THEN THE SOUNDS OF BRICKS FALLING AND AUTOMOBILE HORNS HONKING.
THE JANITOR LOOKS OUT THE WINDOW, WHISTLES IN REGRET.

> JANITOR
> This don't look good.

> MRS. MONTEFUSCO
> (HASN'T NOTICED THE TRAGEDY) Do
> you think my marriage is over?

> JANITOR
> Na. Ya can always patch things up with your
> husband. (BEAT) (LOOKS DOWN) But ya
> may need a new lawyer. They both look
> down onto the street with concern.

INT. LARGE PIT -- MOMENTS LATER

CHARLEY LOOKS DAZED AS HE RISES FROM THE FLOOR. HE'S NOT ALONE IN THE PIT; A SHORT, SMILING
MAN, DOMINIC, STARES AT HIM EXPECTANTLY.

> CHARLEY
> Mrs. Montefusco? What happened?

> DOMINIC
> You fell off the window ledge.

> CHARLEY
> (SLIPS OUT OF THE ROPE) That idiot
> must've let go of the rope ... I could've been
> killed.

> DOMINIC
> Well ....

> CHARLEY
> How far did I fall?

DOMINIC
(GIDDILY) Forty-seven floors.

CHARLEY
(ALSO GIDDILY) Whew! I gotta be more careful --

DOMINIC
(LAUGHS) And that's not even the bad news.

BOTH MEN LAUGH HEARTILY.

CHARLEY
(REALIZES) The money fell too!

DOMINIC
Uh-huh; scattered all over the street. It was quite a scene. People on their hands and knees, scooping up money - tryin' not to fall through the hole you made in the subway vent.

CHARLEY
Oh, great. I've got a client up there who probably wants to murder me and I'm ... (PUZZLED) 47 floors? Onto the street?

DOMINIC
Head first. (WAITS FOR REACTION)

CHARLEY
(LOOKS UP) And that's my outline? (PON-DERS) Not a scratch on me. (NERVOUS LAUGH) Must be my lucky ... eh ... what is that?

DOMINIC
Tomorrow's paper. Read for yourself.

DOMINIC HANDS CHARLEY A TABLOID NEWSPAPER.

CHARLEY
(READS) "Attorney leaps out window with stolen money." (UPSET) It was not stolen! It was my retainer fee!

DOMINIC

It doesn't matter anymore. They won't indict you in your condition. You're off the hook - you're dead.

CHARLEY

Ha! (FEELS PULSE) I feel fine. I ... I'm probably in shock. Who are you?

DOMINIC

My name is Dominic and I'm the one who delivers the bad news.

CHARLEY

What bad news? Nobody's dead here.

DOMINIC

I am. I was killed during The Great War; the one that ended all wars, for a while anyway.

CHARLEY

(LOOKS HORRIFIED; THEN LOOKS TO ESCAPE) Is that right? How did you meet your alleged death?

DOMINIC

I was thrown overboard for telling people what they didn't want to hear. So you know I don't enjoy this sort of thing.

CHARLEY

Eh, where ya from, Dominic?

DOMINIC

I'm currently residing in hell.

CHARLEY

(TAKEN BACK) Is that where we are?

DOMINIC

Do you see any of your favorite relatives, all dressed in shimmering robes comprised of tiny diamonds? Or ... or ... do you see any multi-colored flowers which seem to have an intelligence all their own?

CHARLEY
(LOOKS AROUND CAUTIOUSLY) Uh, no.

DOMINIC
Then ya ain't in heaven! This is purgatory, a holding tank. I came to take ya to hell.

CHARLEY
(TRYING TO JUMP OUT OF THE PIT) Hey, you go wherever you feel most comfortable but don't ... why would I be a candidate for hell?

DOMINIC
You're a lawyer, aren't you?

CHARLEY
Lawyers are allowed in heaven. Aren't they?

DOMINIC
Sure. But no lawyer has ever qualified.

CHARLEY
That's slander. I can sue you for that.

DOMINIC
Not really. We have different rules in hell. Fair trials, for instance, are few and far between. Collecting can be kinda difficult.

CHARLEY
Ok, for argument's sake, suppose I am dead. Do I stay in this pit forever?

DOMINIC
When you're ready -- and I don't want to rush you -- I'll take you down, get you acclimated.

CHARLEY
Acclimated to what? (MUMBLES) Oh, I know I'm not going to like this answer.

DOMINIC
Well ... it's kind of an indulgent place; really
too wild for me. As a matter of fact (WHIS-
PERS) I don't even belong in hell. It's a mistake.

THEY HEAR SOUNDS FROM O.C.

CHARLEY
We'll have to talk about that later because
the rescue team has arrived. (DESPER-
ATELY SHOUTS) We're in here!

A THIRD FIGURE APPEARS; AN OLDER, DISTINGUISHED-LOOKING MAN WITH WHITE HAIR, HORACE. HE IS
DRESSED IN A SHIMMERING WHITE ROBE AND STANDS ON ONE SIDE OF CHARLEY WHILE DOMINIC FLANKS
THE OTHER.

HORACE
Charles Merriweather?

CHARLEY
(HOPEFULLY) Emergency Rescue Team?

HORACE
No. I'm an angel. I bring good news.

DOMINIC
Don't tell me he's been accepted.

HORACE
Still delivering erroneous information?

DOMINIC
(HURT) That was only one time!

CHARLEY
What's the "Good news"?

HORACE
I'm pleased to report that we have a job for
you in heaven.

CHARLEY
(DISGUSTED) So we're all dead. That
explains how you two know each other.

HORACE
We work for different agencies.

> **DOMINIC**
> Heaven and hell are separated by a very fine line. It's all, "Who you know."

> **HORACE**
> The other angels are waiting. Ready?

> **CHARLEY**
> (SEARCHING FOR EXIT) No, I'm not ready!

> **HORACE**
> Frankly, I think we should get away from this ... element.

> **DOMINIC**
> Objection! He hasn't even gone through the stages of death yet.

> **CHARLEY**
> Sustained! (TO DOMINIC) What are they?

> **DOMINIC**
> Denial is first.

> **CHARLEY**
> I've been denying this since I got here. I know it's just a bad dream.

INT. TORTURE CHAMBER -- CONTINUOUS ACTION

CHARLEY STARTS SCREAMING, AS IF HE'S BEING BROILED ALIVE.

INT. PIT -- CONTINUOUS ACTION

CHARLEY LOOKS PANICKED. HE CHECKS HIS SKIN FOR BURNS.

> **HORACE**
> That was a bad dream. This pit is your new reality.

> **CHARLEY**
> (ANGRY; PUNCHES WALL) Why is this happening to me?

> **DOMINIC**
> Anger is the second stage.

HORACE
(TO CHARLEY) It's happening because the angels have called you.

CHARLEY
You mean they murdered me!

HORACE
Sometimes the good die young.

CHARLEY
I'm no good! I tell my clients to lie. I lie all the time; even to the jury for the sake of a lousy few grand. I'm slime.

DOMINIC
Then why play hard-to-get with me?

CHARLEY
(SHOUTS) I don't wanna go with you! I can tell just by looking you at you that you're bad news. If I looked up "bad news" on the Internet, I'd see your photograph!

DOMINIC
The Inter-what? I've never heard of that. I have seen a photograph, though. Once.

CHARLEY
(COMPOSED; TO HORACE) I'll make a deal.

HORACE
(LOOKS BORED) Third stage; bargaining.

CHARLEY
It's called negotiation, my favorite sport. I'll work for you on Earth, as a living --

HORACE
Sorry, but once you're called ...

CHARLEY
What's it gonna take: an act of God?

HORACE
Get to the depression stage so we can proceed.

CHARLEY
(FALLS TO HIS KNEES)
I can't believe I'll never see my family again. Why did I postpone that vacation? And my asbestos case. The jury would've awarded us scrillions! (SOBS; DEVASTATED) The Eagles were about to win the Super Bowl ... (SUDDENLY CHEERFUL) But I'm not depressed. I'm still bargaining.

INT. HEAVEN -- CONFERENCE ROOM -- DUSK EXECUTIVE ANGELS, #1 & #2, THEIR GENDERS INDISTINGUISH-ABLE, WATCH CHARLEY'S ANTICS ON A MONITOR.

#2
Are you sure he's the guy?

#1
We know about his life; let's see how he han-dles his death.

#2
I don't see any improvement.

#1
Get him up here. All mortals deserve a chance to make good.

A TUNNEL FORMS ABOVE CHARLEY, DOMINIC AND HORACE. CHARLEY

HEARS CHIMES; SEES SOOTHING BRIGHT LIGHT. THE MEN ARE SUCKED INTO THE TUNNEL.

INT. A WHITE TRAIN - CONTINUOUS

CHARLEY, A PASSENGER ON THIS WHITE TRAIN, SEES MEADOWS AND GARDENS; CRYSTAL BRIDGES OVER SPARKLING RIVERS. HE READS THE HEADLINE ON HIS NEWSPAPER, "ATTORNEY LEAPS OUT WINDOW WITH STOLEN MONEY," THEN STASHES THE NEWSPAPER BEHIND THE SEAT.

EXT. MEADOW -- DUSK

MAGICALLY, CHARLEY, DOMINIC AND HORACE ARE LEFT STANDING IN A MEADOW. CHARLEY SEES SILHOU-ETTES OF FIGURES IN SHIMMERING ROBES AND UNUSUAL, COLORFUL FLOWERS. A FLOWER SEEMS TO BE SWAYING TO THE MUSIC; IN TOUCH WITH CHARLEY.

THE FLOWER WINKS AT HIM.

THE SILHOUETTES OF ANGELS #1 AND #2 ARE SUDDENLY IN FRONT OF CHARLEY, DOMINIC AND HORACE. CHARLEY GOES RIGHT ON NEGOTIATING.

CHARLEY
I'll give you my home in the country, my mutual funds; take my dog ... where am I?

#2
You're home, Mr. Merriweather. This is where you'll reside and work.

CHARLEY
That's fine except for the fact that I've got a client waiting for me ...

DOMINIC
I've made it to heaven! My ordeal is over!

HORACE
(TO DOMINIC) Enjoy. It'll be a short visit.

#1
And you're here, even though you're quite flawed, because you're the best overall choice from a long list of nominated attorneys.

CHARLEY
Excuse me, Your Honors. Whattya mean, "flawed"?

A HOLOGRAM FLIES AT CHARLEY, SHOWING HIM HIS ENTIRE LIFE IN A FEW SECONDS. HE WINCES, AGHAST AT HIS MISTAKES.

CHARLEY
I see, uh, what were you saying -- best choice? Best choice for what?

#1
The newly created position of heavenly counsel.

CHARLEY
You mean this guy wasn't kidding? There aren't any lawyers in heaven?

#2
That's right, but things are changing here. Spirits are returning with new experiences that affect their attitudes toward the afterlife.

#1

Except for a chosen few, everyone is equal in heaven. And the only vice is debate. Consequently, the lobbying can get vicious.

#2

When we realized the political maneuvering was out of control, we sent for you to arbitrate our internal conflicts.

#1 AND #2 SMILE PEACEFULLY. CHARLEY LOOKS FURIOUS.

CHARLEY

"Sent" for me! Why didn't you "send" for a Supreme Court Justice?

#2

Because we also need you to negotiate with the other side.

CHARLEY SEEMS CONFUSED; LOOKS AT DOMINIC, WHO POINTS DOWNWARD.

DOMINIC

There are only two places to be and you're in one of 'em!

CHARLEY

Wait. Why do ya need me to negotiate with hell?

#2

You were most qualified due to your basic understanding of deceit, corruption, greed --

CHARLEY

(HUMBLY) I may need a refresher course on some of those --

A HOLOGRAM FLIES TOWARD CHARLEY AGAIN, SHOWING HIM HIS CORRUPT, DECEIT-FILLED ACTIONS ON EARTH. HE WINCES AGAIN.

CHARLEY

Eh, I can explain some of those seemingly devious measures --

HORACE

That's the purpose of your life review.
    (ROLLS HIS EYES)

>   CHARLEY
> In that case, I'd give myself a B, maybe a
> B+.

CHARLEY SEES MORE OF HIS LIFE REVIEW. HE LOOKS NAUSEOUS.

>   HORACE
> You're experiencing the pain that you've
> inflicted upon others; what it felt like to be
> on the receiving end.

>   CHARLEY
> Well, that scene was from my divorce. She
> was trying to hurt me, too. And what ...
> who's that, Wanda? That guy she's dating is
> no good. That lousy bum ... wait a second,
> this is from the future.

>   #2
> You must forgive everyone, from the past
> and future, or be stuck at a low spiritual
> level.

>   CHARLEY
> Sorry, but once someone backstabs me ...
> (STARTS VIBRATING SLOWER) ... OK,
> I get it, maybe I will try to forgive my ene-
> mies.

CHARLEY STARTS TO LOOK ALMOST TRANSLUCENT; LESS DENSE. HE VIBRATES UPWARD, LIKE A HUMMING-
BIRD.

>   DOMINIC
> Hey, Charley, does your body feel light? Is
> your mind expanding?

>   CHARLEY
> Yeah! I feel really alert, like waves of infor-
> mation are flying into my head. I feel like
> I'm surrounded by velvet or somethin'.

>   DOMINIC
> Can I try it, too?

>   HORACE
> (TO DOMINIC; STERNLY) Just stay where
> we can see you. And try not to talk.

#1
Mr. Merriweather, you won't be afraid to deal with the unscrupulous minds which control the other side. In fact, our scout Horace says you're sneakier than any of them, in your own, righteous way.

CHARLEY
First of all, I think you've badly underestimated a lawyer's value to society. You need us to interpret laws, protect the average angel ....

#2
Self-promotion is not allowed here.

CHARLEY
Oh, was I supposed to check my ego at the gate? Lawyers have egos. (SIGHS) Well, if you don't have lawyers, you must have some kind of negotiating team. How do they manage?

#1
We wouldn't know.

CHARLEY
You never tried to hash things out with the devilishly unscrupulous competition?

#2
We made believe they didn't exist. So they kept taking advantage of us.

CHARLEY
Seems to me, we have no alternative but to beat 'em at their own game.

#1
That's the spirit! (POUNDS FIST) We won't be pushovers any longer!

#2
(TO #1) If you're going to make this a revenge thing, then ....

#1 LOOKS AWAY GUILTILY; TRIES TO HIDE A SMILE.

            CHARLEY
(SOTTO) I want to remember this dream.

            #2
We need your brand of representation if we hope to deal successfully with the other side. You will outline our complaints, demand the safe return of our hostages and negotiate unresolved matters. Any questions?

            CHARLEY
What kind of salary will I receive?

            #2
You may accept our offer or go live with Satan in the darkness of hell.

            CHARLEY
Uh-huh. How about a pension plan?

            HORACE
Shall I show them to the one-way elevator?

            DOMINIC
Charley, take the deal!

            CHARLEY
(DECIDING) So I'll be negotiating for the return of angelic hostages.

            #2
That will be part of your job.

            CHARLEY
(SIGHS) Why not? (BEAT) It might add a little life ... to my death.

                                   FADE OUT

FADE IN:

INT. HEAVENLY TRAIL - DUSK

HORACE LEADS CHARLEY AND DOMINIC ALONG THE TRAIL.

> HORACE
> Follow me.

> CHARLEY
> Where are the lions, tigers and bears?

> HORACE
> Reading.

> CHARLEY
> (DISTURBED BY THIS
> NEWS; QUIETLY) Horace,
> where are my folks?

> HORACE
> They've begun new lives already. They're on
> Earth, in grade school.

> CHARLEY
> Can I see them?

> HORACE
> Maybe in your next life. If you study and
> achieve spiritual growth.

> CHARLEY
> (TO DOMINIC) I used to think all the good
> ones were dead. Now I'm dead and they're
> alive!

> DOMINIC
> No one ever said the afterlife was fair.

> HORACE
> Death is a "wonderful journey home.

> CHARLEY
> (GRUMBLES) Yeah, all but the "wonder-
> ful" part.

> HORACE
> You can start working immediately.

                    CHARLEY
          Where?

                    HORACE
          Right here -- in what looks like your old
          office.

INT. LAW OFFICE -- CONTINUOUS ACTION -- DUSK THE THREE SPIRITS ENTER THE OFFICE. SOMEHOW, THE
ANGELS HAVE RE-CREATED CHARLEY'S OLD LAW OFFICE IN EVERY DETAIL.

                    HORACE
          I must attend a very important meeting. If
          you have a problem, contact me telepathi-
          cally.

                    DOMINIC
          (WAVES) We'll do that.

                    HORACE
          And you -- go back where you belong!

                    DOMINIC
          I belong here. I need Charley to prove it!

                    HORACE
          You can only stay if you make yourself use-
          ful.

                    DOMINIC
          I'll prepare him for his first business trip to
          hell.

                    HORACE
          All right. But no roaming around!

HORACE EXITS.

                    CHARLEY
          Sit down, Dominic. You can be my first cli-
          ent; help me forget about my predicament.

                    DOMINIC
          What   predicament?   (REALIZES)   Oh!
          About being dead. Don't worry. I got used to
          it in no time.

CHARLEY
(PLEASANTLY SURPRISED) No kidding?

DOMINIC
Because time doesn't exist in hell, or in heaven. It's always dusk, everywhere. You'll adapt.

CHARLEY
I'm still a little confused. If you can do anything you want in hell, why doesn't everyone just come down for the party?

DOMINIC
You can indulge in vices there but you'll never make it back to Earth. You won't earn another life.

AS CHARLEY REFLECTS, A BEARDED, YOUNG POET ENTERS CHARLEY'S OFFICE.

POET
(FERVENTLY) I had a drink or two to toast a life with my new bride. I had a drink or three to mourn the friendships that had died. I had a drink or four when the welfare check would come. I had a drink or five because it almost made me numb.

DOMINIC
(WHISPERS TO CHARLEY)
Poets get automatic berths in heaven. God knows why.

POET
Wait! There's another verse! Dominic rises as Charley assists the Poet.

CHARLEY
Sit down and we'll talk --

POET
I had a drink or twenty when I bet or voted wrong. They told me that my problem was my drinking, all along.

CHARLEY
Is there anything I can do to help?

POET
The other angels mock me.

CHARLEY
All you need is a restraining order.
(WRITES) No angel can harass you until
you're reincarnated. That OK?

POET
What can I do to repay you?

CHARLEY
(PUTS ARM AROUND THE POET) When
you get back to Earth, I'd like you to send
my love to a wonderful gal named Wanda.

POET
It will warm my heart to bring a message of
love to the mortal world.

CHARLEY
And ... there's this clumsy janitor I met just
before I died. I want you to follow him into
the subway station, then casually bump into
him just before the train pulls in --

CHARLEY SMILES VENGEFULLY AS THE POET SHAKES HIS HEAD MOURNFULLY. DOMINIC HIDES HIS FACE IN
HIS HANDS.

POET
Revenge is not yours, nor mine ...

CHARLEY
Come on! Revenge belongs to everyone.

POET
Don't let Muck hear you!

CHARLEY
No one can hear us. All I'm saying is I want
the janitor to wake up every morning feeling
guilty and afraid for his life.

POET
(MAKES PRAYING MOTIONS) Muck, he
doesn't mean what he says.

CHARLEY
Tell me something: what is the official religion around here? I always wondered.

POET
Muckism.

CHARLEY
I knew that was gonna be the answer! What's so great about this guy Muck?

POET
Ask him yourself. How are you today, Muck?

MUCK, LOOKING ANCIENT AND WIZENED, STROLLS IN, PATS THE POET.

MUCK
Fine. Now run along son. Write more poems. Try to keep outta trouble.

CHARLEY
(TO POET) You can do a good deed: give Dominic a tour of heaven.

DOMINIC
(IGNORING POET AND CHARLEY; TO MUCK) Could ya write me a letter of recommendation?

CHARLEY
(STERNLY)
Take the tour, Dominic!

CHARLEY POINTS TOWARD EXIT. DOMINIC SHRUGS; RELUCTANTLY LEAVES WITH THE POET.

CHARLEY
It's an ... honor to meet you, sir.

MUCK
Knock it off. Ya never heard of me.
(HOPEFUL) Did ya?

CHARLEY
Not until recently --

MUCK
I was big before the dawn of history.

CHARLEY

No wonder. Your charisma --

MUCK

The Caveman Messiah was my tag. Before public relations. Before page one of the bible!

CHARLEY

I thought the bible started, "And God created the Heavens and the Earth."

MUCK

(POINTS) Just testing. Get used to it. Anyway, I was born just after the dinosaurs died, when the dust settled.

CHARLEY

Sounds like you were under-appreciated. And before your time.

MUCK

Who knew? How could I guess that all record of me would disappear?

CHARLEY

Nothing survived?

MUCK

One picture of me; a mural, really, on a wall in a cave in Southern Alaska.

CHARLEY

Not the Middle East?

MUCK

Too hot. Bad sleeping weather.

CHARLEY

But it's a central location.

MUCK

I figured Alaska was too. Right between the two continents.

CHARLEY

The land must have been unspoiled.

MUCK

We hadn't even invented trash.

CHARLEY

No wars.

MUCK

For a while, the bear and the salmon were friendly. Ah, what's the use in complaining about lost opportunities?

CHARLEY

Serenity is very important up here.

MUCK

(LESS THAN SERENE) Ya know, I could've been Elvis! I had my choice: Messiah or gospel singer. It seemed like a good decision at the time. Who knew?

CHARLEY

You can get reincarnated. Uh, I guess.

MUCK

Why? I'm revered up here. The angels say,
  (NEAR TEARS)
"Know who he used to be?"
  (COMPOSES HIMSELF)
So, do ya like the job?

CHARLEY

I'm eh ... just starting.

MUCK

I know. I'm supposed to check ya out; see if you're really qualified.

CHARLEY

You mean I'm on probation?

MUCK

No, I'm offering some friendly warnings.

CHARLEY

Hey, I've been warned about hell --

MUCK

I meant the problems up here.

CHARLEY
What problems can the angels have?

MUCK
The only vice up here is debate. So, now, they're arguing over the dress codes.

CHARLEY
(SERIOUS) How do you feel about that, sir?

MUCK
Well, I wrote the commandment: "Go forth to wherest thou climate suits thy clothes." Hey, you've got another client coming in. Don't mind me. I'm just observing.

CHARLEY
Sure thing. Send in the next angel.

THE JANITOR ENTERS THE OFFICE, SITS DOWN. HE'S WEARING A NICE SUIT.

CHARLEY LOOKS SHOCKED; ANGRY.

JANITOR
(DIM SMILE) How are ya?

CHARLEY
I'm at the end of my rope.

JANITOR
Have we met?

CHARLEY
You promised to hold onto the rope!

JANITOR
(RECOGNIZES CHARLEY) Oooohhh! (BEAT) You're still mad about that?

CHARLEY
Your carelessness cost me my life!

JANITOR
(TO CHARLEY) What's the real deal here? Are you some kinda vigilante? (SHRUGS) I didn't do it on purpose.

CHARLEY
Then you lied and told the press I was trying to steal the money.

JANITOR
I had to -- so the insurance company would pay off Mrs. Montefusco.

CHARLEY
(TO MUCK) I'm supposed to help this guy or what?

MUCK
It's your first day on the job. Do what you feel is right.

CHARLEY
This has gotta be a set-up. (THINKS; TO JANITOR) Who sent you here?

JANITOR
Horace. Said he was a big shot.

CHARLEY
I see. He's giving me a chance for revenge; or enough rope to hang myself.

JANITOR
If you think killing me will make me more truthful, then go ahead.

CHARLEY
Killing you will definitely make you less careless! But there's a problem. You're already dead.

JANITOR
I guess you'll have to find another way to get even.

CHARLEY
But that would just keep the bad karma in motion. You had my fate in your hands. Now I have your fate in my hands. I have to forgive you to break that downward spiral.

JANITOR

Good. Can ya give me a cushy job in the heavenly health club?

CHARLEY

Yes. (WRITES) First, take a carelessness prevention course at the academy, then report to the heavenly spa. And stay away from heights!

THE JANITOR TAKES CHARLEY'S NOTE, EXITS. MUCK PUTS HIS ARM AROUND CHARLEY.

MUCK

I can tell you'll be a real asset to us.

CHARLEY

Hey, are you hungry? Wanna grab a bite?

MUCK

My spirit's willing but my stomach is dead and buried. You'll get used to not eating. And you'll never know hunger or pain.

CHARLEY

Or pleasure.

MUCK

You're catching on. Hey, I think you're ready for your first road trip.

CHARLEY

Business trip to hell? So soon? Maybe you're right; I should immerse myself in the excitement and vice.

MUCK

Your days of excitement and vice ended when The janitor let go of that rope.

DOMINIC MATERIALZES.

MUCK

We want you to start negotiations at once. Dominic will be your tour guide.

CHARLEY

And in return for his diligence, you'll grant him Eternal peace in heaven, right?

MUCK
If he doesn't lead you astray.

CHARLEY
Don't worry. My oats have long been sowed.
Noooo sir, there's nothing in hell that could
possibly attract me.

INT. HELL - ANYTIME

A WILD PARTY IS UNDERWAY. IT LOOKS MORE LIKE A RIOT. AS THE VISITORS EXIT A CREAKY, OLD ELEVA-
TOR, DOMINIC SMILES SHEEPISHLY; CHARLEY'S MOUTH OPENS IN WONDER. A DRUNKEN MAN, HOLDING A
WINE GLASS IN EACH HAND, FALLS TO HIS KNEES.

DRUNKEN MAN
I've died and gone to heaven!

DOMINIC
Guess again, glutton. (TO CHARLEY) You
can tell I don't fit in.

A SEXY, VAMPIRE WOMAN, KARLA, EMBRACES DOMINIC.

KARLA
Ready for another half-moon howl?

DOMINIC
Not now, Karla. (EMBARRASSED, TO
CHARLEY) We're in the glee club.

CHARLEY IS DISTRACTED WHEN KARLA RUBS UP AGAINST HIS BODY. HE SEEMS PUZZLED AT HIS RENEWED
INTEREST IN THE OPPOSITE SEX.

CHARLEY
(FINALLY) Can I get a beer?

DOMINIC
You really shouldn't. Well, you don't want to
look conspicuous. Just sip it.

KARLA GIVES CHARLEY A BOTTLE OF BEER, THEN GRABS HIS RUMP.

CHARLEY
(LEAPS IN THE AIR) Whooaaaa!
(LAUGHS; READS LABEL ON BOTTLE)
Fire-brewed.

CHARLEY GUZZLES SOME BEER, SITS DOWN AT THE BAR WITH DOMINIC.

KARLA SITS DOWN NEXT TO THEM. SHE SEEMS ENAMORED WITH CHARLEY,

WATCHING HIS MOVEMENTS, LIKE HE IS HER NEXT MEAL.

> KARLA
> (PURRS) I'm looking for a nice guy.

> CHARLEY
> (TO DOMINIC) She's starting to look good.

> DOMINIC
> Come on, Charley. Ya need protection from
> yourself. I'll take ya to see the boss.

DOMINIC PULLS CHARLEY THROUGH THE CROWD. IT LOOKS FESTIVE

ENOUGH BUT MANY EXPRESSIONS REVEAL AN UNDERLYING TENSION.

CHARLEY SEES A FEW EVIL-LOOKING JUDGES, STILL IN THEIR ROBES. THEN HE SPOTS SOME MEN IN RUM-
PLED SUITS, DRINKING AT THE BAR.

> CHARLEY
> I know those guys. Hey, Harper, Thorton
> and Brookstein!

> HARPER
> (RECOGNIZES CHARLEY;
> LIFTS RUM BOTTLE) Hello,
> Merriweather. Think any of us
> lawyers will make it to
> heaven?

> DOMINIC
> Try to keep a low profile.

CHARLEY SMILES CROOKEDLY AT THE THREE MEN; KEEPS WALKING.

> CHARLEY
> Those guys did the same things when they
> were alive. Looked and acted the same....

> DOMINIC
> Some people can't even tell the difference
> between life and death. To me, that's scary.
> OK, here's the place. Don't let him intimi-
> date you.

CHARLEY GULPS DOWN HIS BEER, THROWS THE BOTTLE AWAY, FIXES HIS COLLAR, NODS. MEANWHILE,
DOMINIC HIDES BEHIND AN INDECENT PAINTING IN AN ALCOVE. CHARLEY KNOCKS ON A GOLD DOOR.

VOICE
Who is it?

CHARLEY
I'm Charles Merriweather, an attorney, sent
from heaven to negotiate the --

CHARLEY IS SUCKED UP IN A WIND CURRENT AND WHISKED THROUGH THE DOOR. DOMINIC MEEKLY FOLLOWS.

INT. LAVISH ROOM IN HELL -- CONTINUOUS ACTION

CHARLEY BRUSHES OFF THE GOLD DUST. HE APPEARS UNHARMED.

CHARLEY
... exchange of hostages. Now, I know you
don't negotiate with strangers but --

A SINISTER-LOOKING MAN WITH A REDDISH GLOW, THE BOSS, EXAMINES CHARLEY. THE BOSS STROKES A PET SITTING AT HIS SIDE. THIS "PET" IS A COMBINATION OF A LION, HIPPO AND CROCODILE.

BOSS
A lawyer made it into heaven?

CHARLEY
New policy, from what I hear.

DOMINIC
It's an experiment --

BOSS
(TO DOMINIC) Shut up.

DOMINIC
Yes, sir.

BOSS
Lawyers come here! Always. Go away. Tell
the angels they're recruiting on my turf.

CHARLEY
Why shouldn't the angels solicit lawyers?
You're going after the ultra-religious.

BOSS
We have to go into new markets: We're not
allowed to advertise!

CHARLEY
Maybe that will change. If you develop a
good relationship with us --

BOSS
That's impossible! We're not even allowed
in heaven. How could we ever --

CHARLEY
I'll pull some strings; get ya in. As long as
ya promise not to steal things, which would
make me look bad.

BOSS
You're making me very angry!

CHARLEY
(TAUNTING) So what are ya gonna do?
Kill me? Condemn me to hell? I'm already
there, Mr. Darkness Prince, or whatever you
call yourself.

BOSS
(PANTOMIMES A ROCK AND ROLL
SINGER) Please allow me to introduce
myself. I'm a man of wealth and taste.

CHARLEY
Yeah, you've laid many a man's soul to
waste. Congratulations. Your mother must
be very proud, whoever she is.

CHARLEY LOOKS AT THE WALL, NOTICES A PORTRAIT OF A JACKAL WEARING A HEART-SHAPED NECKLACE
THAT READS, "MOM".

CHARLEY
Whatever she is. But the fact remains: I've
dealt with judges who'd make you look like
a total wimp!

DOMINIC PULLS CHARLEY OFF TO THE SIDE.

DOMINIC
You just called Satan a wimp.

CHARLEY
I know what I'm doing; standing my ground.
It's a negotiation tactic.

THE BOSS PACES AS A 12 YEAR-OLD PAPERBOY APPROACHES CHARLEY.

> PAPERBOY
>
> Mister, wanna cigar? Latest edition of your "Crime News"?

CHARLEY READS THE HEADLINE: "COMPUTER CRIME WORKS AGAIN!"

> CHARLEY
>
> Just the cigar.

> PAPERBOY
>
> That'll be 10 years outta your next life.

CHARLEY SMELLS THE CIGAR; SEEMS TO BE WEIGHING THE OFFER.

> DOMINIC
>
> He knows you're an angel and he's trying to tempt you.

> CHARLEY
>
> (FINALLY) Maybe later.

CHARLEY RETURNS THE CIGAR TO THE PAPERBOY, WHO EXITS.

> CHARLEY
>
> (TO BOSS) Whattya say? Let's cut through the formalities and talk about it.

> BOSS
>
> (SIGHS) This might be overdue: a dialogue between heaven and hell. We can cut out the bickering; the cutthroat rivalries.

> CHARLEY
>
> Let's all act like adults.

> BOSS
>
> We'll still have cutthroat rivalries down here. They just don't have to exist between your world and mine.

> CHARLEY
>
> Decide what it is you need from this deal and I'll return with proposals. Meanwhile, thanks for your time.

> BOSS
>
> Time doesn't exist down here.

> CHARLEY
> So you've eliminated the sin of being late.
> (WINKS)

> BOSS
> You're right. (LAUGHS) Devils, we've accidentally eliminated a sin. Let's find something to replace it with!

A LOUD CHEER IS HEARD. DEVILS BEGIN RUNNING AMOK.

> DOMINIC
> Wanna leave now or stay for the riot?

> CHARLEY
> I'm ready to .. .(SEES KARLA; HIS EYES
> WIDEN) ... what do you want to do?

AS THEY TURN TO LEAVE, KARLA, APPROACHES. SHE TRIES TO BITE CHARLEY'S NECK WITH HER FANGS.

> KARLA
> Just one bite; for old time's sake.

> CHARLEY
> Lady, I'm going up to heaven now. How will
> I explain vampire bites on my neck? Huh?

CHARLEY AND DOMINIC ENTER THE SELDOM-USED ELEVATOR. KARLA RUNS AFTER THEM BUT ARRIVES JUST AFTER THE ELEVATOR DOORS CLOSE. SHE PUTS HER BACK UP AGAINST THE DOORS, SLIDES DOWN TO A SITTING POSITION. SHE LOOKS HEARTBROKEN.

> KARLA
> I don't get it. They loved me on Earth.

KARLA'S EXPRESSION SLOWLY CHANGES FROM SAD AND DOLEFUL TO INSPIRED AND DEVIOUS.

> KARLA
> They did love me on Earth. Now I remember. I prowled around, enticing people, then
> draining their blood. But I always wanted to
> live in heaven. (Rises, eyes elevator) And
> there's my ride!

KARLA STEERS HERSELF THROUGH THE CROWD, WHICH IS STILL TRYING TO CONJURE UP NEW SINS.

                    KARLA
Heaven has to be more challenging than this
place. And it's got that heavenly attorney.
(GIGGLES)
Heavenly attorney. (SHAKES HER HEAD)
Doesn't sound right.

KARLA KEEPS WALKING, SEES THE DRUNKEN MAN WE SAW EARLIER.

                    DRUNKEN MAN
I took a steam bath; now I'm more wasted!

                    KARLA
I know the feeling.(SEES BOSS) Oh, honey.

                    BOSS
Karla, my favorite fiance! What's wrong?

                    KARLA
I wanna go to heaven and bite that lawyer.
He acted so hard to get.

                    BOSS
It's a good thing I'm not a jealous guy.
(QUICKLY) But I am working on it. Devils!

THE DEVILS HUSH UP.

                    BOSS
I'd like to share something with you:
revenge! That heavenly counselor snubbed
my lovely fiance, Karla. You know Karla --
the gal with the great singing voice.

THE DEVILS SNICKER AT THE SUGGESTION.

                    BOSS
That demonette who's been entertaining
down here for 700 years --

                    KARLA
                (WHISPERS TACTFULLY)
Six hundred.

                    PAPERBOY
Whattya gonna do, Pop?

>   BOSS
> Take advantage of 'em, like always. Can you
> believe they sent a clown like that to negoti-
> ate with me, the master?
>   (SUDDENLY INSPIRED)
> Now I'm feeling it.

>   KARLA
> What?

>   BOSS
> Jealousy. Yeah, there it is. Feels good. Not
> as heavy as hatred; doesn't have the zing of
> lust ... but I like it.

>   PAPERBOY
> How will ya take advantage of him?

>   BOSS
> By fooling him into thinking I'll make a
> deal. And then I'll take over heaven!

>   KARLA
> But you could be a legitimate angel if they'd
> give you a chance.

>   BOSS
> Are you kidding? Can you imagine me trad-
> ing in my horns for wings? Glowing red in a
> sea of white? Wait a minute. I was a legiti-
> mate angel; a very important one!
>   (SHAKES HEAD; DISAPPOINTED IN
>   KARLA) Didn't you read my autobiogra-
> phy?

INT. EXECUTIVE CONFERENCE ROOM -- HEAVEN -- DUSK

CHARLEY MATERIALIZES NEAR #'S 1 & 2, MUCK AND HORACE.

>   HORACE
> The meeting may now commence.

>   CHARLEY
> What's going on?

>   MUCK
> We've got good news.

> CHARLEY
>
> What?

> #1
>
> You've passed the test. You've officially made it into heaven!

CHARLEY'S EYES OPEN WIDE WITH HAPPINESS.

> #2
>
> We tell everyone they're the only one of their kind in heaven. Then we send them out to test them.

> CHARLEY
>
> I passed the ... heavenly bar exam!

> #2
>
> The manner in which you handle your death determines whether you belong in heaven or hell.

> #1
>
> You've done so well that we really are appointing you heavenly counselor.

> #2
>
> As well as special consultant to Muck.

> CHARLEY
>
> What could be better? Yes! Yes! Yes!

> HORACE
>
> Celebration is shunned here, sir.

> CHARLEY
>
> (TO MUCK) Am I Horace's superior now?

> MUCK
>
> Yes you are, my son.

CHARLEY GOES NOSE-TO-NOSE WITH HORACE.

> CHARLEY
>
> I'm gonna watch you so closely, you'regonna wish you were alive!

HORACE SNEERS, THEN EXITS.

#1
Have you decided on a negotiating strategy
with the other side, Mr. Merriweather?

CHARLEY
Well, I've learned a lot from Muck.

MUCK SMILES BASHFULLY.

CHARLEY
And I've decided to lie to those demons! I'll
promise `em the moon, then give `em nothing. Let them bleed; let them make the first
concession, for once!

MUCK'S SMILE DISAPPEARS.

#1
You mean we'd bluff them into returning our
spirits, then we wouldn't return theirs?

CHARLEY
Bait and switch. Simple yet effective. The
devils will respect us for using such a classic
device. And they'll never expect it from our
side. They'll be totally unprepared.
(SMILES PROUDLY)

MUCK, #'S 1 & 2 ARGUE ABOUT THE MERITS OF CHARLEY'S PLAN.

CHARLEY
(LOOKS AROUND; SOTTO)
I've got to remember this
dream.

FINALLY, MUCK TAPS CHARLEY ON THE SHOULDER.

MUCK
You have our support. Do whatever it takes
to help the angels.

DOMINIC RUSHES IN.

DOMINIC
Charley, the devil's boss wants to see you
again -- right away!

CHARLEY
Tell him to wait until I'm ready.

DOMINIC
You might miss the food and liquor orgy.
And they've got the Super Bowl on HDTV.

MUCK
It sounds like you can catch him in aweak
moment.

CHARLEY
Exactly what I was thinking. I should
getright to work.

DOMINIC
(LEADING CHARLEY AWAY) And his
girlfriendhas a sister they all want you to
meet. You know, sex is unknown in heaven
but it's very popular down there ....

CHARLEY
Angels, don't wait up. I'll be negotiating - it's
my favorite sport!

FINAL FADE OUT

Appendix C: Feature Film Treatment

"Technobred"

Feature Film Treatment

by

Donald Paul Rutberg

© 2000

CONCEPT

Genetic engineering can eradicate disease and famine or introduce problems that are even more deadly.

It can also bring together an orphaned girl and a loving pet.

"Technobred" is a story about the abandoned and unwanted triumphing through love and courage. It is a contemporary "boy and his horse" story: The "boy" is an orphaned girl and the "horse" is a secret genetics experiment, created in the lab of a dairy magnate. Desperate to acquire the best yearlings, this ego-starved dairy magnate illegally creates his own $10 million race horse -- at the same cost as one of his milk cows. He implants the embryo in a surrogate mother on Jessie Monroe's obscure farm, then he and his scientists are killed in an accident ... and no one knows this newborn foal was bred to be a champion.

Jessie, in her mid-teens, saves the foal, Techno, when the surrogate mother tries to kill her offspring. Techno saves Jessie's life when her stepfather's farm is set on fire, killing the greedy, abusive man.

The girl and her horse, both orphans, are adopted by a trainer, Bob Cougar, who is a recovering compulsive gambler. For the first time in his life, Bob has a champion, albeit a horse that comes from nowhere, in his stable. In order to cash a big bet, he takes an unacceptable risk and enters Techno in a claiming race, where other trainers can purchase any horse entered. When Techno is claimed by a new owner in another stable, Jessie feels betrayed and heartbroken.

Techno won't run for his new owner and the man is happy to sell Techno back to Bob and Jessie for a profit. Back in his own "family," Techno wins the world's most prestigious race, The Breeder's Cup Classic. But there is some concern when they realize the entrants in the race are all the same horse! They were all cloned from the same illegal embryo by the dairy magnate's top scientist, who orchestrated the "accident" which killed his boss.

Bob and Jessie decide they have to stop the cloning conspiracy, which could eventually ruin the sport, even if it means losing their own champion runner.

"Technobred" explores the ramifications of genetic engineering. When it is used recklessly for greedy purposes, bad things happen. When it is used to create a loving pet for an orphaned girl, even though it's accidental, good things happen.

MAIN CHARACTERS

JESSIE MONROE is a strong-willed, teenaged orphan who yearns to become a leading female jockey. Constantly threatened by weight problems, unscrupulous horse owners, greedy trainers and race fixers (among other obstacles) she rises to the top of her profession with considerable help from another orphan -- her beloved thoroughbred, Techno.

TECHNO is an impeccably bred, highly intelligent thoroughbred race horse. If his real breeding were known, his value would be about $10 million -- before he ever raced! Unlike his "twin brothers" who were cloned from the same embryo, Techno is raised like a pet on Jessie's farm, reducing the stress on his fragile legs. Jessie is the only jockey Techno will abide.

BOB & SONDRA COUGAR are Jessie's foster parents. Bob is a failed horse trainer with a compulsive gambling problem; Sondra is an equine bone specialist. It is the Cougars who discover that Techno is an illegally bred race horse -- part of a conspiracy to secretly race cloned thoroughbreds, each valued at $10 million, and all likely to dominate, and possibly destroy, the sport. Bob tries to expose the conspiracy but, in doing so, collects blame for the crime and jeopardizes his own (and only) valuable race horse.

LANA ARMSTRONG, the wife, then widow of EDWARD ARMSTRONG, the man who created the cloned race horses, owns most of the "Technobreds." If she's successful, she'll earn millions and become the most prominent owner in the history of the sport -- or any sport. Bob Cougar is the only man who can expose her criminal activities -- which may include murder.

DR. JERRY OLSON is the scientist who carries out Edward and Lana Armstrong's plan. Olson becomes Lana's lover and evolves into her scapegoat.

FRANK PRUDO is a competitive horse owner who unknowingly acquires a valuable "Technobred." He's the one who claims Techno for his stable, before selling the colt back to a hysterical Jessie and guilt-ridden Bob. Frank starts out as Bob's adversary but eventually becomes Bob's closest ally.

ADAM CROWLETT is a Canadian youth who falls in love with Jessie when the girl jockey and her mystery horse are in hiding.

JIM COUGAR is Bob's scheming brother who lives in Canada. He provides a shelter for Jessie and Techno but, when he realizes that Techno has impregnated Adam's mare, he tricks Adam into selling the mare to him for 1/1,000 of what she's really worth.

HERBERT BOGGS is Jessie's greedy, misanthropic step- father who makes a deal with Edward Armstrong. Then, like Edward, he dies in mysterious fashion.

DR. SABLE is a small-town veterinarian who first suspects that Techno is not the natural offspring of Herbert Boggs' slow gray mare and Edward Armstrong's sterile stallion.

DR. WILLOT quits his job at Armstrong Dairies when he realizes that he's a vulnerable pawn in a crime. Willot eventually tires of running from Olson and Lana and joins forces with Bob and Dr. Sable in an attempt to expose the crime and save the sport.

RAMON is a professional race fixer who also sells drugs to jockeys. He pressures Jessie to "throw" the $4,000,000 Breeder's Cup Classic, the world's most prestigious race. Ramon, as it turns out, is a man whose testimony can put Lana Armstrong in jail.

STORY OUTLINE

The story begins at the Keeneland, Kentucky horse auction, where Edward Armstrong, a dairy magnate, is again outbid by richer men for the best yearlings. Embarrassed, he makes plans to create his own champion.

Armstrong orders his top scientist, Dr. Jerry Olson, to secure reproductive materials from the top sire and dam in racing, in order to illegally breed a $10 million thoroughbred in his dairy lab. Olson passes those orders on to Armstrong's veterinarian, Kenneth Willot, who, against his better judgment, leads a team of mercenaries into two separate barns and secures the valuable materials.

Dr. Olson creates an embryo in his lab, then clones the embryo. He creates 12 horses -- each potentially worth $10 million -- in test tubes and stores them in liquid nitrogen. Olson suggests that Armstrong test only one clone initially; to see how the experiment develops. Olson has a surrogate mare already picked out.

The slow gray mare that is chosen lives on Jessie Monroe's obscure farm. Jessie sees that Armstrong's stallion is not interested in breeding with the old mare (the stallion is sterile) but Jessie's misanthropic stepfather, Herbert Boggs, is thrilled that his "prized" mare was chosen. Boggs will be paid handsomely when the foal is born.

Armstrong and Olson visit Jessie's farm, where Olson implants an embryo into the gray mare, then announces, "She's carrying!" On the way home, Armstrong's helicopter crashes, reportedly killing all aboard. Boggs is delirious with joy: "That's gonna be my horse! There's no one alive to claim it!"

Indeed, a $10 million thoroughbred was waiting to be born and no one knew of its existence or its value.

The foal, Techno, is born on Boggs' farm. The local veterinarian, Dr. Sable, can't understand why the foal was abandoned or how a sterile stallion could be the sire. A few nights later, the gray mare tries to kill her unnatural foal. Jessie saves Techno's life, then Boggs beats Jessie for allegedly trying to injure his "prized" mare.

Two years later, Techno is ready to race and Jessie aspires to be his jockey. Boggs claims that neither are ready but he really wants to keep Techno's existence a secret for as long as possible. Dr. Sable, still suspicious, calls Dr. Willot to find out why the majestic-looking horse was abandoned by Willot's former employers. Willot warns Sable to forget his misgivings. Willot makes a phone call, then, a few nights later, Jessie's farm is burned to the ground. Techno saves Jessie's life but Boggs and Techno's equine "parents" perish in the fire.

Jessie and Techno are sent to an orphanage. Techno nibbles on some grapes at a neighboring farm and the farm owner shoots at the frightened colt. Techno hurdles a fence and keeps running, soon becoming very lost. Jessie goes looking for him and gets lost herself. But her beloved colt finds her and both orphans ride off in the opposite direction of the orphanage.

Bob and Sondra Cougar take in the two orphans after horse and girl simply ride up to Bob's rural porch as he fetches the morning newspaper. Bob is a horse trainer but is also a recovering compulsive gambler. Against Sondra's wishes, Bob begins to train both horse and jockey.

At the California State Fair, Techno and Jessie win their first race easily. Bob collects on his bets. But Dr. Sable confronts Bob with the prevailing circumstances at the time of Techno's birth. He asks Bob to help him solve the puzzle of a horse that comes from nowhere.

Bob calls Edward Armstrong's widow, Lana. When Bob mentions her stallion, the supposed sire of Techno, Lana hangs up on him. Bob travels to Kansas City to see her. Lana tells Bob to race his "gift" horse and keep his mouth shut! Her late husband did nothing wrong and if he did, Bob was just as guilty as anyone for racing a "Technobred." Bob realizes that Lana has more than one "Technobred" and vows to stop her from ruining the sport.

Techno, now at a major race track, trains brilliantly for his first major race. But his workout is seen by a shady jockey's agent, who tips off an owner, Frank Prudo. Prudo unknowingly owns another "Technobred," Experimental Dancer, his fastest and most fragile horse.

Dr. Sable, continually looking for clues to the mystery, tells Bob that Dr. Willot is missing. But Bob has more pressing matters on his mind and he enters Techno in a $50,000 claiming race, where any horse can be claimed by another owner for a predetermined price. Bob thinks that no one will pay $50,000 for a mystery horse but Frank Prudo knows how fast the colt can run. Bob collects a small fortune from betting on the race, which Techno wins, but he breaks Jessie's heart when Frank Prudo claims Techno for his stable.

Sondra and Jessie are understandably upset with Bob. Sondra forgives her husband when she learns that Bob wasn't simply trying to cash a big bet; he had lost confidence in himself and thought no one would claim a horse from a failed trainer. Jessie threatens to move away. Sondra tells Bob he has to buy Techno back from Frank Prudo, no matter what the cost.

Techno acts like a wild beast for his new owner. He breaks free of his training bridle, runs away and hides. He's finally shot with a tranquilizer gun and brought back to his barn. Bob and Jessie try to make a deal with Frank Prudo. Then Jessie sees her horse lying on some hay, unconscious. She tries to free Techno but the colt is too groggy. Frank tells Bob to buy Jessie a dog or cat to soothe her nerves. Techno is entered in a race but throws his new rider, drags him around in the mud, bites a few of his opponents, then refuses to run. When Bob offers Frank $100,000 for the wild horse, Frank immediately accepts the money and Techno once again belongs to Bob and Jessie.

Weeks later, Frank Prudo brings Experimental Dancer to Bob's farm, hoping that Bob will train the talented but moody horse. Frank admits that he had purchased the colt's broodmare without knowing the mare was pregnant. He acquired his horse accidentally, like Bob had done.

Frank gives Bob an application form. It seems that Techno had been nominated by Edward Armstrong to run in the world's richest race, the $4,000,000 Breeder's Cup Classic. Techno begins training for that race. Meanwhile, Sondra, a bone specialist, tests Experimental Dancer's general health. Her DNA tests prove Techno and Experimental Dancer are the same horse!

At the Breeder's Cup party, Dr. Sable tries to dissuade Bob from running Techno in the next day's $4,000,000 race. Rumors of cloned horses are circulating through the crowd of owners and trainers but no one wants to take these rumors seriously. Lana Armstrong, dancing with Dr. Jerry Olson, who not only survived the helicopter crash but orchestrated it, asks Bob, "How do the gamblers handicap the race?" Bob needs the testimony of Dr. Willot to prove that Lana Armstrong and Jerry Olson, for their own greedy purposes, created cloned thoroughbreds and hid their identity from the betting public. Bob also wanted to know who had murdered Edward Armstrong. Bob knew why he was killed. The "Technobreds" were making millions for Lana and Olson. It would be up to Bob to stop them but if he did, he'd risk losing his own prized colt.

As the 12 horses stand in the starting gate before the Breeders' Cup Classic, Techno sniffs around at 11 horses who smell exactly like he does. Each horse wears different color silks and different equipment but they all look identical. Jessie tries to soothe Techno, who can sense that his rider is also uncomfortable in the starting gate. And then the gates open.

In the clubhouse, during the running of the Breeder's Cup Classic, Olson tells Bob everything about the cloned horses. All of them are running in this race. All 12 horses are genetically identical, including Techno. Olson is 100% certain that Bob won't repeat the secret information and risk forfeiting a multi-million dollar (and sole) asset.

Jessie and Techno win the race, after which Jessie tells a stunned broadcaster and national TV audience that all 12 horses are clones. Dr. Sable approaches Bob with Dr. Willot. Both veterinarians want Bob to refuse the trophy and the $4,000,000 purse. Bob, who has never before won a major race, accepts the prizes but promises to do something to stop Lana Armstrong.

Bob calls a press conference to tell all he knows about illegally bred race horses. Frank Prudo tries to talk him out of it, warning Bob that he'll lose his horse. Bob goes through with the press conference (with his wife's blessing) aided by the testimony of Sable and Willot.

Jessie and Techno, meanwhile, flee the country. They drive to Canada to stay on an anonymous farm owned by Jim Cougar, Bob's scheming brother. Techno travels with a high fever. Once inside Canada, Jessie's van gets a flat tire. A Canadian youth, Adam, helps the girl and her sick horse get to Jim's farm.

Lana Armstrong reads the newspaper account of Bob's press conference, realizes that Olson told Bob the truth, and fires her top scientist/lover. Frank Prudo hides Experimental Dancer to protect his investment. Jessie discovers she hates Jim Cougar but likes Adam.

Bob is told by racing officials that he can't race Techno again. They insinuate that he created the entire problem called "Technobreds". He's being punished for his honesty.

"I reported the crime; I didn't commit one!" Bob reminds the nervous racing officials.

Sondra knows that her husband has regained self-respect through this ordeal. She just hopes he doesn't explode while arguing with closed-minded racing officials.

Olson, meanwhile, visits his attorneys who advise him to find the man who burned down Jessie's farm. Otherwise, there is no case against Lana and he'll get blamed for crimes which she alone conceived.

Jessie and Adam fall in love during the Canadian winter. Techno and Adam's mare, Shadow, do the same. Jim learns that Shadow is carrying Techno's foal and buys the mare from Adam for a few thousand Canadian dollars. Jim then reveals that Shadow is pregnant with his horse's foal. Jessie reminds Jim that his horse died before Shadow became pregnant! The foal, Techno's son or daughter, will be worth millions and belong to Jim.

Bob tells Jessie that Techno can't race or breed so she may as well come home. With the $5,000 that Adam gained when he sold his mare, the two lovers drive back to California.

Olson is indicted in the killing of Edward Armstrong. Lana finds a new scientist who will create more "Technobreds".

Bob offers to buy Shadow from Jim. But Jim just laughs at his brother's modest offer and says he'll get a fortune for the mare at auction.

Frank Prudo bluffs the racing commission into thinking that Bob will ruin the integrity of the sport by claiming that most thoroughbreds were illegally bred. Bob is allowed to race and breed Techno. All "Technobreds" are allowed back on the track. But Techno is discovered to have bone chips in his knee and undergoes arthroscopic surgery.

Bob travels to the Seattle horse auction where his desperate brother is selling Shadow. Bob is the only one who knows the real value of Shadow's unborn foal. He buys Shadow at the auction for less money then he had originally offered Jim.

Jessie fights a weight problem as she and Techno prepare for their return to racing and a possible second straight Breeder's Cup Classic victory. But a criminal named Ramon wants Jessie to help him fix races. He threatens her if she doesn't hold Techno back from winning some prep races. Ramon also brags about how he once burned down her farm and could do it again.

Jessie and Bob call the FBI. Techno is scratched from the races he's supposed to lose. Finally, the FBI catches Ramon in the act of fixing a race. No one can find a link between Lana Armstrong and a crime. But Ramon can. He is that link. Ramon makes a deal with the FBI and tells all he knows about Lana Armstrong's crimes.

At the Breeder's Cup party, Bob asks Lana, "How do the murderesses handicap the race?" The FBI arrests Lana for ordering the fire which killed Jessie's stepfather. In the Classic the next day, Techno beats Experimental Dancer by a head to win a consecutive $4,000,000 race. Jessie tells a national TV audience that she's engaged to marry Adam.

Jessie's weight again becomes a problem and she decides to retire from riding. But then Shadow delivers a majestic-looking foal, a colt who looks just like his father, Techno. After taking one look at the foal, Jessie announces, "I just came out of retirement!" THE END

Appendix D: Children's Picture Book

"A Leprechaun Named Levity"

by

Donald Paul Rutberg

Don Rutberg

"A Leprechaun Named Levity"

In a town not very far from you;
On a day much like today,
A leprechaun named Levity
Asked, "Who else wants to play?"

No one gave an answer.
No one asked the elf his name.
No one here had time to greet
This stranger or play games.

Levity, who lived out where
The forest almost ends,
Walked smiling down the empty streets.
He'd try to make new friends.

Faces that he saw were pale
And looked a little worried.
No one's work was getting done
But everyone was hurried.

He asked around, about this town,
With his normal, carefree style.
Residents were more inclined
To whine at him than smile.

"I don't take things seriously,"
He said to folks he met.
"You have highs and you have lows ...
But I have no regret."

"What's so darn important, Folks?
What's the harm in telling jokes?
Be the best that you can be
Then say, `So what?', like me."

No one seemed to trust him
With his "What's-the-difference?" smirk.
He was the kind of leprechaun
Who'd take a day off work.

The town folk took work seriously
And covered up their ears.
No one had vacationed here
In seven hundred years!

So Levity, uncaringly,
Moved on with nothing gained,
To sleep out in the forest
Since he didn't mind the rain.

"I don't take things seriously,"
He said to trees he met.
"You have highs and you have lows ...
But I have no regret."

Well, one tree had a sweaty palm
And wrinkles in his bark.
He worried he'd go, "Timberrrrrrr!"
Then be benches in a park.

His friends got jobs as weapons,
Though they weren't mean at all.
Cut, then shaped to baseball bats
That crushed the little ball.

The Tree said, "Trees would never
Hit a baseball -- people do!
I'm antsy 'cause we trees
Deserve consideration, too."

"Don't take it all so seriously,"
Levity replied.
"Why upset your woodwork
Over games you haven't tried?

"What's so darn important, Tree?
Why take life so seriously?
Be the best that you can be
Then say, 'So what?' like me."

The Tree soon felt uplifted.
His attitude improved.
He waved his leaves and told the elf
Of jobs that he approved.

"I'd like to be a hospital --
A very helpful thing.
Or else a fine piano;
Maybe I could learn to sing."

"... I could dance to my own music
With the pedals and the keys.
And build appreciation,
Earn respect for all us trees.

But if I'm just a toy, I'll be
The best that I can be.
Giving from my roots because
I take things seriously."

Levity moved onwardly
And didn't even care
If he might lose his way
Or if the turtle beat the hare.

Well, soon Lev met a worried dog,
"I'm a ruler," was his claim,
And since the day that he was born,
"King" had been his name.

"Why am I in charge?" King asked.
"I don't have time to sneeze.
Digging, sniffing here and there
And holding all these keys.

"Governing is serious
To everyone I know.
I have highs and I have lows ...
Now I have got to go!"

"Wait," Lev said. "Why can't you see?
You take your job too seriously.
Just be the best that you can be
And say, 'So what?' like me."

"So what?" King sneered. "Why you dumb elf,
I'd slap you if I weren't a prince.
Once I hit a boxer ...
And he hasn't battled since.

"Naturally, dogs look to me
As leader of the pack.
I tell 'em when to miss a meal
And when to hit the sack.

"But this responsibility
Has got me chewing claws.
I'm the judge and jury ...
And I don't know the laws!"

Shouts of, "King, get back!" made King
Run off; still serious.
Then in the sky, Lev saw some lights
That looked mysterious.

Suddenly, he saw a spaceship!
It was landing ... on the grass!
An alien popped out and mumbled,
"I think I'm out of gas.

"I tried to find a station
When I stopped off for a bite
Near Mercury, but golly gee,
My money's getting tight.

"I didn't take it seriously
That I was low on cash.
Lucky I had credit cards
Or else I would've crashed.

Maybe you can help me
With a temporary loan.
I need a little extra
To help repair my phone."

"You see, the nearest spaceship shop
Is ten light years away.
I'd like to call them up --
See, they won't come if I can't pay."

"Sorry," said the leprechaun,
"But I don't have a cent.
I live in the wilderness
And don't pay any rent."

"What's so darn important, Friend?
How much money can you spend?
The richest things in life are free.
Just say, 'So what?' like me."

"All I need's a Geezorp
To fill my empty tank."
The Alien said, "I didn't come
This far to rob a bank.

"A Geezorp is the money
That we spend throughout the stars.
I hope that I have better luck
Borrowing on Mars!"

Lev thought that he might someday
Like to travel out in space.
But he thought this guy's planet
Was too serious a place.

Lightening, thunder; everywhere
But Lev did not complain.
He found a cave while climbing;
Went inside, expecting rain ...

... That never came. He wondered why
The ground and leaves were dry.
An old man said, "You -- droopy ears;
I suppose you'd like to try!

"I'm the weathermaker.
I take orders from the top,
To end the droughts in deserts
And let farmers grow their crops.

"But I can't start a sprinkle.
This machine just won't respond.
Frightened fish are thinking
That the plug's pulled from their pond."

Lev said, "I never take life seriously
When it forgets to rain.
Don't let minor setbacks
Wash your good work down the drain.

"Look at all the snow you've made;
We play in it and ski.
Be the best that you can be
And say, 'So what?' like me."

"I, for one, am serious."
The Weathermaker said with pride.
"I hear trees asking, `Where's the rain?'
By now, they're petrified.

"Trees can tell when something's wrong
With nature, right away.
Then the blame will fall on me --
I won't know what to say.

"The rain is late? That's no excuse.
They'll think that I don't care.
I'd better think up something good
 To tell that eight-foot bear!

He believes it's serious
When rivers don't run deep.
Rain improves his fishing
And he says it helps him sleep."

"So leave me now. You won't get wet
Until I fix what's stuck.
But don't go West because you'll find
A lot of angry ducks!"

Outside the cave, the angry ducks
Were waiting, their wings folded.
"Couldn't you do anything?"
The angriest duck scolded.

Lev said, "The man apologized
Because the rain is late.
I'm certain that he'll do his job
If we just let him concentrate."

So Lev, the ducks and bears walked west;
They reached the rain-washed sea.
Lev saw an Angel surfing in ....
She told him, "Come with me!"

He wouldn't listen seriously
To the few words she said:
"Sorry, little fellow,
But, officially, you're dead!"

"You want to know what happened?
Well, I researched and I found
That what's-his-name made too much rain.
It says right here you drowned."

"I don't take life seriously."
Lev said, "I'm not upset.
I had highs and I had lows
 I have no regret."

The Angel said, "You're wrong,
You had no highs or lows.
You never frowned or smiled one smile.
That's what my research shows.

"But I think you'll smile
When I tell you super news:
You've been good so you'll come back
At any time you choose!"

"So what?" Lev said, "It's not so great
To be all by myself.
No one takes me seriously
Because I'm just an elf."

The Angel whispered, "That is why
You never felt a thing:
You numbed yourself to happiness
As well as suffering.

"Now you'll have another chance
To see what you have missed.
And you will learn the difference
Between being punched or kissed.

"If no one took things seriously,
None of us would feel
Friendship, love or decency;
The things that make us real."

Levity was crying now;
His heart was touched, at last.
He was feeling those emotions
That he hid from in the past.

"I'm gonna take it seriously,
No matter what the cost!
Dancing when I'm happy ...
And screaming when I'm lost."

"Even if I hear a couple
Words that hurt my pride,
I will still be comfortable
With what I have inside.

"That's what's so important, Miss."
Then the Angel said, "How about a kiss?
A little peck right on your cheek.
To get you started, so to speak."

And so they laughed and kissed until
Lev's spirit was repaired.
"Send me back to live my life --
I'm totally prepared.

"I'll start from the beginning
In a second childhood,
To feel all those emotions
That I never understood."

The Angel told him, "Do your best,
Leprechaun Named Levity.
'Cause what's the use in being free
If you don't take life seriously?"

It's been some time since Levity
Got his second chance on Earth.
He's seen his loved ones growing old
And known the joys of birth.

He started taking seriously
Everyone he met.
Now he has highs and he has lows ...
But he feels no regret.

In a forest pretty close to you;
On a day much like today,
A Leprechaun Named Levity
Mixes work with play.

He knows that he will manage to
Rise up if he should fall.
He knows that he has made
Some special, new friends after all.

So think about young Levity ...
Who's mainly feeling good
'Bout taking life more seriously.
Sometimes, you know, you should.

THE END

Appendix E: Children's Middle Grade Fiction

"The Traveling Monarchs"

by

Donald Paul Rutberg

3,500 Words

The Traveling Monarchs

Summer was about to end and Beverly was already missing it. She was walking slowly along the beach in Atlantic City, New Jersey, tossing up raw clams to grateful seagulls, watching the sun set over her shoulder, thinking about ... school?

Yes, school, and how the first day of seventh grade would be embarrassing for her because she couldn't think of one important thing she'd done all summer. She'd have to tell the whole class how she went to the shore for three weeks and had a bad cold for a month. How could she admit the highlight of her summer was getting over a cold?

Beverly suddenly felt nervous about the possibility of a 12 month school year. She needed some time off every summer to make new friends, create art, explore nature and, of course, sleep really, really late. But now this summer was screeching to an end. So she walked slower and willed the sun to stay in the sky a while longer.

Beverly's walk had slowed to a near stop when she felt surrounded by something swarming in the air. Bees! No, there weren't any bees by the ocean when the breeze came in like this. But some very small creatures in a very large group were flying near her head and shoulders and she was spinning like a sand crab trying to figure out what they were.

One hundred thousand tiring butterflies were flapping onto the beach from out in the ocean. They were orange and black and lined up in precise rows of twenty, one row after another. Every few seconds, a butterfly captain would flutter ahead of a group and an occasional sergeant of arms flew off to the side to keep formation.

Beverly had never seen a group of butterflies that looked this large, this organized or this exhausted. One hundred thousand of them barely had the strength to land heavily (for them) on the beach. They were groaning and when this many butterflies groan, people can hear it.

Beverly wasn't sure her eyes or ears were working properly. She shook the wet sand off her face, tilted her head and focused on these tired butterflies, who had all dropped onto the beach in perfect alignment.

The butterflies seemed to be looking at her but they weren't saying anything. So Beverly found an ice cream stick and wrote a note in the sand: "Can I help you? Sincerely, Bev Flyer."

The butterflies had to turn around because the note Bev had written in the sand was upside-down to them. All 100,000 butterflies moved closer to the boardwalk, did an about-face and read Bev's note.

Then the butterflies arranged themselves in the shapes of letters that spelled words. A group of butterflies formed the letter "H," then another group formed an "i," until they spelled out, "Hi, Bev. We need a ride to Mexico."

Bev spelled in the sand, "Let's talk to my Dad about this."

Dad was sitting on a bench on the boardwalk, a laptop computer by his side, carefully reading the news on the screen.

Bev asked, "Can butterflies spell?"

"No they can't."

Dad didn't look up.

"Uh, I think they're in trouble," Bev said, as she noticed hundreds of butterflies fluttering weakly into the sand.

"They'll be fine, dear," Dad said as one butterfly floated onto his nose. "They fly through New Jersey ... oh, that tickles ... every September. They aren't in trouble and they certainly can't spell ...."

The butterflies spelled out a message while fluttering above Dad's head on the boardwalk: "We might freeze."

The butterfly who had drifted onto Dad's nose danced off his nose and dotted the "i" in "might."

"Let's talk to your mother about this," Dad said as he picked up his laptop, got off the bench and rushed toward the house.

The house was only a few feet from the boardwalk. Bev looked for stray butterflies but couldn't find one who was out of formation. The entire group followed, 20 in a row, toward the house, where Mom was using her computer.

"What's the weather forecast?" Dad asked, sounding as calm as possible for a man who believed he had just communicated with winged creatures; part of a species which has been on Earth for ten million years.

Mom checked with the computer she used mostly for business -- she owned a small travel agency -- then said, "The temperature is going to drop 30 degrees tonight."

"Can these butterflies come in?" Bev asked as she pointed outside the door. "They'll catch cold."

"As long as they wipe their feet," Mom said, then she got a towel and, thinking this was a joke, put it on the floor.

One hundred thousand butterflies cruised into the house, all carefully wiping off dirt as they entered. Due to their great numbers, they spread to every room, every square inch of the big, old house. Even the fireplace, which was never used, was jammed with colors orange and black. And when the butterflies fluttered their wings, the entire fireplace seemed to be moving.

It was as if the Flyer family had ordered way too much orange and black wallpaper for their summer house.

Mom looked at Dad like it was somehow his idea but Dad shrugged and said, "Bev adopted them."

Mom was suspicious because once Dad had said the same thing about the family basset hound, Scooter. (Dad later admitted it was he who had adopted Scooter.)

Scooter woke up from his nap to greet the butterflies. When he barked, the butterflies laughed and when 100,000 butterflies laugh, people, as well as dogs, can hear it.

"What's so funny?" Bev wondered because, to her, Scooter's barks all sounded pretty much the same, except when he howled at sirens and fireworks.

A group of butterflies floated over to Mom's computer, piggyback style, and typed firmly (for them) on the keyboard, "Scooter said, 'I'm Scooter and this is my home!'"

Bev told Scooter, "You live here with us, not the other way around" but Scooter just tilted his head politely and barked again.

The butterflies at the computer translated Scooter's bark: "We have food here. I'll help you find some."

This is how Bev and her parents learned that basset hounds and butterflies have been friends for a long time.

"What kind of butterflies are they?" Bev asked.

Mom used the computer's encyclopedia and downloaded butterfly pictures on the monitor.

Meanwhile, some of the butterflies formed themselves into the shape of a crown.

"King butterflies?" Bev guessed. "No, that's not it."

Then Mom found a picture of orange and black butterflies and announced, "They're Monarchs! They lay eggs in milkweed as they migrate from Kansas to California, or ... a different group of Monarchs migrate from the east coasts of Canada and the U.S. to south central Mexico. These are the Eastern Monarchs, isn't that right?"

The butterflies saw the Monarchs on the monitor and spelled out, "Si," which means yes to anyone who lives in Mexico.

"Am I the only one paying attention?" Bev wondered. "They're too tired to fly by themselves. And if the temperature really does drop 30 degrees, they'll freeze without our help."

Bev's house was not big enough to comfortably hold this many butterflies, who probably all had dirty wings, for a long period of time. Just walking from room to room was difficult.

"We have to get them a ride to Mexico!" Bev insisted. "The sooner the better."

Mom phoned the airline and explained the problem. Then she hung up the phone, half-smiled and typed out, "Good news. Butterflies are allowed on the plane!"

One hundred thousand butterflies applauded and when this many applaud, people can hear it.

Then Mom typed, "The bad news is that it will cost $1 per butterfly."

Bev started counting butterflies. She stopped counting a few seconds later, when she realized that, if she used all the money in her savings account to transport these creatures to sunny Mexico, she would still be $99,000 short of accomplishing her goal.

Meanwhile, Mom typed out more bad news.

"Space is limited. There's only one flight per day. They must fly on a Wednesday, leave at 1 am and stop three times along the way. Hmmm, that means no in-flight movie."

Beverly sighed.

Mom typed, "Plus, there's tax."

Dad groaned.

The butterflies sagged heavily (for them).

Mom left the computer work station; moving carefully, not wanting to squash any of her invited guests.

Bev sat down at the computer and soon learned even more disturbing news.

"There's no milkweed in Mexico. The butterflies live in evergreen trees down there."

"What's wrong with evergreen trees?" Dad asked. "When I was in Pismo Beach, California, the butterflies loved hanging out in those trees. When they flapped their wings, it looked like the trees themselves were shimmering."

Out of the corner of his eye, Dad thought he saw the fireplace shuffle back and forth.

"Just like that!" he shouted.

"Well, in South-Central Mexico, the evergreen trees are disappearing!" Bev explained. "The people there are so desperate for money that they chop down evergreen trees where butterflies roost. All Monarch butterflies who migrate from the eastern U.S. and Canada will die before next spring and no new ones will be born."

Scooter barked and the butterflies typed out, "We agree with you, Scooter. We'd like to bite them but butterflies have no teeth."

Bev had never seen Scooter so upset. Mom and Dad didn't look so happy either.

"What about the Kansas to California monarchs?" Mom asked. "How will they survive?"

Bev read the computer screen and answered, "The people of California have bought the land and the milkweed where butterflies breed and roost. The Western Monarchs are safe in California but the Eastern Monarchs aren't safe in Mexico."

"Maybe some people are thinking, 'What's the big deal?'" Dad guessed. "After all, we still have Western Monarchs."

Bev asked, "What will they say after all the Monarchs are gone? 'Well, we still have grasshoppers.' Then grasshoppers will be wiped out and they'll say, 'We still have beetles and crickets.'"

"We can't stop cold weather or the illegal logging in Mexico but we can do something. Can't we?" Mom asked.

"If we don't," Dad said glumly, "these may be the last butterflies we'll ever see."

"Even if we could afford to charter a few planes, they're not going to survive in their usual spot in South-Central Mexico," Bev insisted. "According to the computer, the evergreen trees are most plentiful in a remote region near Acapulco, Mexico."

"So let them wait here until it gets warm again in a few days, then they can fly to Acapulco themselves," Dad suggested. "After all, they're the greatest navigators in the world, right?"

It was true.

Bev's parents were happy with the new plan and went to sleep. But Bev was still worried about her new friends and stayed up late to keep them company and solve any last minute problems.

"What will you eat on your trip?" she asked the butterflies out loud, as she and Scooter shared a late night snack in front of the computer.

She stared at the pictures on the monitor.

"OK, in the Southern United States you can eat milkweed, which grows near corn fields. Sound good?"

The butterflies all nodded and rubbed their bellies, recognizing the milkweed in the picture. Scooter licked his lips.

Bev kept reading until she saw a headline: "BT corn killing monarchs."

"Oh, no!" she shouted.

"What's BT corn?" the butterflies spelled out.

Bev read aloud: "BT corn has bacteria in it that's safe for humans but deadly to insects called European corn borers. This is used so the borers don't ruin the crop. One-third of all corn growers use BT seeds. It saves farmers one billion dollars in lost corn crops. It's used instead of poisonous pesticides, so farmers don't pollute their land and water. They spray bacteria from helicopters or add it to the water and the corn thrives. But the butterflies suffer."

The Monarchs formed the shape of a question mark.

Bev kept reading, printing out copies for the butterflies, hoping that by educating the creatures, she could help save them.

"BT corn doesn't kill butterflies. But the corn produces pollen in the summer and the pollen flies around and gets on your milkweed. And it's the milkweed, dusted with BT pollen, that's so bad for you. You eat less, grow slower and die younger and more often. You lay three generations of eggs between July and September when you migrate to Mexico -- and that's the same time of year the corn pollinates! The timing couldn't be worse. The pollen flies onto your food just before you get there for dinner."

Bev pounded her fist on the table and accidentally crushed a couple of crackers. She ignored the mess and kept reading.

"Some experts say butterflies don't actually eat the corn. So what? The corn pollen is just as bad! These experts also say that honeybees and ladybugs are not affected by BT seeds or pollen from BT corn. Is that supposed to cheer us up. Huh?"

The butterflies shook their heads, "No."

"The Monarchs could disappear because of BT dust or evergreen forest destruction. It's double-trouble for you poor butterflies. I can't stand it," Bev moaned.

"Can you help us?" the butterflies spelled out.

Bev tried to appear calm. Hands shaking, she typed on the monitor: "Don't worry. I'll save you."

She kept typing instructions for the butterflies.

"The first thing you should do is forget about flying to your old spot; where the evergreen tree forests have been destroyed. All in favor, raise their ring wing."

All butterflies raised their ring wing.

"Next, don't try to migrate through the Southern U.S. It would spell certain doom."

The Monarchs spelled out, "Certain Doom."

So, through the late evening and early morning hours, Bev walked around the living room, carefully, trying to think of ways to fly her endangered friends to Acapulco, Mexico. She had to get them directly and inexpensively to that hard-to-find, Mexican, evergreen tree forest. Anything less would be a disaster.

Bev noticed a travel brochure on her mother's desk. "Fun in the Mexican Sun" was the promotional brochure sent to her mother's travel agency by Javiar, the entertainment director of a resort in Acapulco.

"I know this man, Javiar," Bev said out loud. "And he knows who I am. My Mom calls him once a week on the videophone to check out the entertainment in his resort, so her customers can decide if they want to go there. Maybe I can call him and see if he needs any more entertainers."

The girl looked at her watch. It was 1 am. She typed out a question: "If it's 1 am here, what time is it in the Acapulco, Mexico time zone?"

The butterflies formed themselves into the shape of a clock and indicated the time would be 11 pm in Acapulco.

Bev said, "An entertainment director should still be up at 11 pm. I mean, entertainers are known for staying up late, aren't they? You butterflies need a name for your group. Try to think one up while I'm calling."

Bev made the long-distance call (it was more like a video conference) telling Javiar's secretary that she was a booking agent, not a travel agent like her mother. Within moments, she had reached Javiar at his Mexican resort hotel.

"Of course I remember you, Beverly. How is your mother?" Javiar asked on the monitor.

"She's fine. She's sleeping," Bev said.

"So you're playing around with the videophone, is that it?" Javiar wondered.

"No, this is a business call," Bev assured him. "Can you see the thousands of butterflies behind me?"

Javiar squinted through the videophone. "Is that what they are?"

"Yes. And they're very talented. They can spell almost any word."

"In English or Spanish?" Javiar asked, chuckling.

Bev typed in Javiar's question.

The butterflies spelled out "Inglis y Espanol." ("English and Spanish.")

Javiar saw this and nearly choked on his mango juice.

"How did they do that? What are they, puppets on wires?"

"They're Monarch butterflies," Bev said patiently.

"But ... are they alive?"

"They are, for now. But if they want to stay alive, they have to get to the evergreen forest near your resort. Will you hire them and transport them down there? You won't regret it."

"Tell them to spell out, 'Snacks are being served by the waterfall.'"

Bev typed out, "OK, this is your final audition, boys and girls" and she asked the butterflies to spell out, in midair, Javiar's words.

Not only did they complete the spelling job, they formed the "C" in "snacks" to look like a pizza with a missing slice and the "V" in "served" to look like a waitress carrying a tray! Then they finished the sentence with a cascading double "L" in "waterfall" that looked just like a waterfall!

Javiar took one look at the perfect sentence structure and artistic style and announced, "They're hired! They're going to be the best beach entertainers we've ever had at this resort. I'll send a plane for them tomorrow morning!"

"Fax me a contract," Bev demanded. "They want a two year contract, with an option for a third year. Don't forget they need guaranteed, unlimited use of the evergreen forest."

"Anything else?" Javiar asked.

"Yes. They want their summers off so they can migrate through New Jersey to Canada. The people up here love to see them, including me and my family."

"I believe you," Javiar said and agreed to Bev's terms.

The next day, which was sunny and chilly (but not too cold) Javiar sent a plane to pick up the butterflies in Philadelphia.

The whole family drove to the Philadelphia airport, slowly so the butterflies wouldn't get lost.

In the parking lot, the butterflies hugged Scooter, who had to wait in the car. When Scooter barked goodbye, the Flyer family didn't need the butterflies to translate their basset hound's thoughts. They knew he was saying something like, "Good luck, have a safe flight and come back soon. I'll find more food!"

If and when they did return, Scooter, with his terrific sense of smell, would be the first to know it. Just as the butterflies relied on their super wings; Scooter had his super nose. He stuck his head out of the car window and sniffed each and every one of them as they approached the airport terminal. Some people never forget a face; Scooter never forgot a scent.

The Monarchs followed Bev and her parents to the departure gate. Bev asked the people who were flying to Acapulco, "Does anyone mind if these butterflies share the plane with you? They're going to be your beach entertainers. They're a little nervous because they've just been hired and it's their first gig."

"What's the group's name?" one tourist, carrying a guitar, asked.

Bev hadn't had time to invent a name during the night, so she blurted out the first thing that popped into her mind.

"They're called, 'The Traveling Monarchs!'"

"Cool," the guitar player said. "They're different and that's totally cool. I like that. Who designed their outfits?"

The passengers were thrilled to share the plane with "celebrity" entertainers. And once they learned the butterflies could spell and sketch in midair, they couldn't wait to play word games with them on the plane.

Bev waved goodbye to her many friends as the butterflies spelled out, "Thanks Bev. See you next year, we hope."

Then, more than a hundred thousand butterflies hoisted her onto their backs and carried her around the airport lounge in celebration. And when this many butterflies carry you around in the air, you can feel it.

Bev and her family returned to their winter home in Pennsylvania. The day was cold and felt like late autumn or early winter. But the butterflies were safe. They were all in Mexico now where extreme weather and starvation couldn't touch them.

Bev missed her orange and black friends but knew she would see them again next summer. She had done something important this summer, after all. She couldn't wait to get to school and make new friends; friends who would be with her on the beach next year, when the butterflies returned.

On the first day of school, the teacher asked Bev what she had done over the summer. Bev told the truth: she had helped save tens of thousands of Eastern Monarch butterflies. The teacher didn't think Bev was telling the truth ... until 100 butterflies floated into the classroom. These Monarchs had gotten lost and stayed warm thanks to a kindly farmer in Pennsylvania who let them rest in his farm house. Through their instincts, they were drawn to Bev and felt the need to approach the blackboard and spell out, "THANKS BEV!"

The End

Appendix F: Children's Nonfiction

"Why Homing Pigeons Come Home"

by

Donald Paul Rutberg

7,000 Words

© 2002

Why Homing Pigeons Come Home

TABLE OF CONTENTS

PART ONE:

INTRODUCTION: WHAT ARE HOMING PIGEONS?

Most people know just three things about the wild pigeons we see flying free:

1. They are tough birds who hang out everywhere.

2. They don't mind flying near your face.

3. If you drop a piece of popcorn, a pigeon will eat it.

This book is not about wild pigeons. It is about their brave and noble cousins, called Homing Pigeons or Homers.

Homing Pigeons are offspring of the Rock Pigeon or Rock Dove that lives wild in Europe, Asia and Africa. They may enjoy eating popcorn just like their wild cousins but Homers are a special breed of pigeon. They have more strength, endurance and speed than wild pigeons; much like comparing a thoroughbred to a plow horse.

Homing Pigeons are known worldwide as war heroes. They have saved the lives of countless soldiers and civilians through their special ability and desire to return home. These sleek, athletic, handsome and loyal pets have earned medals from governments and saved communities because they always use their natural home-finding skills to deliver important messages.

These birds can be driven to foreign countries or across mountain ranges or dropped from airplanes out over the ocean and still find their way back home to their families. They've been flying home with notes tied to their feet, often through unfamiliar territory, for thousands of years. People would read the messages (warnings such as, "RUN FOR YOUR LIVES!") and then decide on a course of action.

Usually, they would run for their lives because someone was chasing them. But when they ran, they took the pigeons with them.

HOW DO HOMING PIGEONS FIND THEIR WAY HOME?

Homers are one-way fliers. They are transported to a starting place, where they are released. Then they fly home.

How do they find their way through strange territory to reach home, sometimes flying more than 1,000 miles in two days?

No one is really sure because we can't understand their homing mechanism. We believe they use the magnetic forces on Earth in ways we can't comprehend, flowing with magnetic winds, like a compass. They may feel magnetic breezes like we feel the wind change or smell a delicious bar-b-que. We believe that Homers never forget a landmark once they see it. But they don't necessarily need to see landmarks to reach home.

- Try this at home: have the family chef prepare your favorite meal in the kitchen. Meanwhile, walk to the room farthest from the kitchen. Cover your ears and sniff the air. Then try to find your family while they're eating dinner.

It's doubtful that Homing Pigeons can sniff out their homes but they may use one or more of their natural senses to reach their home loft.

Homers may very well use the sun to navigate. Whether they are flying compasses or flying sundials, both or neither, all we know for sure is they use their instincts; instincts that we don't have.

WHY DO HOMING PIGEONS COME HOME?

The answer is not because they recognize the importance of the messages they deliver. They can't read or write. It's because ... maybe you can figure it out for yourself. One clue has already been given away.

PART TWO:

GENERAL PIGEON HISTORY: WHO ARE THEY, REALLY?

All pigeons, including Homers, descended from the Rock Pigeon or Rock Dove, who descended from plain old doves. (These were same doves that Noah sent from his ark to see if the waters had gone down and if there was any land left on Earth.) Therefore, all pigeons are related to doves, although doves are usually smaller than pigeons.

That's right; those popcorn loving, get-in-your-face, wild pigeons that you see using the Earth for a toilet are basically doves. There are hundreds of dove/pigeon species. They live everywhere except for frozen zones and are most abundant near the tropics.

Today, the Rock Dove nests on cliffs in Europe, Asia and Africa. They are most often slate blue in color and have two black wing bars, a white rump, a black tail band and a green and purple gloss on their necks. Many modern pigeons differ greatly from their original Rock Dove ancestors. But when domestic pigeons run wild, they return to their original ancestral colors. Big city pigeons, as wild as pigeons can get, look much like their European ancestors.

Pigeons are known for making soft cooing sounds during mating season. They show great affection for their family members and are considered gentle; a symbol of peace. However, they fight viciously amongst themselves -- as you probably know if you've ever dropped a piece of popcorn right in the middle of 50 pigeons.

VARIOUS BREEDS OF PIGEONS AND DOVES

The many different breeds of pigeons are raised for racing, carrying messages, recreation, show or food. (Large birds produce fat, little babies, called "squabs" which are consumed as a delicacy when they're one month old.)

The English Carrier Pigeon is a large, stately bird, bred for show, like some dogs are bred for elegance and beauty. Carriers may be black, white or colored and, like Homers, are descended from the European Rock Dove. Carriers are larger than Homers and walk proudly erect. They have a long beak, head and body and strong wings and feet. Their feathers are always well groomed but they have to go through life with large, fleshy growths that surround their big yellow eyes and their bills. Sometimes, these growths completely cover their noses. Carrier Pigeons are thought to be the only animals bred for elegance and beauty that have large, fleshy growths completely covering their noses.

Fantail Pigeons are the fanciest of the show birds. They dance on their toes, hold their heads far back and spread their enormous fan-shaped tail. The Fantail has 30 feathers, two or three times more than other pigeons. The vain and pompous Fantail struts around with its neck puffed up like a balloon. It has special sacks in its neck that fill up with air to gain this effect.

The Tumbler Pigeon performs acrobatics in the air, doing backward loops. The Roller Pigeon is another acrobat, who flies in a circle, then rolls about 100 feet while holding his head and neck downward.

The Crowned Pigeon of New Guinea is one of the most beautiful and the largest, about the size of a large chicken. The Band-tailed Pigeon of the Western United States has a black band across its tail. Hunters shoot large numbers of them for sport when the birds gather to eat wild fruits.

The pinkish-gray Passenger Pigeon, from North America, used to number in the millions. In the early 1800's, naturalists in Kentucky spotted over 2 million in one group and another flock that blocked out the sun and took three days to fly past . Their wings sounded like thunder and their nesting areas covered thousands of acres. Hunters killed so many that now they're extinct.

Hunters flashed bright lights into their nests at night to blind the birds, then knocked them from their trees with poles. Then the Passenger Pigeons were shot or choked with burning sulphur and eventually eaten or sold for food. Carloads were shipped each day to markets in New York and Chicago. The Passenger Pigeons sold for 1-2 cents each! The last one died in 1914 in the Zoological Gardens in Cincinnati.

The Bleeding Heart Pigeon, from the Philippines, has underparts that are completely white except for a great splash of red over its chest that resembles a gunshot wound. Maybe the Bleeding Heart Pigeons are protesting the plight of their extinct cousins, the Passenger Pigeons, by developing this red splash on their chests. Maybe they're thinking that if they look like they've already been shot, no hunter will shoot them again.

As far as we know, no breed of pigeon has developed a bulls eye design on its chest -- good news for pigeon lovers everywhere.

EARLY PIGEON HISTORY

Homing Pigeons carried messages for ancient Egyptians and Persians. They were used to bring home Olympic Game results 2,500 years ago. This "Pigeon Network" brought us sports scores and highlights before we invented radio, TV and the Internet.

Romans used Homers to send military messages, as did the French during the Franco-Prussian war in 1870. The French used Homers to send some of those "Run For Your Lives" messages. Unfortunately, the Germans (Prussians) used hawks to kill the Homers. The pigeons knew the hawks would try to kill them in the air, yet they still tried to fly home as quickly as possible.

Although Homers have been racing for thousands of years, the original pigeons could only travel 40 miles or so per day. (By 1919, they could travel 200 miles per day; now they've improved to 600 miles a day.) In ancient times, 40 miles was a great distance because there were only two available ways to travel -- on foot or horseback. Early Twentieth Century pigeons were fast and reliable enough to be used by newspapers to bring stock market quotes across the English Channel from England to Belgium.

COMING TO AMERICA: PIGEONS BECOME WAR HEROES

Homers were imported to the U.S. for racing in the 1880's. European immigrants would bring their birds with them to big cities. They'd buy houses near landmarks, like rivers, and race against their neighbor's pigeons, just as they had done back in Europe. Houses near rivers were in demand because they provided the pigeons with an easy flight path.

But new neighbors eventually moved onto these streets near the rivers and they didn't respect the sport, the different culture or the birds themselves. They also didn't appreciate pigeon poop landing on their clean clothes, hanging on back-yard clotheslines. There were many heated arguments surrounding pigeon flights. The worst part was, they couldn't even argue in the same language. English was foreign to many of these new arrivals in the U.S., even though it was spoken all around them.

In those days, early in the 20th century, houses were built right up to the street and most homeowners had a big yard in the back. Now, houses have large front lawns and small back yards, which is better suited to owning dogs than Homers.

Still, the introduction of racing Homers, via Europe, turned out to be a fortunate move for the U.S. When radio silence was needed or all communication was cut off (because radios were being blown up in battle) the use of Homing Pigeons was considered the best way to transmit messages. (There were no cell phones, beepers, computers, fax machines, videocameras or TV's.) American Homing Pigeons carried vital messages and brought back war results in World War I, World War II and the Korean War.

They traveled over oceans and high mountains; through rain, fog and wind. Even when they were mangled by shellfire, they bravely brought back messages anyway, saving thousands of lives at a time.

Homers served in the U.S. Army signal corps. In World War I, there were some amazing reports of brave pigeons delivering messages during combat. One bird carried a message 24 miles in 25 minutes! It arrived with one leg shot off and its breast injured by a bullet.

One pigeon received government medals and honors. He was a United States' bird called "GI JOE," who saved over 1,000 British soldiers by himself in World War II. "Joe" was given a medal for bravery; at the time he was the only animal in the U.S. to be honored in such a way.

What did "Joe" do to deserve such glory? He brought a message to 1,000 British soldiers indicating that the enemy had changed direction, added troops and was headed toward their camp.

In other words, "Run For Your Lives!"

These brave birds have worked together with people in mysterious yet inspiring ways. Still, the U.S. army sold the last of its birds and replaced them with electronic devices in 1956.

PART THREE:

THE SPORT OF RACING HOMERS

Pigeon racing has been popular throughout history because people have always appreciated the Homers' athleticism. The birds' antics (like accidentally whacking one another in the face or zooming through small openings) can be delightful and fun.

Through the hobby, you will learn about sportsmanship, nutrition, psychology, weather, math and carpentry. Millions of people race competitively; a hundred thousand in the U.S. It is an active, not passive hobby for children, who usually love the birds as pets.

The sport started in Belgium, then spread to Holland and England. Racing a stable of pigeons is almost like playing baseball or football for children in Belgium. In that pigeon-happy country, people build pigeon lofts in the attics of their homes. Families with big houses hire a loft manager to live with them. The loft manager just has to whistle and the trained pigeons fly home to the top floor of the house they all share.

In New York City, people rent out their roofs to pigeon racers. Of course, not everyone wants to share a balcony with a stable of Homers, no matter how swift and handsome they seem.

Despite their reputation for being ... not as clean as you and me, Homers harbor fewer germs than dogs and cats.

- Try this at home: put an important message on your cat's collar. See if the cat attempts to deliver the message.

Today, most towns in the U.S. have a pigeon racing club -- there are over 700 clubs nationwide. You can find out more by calling the American Racing Pigeon Union at 1-405-478-2240 or the Racing Pigeon Digest at 1-318-474-1289.

THE MATERIALS YOU'LL NEED FOR RACING

Homing Pigeons eat whole grains such as wheat, corn, barley and peas. They consider peas their dessert. Some trainers mix garlic in with their food, which cleanses the birds' systems. But they must also eat sand or some other kind of grit or stone. This gritty material helps Homing Pigeons digest by breaking up the food in their powerful gizzards.

As we know from observation, pigeons eat a lot. They don't, however, drink like most other birds, who gently tip their heads up with each dainty sip. Homers drink more like horses, thrusting their beaks into water and pumping it down their throats.

Usually, Homing Pigeons live in separate lofts, such as packing crates. You don't have to build anything elegant for them -- pigeons are not fussy housekeepers -- just a modest coop or loft that blends in with the neighborhood.

The loft needs a floor, four walls, a roof, external fixtures, a landing board, a trap, ventilators, turbines and aviaries; internal fixtures, storage areas for food, water and an infirmary. See to it that all pigeons are able to land on the board at the same time. Build a picket fence to help them land on their board. When they enter the loft through a type of trapped door, the birds drop in but can't get back out.

The loft should face away from the direction of bad weather and away from all wires. It should face the afternoon sun and have about 8 x 10 cubic feet of air for each bird. Divide them into three sections: breeders, young birds and old birds. When they're older than two or three, separate the males and females. Make sure they're able to stick out their heads to reach food and water but aren't able to reach others, or walk on their food.

Also, you must design the loft to keep out intruders such as mice, rats, opossums, raccoons, weasels, snakes, cats, dogs, wild birds, sparrows and thieves. Remember, pigeons have been attacked throughout history so don't give any creature an easy opportunity to do it again.

Forty years ago, Homers sold for a few dollars each. Today's birds sell for a hundred dollars or more and top breeders can cost tens of thousands. Pigeon feed used to cost $4-5 for a 100 pound bag. Now it costs $25 for 100 pounds, and it's not even the "good stuff." They also need grit for their gizzards. The plain variety of grit consists of oyster shell, granite and charcoal.

Can you imagine a bird so tough he wants to eat charcoal and actually needs it in his diet. Also, if these birds eat shell, granite and charcoal grit, and it's considered the "plain stuff," what's in the "good stuff"? I'm not sure we want to know but my best guess is: it's probably a gritty substance that tastes better than granite but not as good as unpopped popcorn.

No matter what the answer may be, the next time you see a pigeon chewing on the side of a high-rise building, acknowledge the fact that he's simply enjoying a little granite salad. But try not to call out, "Good appetite" because people may become concerned for your sanity.

To summarize, some hobbies for children cost more than pigeon racing; some cost less.

Give them a few baths a week -- and a yard if you've got one -- and they'll be happy.

TRAINING YOUR PIGEONS

- Try this at home: once the homers are familiar with their home loft and surrounding areas, put them in a basket and take them two or three miles away, then release them. They will fly home. gradually increase the distance from home and release them 10 miles away, then 30 miles. Have your own race with the birds over areas they know. Nine out of ten probably will beat you home.

Like a pigeon is to a rock dove, Sam Rosenberg and I are cousins. Cousin Sam has owned a pigeon feed store in Philadelphia for over 50 years. He and his family supplied food and medicine for thousands of U.S. pigeons during World War II, including GI Joe, the world's most honored pigeon.

As a boy, Sam used to take his Homers on the elevated train in crates. He'd take the 6 AM shuttle to the end of the line and, a few minutes later, release the pigeons in the park. He'd watch them circle to get their bearings, then a few leaders would lead the rest back home. Young Sam (he's 72 now) would get back on the train and hope the pigeons beat him back home.

"It was very exciting," Sam remembered. "And it was easy for kids to read about the hobby. The newspapers used to run a daily column about pigeon racing just for them."

The chances of your hometown newspaper running a daily pigeon column are very slim. But you can be successful if you start with two pairs of really good birds. They should be ready to race in 6 months; ready to fly for 15 hours at one time or in 300 mile per day races.

When a bird is about one week old, place a permanent band, with an ID tag, on his right leg. The pigeons wind up growing into these tags, which look like ankle bracelets. You can figure out how fast they really flew and in what position they finished in the race.

Training pigeons is hardly an easy task. It takes time and effort. You could find yourself releasing the birds in different states every weekend.

HELPFUL HINTS:

Homers do not like to fly in Northeast winds! Windy weather from the Northeast disturbs their flight dramatically. We're not sure of the reason but it may be because magnetic fields are especially vulnerable to Northeast winds.

A pigeon will lose feathers every year and feel sore, like a baby losing a tooth. When the feather falls out, it is replaced by a more beautiful feather, provided by nature. In what is called "molting season," they start losing feathers one at a time.

You'll find that birds with young in their nest are especially dependable homers. Don't put a male and female in the same race. Concern for their mates and babies make them eager to perform their best and reach home. No matter where you take them, by car, truck, train or airplane, they will attempt to reach home as soon as they can.

Some people think Homing Pigeons mate for life. Others believe they mate for a long time but maybe not forever. A pair can raise as many as 11 broods (youngsters) a year but the average allowed by serious pigeon breeders is three or four.

Sometimes, trainers switch mates to get faster offspring.

As previously suggested, it's a good idea to separate the males from females during winter months. This keeps adults in better physical condition and helps the young birds stay more vigorous. When they don't mate, they get new feathers faster. It keeps their minds on racing, not having families.

The female lays two white eggs in her grass and twig (and sometimes messy) nest. Both male and female take turns sitting on the eggs (proving pigeons can be tender) until they are ready, in 17 days, to hatch. It is difficult for us to identify the males from the females in the early weeks after hatching.

The babies, called squabs, are almost naked and blind when hatched. Yes, they are ugly. But they develop rapidly and are soon covered with spiny pin feathers. (At least they don't have fleshy growths covering their noses, like Carrier Pigeons.) Baby Homers are fed a brownish liquid called "pigeons milk" which forms in their parents' necks. The milk is pumped down the babies throats by both Mom and Dad Pigeon; quite a unique trait in the animal world, proving once again that pigeons, though tough, can be tender.

Keep track of every pigeon that you breed in order to improve the stock. Breed the fast ones to the faster ones and keep the bloodlines going.

One pigeon racer recently raced from Spain to Holland and won a $150,000 prize. Good trainers do get rewarded in this sport. But it's more about prestige than money. Most owners of champion pigeons wouldn't sell them for any price.

WHAT HAPPENS DURING A RACE?

Just like all horses will run around the pasture, all Homing Pigeons will fly home. The question is: how fast will they fly?

Not every pigeon is fast. Some may be fast but have no stamina for distance races.

Typically, pigeon races cover hundreds of miles over known terrain. The birds can travel 600 miles per day without stopping for food or drink. (These "old" birds race in the Spring of each year.) A Homer's prime racing age is considered to be two-four years old. But yearlings, or one-year olds, also compete.

Older birds race better in bad weather because they have more experience navigating through magnetic distortions and clouds. Homing Pigeons usually need sunlight to fly directly home, although older birds seem to need less of it.

Special clocking devices record the exact time that each contestant reaches home. Trainers remove the leg bands (the ones that look like ankle bracelets) when they enter the loft and record the official time.

Five pigeons recently flew from Georgia to Pennsylvania in one day. No one knows how they did it, exactly. They had no maps, no compasses and no one directing them North, yelling the state motto, "You've Got A Friend In Pennsylvania." These five pigeons just depended on the personal radar screens in their heads. No other animal, including hunting dogs like bloodhounds, with their incredibly sensitive noses, could've returned home so soon.

One trainer raced 15 pigeons from Stubenville, Ohio to Maple Shade, New Jersey. He lost 14 of the pigeons. Only one got home -- and he was the winner of the race!

What happened to the other 14 birds? Most likely, the mountains trapped them; pushed them down into the rocks, where skunks, foxes, falcons and hawks could have easily killed them. (Even a rat can kill a pigeon.)

Some return home so tired they can hardly walk.

Hundreds of Homing Pigeons recently got lost racing from Virginia to Pennsylvania. In a France to England race, many pigeons got knocked down by a storm and drowned in the English Channel. High tension wires kill pigeons all the time.

Scientists have tried to put transmitters on pigeons' shoulder harnesses. One scientist/trainer knew exactly where a certain bird was flying from 40 miles away. The transmitter was the size of a pack of matches. Someday soon, it will be possible to send a video signal from your pigeon's leg band to your television set. You'll be able to sit in your living room and see what your pigeon is seeing from the sky, on Pigeon-Cam.

PART FOUR:

THE PIGEON MAN

Cousin Sam recommended I visit his friend, Ben Garberman. Ben is 74 years old and has been racing pigeons for 68 of those years. I set out to find him, thinking he might know something about the sport.

He was easy to find, due to the fact he had 200 pigeons flying around his backyard in New Jersey.

"I'll be honest with you, I love pigeons," Ben said proudly. "I don't know why. I call it an addiction, like I'm addicted. If I want to relax, I just go in the back to my birds. It's relaxation and fun for any age, especially for children and senior citizens. It stimulates and challenges the mind."

"Isn't it a lot of work?"

"Yes but it's wonderful work. Everyone who does well in racing puts in a lot of time. I give them a bath three-four times a week. I used to take them on training flights four-six times a week. I'd leave the house at 4 AM, drive a hundred miles, release the birds, then go to work. It used to be pretty cheap; now it can be costly but still less expensive than a lot of other hobbies, like golf. But the prestige when I won a race ... it was great. I won a lot of races and trophies. Most of the time, before the race, you could tell who was eager to fly. Those eager pigeons usually won.

"For long races, I'd get the birds to the starting spot a week early, for a training toss. They'd get really eager to fly home so they could sit on their eggs at their home loft. When that strategy worked, I'd say, `See, I did a good thing.' When it didn't work, I tried something else the next race."

"I think I was flying pigeons in my mother's belly, before I was born. My father didn't like animals of any kind. But he didn't stop me from having ten birds, in what is now Lithuania. My own children are not so interested in them. But I loved pigeons when I was a boy in Europe. I don't know why, really. When I was about five years old in 1930, my parents had to carry me away from the pigeon coop to put me to bed.

"I didn't race them in Lithuania. I just watched them fly home. Who gave me my first pigeon? Myself, in 1930. The only time I didn't race them or even think about them was during World War II. I was only thinking about how to get a loaf of bread."

Passenger Pigeons were wiped out in 1914 and Ben was trying not to get wiped out in 1945. Right after the war, he stayed in Germany (which lost the war) for four years. He couldn't come to the United States (which won the war) because of a quota.

"A loaf of bread and a bowl of soup made us happy in those days," Ben recalled. In 1949, the quota was lifted and Ben came to South Philadelphia.

"My aunt was here. I went to work."

He got his first pigeons a few weeks later. They cost a few pennies each and were kept in a cage outside. Ben had 75 pigeons by 1954.

"I had some pigeons ... and children, too. My wife and I were from small towns in Lithuania, where a seventh grade education was considered a great education."

Ben's wife excused herself to mail money to an old friend in a Russian town near Minsk.

"In White Russia," she said and later I learned that White Russia is what we now call Belarus.

The Garbermans' love people, as well as pigeons.

"The King of Holland and Queen of England love pigeons but some famous Americans have also owned pigeons. Actor Yul Brenner, who was one of the most famous movie stars of his era and one of the first to have absolutely no hair on his head, had two lofts, one in California and one in New York

City. Mrs. Stetson, who used to own a hat factory, raced pigeons. Mrs. Stetson was like everyone else at the Pigeon Club. The only way to tell she was wealthy was when she didn't have to carry her own pigeons. Her servants did that but she was just like everyone else in the club who loved those birds. She had a loft in her house and on her factory roof. Factory workers would go to conventions and spend most of their paychecks buying the best breeders."

(In recent years, boxer Mike Tyson and NYPD Blue's "Bobby" have been depicted as pigeon owners on TV.)

Ben took me into his backyard and showed me his 200 or more pigeons. They stood on the roof like soldiers on duty. One dark bird looked just like a wild city pigeon but was a Homer. They sensed that I was a stranger and flew a few feet away.

"Don't be nervous," I told them and offered rice.

Pigeons, Ben explained, love rice. Their "Uncle Ben" regularly buys 25-50 pound bags and carries them out back for the pigeons, even though he's 74 years old and has a heart condition.

Ben took me into an enclosed trailer. "These are the most valuable racers," he said. They are locked inside the trailer but can use a door to go outside into the screened-in aviary for some fresh air.

"These birds are great athletes; champions," Ben bragged. "I wouldn't hesitate to put any of them in a 600 mile race. That one over there went 600 miles in one day, from Georgia to New Jersey."

They flew past me like doves and my jaw dropped in their splendor.

"See the wild baby?" Ben asked and then he removed and reattached the band on her ankle. "Her foot grows into it. I know the father of this baby, the grandfather, great-grandfather; everyone in her family.

"With babies, you have to settle them; let them get used to the loft. When she's 10-12 weeks old, I'll start training her."

I started petting the pigeon without being aware of it, like she was a miniature, flying pony. Being with these pigeons and touching them is the best way to learn about their habits; the best way to appreciate them.

Then the "wild baby" flew out the door into the aviary. She wasn't in the mood to be settled. All the champions went outside for fresh air except for ten, who sat nervously in their little shelves in the pigeon coop/trailer. My videocamera zoomed in on a white pigeon with red splashes on her chest.

"The Splashes are better at long distance races," Ben reported. "They have more stamina bred into them. They can take more punishment. The dark birds are good for shorter races."

I looked closer at the Splash, then realized it was a Bleeding Heart Pigeon, in person! I felt like I knew her.

One bird was hiding on the bottom shelf, afraid of the camera. I learned that pigeons are really camera-shy.

A male Homer cooed as I tried to pick out the fastest birds by looking at them, like they were race horses in the paddock. The difference was ... birds don't need to be saddled; only tagged.

In another loft, Ben showed me his Roller pigeons.

"Do they race?" I asked Ben.

"They're too dumb to race. They get lost every time," Ben admitted.

But they looked much like Homers.

Outside the aviary, I noticed what looked like a wild pigeon sitting on a canopy. This one was a wild pigeon, called "Corny."

"He loves to eat corn," Ben said, smiling at a bird who adopted him.

"The real McCoy's are over there," Ben told me and showed me a small coop filled with a dozen beautiful, streamlined Homing Pigeons. But they kept flapping their wings and hitting each other in the face. It looked like a pigeon version of pushing and shoving at a Miss America contest.

"That's OK," Ben insisted.

I reminded Ben that they're related to peace-loving doves, yet were whacking each other in the head.

"It keeps them competitive. Let them fight."

These beautiful, flapping Homing Pigeons looked like wild ones.

"Look closely," Ben suggested. "They're bigger than wild city pigeons."

On top of another shack, non-breeding Homers and Rollers stood together, free to fly away.

"They won't leave this yard," Ben said. "They know they live here. This is where they eat and bathe."

Ben showed me his pigeon bathtub. It looked like a miniature, plastic sink.

Then Ben showed me the clocks used to track the speed of each bird. They were the same clocks used in the 1800's to keep track of each racer's time.

"I flew racers for many years," Ben said. "I knew the exact distances of the races; knew exactly where they started out, how long it took and how fast they went."

Ben took out a very old chart that had been folded up in his wallet for decades. The reference chart measured distances and was issued by the U.S. government. It is dated 1866!

"For example," Ben stated, "the distance from Indianapolis, Indiana to my home in New Jersey is 592.4 miles."

Then Ben showed me an even older clock. It looked like a real museum piece, from an era, I guessed, just after the dinosaurs died. I looked for dinosaur teeth marks or damage from a prehistoric foot that may have stepped on this old clock but couldn't find any. I guessed that anyone new to the sport would not have to go out and buy a high-tech clocking device. Ben assured me the old clocks (and old charts) still work fine. After all (the last time I looked) Indiana was still the same distance from New Jersey as it was 134 years ago.

"Do the neighbors complain about all these birds living so close to their yards?" I asked.

"No, I have no problems. The neighbors help me build new lofts."

"Do your birds know who you are; do they recognize you?" I asked Ben.

"Sure. They greet me and know my smell. And they stay away from strangers. Do they love me?" Ben wondered. "I hope so."

"What do you do when the birds come back with injuries?"

"I've seen a lot of them come back injured," Ben reported. "It happened many times. They get hurt fighting with cats or flying into high tension wires. Wires are very bad for birds -- and for people too. In World War II, Germans would use wires to kill United States soldiers driving in jeeps. The soldiers had to put iron bars on the front of their jeeps to protect themselves.

"Anyway, when the birds came back injured, my wife would hold them and I would stitch them up like a doctor. I'd put vaseline on the wound, push the skin together, then stitch them up; sew them up with silk thread, just a little bit. Four or five days later they would be OK to fly. The only ones I couldn't help were the birds who got lost and never came home."

ADD THESE ITEMS TO YOUR LIST OF MATERIALS YOU WILL NEED:

   -- VASELINE

   -- SILK THREAD

   -- SEWING NEEDLE

FINAL THOUGHTS

Many of us believe that dogs are our best friends. Don't you think Homing Pigeons, brave and loyal, should rank about second or third?

Our second or third best friends are ... pigeons?

Even if you decide not to train a stable of pigeons, the next time you see a pigeon in the park when he flies right past your face, smile at him. Show him that you know pigeons are actually doves and they've saved people's lives in wars and are really nice.

Don't chase them away shouting, "Go use the public restroom, not the public park!"

Don't scream, "Get away from my sandwich, you poor excuse for a flying squirrel."

Don't make them feel unwanted.

Instead, open a can of peas for them. Then, keeping your hands up to protect your face, say, "Thanks" and wave to the cousin of a brave buddy, the noble Homing Pigeon.

Why do Homing Pigeons come home?

The answer is simple: Because they desperately want to come home to be with their families.

They do it for love.

PIGEON POINTS

   -- The wilder the pigeon, the greater its chances of looking like its ancient ancestor, the Rock Dove.

   -- Considered gentle and symbols of peace, pigeons fight viciously amongst themselves.

   -- Homing Pigeons have a special gift that enables them to flow along with the Earth's magnetic fields. They also remember everything they see on their trips; memorizing the location of all landmarks, no matter how insignificant.

   -- In 1900, food markets in New York City and Chicago sold Passenger Pigeons for a penny-a-piece to anyoneinterested in a cheap meal. By 1914, the penny-a-piece deals

were gone forever ... and so were the Passenger Pigeons.

   -- Wild pigeons are considered lousy housekeepers. They often take over a decaying nest of a bird family that has left the region. Their nests are so flimsy that pigeon parents have to sit on the messy twigs so their eggs don't blow away in the wind.

   -- In World War I, a Homer carried a message 24 miles in 25 minutes. It arrived with a leg shot off and its breast injured by a bullet.

-- Homing Pigeons delivered secret messages for persecuted Polish Jews in the Warsaw ghetto during World War II.

-- The Queen of England, Disneyworld and Mike Tyson have Homing Pigeon stables. Which flock and which bird is the fastest? No one will know until they race.

-- One day, we may be able to attach super-lightweight transmitters or video cameras to Homing Pigeons and follow their flight on TV monitors.

Appendix G: Novel Sample

"Summer At Saratoga"

Sample Pages From

A Novel By
Donald Paul Rutberg

46,000 Words
(in manuscript)
© 2001

Summer At Saratoga

PART ONE

CHAPTER ONE

She sat by herself in the food court, massaging the veggie sandwich she had brought in her brown-bag as if it were a once-in-a-lifetime treat. Janice was 30 years old, tall and slender, with waist-long, auburn hair. She wore an old-fashioned dress and a provocative smile. Her plain looks, un-enhanced by make-up, were overshadowed by a mysterious aura. Maybe she was a witch. And maybe she wasn't shaving her armpits. But this was a trade show in Pittsburgh. My expectations weren't that high.

At least she was interesting. I had noticed her in the Monroeville Expo Center while I was selling "old lady" dresses; the kind your great-grandmother would wear if she came back to life tomorrow at age 124. And please don't ask what I really do. Everyone asks that question.

I dropped out of college after three and a half years. I couldn't take the phony L.A. crowd anymore and I couldn't sit through one more business class. I had proven to myself -- and my professors -- that I wasn't cut out for business. So, caving in to the subtle pressure from my family, I moved back home to Philadelphia and went into my father's dress business, opting for the "easy" money. Everyone said there were worse things out there than "easy" money and I believed them.

Dazed and confused were conditions I would've considered upgrades.

In Pittsburgh, I was less absorbed in selling dresses than I was in meeting interesting women. Janice seemed out of place by at least a century. She looked to me like a woodcarver or pottery-maker or some kind of Indian doll artist. I could imagine her sitting around all day painting faces on dolls. There was a secret smile on her face as I cruised around the Expo Center's food court. I knew her smile was only for me ... yet she wasn't even looking in my direction.

I kept cruising, like I was looking for my friends at a particular table, even though my only friends in Pittsburgh were my sales partner, 75 year-old Ben and my old high school buddy, Jack, who was next door in his hotel room indulging in one of the many vices he needed every day of his salesman's life.

I nodded to some imaginary acquaintances, ignored several beautiful women sitting by themselves and sat down, like a small piece of iron drawn to a powerful magnet, next to Janice. She smiled and, this time, I knew her secret.

"Usually, when I'm attracted to someone, I know why," I told her. "But I have no idea why I was drawn over to you. All I know is I was definitely pulled over here."

"What do you really do?" she asked.

"You mean, when I'm not selling old lady dresses."

"Um-hum."

She knew what I was selling. She had probably seen me in my little sales booth with Ben, yawning. I told myself to monitor my thoughts; she could be psychic.

"I've got a hunch but tell me anyway," she said, her lips tightening.

"I'm a sportsman," I said.

"Oh, yeah? What kind of sports?"

"Horses. Thoroughbreds," I said, even though my dad and his partners were merely considering buying a few race horses and letting me manage the stable.

"That's why you were drawn to me. I train horses. Here's my card."

Her address was in Saratoga Springs, New York, where the big-time Saratoga race track was located.

"What the hell are you doing in Monroeville?" I asked.

But I already knew part of the answer.

"Meeting me, right?"

"Um-hum," she cooed.

I knew she was omitting 99% of the story. But that was all right. Her secrets made her more interesting. Besides, I couldn't learn them all in a trade show's food court.

"You know, I'm not busy later. I'm not busy anytime. I'm just baby-sitting this cranky, old guy named Ben. He's been a road salesman for more than 50 years."

"I saw him. He looked strict."

"He's ... sick. And he needs his rest. Maybe we could get together later --"

She wrote her local address on my hand.

"Meet me at my place at eight o'clock. I'll go to the market now and cook dinner for us. What kind of wine do you drink?"

"I'm sending that to you telepathically," I said as I touched her shoulder with my left hand, the one without the writing on it.

She just smiled, that secret smile.

And that's how I got invited to her apartment on the night I was nearly killed.

Hours later, Janice kissed me hello and if it weren't for the smell of broiling fish from the oven I would've suggested moving right along to the bedroom. I politely examined her collection of rare dolls from around the world and was impressed. This lady had style. And if I had lied and said I was impressed when I really wasn't, she would've known. So I marveled at the Oriental, Norwegian and, yes, Indian dolls in her glass case and took her hand as she led me comfortably to the balcony in her Pittsburgh suburb.

I've been with long-term girlfriends and felt so tense that it seemed like a first date. This was the opposite; a first date with someone who felt like a trusted, long-time lover.

We drank wine and talked about everything except business. She told me she was on-again, off-again with a guy (her boss in a craft store) she pitied more than loved. This poor fellow had been in a horrible car accident that left him in a coma for six months. He had trouble walking a year after the crash. But when he awakened from the long coma, he developed telepathic, telekinetic powers, or so she claimed.

"He can talk to you without saying the words?"

"Uh-huh. And I'm learning to talk back, telepathically."

"She is a witch," I thought, then tried to erase the words from my mind in case she could read them.

She did flinch a bit when the thought about her being a witch flashed through my mind. But as she told me this sad story about her dissolving love affair with the "Dead Zone" wannabe, I sort of believed her; well, not the telepathic, telekinetic part but all the rest. Her tone was honestly sad.

I didn't tell her about the girlfriend I had just broken up with in Philly. I felt the story of a beautiful yet dull, spoiled, Italian Princess who loved her job with Amway just wouldn't add anything to our conversation. I even kept the ex-girlfriend's image out of my mind so Janice wouldn't pick it up through supernatural powers.

We talked about poetry and our dream diaries; interpreting each other's best we could. Janice felt like I wasn't enjoying my work and was selling dresses just for the prospect of "easy" money. I told her she didn't need any psychic skills to come to that conclusion.

I took off my shoes as we finished the second glass of white wine. We were relaxed, like reunited lovers, before our first passionate kiss, which came moments after our introductory kiss and before the fish was fully broiled.

That's when the "Here Come Trouble" truck came rumbling across the lawn and into the driveway, braking at the last second, too late to avoid smashing into the garage door beneath the apartment. I looked down to my right, puzzled, almost amused.

My first thought was, "Somebody's real mad" and this somebody drove the kind of bad news truck that you see on "Most Shocking Police Videos." He had the gun rack, the flood lights, the rebel flag, the pirate flag, the blackened windows and the broken license plate positioned where no human could possibly make out all the lettering. Whoever this guy was, he hated authority and was insecure about something, probably for good reason.

As he flew out of the truck in a rage, screaming like a wounded Sasquatch, Janice jumped out of her chair and said, "It's my boyfriend! Quick, hide in the bedroom!"

I knew I'd make it to her bedroom within a half-hour but this wasn't the way it was supposed to work.

"Whattya mean, 'boyfriend'? The coma guy?"

"Hurry! Please!"

She pulled me to the bedroom door, looking so worried that I started to worry. I thought about retrieving my shoes but she was pulling me like a mother zebra pulls her baby from a hungry hyena.

"Is this the guy with the telepathic, telekinetic powers?"

"Yes!"

"Then why am I hiding? He knows I'm here."

She shoved me into a dark, windowless room. Just before closing the door, she said, "And don't come out until I say so!"

I stood in total darkness, in a room, an apartment and a suburb I was visiting for the first time, smelling overcooked fish. I was also listening to a loud argument from down the stairs that had a 50-50 chance of ending with a shotgun blast.

I looked around anyway. It was still dark. The decibel level was rising down the stairs. I breathed as quietly as I could and planned the next minute carefully. First, I tried to combat the angry guy's telepathic edge by concentrating on putting up a huge, cement wall in front of me so when he probed the apartment, he'd see only the cement wall and not me.

"That's crazy," I thought. "The guy will see a cement wall right in the middle of the room and know someone was here, creating this artificial wall."

I was out of ideas. And I figured the more I thought, the more I'd be revealing to the telepath who wanted to hurt me. So I opened the door a crack and heard bodies bouncing off the stairway walls.

I thought, "God bless this girl. She's gonna protect me or die trying. She's got guts."

"You're not going up there, you bastard!" she screamed.

A moment later, I heard a man scream, "Get off my hair!"

That's when I heard the thud and knew she was unconscious and unable to protect me, even for another second.

It was time for "Plan B." But before I could implement "Plan B," I had to erase it from my thoughts. As I stood there, one ear in the hallway, erasing files from my own brain, like in a Phillip Dick story, I heard heavy footsteps limping up the stairs. I sprinted across the living room, onto the balcony, said a quick goodbye to my shoes and vaulted from the second floor balcony onto the front lawn.

The last time I did something like this was when I was 12 and the cops kicked me off the school's annex roof. I didn't stop to see if the guy had left his keys in the ignition, although he was in such a hurry to inflict pain, he probably had. I just sprinted up the street, cut in-between buildings like I did as a child after throwing snowballs at the older guys, and kept running until I could duck into a pizza parlor on a side street and call a taxi.

When the sun came up in a few hours, I was going to strongly suggest to my partner, Ben, that it was time to leave Pittsburgh. He would understand.

CHAPTER TWO

There were only two times in my life when I was actually happy to be cruising on the Pennsylvania turnpike at dawn -- when I drove to the Kentucky Derby and this time.

The Derby was a party for 100,000 thrill-seekers. Even the presence of the National Guard failed to stop people of my generation from drinking, dancing and sliding naked through the infield mud. In between races, I kept trying to win the affections of a cute national guardswoman and I know I would've gotten a date with her if Churchill Downs had scheduled one more race that day or if there wasn't some kind of bomb scare in Louisville.

Driving on the Pennsylvania turnpike at dawn with my buddies was a memorable experience. And so was driving with Ben, for a different reason. I was happy to escape from Pittsburgh with nothing worse than a swollen ankle.

Ben was a horribly inattentive driver, had poor vision and was so cheap that he wouldn't hit the brakes in life-and-death emergencies because it would, "Kill the gas mileage." For that same reason, he once refused to brake and swerve around a tire rim that was lying on the highway near Pittman, New Jersey. We spent two hours waiting for the auto club to tow us to a repair shop and four more hours waiting for the mechanics to fix the broken axle on the van. Ben spent another hour arguing over the price of repairs. We missed six appointments.

I would've been annoyed but I was only making $175 a week (my dad didn't want to "spoil" me until I had proven myself) and wasn't on commission. (Ben earned a seven percent commission.) I wanted to be where I was the least bored. If that meant driving around in Gettysburg or York, Pennsylvania, gazing at the neat war statues, I was all for it. If it meant traveling around Maryland, eating crab cakes for breakfast, lunch and dinner, I was happy to do it. On one sales trip, Ben let me drive around Penn State's campus where I had spent a few weekends and I had great fun getting lost.

Selling dresses did not matter to me at all. I guess buyers noticed and that's why they were always asking, "What do you really do?"

(Most workers, I found out later, take an active interest in their day-to-day responsibilities. Without their jobs, they can't make a living. But my circumstances were unusual. I had no expenses and couldn't be fired. There were no financial highs or lows in my working life, only a numbing middle-ground.)

We stopped to buy shoes in Harrisburg, Pennsylvania, then had lunch. An older lady asked how my parents were doing.

"Fine," I answered, "except they're 100 miles away and you've never met them."

Once a week, people would stop me in diners and ask about my family, thinking they knew me. After the first few experiences, I would just smile and let the people think I really was the "Jones" boy from down the street.

Anyway, Ben had failed to call the buyer at the Harrisburg department store in advance (as was his practice) so we couldn't see him. Ben didn't like the man, even though he had been selling dresses to him for 45 years.

We drove to Lancaster, where Ben hoped to sell hundreds of dresses to one buyer. Ben parked the huge van on the street, told me to watch the meter (as opposed to feeding the meter) and proceeded to bring the buyer to the van. Two entire lines of half-sized dresses -- missy and petite -- were hanging on racks in the back of the van.

To interpret half-sized dress business code, Missy dresses are purchased by the really old, fat lady customers. Petite dresses are purchased by the really old, fat, short lady customers.

But these darling retail customers would never have the opportunity to buy our Classic Designs' dresses if the department store buyers didn't buy them wholesale and keep them in stock. To Ben, these buyers were the lesser of two evils. He didn't want to go back to selling retail -- ever!

The buyer, a man in his late sixties, seemed to really hate Ben. At one point he told him, "Ben, if you just shut your mouth, I'll buy the whole line!"

Ben wrote the order, a nice order, in silence. The man looked at me like he wouldn't trade places with me for any reason -- even if he had been given just one week to live by his doctors. When he heard I was the boss' son and was only paired with Ben temporarily, he seemed relieved. I shook his hand goodbye and assured him I'd be all right. It would not have surprised me, given his hatred for Ben, if he had given me a cyanide capsule to slip into Ben's medicine bottle late at night.

The buyer didn't understand that Ben didn't bother me. He was entertaining. He treated me well because he wasn't threatened by me; I was the only one in the entire rag business who didn't want to succeed him as the East Coast rep for my dad's business. And I was the only one in the rag business who treated him like a friend. No, Ben didn't bother me at all. The job did.

The highlight of the day came a few hours later when we ate in a Pennsylvania Dutch-owned diner. Ben, no kidding, tried to get the waitress to give him a free lamb chop. We had already paid the check (I was on an expense account so my meals were free) and the waitress asked if we needed anything else; you know, more water or coffee. Ben said, "Yeah, doll baby, can you bring me out a lamb chop from the kitchen? It'll be our little secret."

I once entered the lobby of a motel near the West Virginia border to find Ben arguing bitterly with a motel clerk. I tried to calm Ben down, since he had suffered through seven heart attacks and a diabetic coma, his blood pressure and glucose levels were off the charts and he drank and smoked like a fiend. I figured he didn't need the stress.

"Thirty-four dollars? Thirty-four dollars? Are you crazy? What do I look like? That's gotta be a mistake! Check it again! Keep on checking it till you get it right, you mongrel!"

I had missed the first minute of this argument because I was parking the monstrous van.

"Ben, what's the problem? Ya gotta calm down."

"Calm down? They wanna charge me, they wanna charge us, $34 a night, at this pig-stye!"

"I thought you said you stayed here before and you liked it."

"I did like it. Because it was only $29 a night!"

"When was that?"

"Fourteen years ago."

Ben ate a few chocolate bars and eventually agreed to pay the $34.

We headed back to Philly. Ben let me drive.

"Slow down, you're killin' the gas mileage," he told me.

I ignored him. Ben didn't badger further because my father was his boss and Ben didn't want to get fired from his cushy, $150,000 a year job. Hell, if Ben had ever learned to keep quiet on a consistent basis, he could've earned $300,000 a year in commissions. Ben had made this kind of money for a long time. He made close to six figures a year as a salesman throughout the 1950's and '60's.

The van, meanwhile, was 10 years old. His suits were older. He never spent more than $7 on a meal and tipped so poorly that I would have to run back and leave extra money on the table.

Ben lit a Viceroy and examined the new corn crop.

"Corn looks ready," he proclaimed.

For some reason, the man loved corn as much as he hated people. Then again, corn had never hurt him.

"She was a Haw!" Ben said for no particular reason.

He was referring to one of his ex-wives, the one who had hurt him the most. He told the story to me on every single trip, always on the way home.

"We were at the biggest trade show of the year. I went around to all the pretty woman, asking if they'd marry me," Ben remembered.

I was familiar with the story and helped Ben re-tell it.

"Someone finally said `Yes,'" I narrated. "As the song goes, `Watch out, you might get what you're after.'"

"I knew somethin' was wrong when she said she'd marry me that weekend."

"Why didn't you date her for a couple months? Weren't you already divorced, like, six times?" I asked.

"Five times!" Ben corrected. "She turned out to be number six."

"Why rush into it?"

"She was a hot, hot woman."

"I guess so."

"Because she was a Haw!"

"What was she -- a sixty year-old whore?" I wondered. "I thought they all retired by 40."

"She came out of retirement for me. And do you know what she was doin' while I was working the table?"

Sure, I knew. Everyone in the business knew. Mrs. Ben Stein VI was makin' whoopee with another schmata salesmen on the other side of the drape that separated Ben's booth from the competitor's booth behind him.

"The salesman from Caldwell!" Ben moaned, as if he would've forgiven her had he caught her, pants down and kneeling, with a salesman from a non-competing blouse firm behind drape number three.

Ben did have one happier hooker story. At a dress show in Pittsburgh, in the 1950's, he stayed in a hotel with Westinghouse conventioneers. A hooker knocked on his door, gave him a wild night of fun and left without taking a dime. She was working for (and on) the high-ranking corporate types. She had the wrong room!

We kept stopping for ice to wrap around my ankle. Ben asked me if I had any funny stories about L.A. women.

"My first night in L.A.," I told him, "I picked up a girl in the supermarket and she followed me home. When I finished, she said, `Welcome to L.A.' I never saw her again but it took a week to get rid of the crabs."

"She was a Haw," Ben commented.

"I think a whore would've been cleaner," I said.

"Weren't you happy in California?"

"They say when you buy a boat, the two happiest days of your life are when you buy it and when you sell it. The two happiest days of my life were the day I arrived in L.A. and the day I left. My friends Dick and Patti were gettin' separated, Dick's best friend Bobby was losing a few grand on a football game -- his team fumbled six times in the first half. It's still a record."

"They're all crooked, those games," Ben chimed in.

"We went down to the beach and left my stereo there, like a gift for the Gods or somethin'," I recalled. "A farewell ceremony. The end of an era."

"Why didn't you stay to graduate?"

"Hey, when it's over, take the hint and get the hell out. Don't stand around tilting the machine or trying to get your dollar back; just go home. Try again later or try somethin' else. Come on, you've been divorced six times, you should know that."

Ben nodded in agreement.

"I was more concerned with packin' up my music and gettin' on that plane. I was desperate to leave. Maybe it was a psychic flash or somethin'. And then, a few months later, I heard that Dick and Patti had separated and Patti had moved in with Bobby, Dick's best friend. It was ridiculous."

"They're all Haws," Ben said in his thick New York accent, which was offensive to anyone born outside the five boroughs; maybe even to other New Yorkers.

He thought about what I had said.

"So you think you have psychic powers, too, like that guy who chased you off the balcony last night."

"Maybe we all have psychic talents. We just don't know how to use 'em."

"Maybe it'll help you in the dress business," Ben suggested.

"If I actually gave a damn about selling dresses, I'm sure it would."

Yes, my college era was over; my dress salesman era was underway. I wasn't going to last three and a half years this time, though. I was going to graduate to something, anything, as soon as I could.

Appendix H: Nonfiction Book Sample

"Life After Death"

(Sample Chapter)

by

Donald Paul Rutberg

© 2002

23,000 Words; 92 pages in manuscript

LIFE AFTER DEATH

TABLE OF CONTENTS

INTRODUCTION: IS LIFE AFTER DEATH REAL?

Imagine a place where there is total peace, love, knowledge and wonder; where there is no violence, hatred or greed and where no one judges you.

Millions of near death survivors claim there is such a place -- and the only way to get there is to die.

An estimated twelve million Americans have had near death experiences, called NDEs. These people were often pronounced dead, sent to a morgue or autopsy room, only to start breathing again. They've learned, or claim to have learned, what people have always wondered through myths and legends: What happens next? Where were we before we were born? Where do we go when we die? Is there life after death?

Dr. Raymond Moody, who has researched life after death for more than 25 years, says these are the most often asked and most perplexing questions. Do we cease to exist? Do we frolic with angels in heaven? Do we return to life only if we're nice? And if we do come back, is it in human form, as different people years later, or in the form of animals, as the Hindus believe?

In addition to NDEs, where individuals claim to have visited a sparkling, heavenly world while their hearts were stopped, sixteen percent of all Americans claim to have left their bodies, called an out of body experience (OBE), at least once. Put another way, the odds are good that someone from your neighborhood will have one of these paranormal experiences.

Some say there is no such thing as death; that leaving this world is just another step in an eternal, spiritual journey.

Dannion Brinkley, who had two near-death experiences, says, "Death is OK, it's just getting there that hurts."

The great poet, T.S. Eliot wrote, "It is worth dying to find out what life is."

A Gallup poll indicates that a large majority of American adults believe in life after death. The majority of doctors and scientists, however, do not believe in it because they can not measure facts about the afterlife. All they know for sure is that we die.

Skeptics claim that glowing descriptions of heaven are just reactions to bad drugs or religious visions, brought on by a fear of death that is greater now than at any time in human history.

The ancient Egyptian Book Of The Dead included details of an afterlife that would instill fear in any reader, in any time period. It claimed that if a person failed the heavenly entrance exam, that person would get eaten by a beast which was a combination of crocodile, lion and hippo. But if the person received a good report, he or she would live in a sea of light.

Galileo, perhaps the most famous scientist in human history, saw it this way. He said the world had matter and energy, which acted on matter. If we lost the energy that gave us our sense of smell, for example, would odors still exist? Or would we decide that, because we couldn't measure and classify odors, they couldn't be real.

One doctor changed his mind and started to believe in out of body experiences while conversing with a patient who had been brought back to life. The doctor asked the man how he felt and he answered, "I'm fine. How are you? You were the one involved in a car accident!"

The doctor wondered, how could a clinically dead man have known that his doctor was in a car accident miles away? Could the patient's consciousness have survived death in some way and allowed him to see the crash?

It is possible that all OBErs and NDErs were hallucinating or dreaming. But if they were, how can we explain the fact that many NDErs had nearly the same hallucination, described the same details and brought back the same impressions of the afterlife when they returned to the world of the living? How is it possible that nearly all of these people remembered the same "dream" years later? Do you remember details from dreams you had years ago?

"Death, that great puzzle, is no longer a mystery ... it is the most wonderful, joyous, sensitive journey home," wrote Robert Cubin, a mystical experiencer.

Whether or not we believe in OBEs or NDEs, most people believe there is a heaven and the chances are good they will be allowed in. A slightly lower number believe in hell. (Almost no one thought they would be sent there.) Interestingly, almost all of the NDErs recalled a blissful trip to heaven. Only a small fraction of the NDErs went through a hellish trip. It could be they didn't want to tell anyone about it.

How real is the idea of reincarnation? The rebirth of the human soul into a new body after death is a very old idea, born a few thousand years ago in India. It is believed by hundreds of millions of people, especially followers of Hinduism and Buddhism.

In reincarnation, a soul moves to another body, called transmigration. You can earn points in this life and be born a king next time. Or you can get demoted to a dog or an insect. What we do in this life determines the quality of our next life. Hindus say it is all about good and bad karma and what kind of life you have led. And don't think that you can cheat your karma -- you can't.

Plato wrote about Er, a soldier, who was sent across a river to the afterlife. Er's memory was purposely not wiped and he was sent back to the world of the living to explain it all to the people.

How real are mediums? These psychics call themselves "telephones to the spirit world."

It depends on whom you ask. Some say the advice from mediums are communications from spirits. Skeptics say the advice comes from human ESP or the unconscious mind.

It is hard to explain, however, how mediums are able to tell people where money was hidden, when the only person who knew about the money was the deceased family member. Some spirits, speaking through mediums, reveal their names and offer personal information (about hobbies, replacing patio furniture, etc.) that only their loved ones would understand.

Sometimes, spirits talk to the living without any help from mediums. Some appear before dozens of shocked witnesses to thank their mothers for paying for the funeral. One seemingly normal woman, who was attending a funeral in Haiti, started talking like the recently deceased woman and thanked everybody for coming to the memorial service!

In Haiti, there are many strange burial customs. Relatives believe souls are bored so they perform for them in cemeteries. They often tell jokes to the spirits. Some Haitians supposedly use zombies, the recently deceased, as cheap laborers. They cast a voodoo spell and put them to work. But they are careful not to give these zombies any salt because if they do, zombies will try to dig back into their graves. It is hard to say whether or not that is a good thing.

People of all different cultures in all different time periods have believed in ghosts. Their power has always been respected, going back to the time of the Romans. A ghost is a spirit who isn't ready to leave this world and enter the next. A ghost is always upset about something.

Abraham Lincoln's ghost is said to be in the White House, where his wife heldséances. His ghost has been seen and heard by dozens of respected world leaders, and a few maids.

So many people have recalled past lives or trips to heaven with such vivid detail that it is difficult to dismiss these memories as total fiction. Some have returned from a bout with death or a "joining" with a spirit and suddenly started drafting atomic energy theories or performing surgery, even though they never finished high school.

This book will examine circumstantial evidence of life after death, along with rebuttals to that evidence. As you read, keep in mind the words of Albert Einstein, who wrote, "The greatest experience we can have is the mysterious" and of Voltaire, who wrote, "After all, it is no more surprising to be born twice than it is to be born once."

Appendix I: Fiction Magazine Articles

"Genetically Mapped"

by

Don Rutberg

1,600 Words

© 2002

Genetically Mappoled

I'm the first victim of genetic discrimination and I have to tell somebody how it all happened.

It started innocently, which was the first bad sign.

I volunteered to have my human genome mapped. I figured, "What could go wrong? It could be helpful, learning about my genetic predispositions."

Months later, I'm unemployable and suing the world.

Why? Because everybody, not just me, received a copy of my genetic map; even the car insurance companies.

"Sorry," they said. "Although you've been a perfect driver for almost 30 years, the genetic research says you're a bad risk."

"Risk for what?"

"Going blind."

"When am I going blind?" I asked with alarm.

"Sometime in the next 75 years."

"I'm only 45."

"But it could happen tomorrow, according to these charts. You see, your mother's grandparents had degenerative vision."

"They lived in Europe. They drove a horse and buggy around the village."

"And crashed into a few huts, we suspect."

"Is that what genetic mapping is all about? Branding me a bad driver? Branding me anything you like? Isn't that illegal?"

"It's too new to be illegal. And please don't ask me about life insurance. We don't sell it to your chromosomal class."

Shaken, I walked over to the polling place to vote.

"Sorry," the ward leader said. "We just received your genetic map and the party leaders, both parties, as a matter of fact, decided that your voting rights should be rescinded. Now, don't take this as all bad news. It was the first time both parties actually agreed on something."

"You're rescinding my right to vote? Why?" I asked. "Am I a criminal?"

"No, but we don't want any crazy people voting."

"Are you a psychiatrist?"

"No, but I can read a genetic map all right. And this one clearly indicates that insanity flows through your DNA."

"Not my mother's grandparents again!" I wailed. "All they did was crash their buggy a few times. They weren't crazy. They were blind."

"This map shows that you have the predisposition for psychotic episodes, given the proper stimuli."

"Arbitrarily take away my right to vote and I will get crazy!" I shouted.

"See?" the ward leader said, holding his palms up. "Besides, what's the difference if you vote or not. Elections are never that close anyway."

The ward leader walked away and started wrangling with leaders from the other political party.

"Pizza!"

"No! Chinese food!"

So I couldn't drive or vote but I could still work, or at least that's what I thought. I applied for a job within walking distance of my home, as a typist.

"I have a Bachelor's Degree in Communications, a Master's Degree in Fine Arts and I type really fast," I told my interviewer.

"Sorry," she said, tapping my genetic map.

"Wait a second. How'd you get that?" I wondered.

"Off the Internet," she revealed. "And it says right here that a mutation of chromosome 17 predisposes you to carpal tunnel syndrome."

"I didn't know I had a chromosome 17," I admitted.

"We would be loathe to hire someone like yourself, only to have you incapacitated by wrist pain, unable to perform even a simple task like typing. We'd be paying you for nothing. And even if we wanted to do that, our medical insurance would never permit it."

At least the woman asked if I needed parking validation.

After a long walk, I arrived home and noticed a man waiting at my door.

"Who are you?" I asked.

He handed me his business card. He worked for the Department of Corrections.

"You must be looking for Lois in apartment A," I blurted out. "She spends a lot of time in Florida. I live up here in C."

"I have the right address. I'm your probation officer."

"Excuse me?"

"Your genetic map has that insanity gene, remember? Or have you conveniently and insanely blocked that out?"

"How could you be my probation officer when I've never been convicted of any crime?"

"Insane people commit crimes," he told me as he handed me the front page of my newspaper.

"Read all about it."

"So, if I'm hearing you right, and I know I am because I also lip read, you're simply getting a head start, before I actually do the dirty deeds."

"It's the prudent thing to do."

"Sure. Sure. Tell me, does my genetic map indicate which psychotic crime I'll be committing?"

"You tell me."

"I haven't really thought about it."

"Wow, you really are a psycho."

"Even if I am thinking about it, right now, I can't go to jail for what I'm thinking."

The officer put away his handcuffs.

"You can't. But, fortunately, you can be assigned a probation officer."

"Why don't you come back later?" I asked.

"I will, just as soon as I hear about your crime spree. Do you prefer pepper spray or the stun gun?"

"Both."

"These maps never lie," he muttered as he walked down the steps and began knocking on Lois' door in apartment A.

Trying to stay calm, I made a phone call to inquire about medical insurance.

"How much overweight are you?" the medical insurance agent asked me over the phone, and I could hear her tapping the chart with my genetic map.

"Maybe a pound or two."

"That's not what the map indicates."

"I work out five times a week."

"Try mixing in a salad."

"I have a salad every day."

"Oh!" she half-sang. "I find that hard to believe -- you eating salad, especially carrots, with those bad teeth."

"I have two crowns. Is that --"

"The tip of the iceberg? It sure is."

"I eat a lot of humus. Very little chewing; saves wear and tear," I reminded her but I knew I wasn't changing her mind about my being an unacceptable insurance risk.

"Have any more cyst operations?" she asked warily.

"My last one was in 1966."

"Allergies?"

"Yes -- to poison."

"Do you mean rat poison or the perfume they call, "Poison?"

"Both."

"Click."

With my options waning, I asked for and received a ride to the street hockey court in New Hope. At least I could work up a sweat and release some tension during the spirited game.

The team captain, Al, a friend of mine since high school, a hockey teammate in college, a kindred spirit and my lawyer, approached me. He put his hands on the goalie mask I was wearing.

"I saw your genetic map, man, and I'm sorry."

"I feel pretty good," I answered.

"No, I mean, sorry, you can't play goal anymore," he said as he unsnapped the straps and took off my mask.

"What? Why not?"

"Chromosome 17. I mean, if you get carpal tunnel syndrome during the game, what chance do you have to make any saves? If it affects your left wrist, the other guys will shoot high on your glove-hand side and if it affects your right wrist, which the chart says it will, then they'll shoot high on your blocker side. Either way, goal scored, they win. We lose. Try soccer."

In other conversations, I learned I could eventually be bald, asthmatic, impotent, mole-ridden, insulin-dependent and tone deaf.

But through it all, I never accepted my new label as "genetically less fortunate." And it was this "stubborn" gene, which went completely undetected in all the mapping tests, by the way, that motivated me to overcome my genetic deficiencies.

I became stubbornly litigious, sued everyone mentioned above, including my own lawyer and lifetime friend, Al.

I walked into Al's trendy, downtown office.

He smiled sadly, then unstrapped my goalie mask.

I handed him an envelope.

"Retirement speech?" he asked.

"Consider yourself served," I barked.

"You're suing me because I won't let you play goalie?" he shouted in amazement. "It's not only me. You'll have to serve papers to the whole team."

"I'm walking there now."

"The jury will never take your side. Never. Trust me. I'm your attorney."

The jury was on my side. All of them had recently been laid off because of "genetic predispositions."

I earned $7,300,000 in damages, which were tripled by the Appellate court judge, who was also on my side. He was about to be forced into retirement because his second cousin had Alzheimer's disease. The judge was 49 years old.

I wrote a book about my experiences. At first, no publisher wanted me as an author because it was discovered that my grandmother wore orthopedic shoes.

"How will you be able to stand around, signing autographs at book stores," publishers asked me. "Huh?!"

But then I heard about an agent who had been fired because his great-uncle had diabetes. He started his own agency, read my book and signed me to a contract. Then he sold my story to a publisher who had started his own company after a large publishing house fired him upon learning his grandfather had degenerative vision.

"Someone found out he drove a buggy into a hut in Europe in 1902," he said softly.

"Yours, too!?" I yelled.

I've had three books published about human rights, human dignity and fundamental freedoms. The story of my life will soon be made into a feature film. The movie studio hired a full-time typist to transcribe the screenplay; gently mentioning something about a, "Mutated Chromosome 17," which, by the way, is the film's working title.

I still can't afford medical insurance; not after my dad's prostate surgery or my niece's gallbladder attack.

The moral of my story? That's easy: If you're always feeling sluggish and think you're getting diabetes, lay off the cheesecake. If your siblings need heart surgery, eat less steak. If you feel, deep down, that you've got a mutated chromosome 17, get some wrist-rests for the computer, damn it.

Whatever you do, don't let them map your human genome.

Code Word: "Interview"

by

Don Rutberg

500 Words

© 2000

Code Word: "Interview"

I needed some perspective into the Pete Rose affair so I set up a dugout meeting with Pete's very first baseball coach, Crusty Crapshoot. I peeked into the dugout and saw he was deep in thought.

"Hi," I said, "I'm the one who called about an interview."

"Sit down," he replied, checking his watch. "Like Lacrosse?"

"Kinda."

"I'm gonna go with Hopkins for a deuce. They any good?"

"I think so. I don't know about this year."

"I got killed last week on all 180 races. Exactas, quinellas; your guess is as good as mine."

"I have some questions about Pete."

"One second. Hey kids!"

The coach's 10 year-old players ran into the dugout.

"Captains only," coach barked and two kids stepped forward.

"I got refreshments in this water cooler. The captain who guesses the amount, or comes closest, wins 'em all for his team."

"Ten," one captain guessed. He'd played this game before.

"Twenty-five," the other said.

"Right on the money, 25. Take it away."

All the kids left except for one that looked like he came from the cast of "Oliver.".

"Coach, I got the results of the third at Saratoga."

"I don't want you tellin' me!" coach moaned. "You're like the Black Plague when it comes to horses. Or dogs!"

After the kid apologized and left, coach explained, "He's a good little ballplayer but most of the guys on death row got more luck than him. If the game's close, I send him over to sit with the other team. Got tomorrow's morning line?"

"No," I said. "I came to ask you some questions about your relationship with Pete."

"You're a sports writer?"

"Just a fan."

"So you're not the bookie who called and asked about a ... I get it! `Interview.' That's our code word!"

"What do you mean?"

"If I want an `interview' that means I wanna bet. I thought that -- hey, Pete was a great kid. Not a lot of talent but he hustled. He wasn't bettin' when he played here. I'm pretty sure. Heck, he was only 10 years old."

"How do you feel about his problems off the field?"

"Terrible thing. He should know better."

"Have you ever gambled with him?"

"We went to the race track together but just to have lunch. Hot dogs or somethin'."

"Does gambling have a place in society?"

"I think it does. Except if you're going to the Hall of Fame. Then ya gotta stand on the sidelines while the rest of us have all the fun."

"I'm sure Pete appreciates your support."

"I'm proud of him, too. Except he can't pick the Breeders' Cup winners to save his life. Last year, me and Pete were watchin' at the track and I told him, `Pete, you've got an o-for-ever streak goin'. Even when ya win ya get disqualified. Sit it out; even if it's wrong, sit one out.' But I think he bet anyway. He's a determined guy. He'll be all right. Hey, did ya hear who won the third at Saratoga?"

Appendix J: Nonfiction Magazine Articles

"It's a Green Thing"

By

Don Rutberg

750 Words

© 2004

It's A Green Thing

I don't recall my very first baseball game. It must have been when I was eight, sometime during the 1964 season, just before the Phillies lost ten games in a row and blew the pennant

My Dad, however, remembers his first game vividly - so vividly that he tells the story at almost every family function. He once described on audiotape all the details of his trip to Baker Bowl to see the Phillies play the St. Louis Cardinals' Gashouse Gang in August of 1936. It was such a poignant story of a poor boy realizing his dream to see a major league game that I wrote a book about it, "Hot Peppers For Pop." (Dad, as a boy, earned money to see his first game by entering hot pepper-eating contests.)

Dad described his first moment inside the stadium this way: "I thought I was in heaven when I saw all that green grass."

Recently, I was reading about famous people's recollections of their first baseball game. Many of them said they were mesmerized by the sight of all that green - green grass, green walls, green seats, posts and pillars.

Their comments resonated with me because they were so similar to my Dad's description. Here's what they said:

Pat Williams, senior VP Orlando magic: "The sights, the sounds, the smells captivated me … everything was green, and that riveted me - the grass, the walls, the seats. They were all green."

Dave Schwartz, The Weather Channel: "I remember the brick façade on the outside of the stadium, the thrill of catching first sight of the green of the field."

Billy Wagner, Phillies' pitcher: "The first thing you see is the Green Monster" (at Fenway Park in Boston).

Jim Thome, Phillies' first baseman: "The first thing I saw was the ivy" (at Wrigley Field in Chicago).

David Halberstam, author: "It was 1941. I went with my father to Yankee Stadium. And I remember how green the grass was. I had never seen anything greener in the world … what I remember most of all was the unreal color of the grass, the greenest thing I'd ever seen, and I thought, how exciting it was to be here."

I couldn't help but notice a common theme. I wondered, what were the grounds for all this green loving? Why were there no memories of purple or pink?

It couldn't be as simple as green going out and hiring the better PR firm.

Have you ever heard people say they fell in love with football when they went to a Tampa Bay Buccaneers' game and saw all that pumpkin?

Is there anyone who reported fondly that they became enamored with boxing when they attended their first match and saw all that red blood squirting onto the ring?

How many hockey fans, speaking about their very first game, mention anything about seeing the Vancouver Canucks uniforms, with the mellow yellow stripes? How many trace their love of the game to seeing, "All that white ice"?

Car racing fans don't pine for "pastoral miles of black asphalt" just as horse racing enthusiasts don't yearn for "perfectly brown dirt."

I'm telling you, it's a green thing.

Greenpeace. Greenbacks. The green, green green of home. These are all good things. Bing Crosby sang about a green Christmas. Mick Jagger saw a red door and wanted only to paint it green.

Popular culture also includes mottos like, "Green is Good" and "Show me the green."

These mottos are just the tip of the Greenberg.

But, seriously, there must be something about green that evokes widespread joy. And I don't think it has anything to do with money. It's more about the green in nature, about our roaming around on green grass, in bare feet, as youths. Green grass has always been a soft place to land. It cushions our falls naturally, when we're young and most vulnerable.

Or maybe the green grass is so popular because it reminds us of summer. It symbolizes the warmest of the seasons, when we're off from school and free to explore the natural world; when we're workin' on our "Night Moves," as Bob Seger suggested.

These famous people probably weren't gushing about baseball's green grass. Instead, I believe, they were looking back fondly at the summers of their youth.

In And Out Of The Nielsen Family

by

Don Rutberg

1,200 Words

© 2004

In And Out Of The Nielsen Family

My wife and I were selected by the Nielsen TV Ratings to join their family. We were to represent 28,100 homes in our area, with each household averaging 3.5 persons. It was a big responsibility because our viewing habits, our approval or disapproval of television shows 24 hours a day, 365 days a year, registered in Nielsen's Florida home office as 98,350 votes!

A Nielsen field representative came to our apartment, near Philadelphia. Once he learned that we had no little kids hogging the tube, he rubber-stamped us and explained how we would be assimilated into the family. We told him we didn't mind the responsibility or loss of privacy because we considered ourselves sophisticated and intelligent viewers, eager to endorse worthwhile productions. No wrestling or surviving shows; no Howard Stern or Anna Nicole productions for us.

If he would've left immediately, everything would've been fine. But as this man kept talking, we became less enthusiastic about joining his family.

"The first thing we do is tear apart your TV's," Mike, the Nielsen rep, said.

"You mean, you open up our TV sets and insert your tracking devices?" I asked.

"Uh-huh."

"Can't you just stick a magnetized chip on the side of the TV?"

"No. We have to get inside; both TV's and both VCR's."

My wife asked, "Suppose you break one of the TV's or VCR's?"

"If your devices stop working because of our messing around in there, we'll pay you 50% of the value of the TV or VCR."

Our old Sony TV is probably worth $100 but would cost $700 to replace.

"That means you'll give us $50 for any TV you break?" I asked.

"Sounds fair," he said with a smile.

"That hardly ever happens, I'll bet."

Mike didn't answer.

My wife broke the silence.

"So you'll know everything we watch and tape."

"Exactly. The next thing we'll do is tear up your carpeting in the living room, dining room, hallways and bedroom."

My wife gasped.

Mike explained, "We'll run wires along the walls and floorboards, into the telephone jacks."

"Uh, we only have one phone jack in the front of the apartment and that's in the kitchen," I said.

Mike inspected our walls. The last time someone looked so closely at our walls, the person was about to saw through them, in order to rescue a baby squirrel.

"No problem," Mike replied. "We'll run the wires near the door alongside the heating and air-conditioning systems, into the kitchen, then ... hmmm, you'll have to remove the phone from the wall-mount and put it on the kitchen table."

"Won't there be a lot of wires on our kitchen walls?" my wife asked.

"You won't even notice them," Mike promised.

That's what the cable company had promised my wife. She's still mad at them.

"It sounds complicated," I mentioned. "How long will it take to install?"

"Five or six hours."

"It'll take a guy five or six hours just to install a monitoring system?"

"No, it'll take a team of three-four men five or six hours to install the system."

"We could put in a whole new kitchen with that kind of time and manpower," I suggested.

"We'll want to get this in motion as soon as possible," Mike said. "The day after tomorrow works for us. Is seven am too early to get here?"

"Yes!" I replied. "I go to bed late."

"We'll work around it. How about Friday night, from 5-11 pm, give or take?"

"We have the Mexican fiesta party at the clubhouse on Friday night," my wife reminded.

We were going to need a few margaritas to say "Yes" to this deal, especially if they wanted to bring in jackhammers, port-o-potties and cots.

"Why does it take so long?" I wondered.

"We have to rewire all your equipment. We'll bring in a few computerized boxes, hide them nicely in cabinets, then they'll record all your info ...."

"We don't have cabinets near the TV's," I said.

The fact that we had no children was a plus but having no cabinets, well, that seemed unnatural to the man.

"Don't worry," Mike replied. "We'll hide the boxes somewhere."

"Not in the fireplace," I mumbled.

Mike dredged up an insincere chuckle.

"Here's the neat part," he said. "The boxes will be hooked up to your phone line and they'll auto-dial our home office in Florida every night about two am."

"Say that again," I instructed.

"The computer is set to auto-dial."

"I make phone calls to the West Coast at 2am. Are you telling me that when I try to make a call, the Nielsen box will be on the phone, calling in a report?"

"It won't take long."

"The box isn't going to call its friends in Australia and talk for an hour, is it?" I joked.

Mike didn't answer.

My wife broke the silence.

She asked, "So how much do you pay us for all our help?"

I could see her ears perking up.

"A dollar a month."

"Excuse me?" she blurted out, her head tilted.

"For each TV and VCR," Mike said, adding incentive.

"Four bucks a month?" my wife screamed.

"Before we pay you, you have to sign a contract for two years," Mike told us.

"Two years!" I repeated.

"If you move, you can quit."

"Gee, thanks," I said. "It really is a free country."

"And we pay you six months in advance!" Mike advised.

"Wow, 24 dollars in one lump sum," my wife, the accountant, whispered.

At that moment, executives from my wife's favorite network, PAX, should have jumped in and offered her ten thousand dollars to sign the contract. PAX would have made a hundred times that sum every year from sponsors and could have out-rated the major networks. The Philadelphia Eagles, Flyers, 76ers and Phillies should have been there to offer me incentives, since they would have been guaranteed 98,350 registered viewers every time they played, even exhibition games.

(I mentioned earlier that we considered ourselves sophisticated and intelligent viewers. That doesn't necessarily mean that we are.)

My wife and I are complimentary in nature and have very different tastes. I often joke that, since she mainly uses the left side of her brain and I use the right, together, we use one complete brain. In this case, however, we were thinking exactly alike. I could feel her on my wavelength. It was time to let Mike in on our telepathic secret.

We admitted that we weren't going to live in a construction zone and give up our privacy for $4 a month. We said we weren't up to the challenge. (We weren't psyched to climb Mt. Everest for two bucks apiece, either). He told us he understood but then stood up in a huff and packed his papers, using body language to question how we could turn down this great opportunity.

We looked with relief at the clean walls and smooth carpeting and wall-mounted phone. I told Mike that we always watched CSI.

"It's the number one show, anyway," I said with a consoling shrug. "You don't need us. CSI doesn't need us."

Mike flew out the door.

"Keep your hands off our TV!" my wife shouted out the window.

Alone in our apartment, feeling as if we had regained our rights as private citizens without taking part in a bloody coup, my wife and I hugged. PAX network executives, somewhere, were sobbing at their lost millions. But the truth was, we would've paid the Nielsen family four bucks a month just to leave us alone.

Index

Cover art by

SBeilin@aol.com